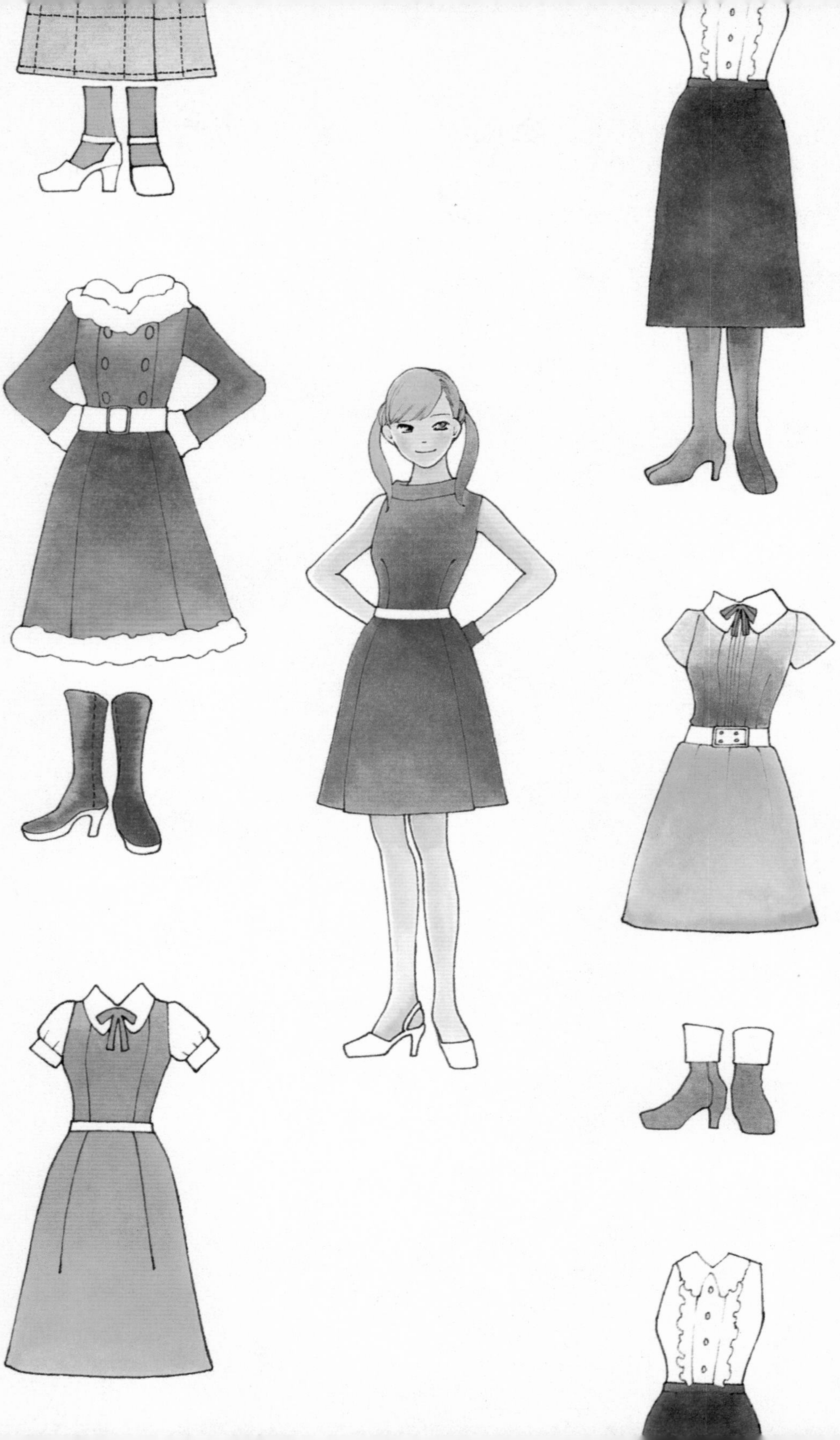

Fantagraphics Books, 7563 Lake City Way NE, Seattle, Washington 98115 | Publishers: Gary Groth & Kim Thompson; Translation: Matt Thorn; Editorial Liaison: Gary Groth; Design: Alexa Koenings; Lettering: Paul Baresh, Tom Graham , Janice Lee and Toby Liebowitz; Production: Paul Baresh and Emory Liu; Associate Publisher: Eric Reynolds | *Wandering Son* Volume 5 copyright © 2005 Takako Shimura. All rights reserved. First published in Japan by ENTERBRAIN, INC., Tokyo. English translation rights arranged with ENTERBRAIN, INC. No part of this book (except small excerpts for review purposes) may be reproduced in any form or by any electronic or mechanical means without the written permission of the publisher. | To receive a free full-color catalog of comics, graphic novels, prose novels, and other fine works of artistry, call 1-800-657-1100, or visit Fantagraphics.com. | ISBN: 978-1-60699-647-8 | First Fantagraphics printing: July, 2013 | Printed in China

WANDERING SON

Volume Five

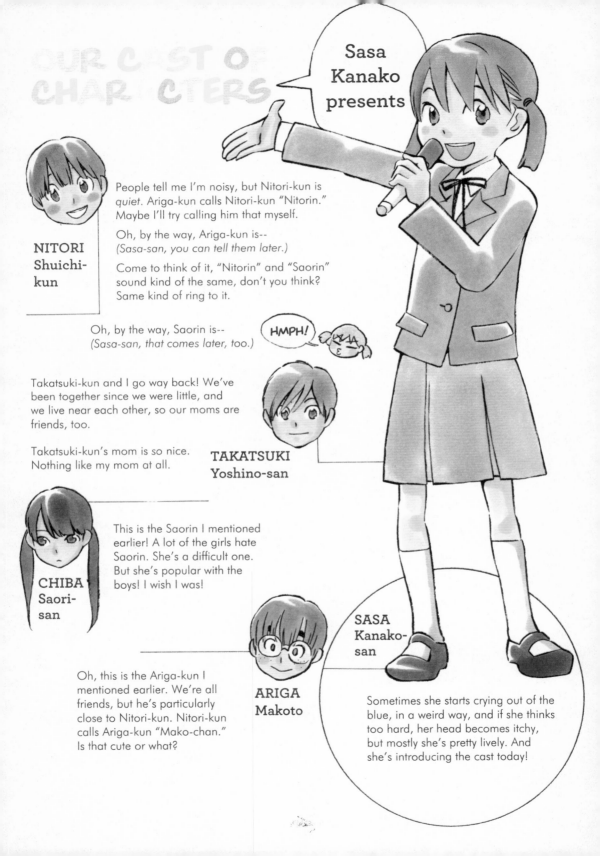

OUR CAST OF CHARACTERS

Sasa Kanako presents

NITORI Shuichi-kun

People tell me I'm noisy, but Nitori-kun is *quiet*. Ariga-kun calls Nitori-kun "Nitorin." Maybe I'll try calling him that myself.

Oh, by the way, Ariga-kun is--
(Sasa-san, you can tell them later.)

Come to think of it, "Nitorin" and "Saorin" sound kind of the same, don't you think? Same kind of ring to it.

Oh, by the way, Saorin is--
(Sasa-san, that comes later, too.)

HMPH!

TAKATSUKI Yoshino-san

Takatsuki-kun and I go way back! We've been together since we were little, and we live near each other, so our moms are friends, too.

Takatsuki-kun's mom is so nice. Nothing like my mom at all.

CHIBA Saori-san

This is the Saorin I mentioned earlier! A lot of the girls hate Saorin. She's a difficult one. But she's popular with the boys! I wish I was!

ARIGA Makoto

Oh, this is the Ariga-kun I mentioned earlier. We're all friends, but he's particularly close to Nitori-kun. Nitori-kun calls Ariga-kun "Mako-chan." Is that cute or what?

SASA Kanako-san

Sometimes she starts crying out of the blue, in a weird way, and if she thinks too hard, her head becomes itchy, but mostly she's pretty lively. And she's introducing the cast today!

NITORI Maho

Nitori-kun's older sister. Nitori-kun was complaining before about how his sister picks on him. But you know, it's not easy being an older sister. The other day my own little brother was-- *(Sasa-san...)*

SARASHINA Chizuru-san

They're both in my class in junior high. Sarashina-san is as tall as Takatsuki-kun and is so cool looking. Shirai-san's always with Sarashina-san. I wonder if they're child-hood friends. They're kind of like me and Takatsuki-kun.

SHIRAI Momoko-san

I hear he's Nitori-kun's sister's boyfriend! I wonder if I'll ever have a boyfriend.

SEYA Riku-kun

SATOH Tamaki-san

HIROSUE Anna-san

Anna-chan and Tamaki-chan are professional models! Nitori-kun's sister is a model now, too, and she's good friends with both of them. They are so cool.

Yuki-san & Shii-chan

I've only met them once. He's so handsome and she's so pretty. Can you believe Takatsuki-kun and Nitori-kun have grown-up friends like this!?

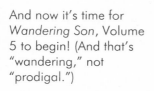

SAISHO Manabu-sensei

Our homeroom teacher. I thought his name was pronounced "Zeisho" at first. I mean, that Chinese character, 税, is always pronounced "zei," isn't it? Who knew?

And now it's time for *Wandering Son*, Volume 5 to begin! (And that's "wandering," not "prodigal.")

CONTENTS

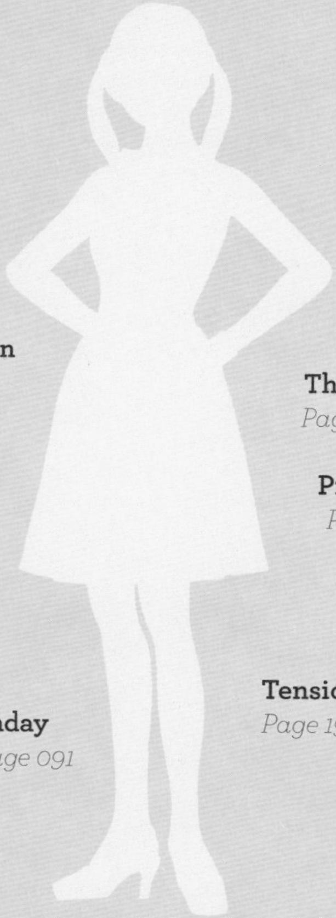

34

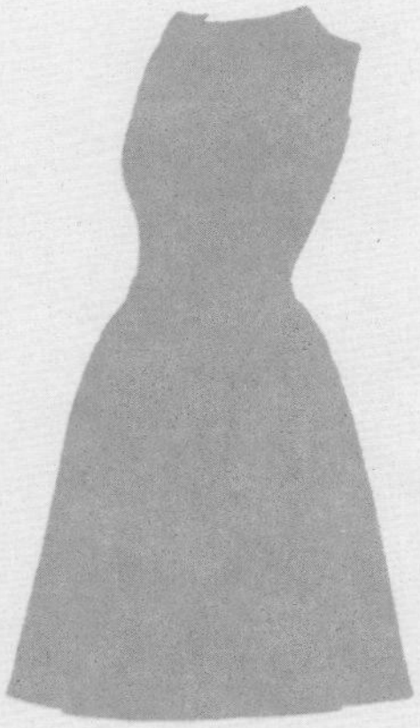

The Curious Sarashina-san

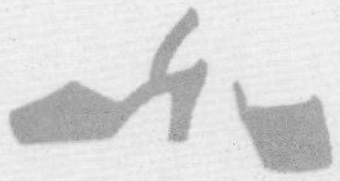

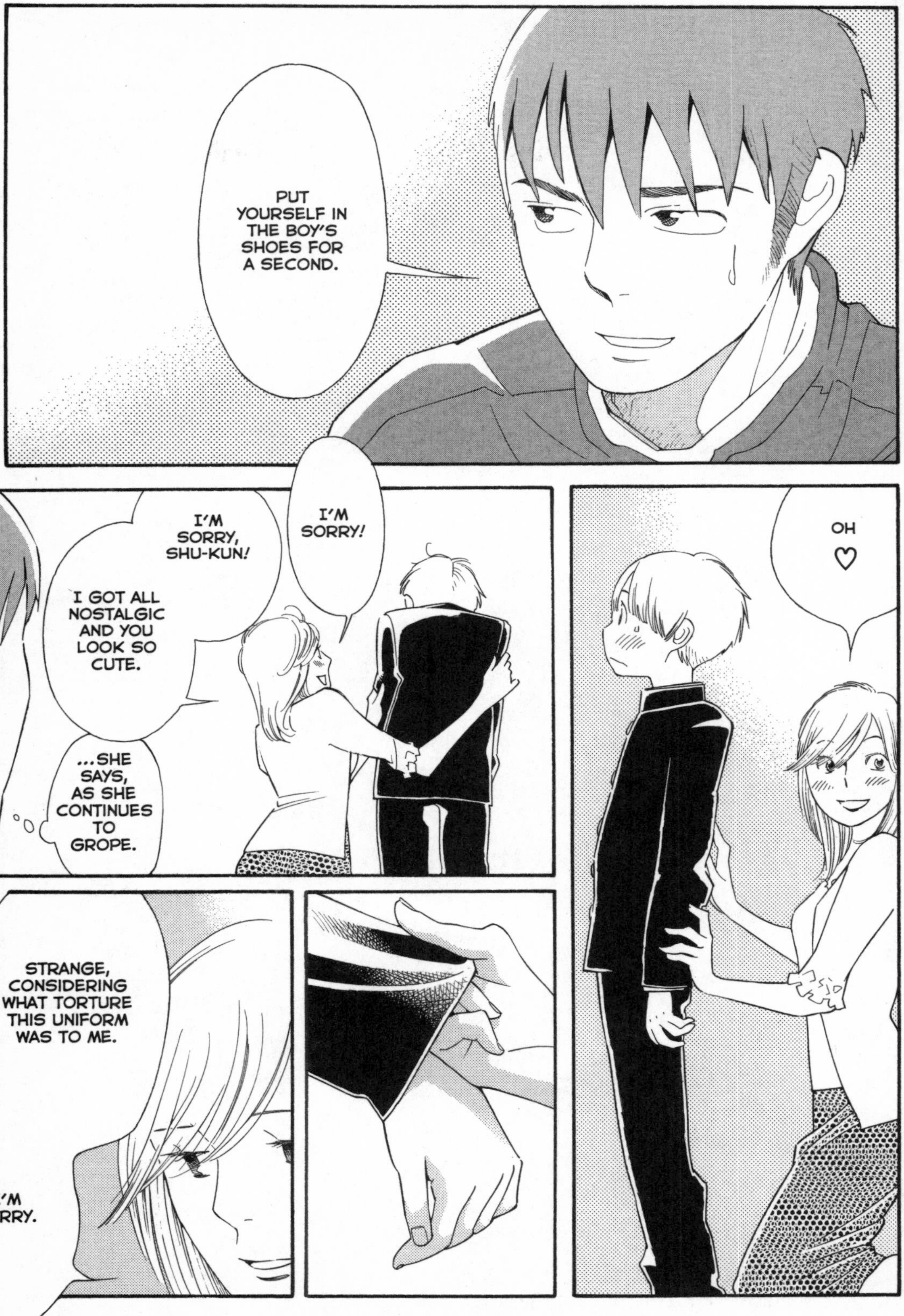
PUT YOURSELF IN THE BOY'S SHOES FOR A SECOND.
OH ♡
I'M SORRY!
I'M SORRY, SHU-KUN!
I GOT ALL NOSTALGIC AND YOU LOOK SO CUTE.
...SHE SAYS, AS SHE CONTINUES TO GROPE.
STRANGE, CONSIDERING WHAT TORTURE THIS UNIFORM WAS TO ME.
I'M SORRY.

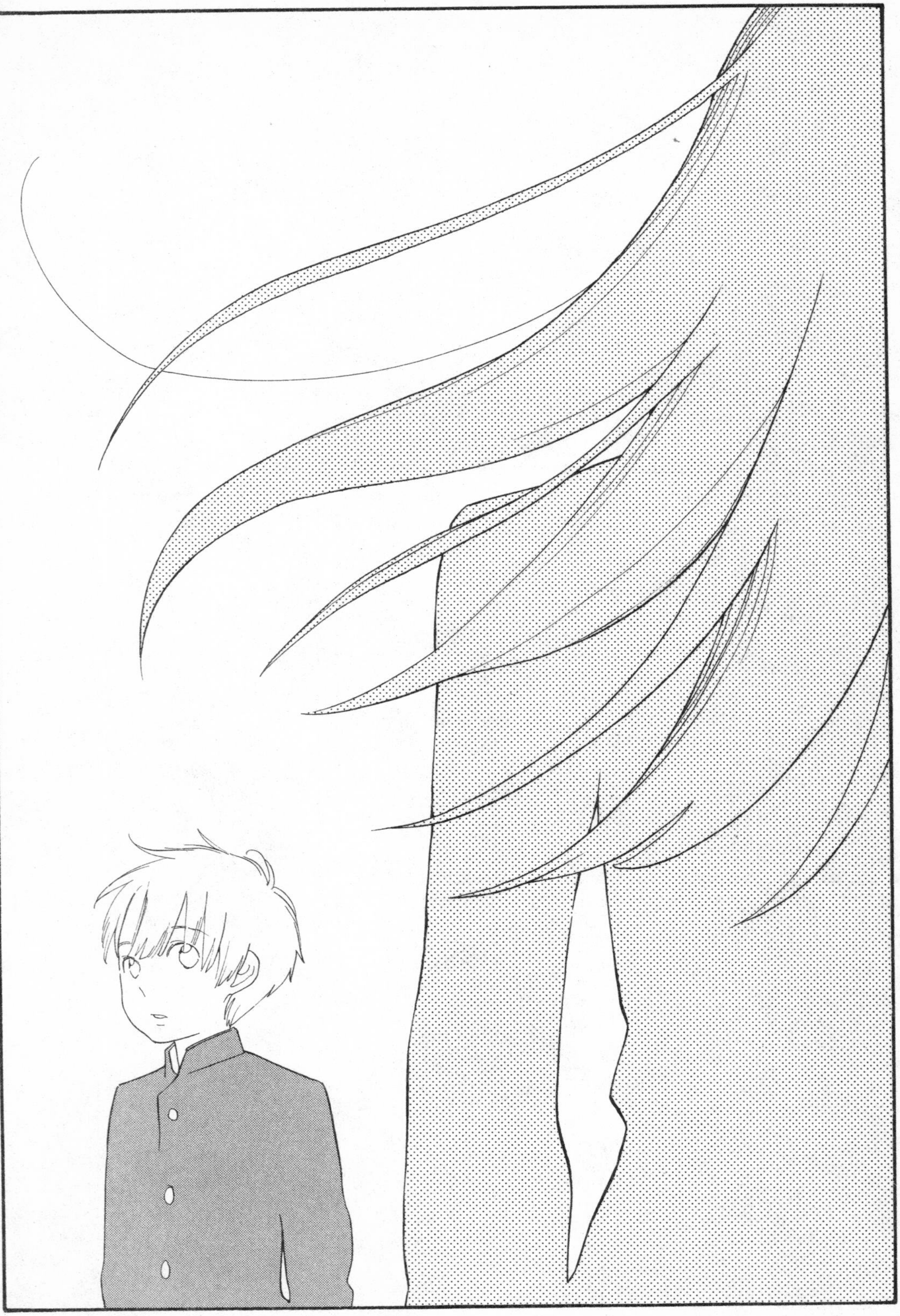

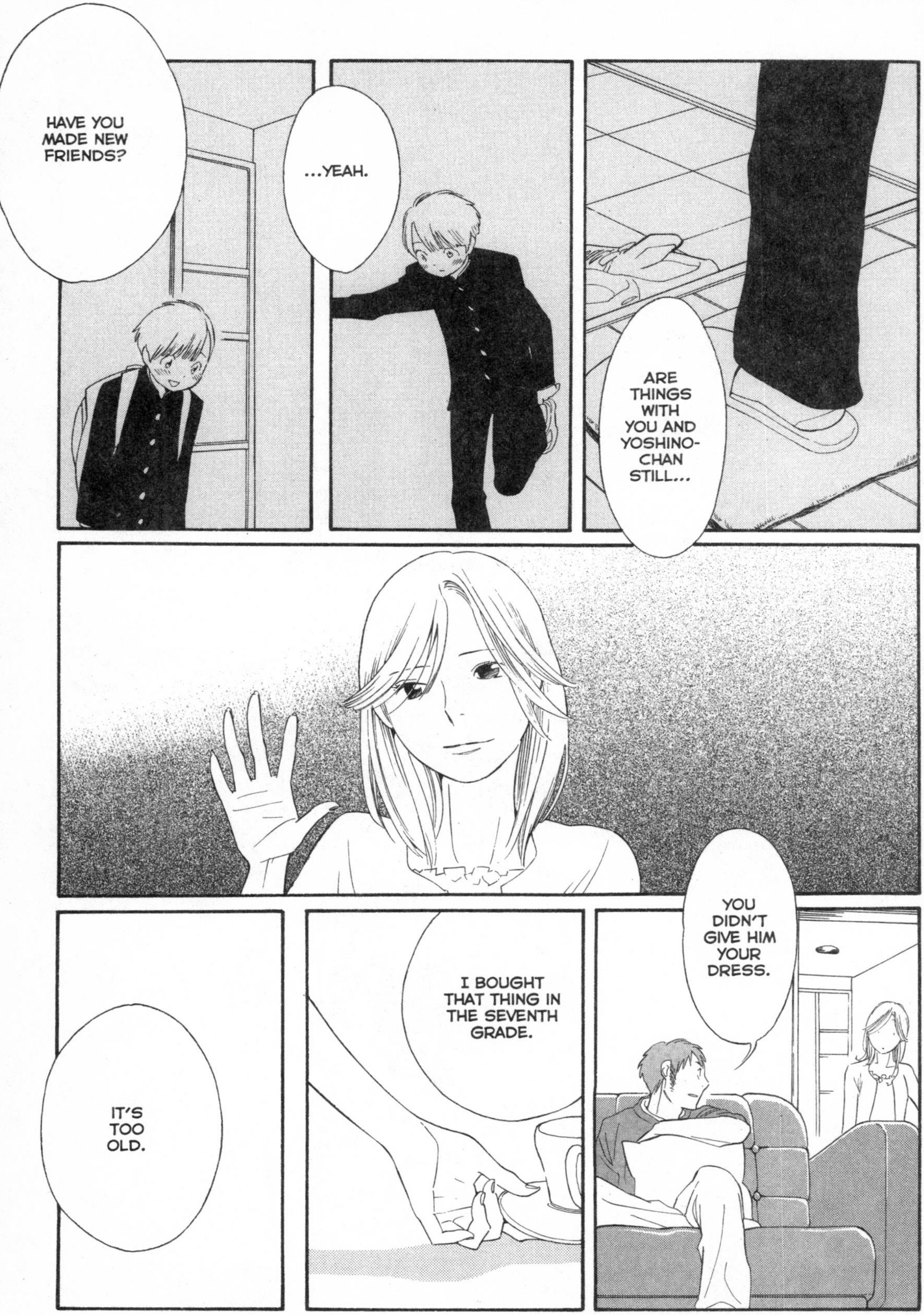
ARE THINGS WITH YOU AND YOSHINO-CHAN STILL...
...YEAH.
HAVE YOU MADE NEW FRIENDS?
YOU DIDN'T GIVE HIM YOUR DRESS.
I BOUGHT THAT THING IN THE SEVENTH GRADE.
IT'S TOO OLD.

HAVE YOU MADE NEW FRIENDS?

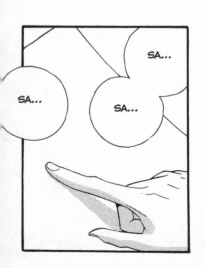

SA...

SA...

SA...

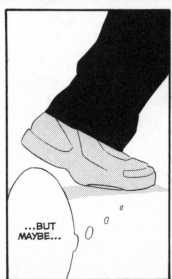

...BUT MAYBE...

NOT EXACTLY...

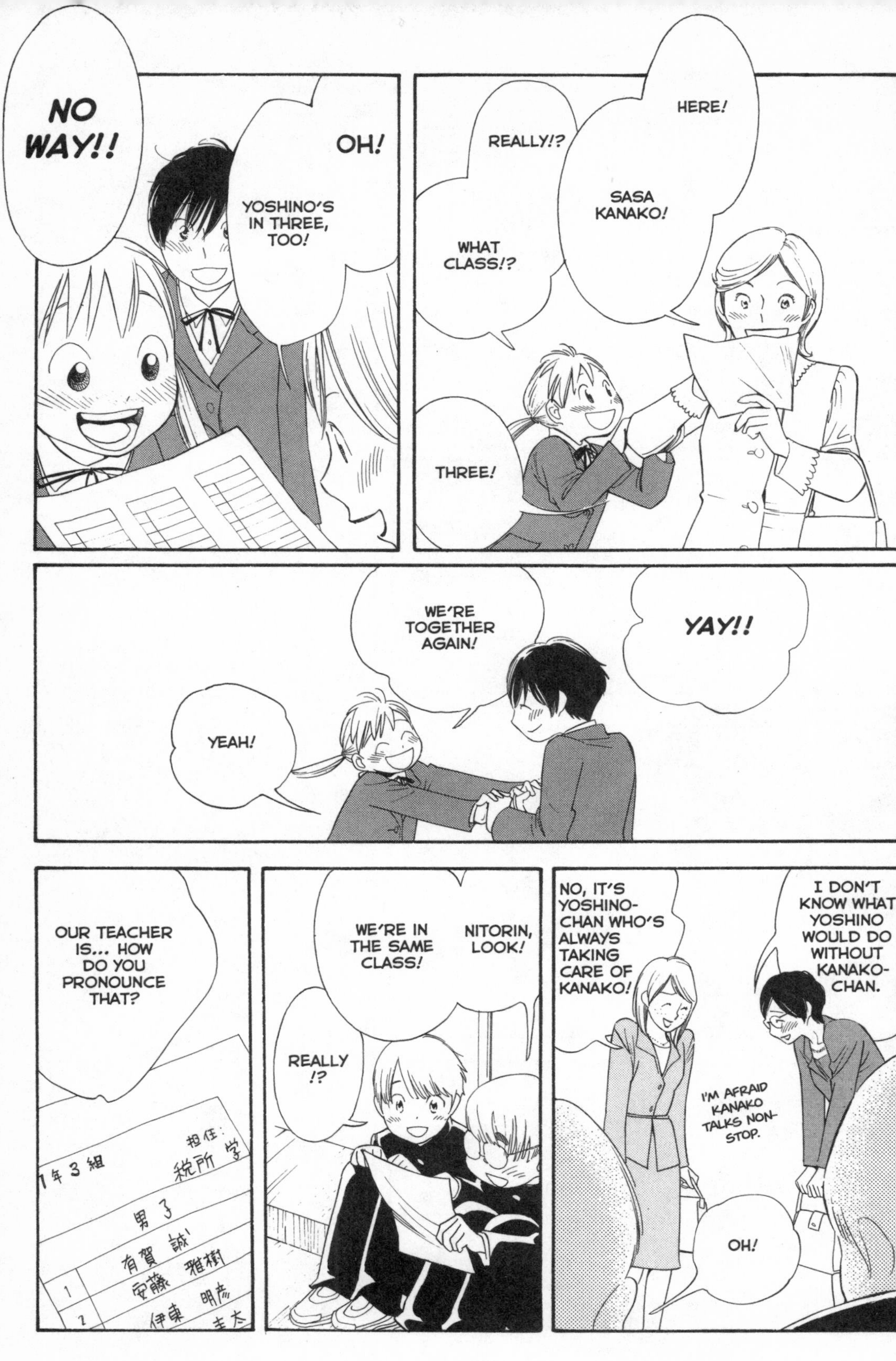
HERE!
SASA KANAKO!
REALLY!?
WHAT CLASS!?
THREE!
OH!
YOSHINO'S IN THREE, TOO!
NO WAY!!
YAY!!
WE'RE TOGETHER AGAIN!
YEAH!
I DON'T KNOW WHAT YOSHINO WOULD DO WITHOUT KANAKO-CHAN.
NO, IT'S YOSHINO-CHAN WHO'S ALWAYS TAKING CARE OF KANAKO!
I'M AFRAID KANAKO TALKS NON-STOP.
OH!
NITORIN, LOOK!
WE'RE IN THE SAME CLASS!
REALLY!?
OUR TEACHER IS... HOW DO YOU PRONOUNCE THAT?
担任:
1年3組
税所 学
男子
有賀 誠
安藤 雅樹

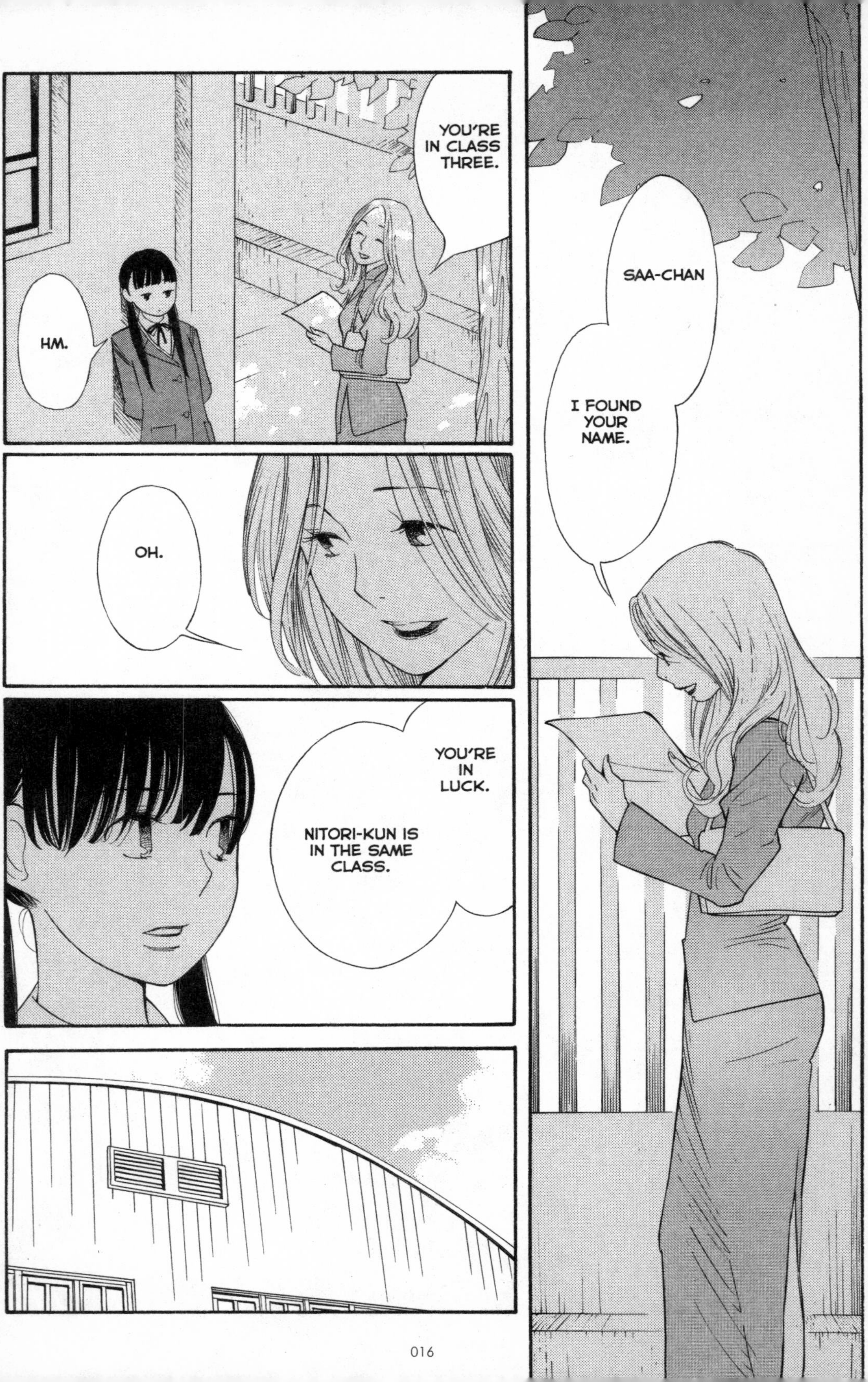
SAA-CHAN
I FOUND YOUR NAME.
YOU'RE IN CLASS THREE.
HM.
OH.
YOU'RE IN LUCK.
NITORI-KUN IS IN THE SAME CLASS.

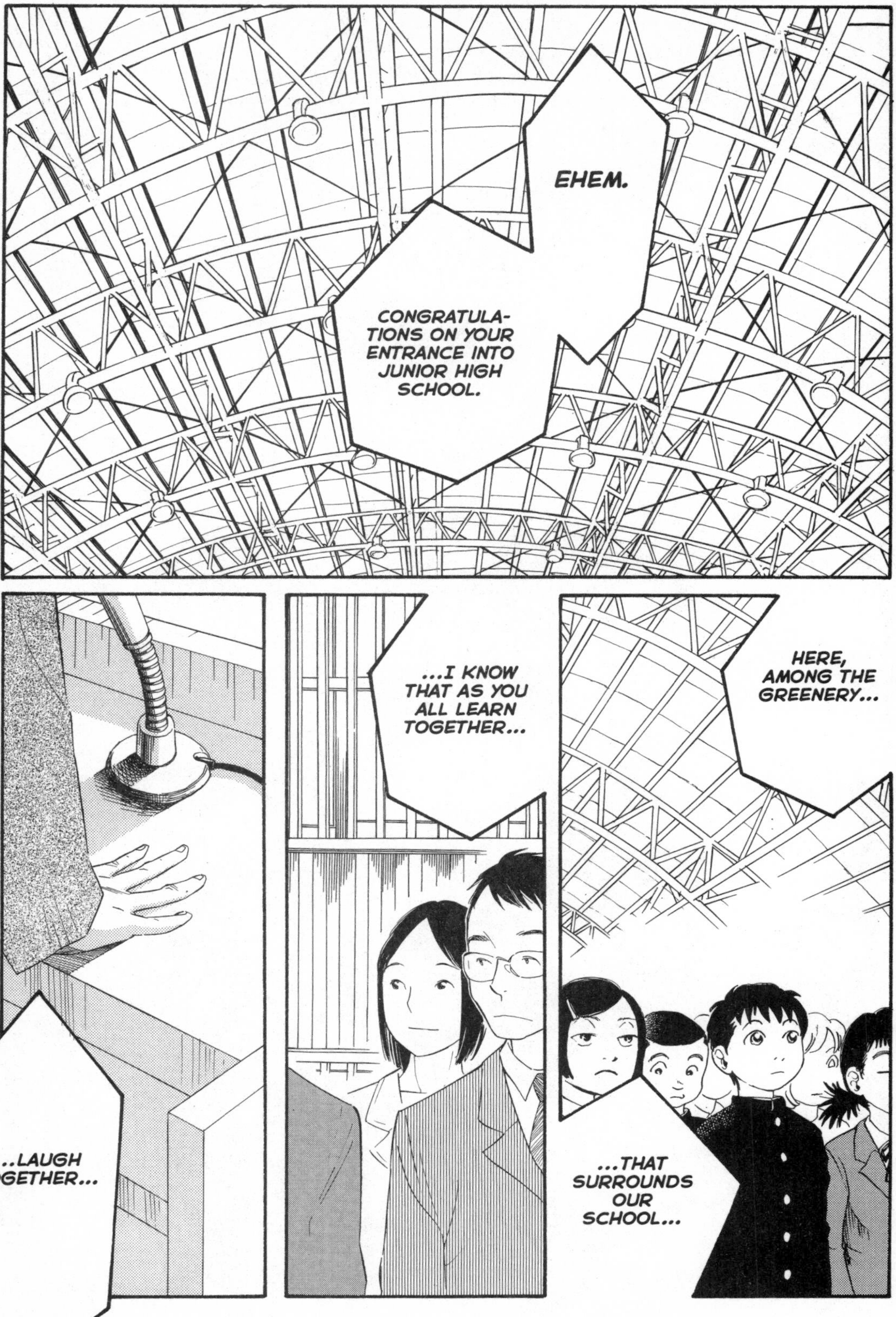
EHEM.
CONGRATULA-TIONS ON YOUR ENTRANCE INTO JUNIOR HIGH SCHOOL.
HERE, AMONG THE GREENERY...
...THAT SURROUNDS OUR SCHOOL...
...I KNOW THAT AS YOU ALL LEARN TOGETHER...
...LAUGH TOGETHER...

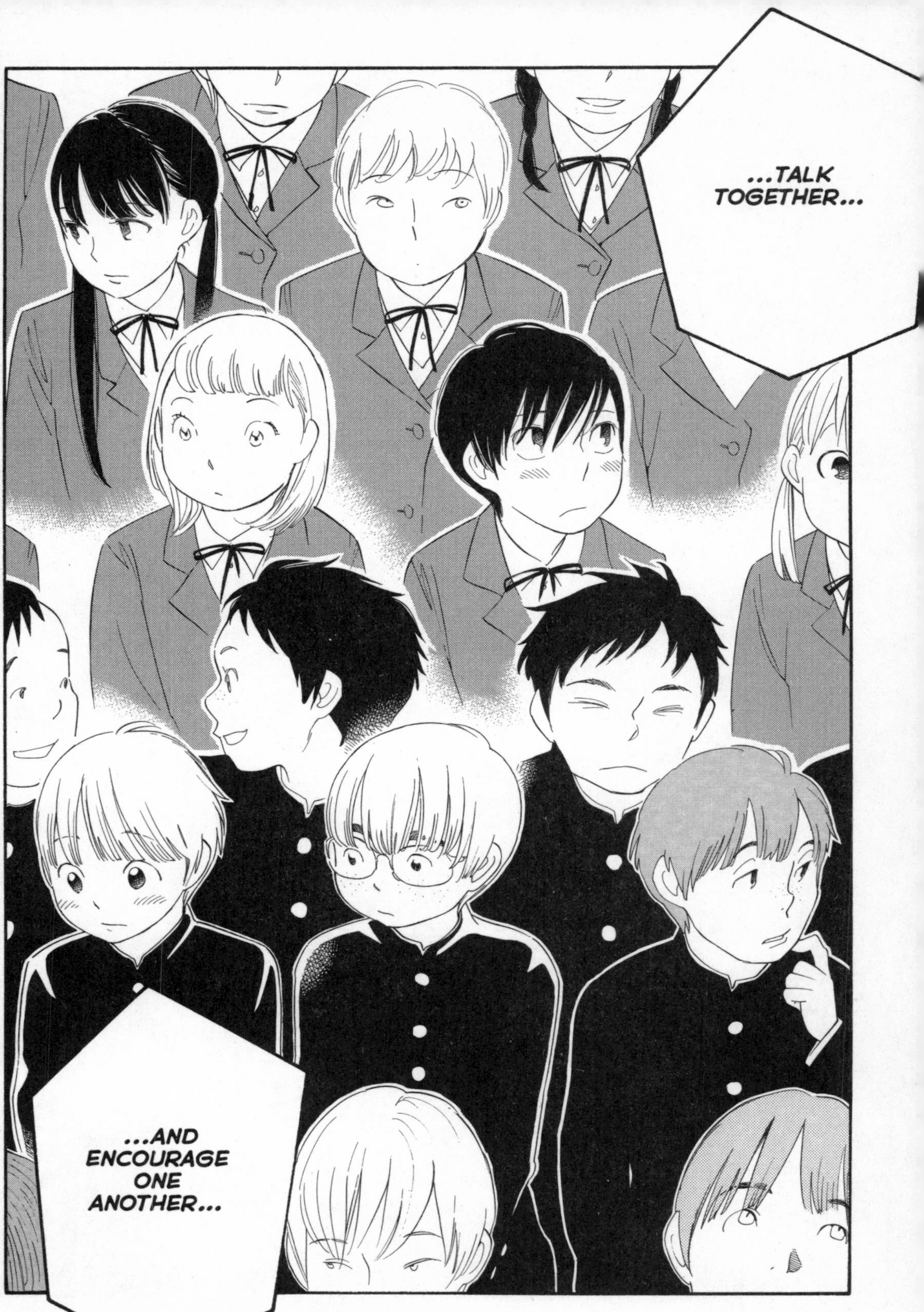
...TALK TOGETHER...
...AND ENCOURAGE ONE ANOTHER...

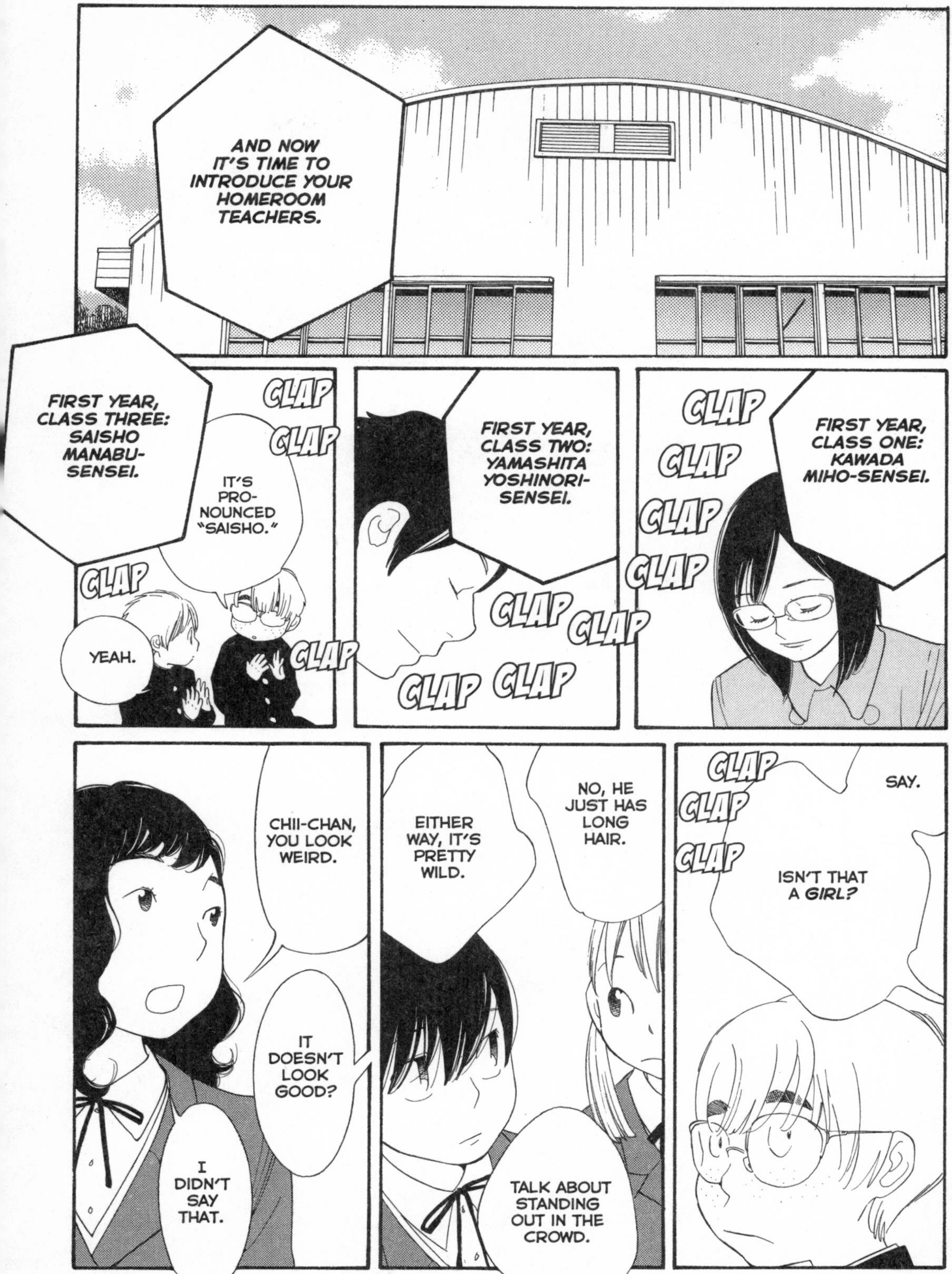
AND NOW IT'S TIME TO INTRODUCE YOUR HOMEROOM TEACHERS.
CLAP CLAP CLAP CLAP
FIRST YEAR, CLASS ONE: KAWADA MIHO-SENSEI.
FIRST YEAR, CLASS TWO: YAMASHITA YOSHINORI-SENSEI.
CLAP CLAP CLAP CLAP
FIRST YEAR, CLASS THREE: SAISHO MANABU-SENSEI.
CLAP CLAP
IT'S PRO-NOUNCED "SAISHO."
CLAP CLAP
YEAH.
CLAP CLAP CLAP
SAY.
ISN'T THAT A GIRL?
NO, HE JUST HAS LONG HAIR.
EITHER WAY, IT'S PRETTY WILD.
TALK ABOUT STANDING OUT IN THE CROWD.
CHII-CHAN, YOU LOOK WEIRD.
IT DOESN'T LOOK GOOD?
I DIDN'T SAY THAT.

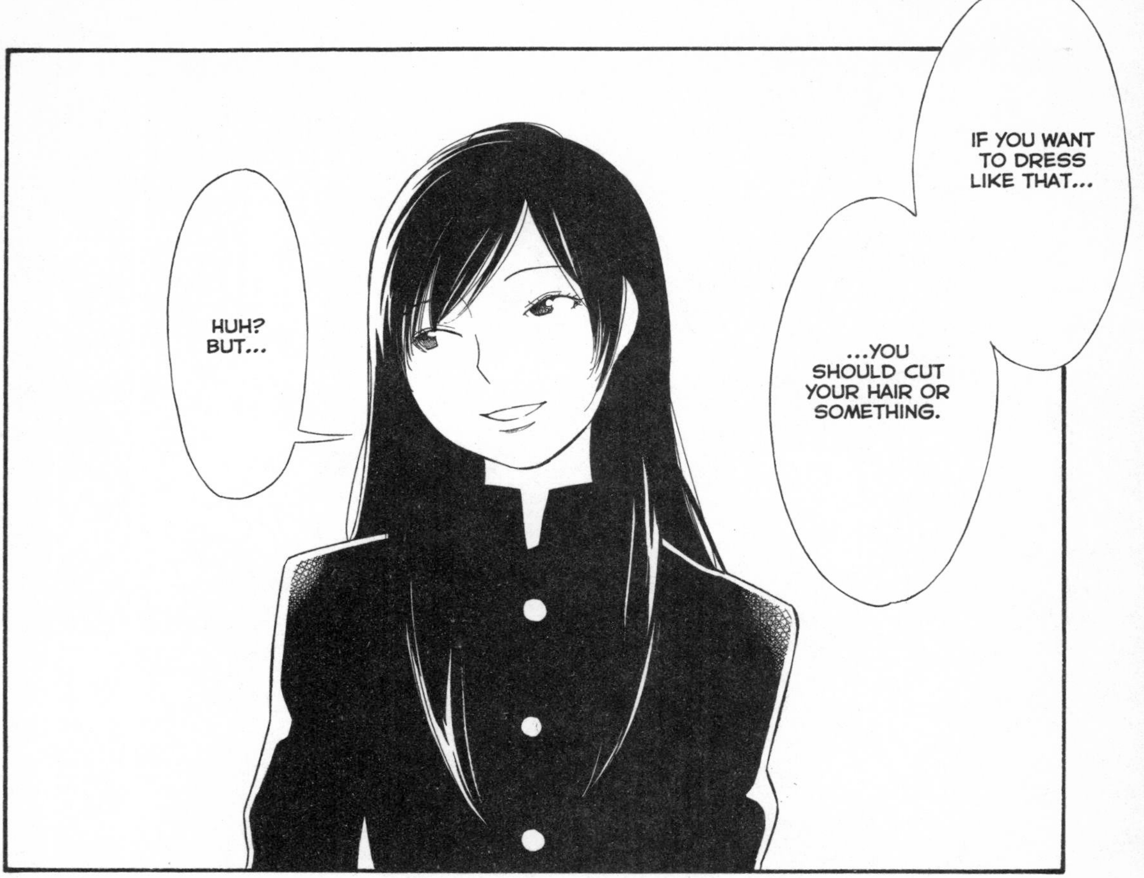
IF YOU WANT TO DRESS LIKE THAT...
...YOU SHOULD CUT YOUR HAIR OR SOMETHING.
HUH? BUT...

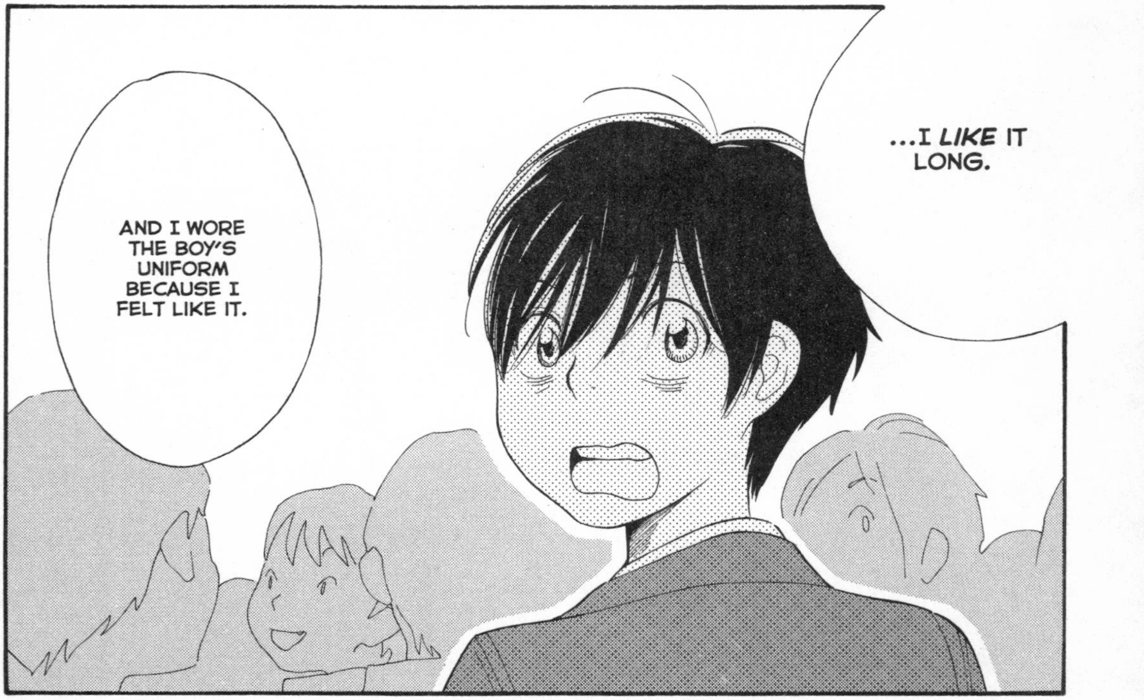
...I *LIKE* IT LONG.
AND I WORE THE BOY'S UNIFORM BECAUSE I FELT LIKE IT.

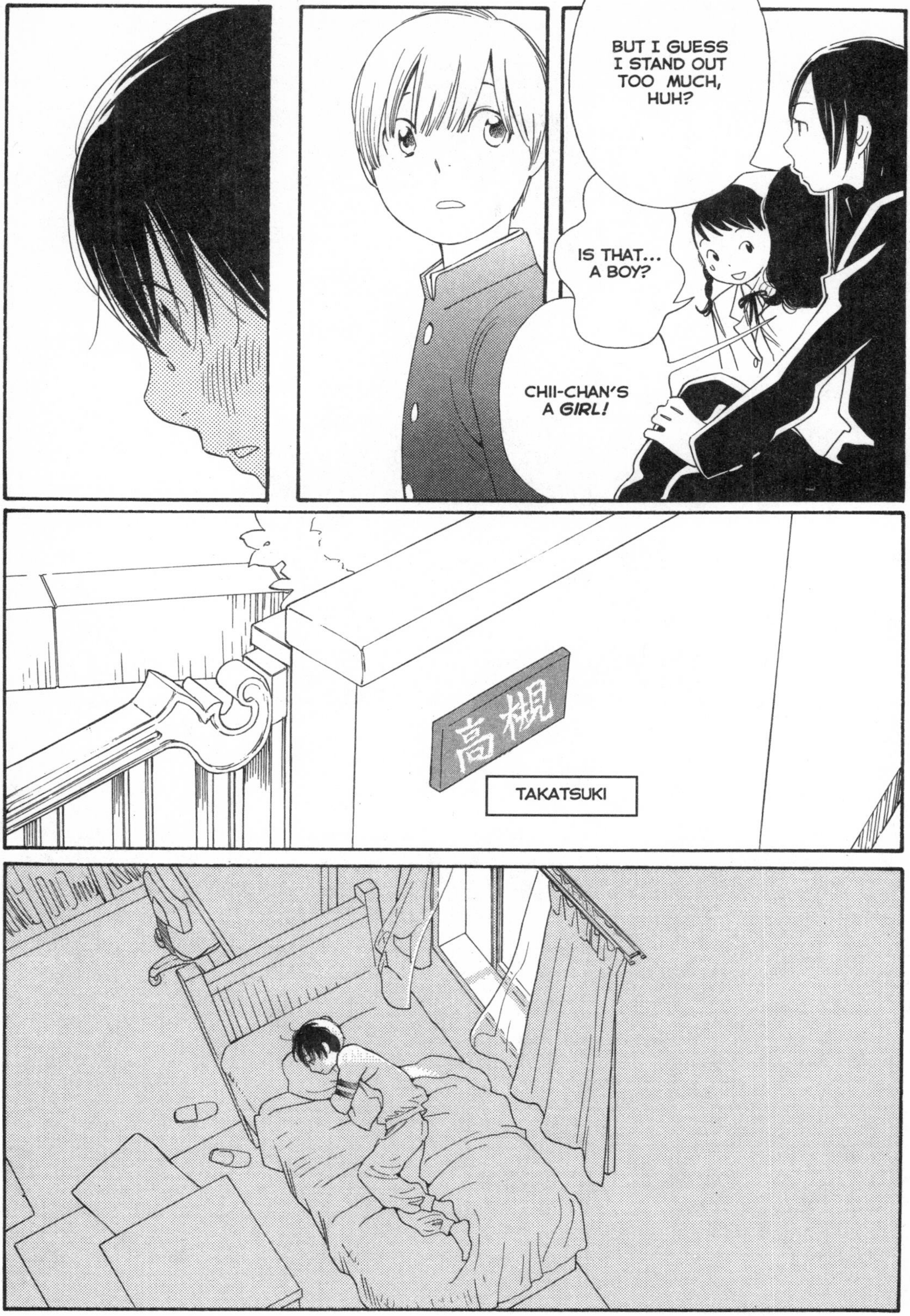
BUT I GUESS I STAND OUT TOO MUCH, HUH?
IS THAT... A BOY?
CHII-CHAN'S A *GIRL!*
高槻
TAKATSUKI

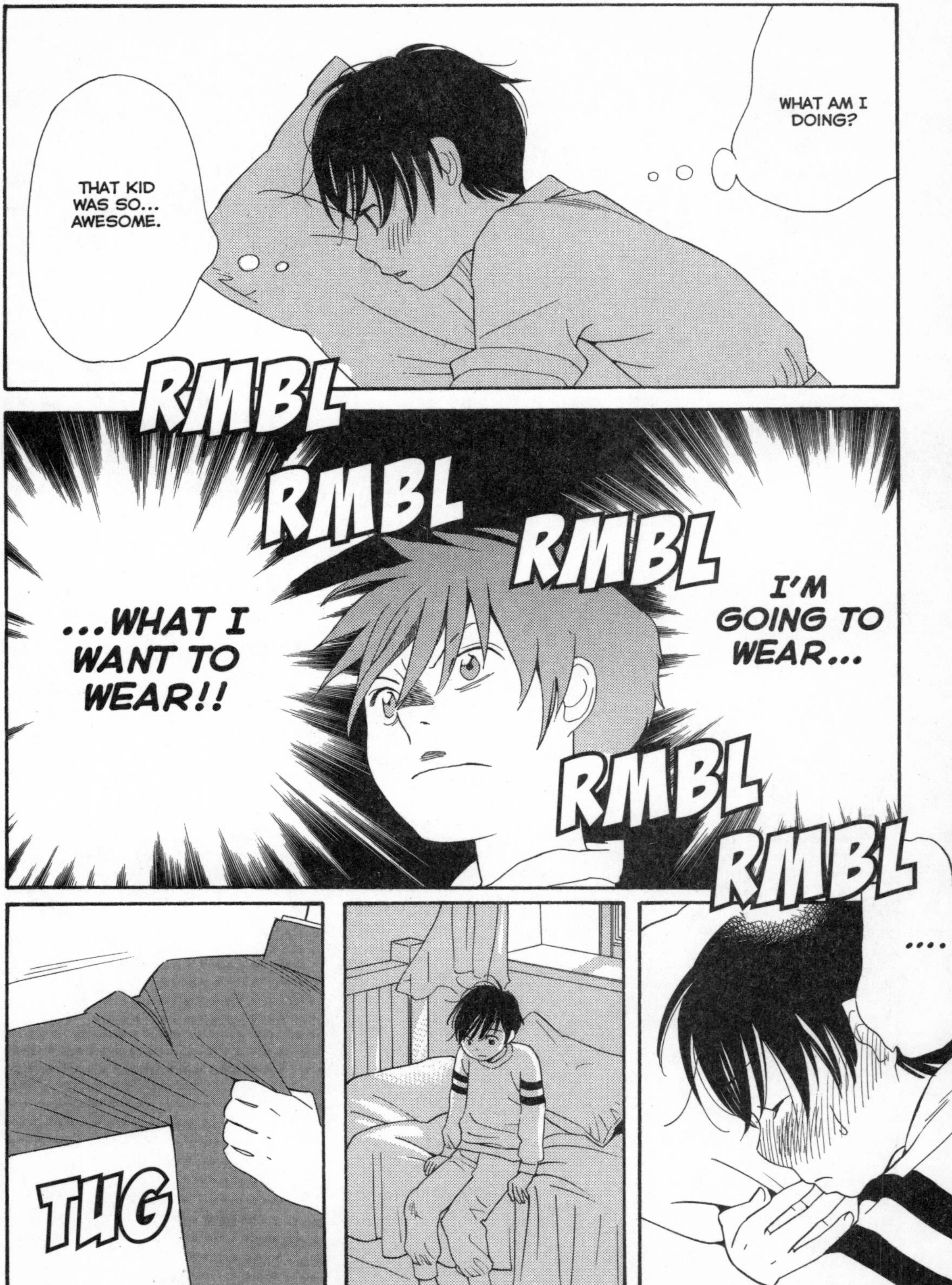
WHAT AM I DOING?
THAT KID WAS SO... AWESOME.
RMBL RMBL RMBL
I'M GOING TO WEAR...
...WHAT I WANT TO WEAR!!
RMBL RMBL
....
TUG

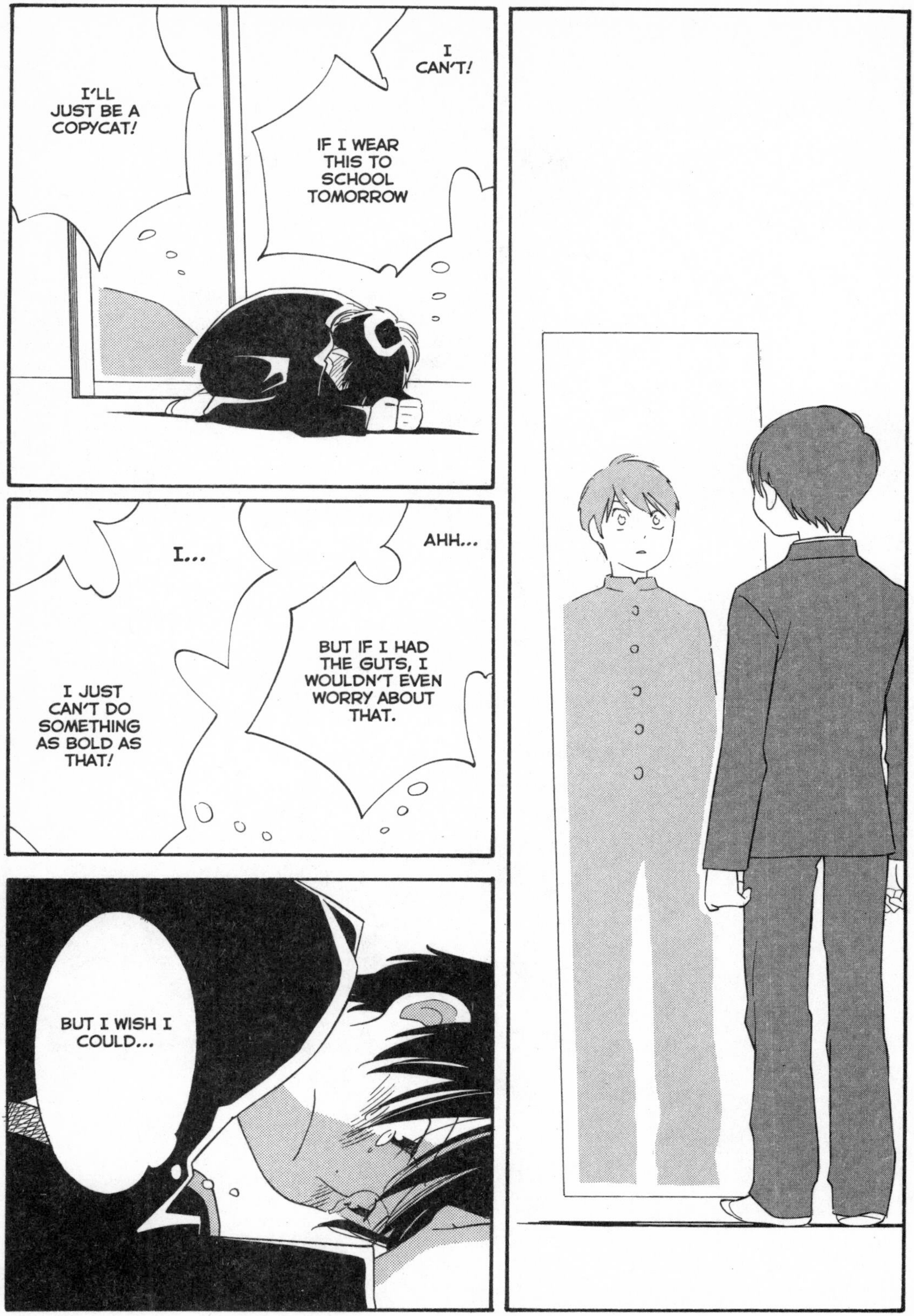
I CAN'T!
IF I WEAR THIS TO SCHOOL TOMORROW
I'LL JUST BE A COPYCAT!
AHH...
I...
BUT IF I HAD THE GUTS, I WOULDN'T EVEN WORRY ABOUT THAT.
I JUST CAN'T DO SOMETHING AS BOLD AS THAT!
BUT I WISH I COULD...

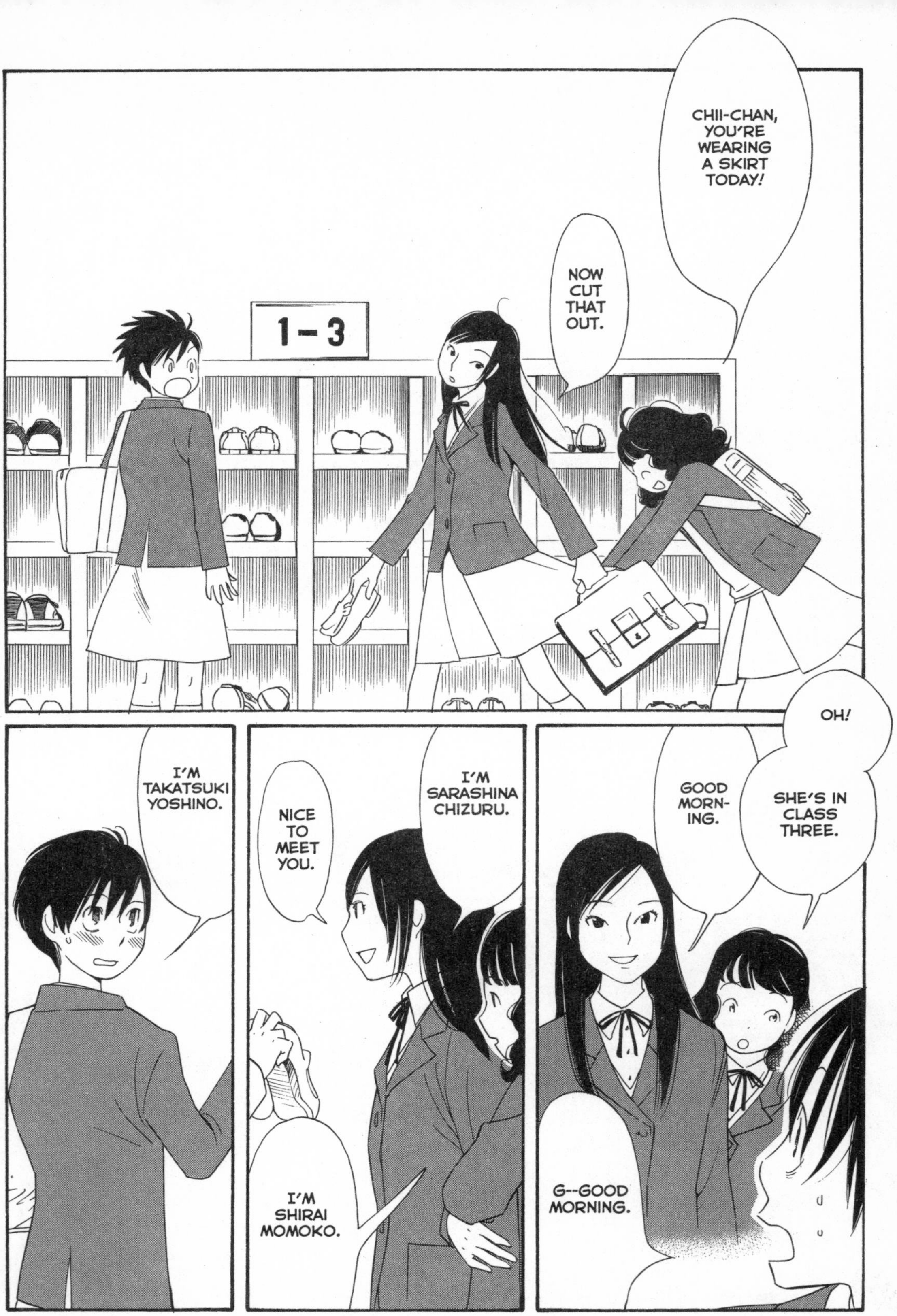
CHII-CHAN, YOU'RE WEARING A SKIRT TODAY!
NOW CUT THAT OUT.
OH!
SHE'S IN CLASS THREE.
GOOD MORN-ING.
G--GOOD MORNING.
I'M SARASHINA CHIZURU.
NICE TO MEET YOU.
I'M SHIRAI MOMOKO.
I'M TAKATSUKI YOSHINO.

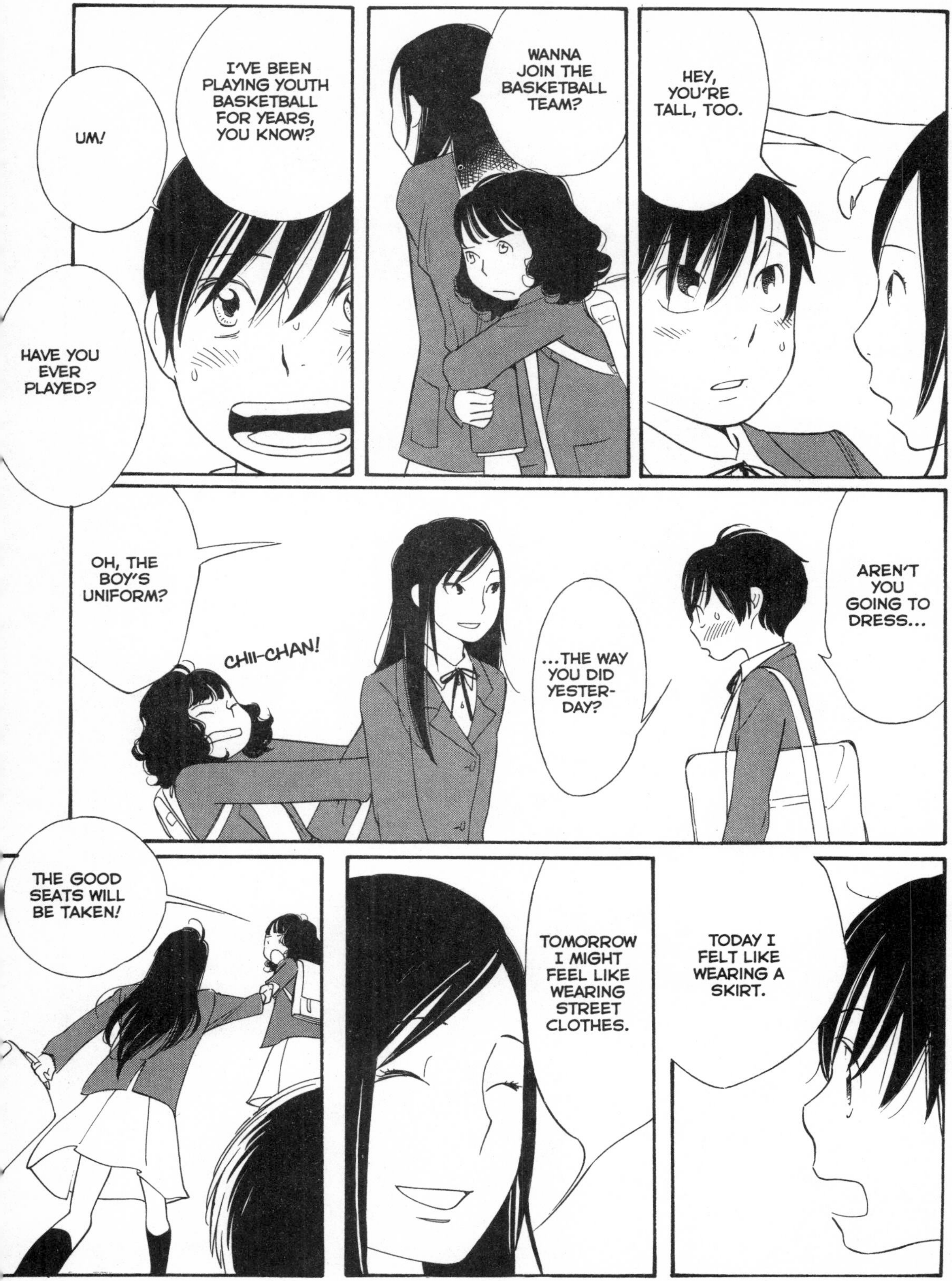
HEY, YOU'RE TALL, TOO.
WANNA JOIN THE BASKETBALL TEAM?
I'VE BEEN PLAYING YOUTH BASKETBALL FOR YEARS, YOU KNOW?
UM!
HAVE YOU EVER PLAYED?
AREN'T YOU GOING TO DRESS...
...THE WAY YOU DID YESTER-DAY?
OH, THE BOY'S UNIFORM?
CHII-CHAN!
TODAY I FELT LIKE WEARING A SKIRT.
TOMORROW I MIGHT FEEL LIKE WEARING STREET CLOTHES.
THE GOOD SEATS WILL BE TAKEN!

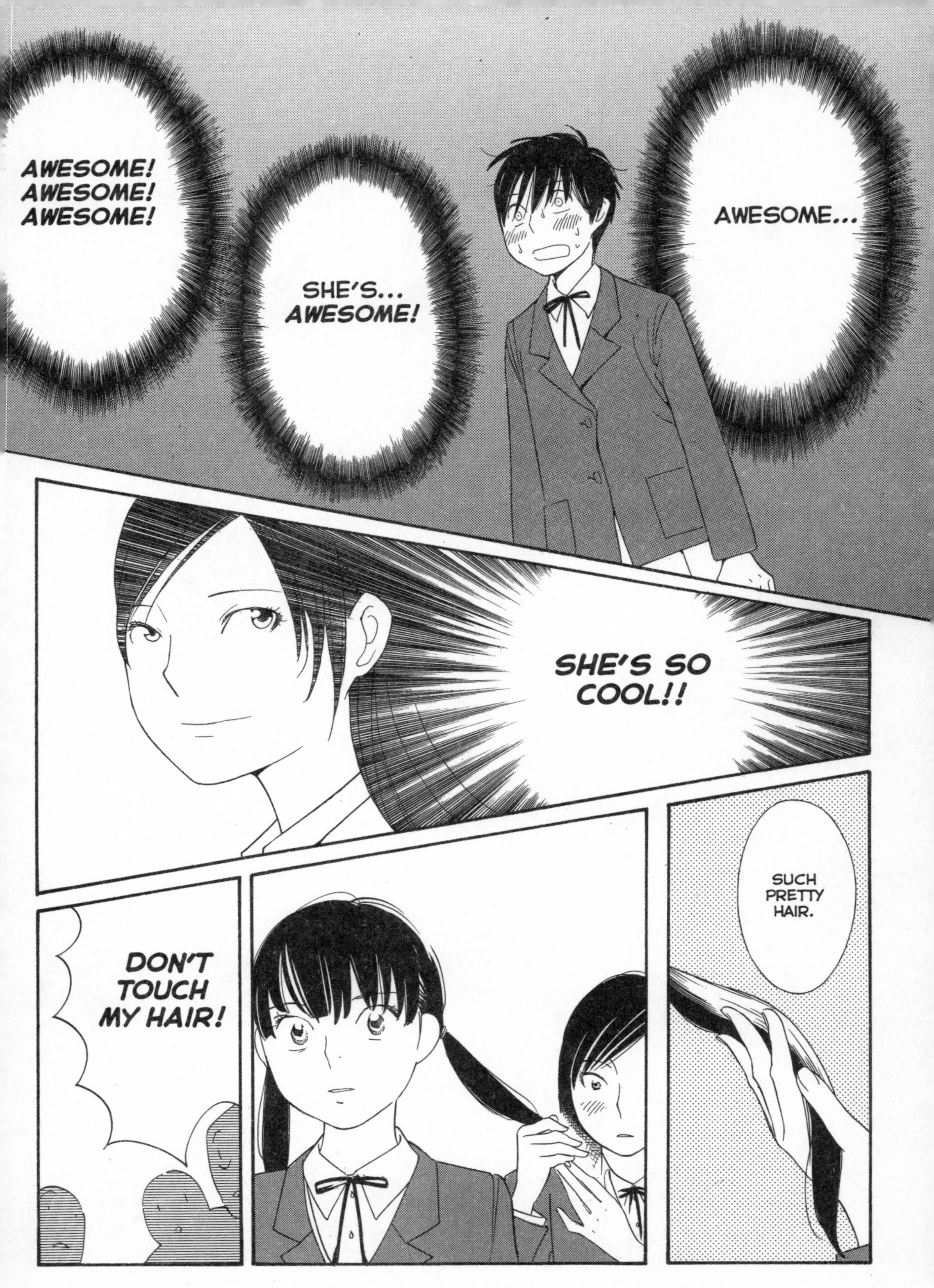
AWESOME...
SHE'S... AWESOME!
AWESOME! AWESOME! AWESOME!
SHE'S SO COOL!!
SUCH PRETTY HAIR.
DON'T TOUCH MY HAIR!

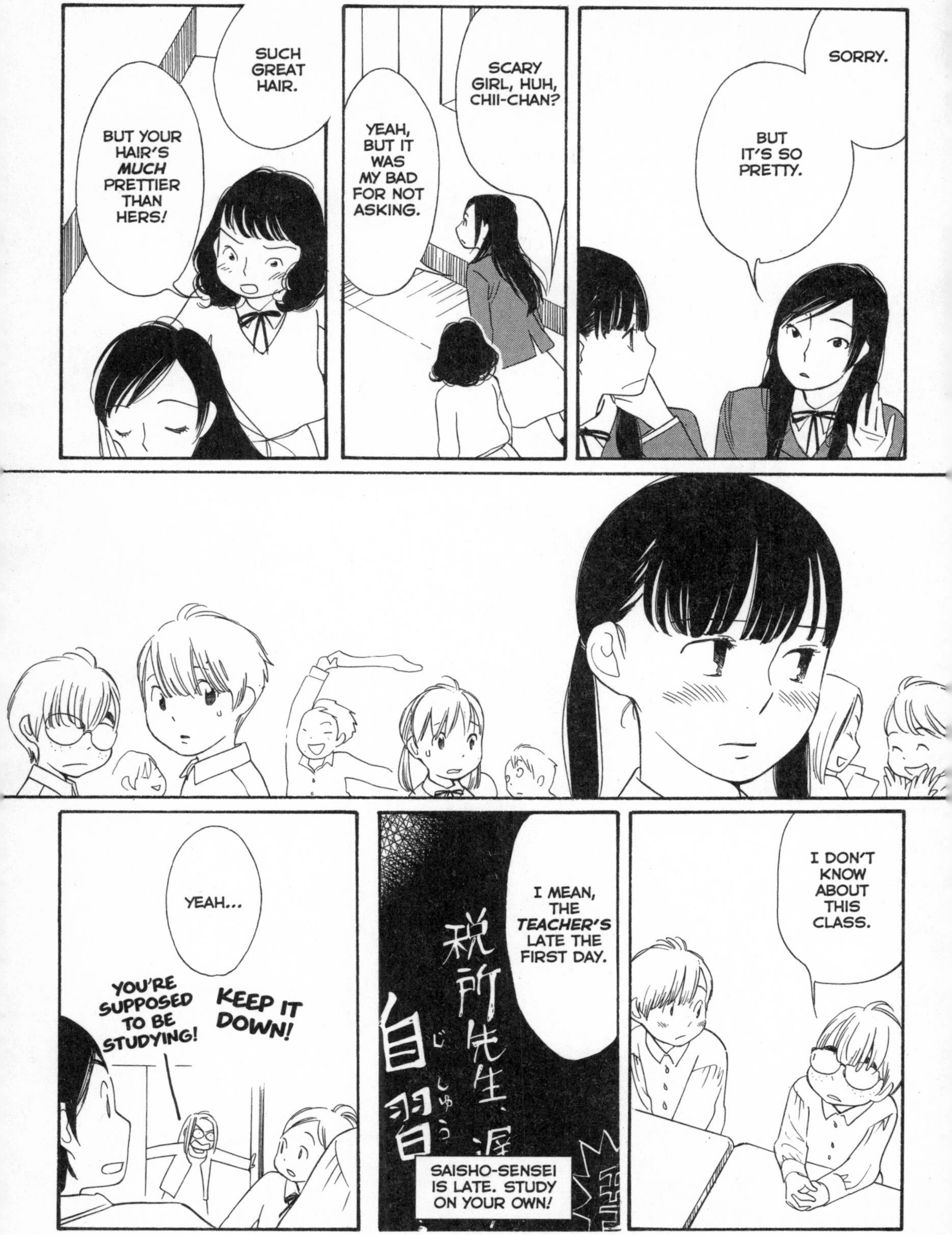
SORRY.
BUT IT'S SO PRETTY.
SCARY GIRL, HUH, CHII-CHAN?
YEAH, BUT IT WAS MY BAD FOR NOT ASKING.
SUCH GREAT HAIR.
BUT YOUR HAIR'S *MUCH* PRETTIER THAN HERS!
I DON'T KNOW ABOUT THIS CLASS.
I MEAN, THE *TEACHER'S* LATE THE FIRST DAY.
税所先生、遅
自習
SAISHO-SENSEI IS LATE. STUDY ON YOUR OWN!
YEAH...
KEEP IT DOWN!
YOU'RE SUPPOSED TO BE STUDYING!

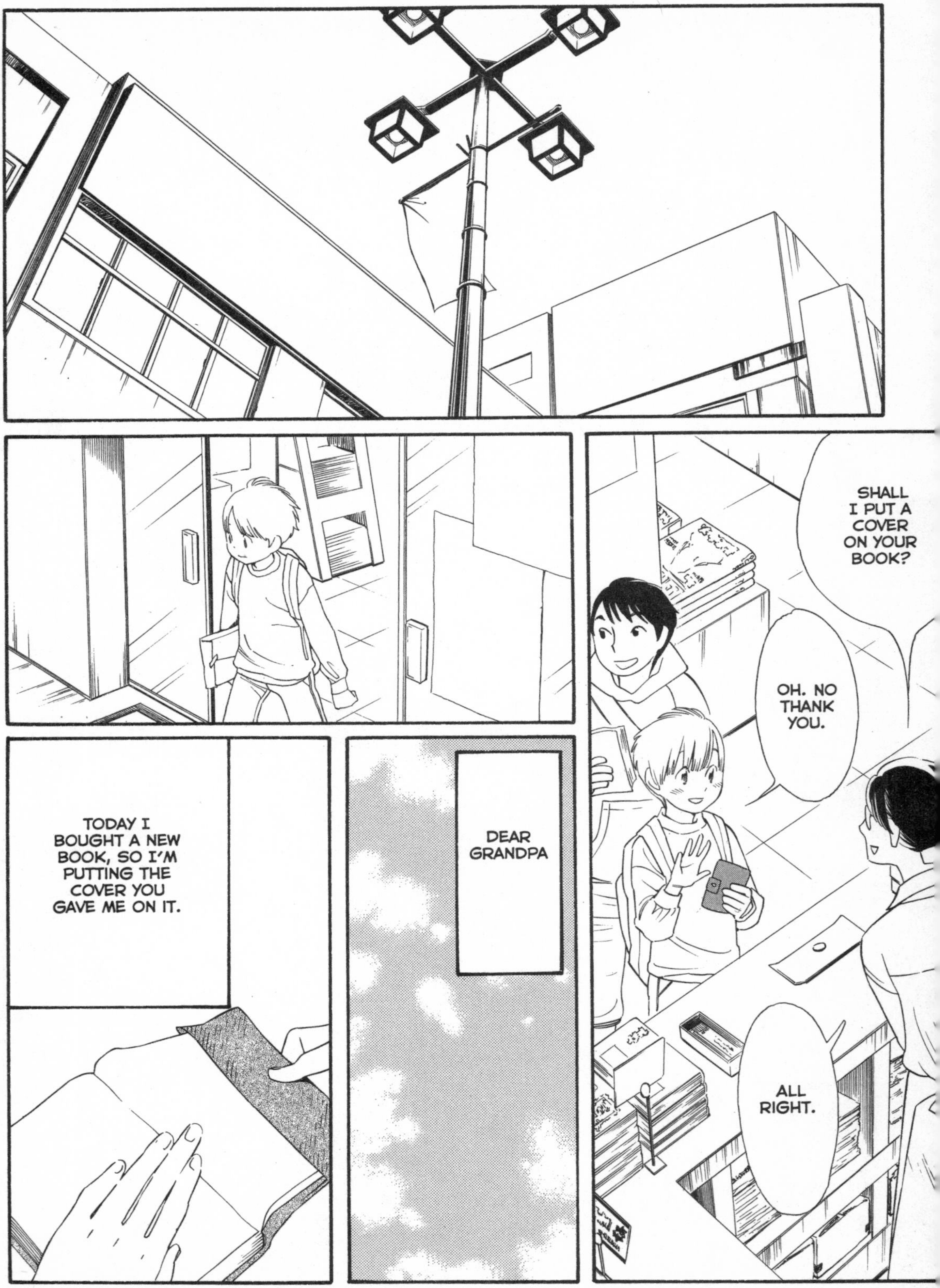
SHALL I PUT A COVER ON YOUR BOOK?
OH. NO THANK YOU.
ALL RIGHT.
DEAR GRANDPA
TODAY I BOUGHT A NEW BOOK, SO I'M PUTTING THE COVER YOU GAVE ME ON IT.

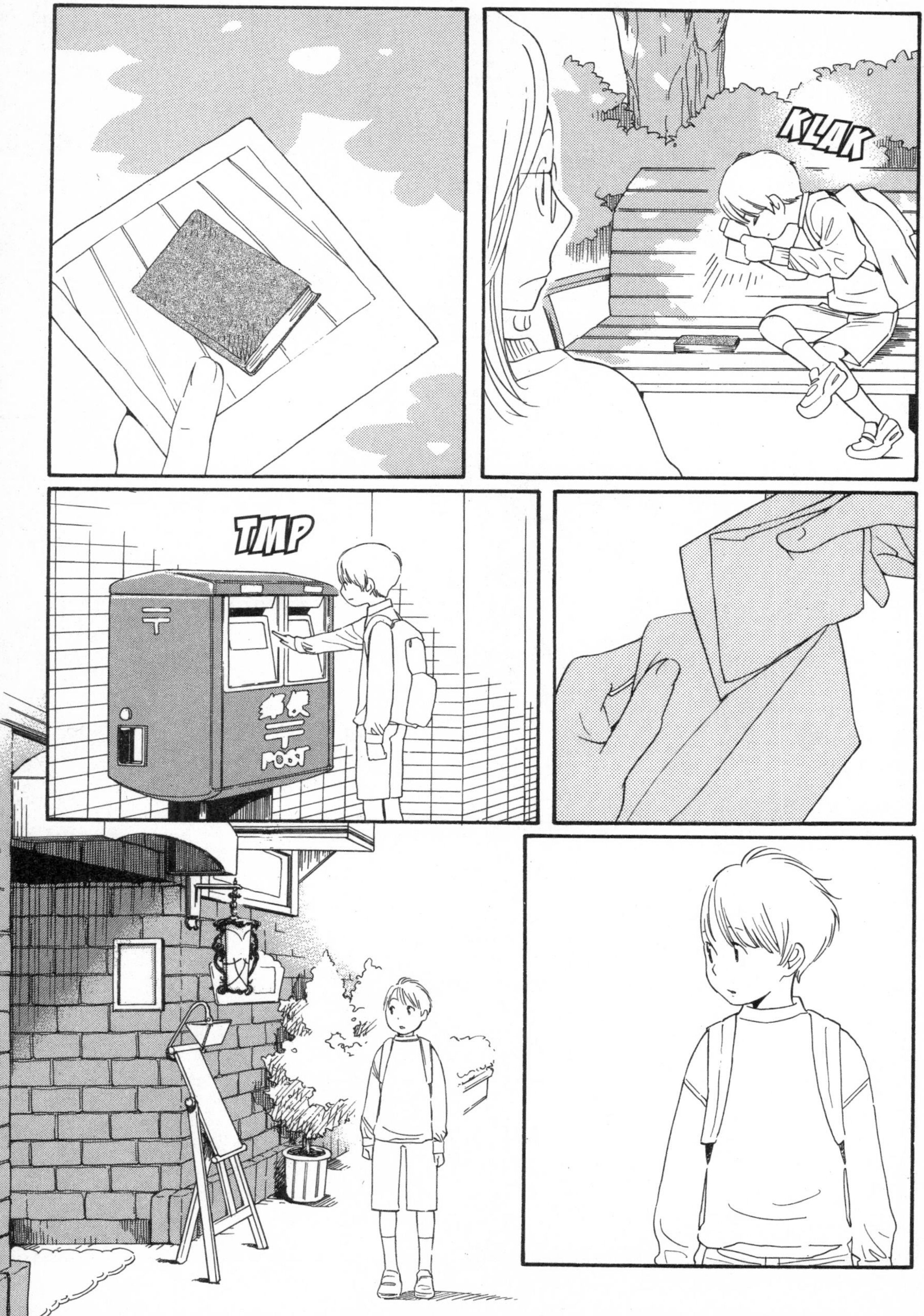
KLAK
TMP
POST

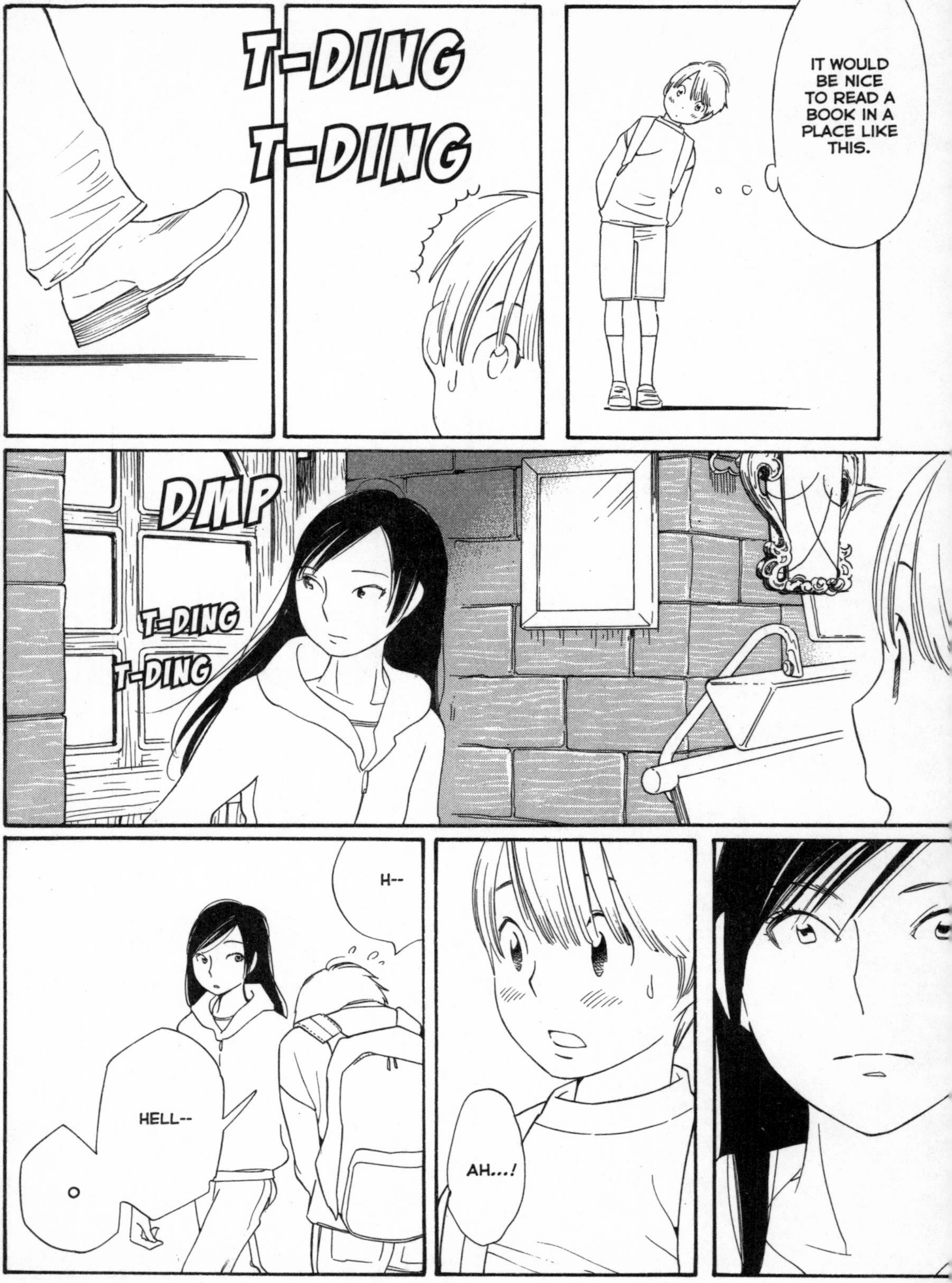
IT WOULD BE NICE TO READ A BOOK IN A PLACE LIKE THIS.
T-DING
T-DING
DMP
T-DING
T-DING
AH...!
H--
HELL--

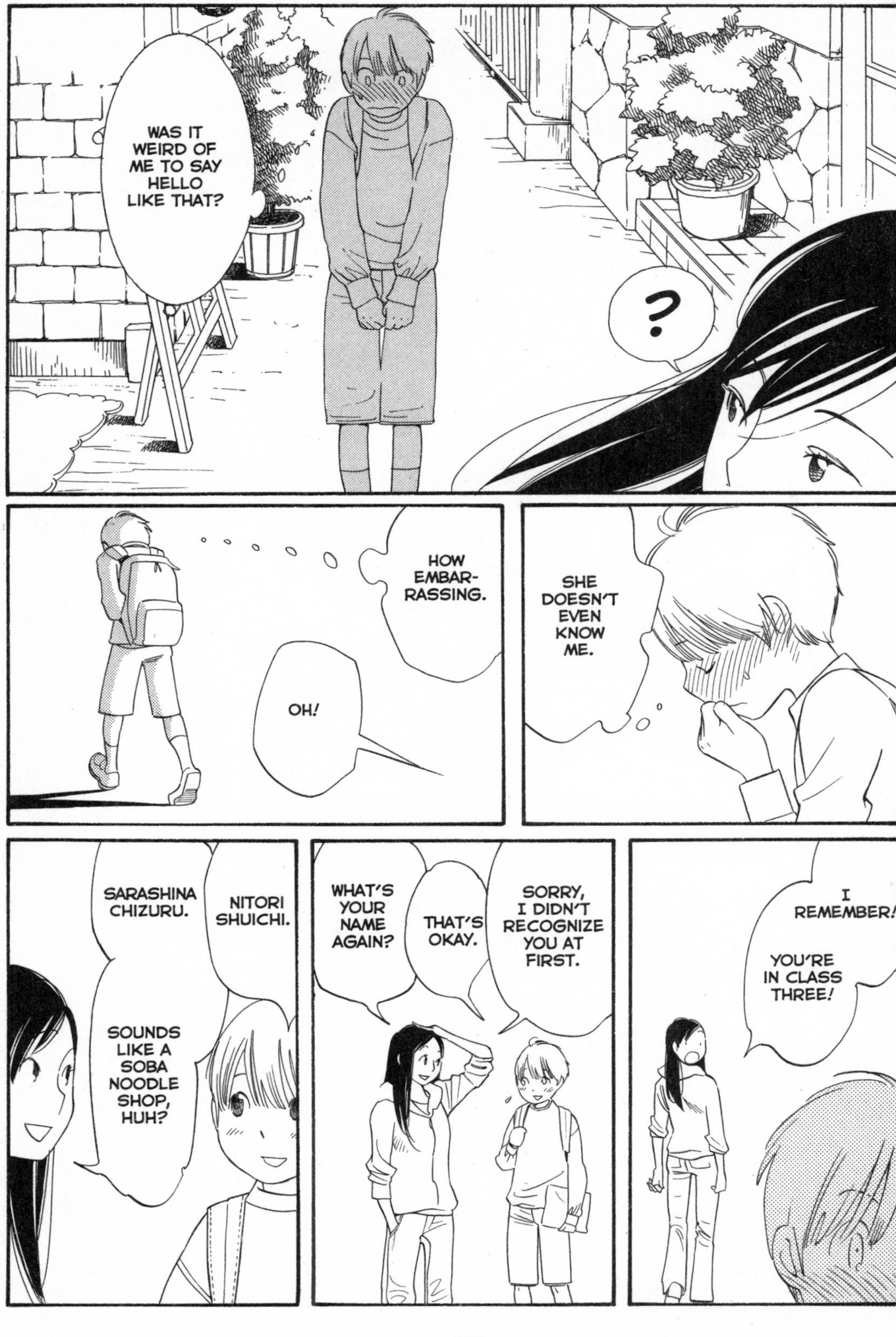
WAS IT WEIRD OF ME TO SAY HELLO LIKE THAT?
?
SHE DOESN'T EVEN KNOW ME.
HOW EMBAR-RASSING.
OH!
I REMEMBER!
YOU'RE IN CLASS THREE!
SORRY, I DIDN'T RECOGNIZE YOU AT FIRST.
THAT'S OKAY.
WHAT'S YOUR NAME AGAIN?
NITORI SHUICHI.
SARASHINA CHIZURU.
SOUNDS LIKE A SOBA NOODLE SHOP, HUH?

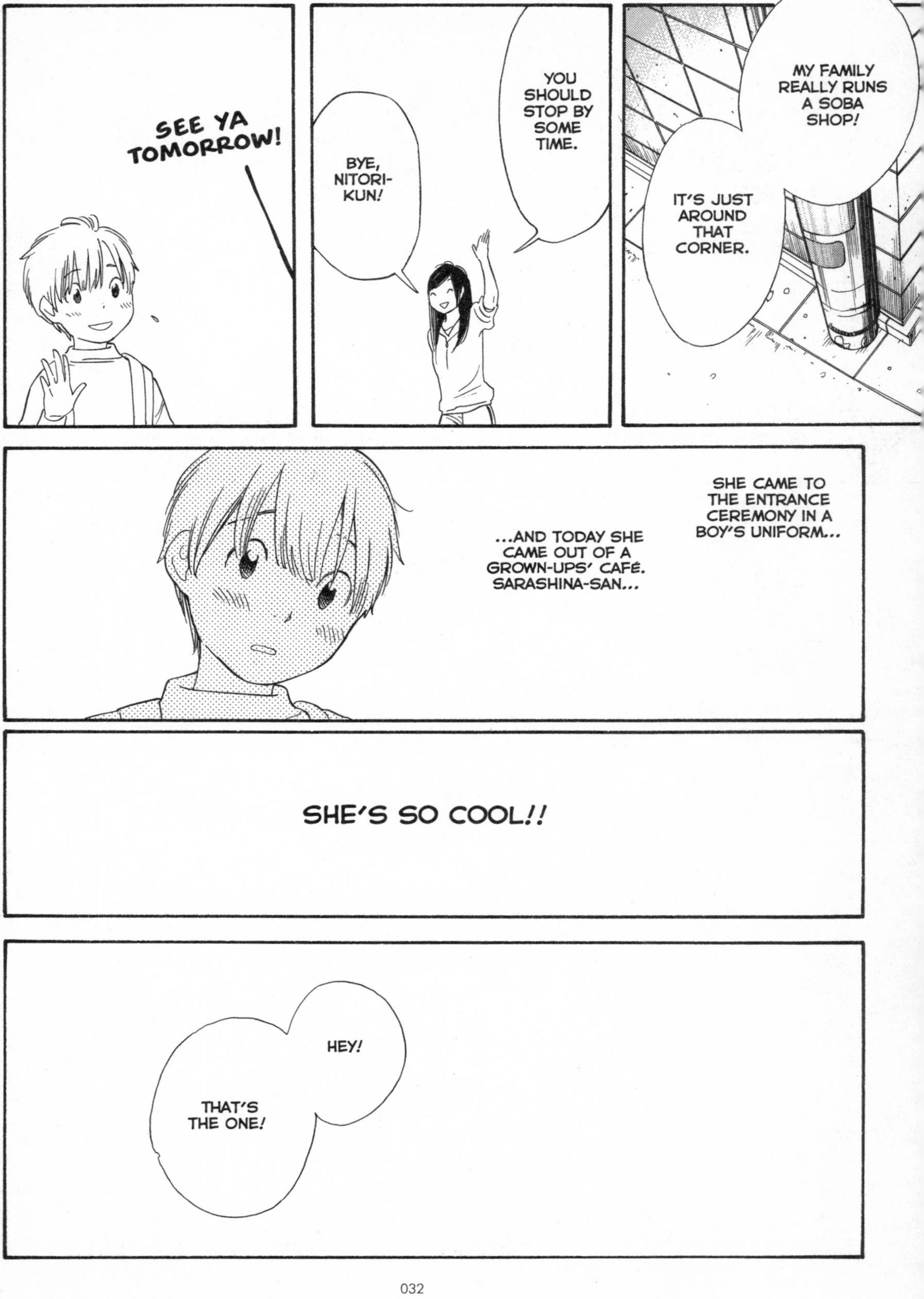
MY FAMILY REALLY RUNS A SOBA SHOP!
IT'S JUST AROUND THAT CORNER.
YOU SHOULD STOP BY SOME TIME.
BYE, NITORI-KUN!
SEE YA TOMORROW!
SHE CAME TO THE ENTRANCE CEREMONY IN A BOY'S UNIFORM...
...AND TODAY SHE CAME OUT OF A GROWN-UPS' CAFÉ. SARASHINA-SAN...
SHE'S SO COOL!!
HEY!
THAT'S THE ONE!

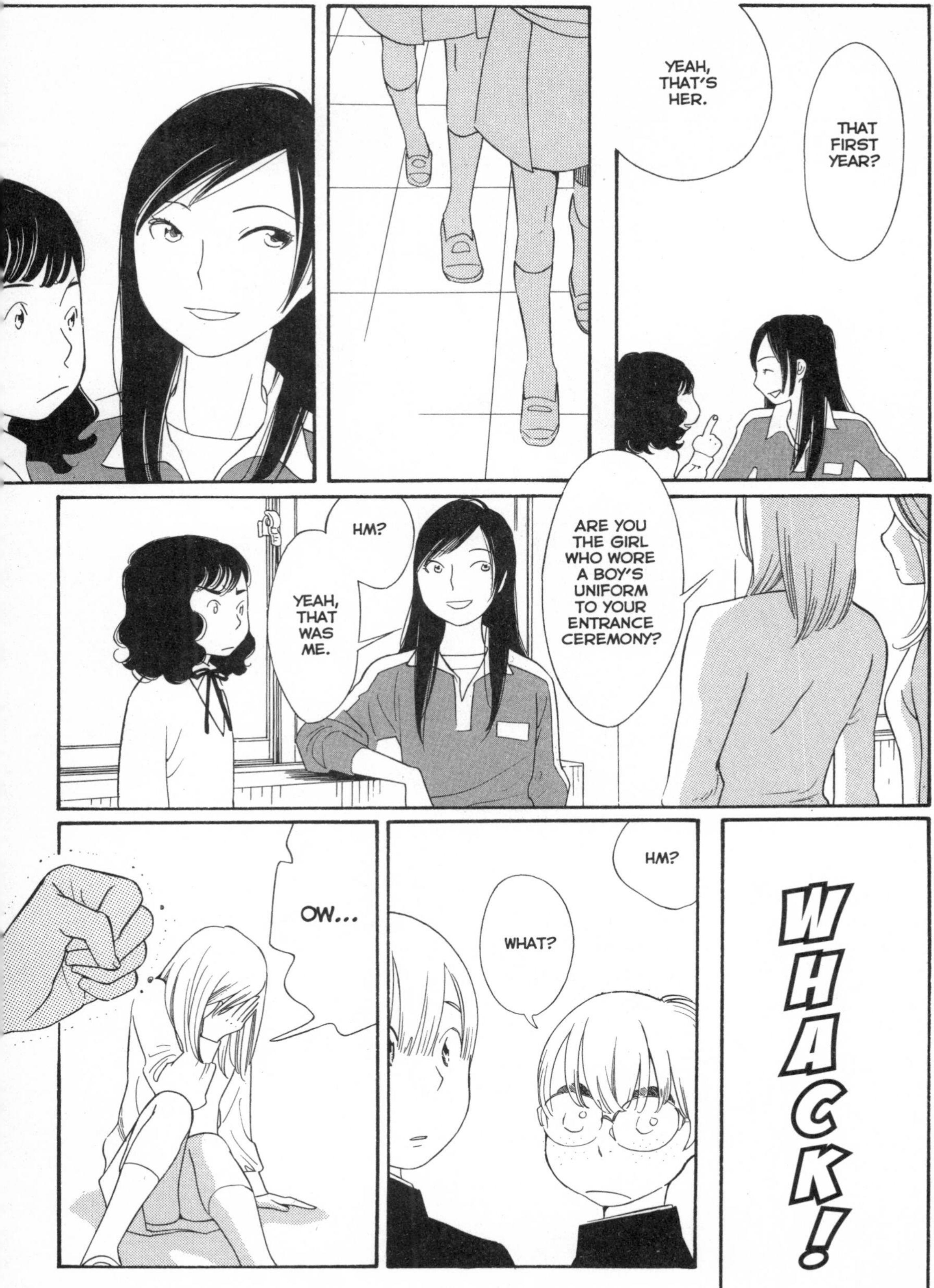

THAT FIRST YEAR?
YEAH, THAT'S HER.
ARE YOU THE GIRL WHO WORE A BOY'S UNIFORM TO YOUR ENTRANCE CEREMONY?
HM?
YEAH, THAT WAS ME.
WHACK!
HM?
WHAT?
OW...

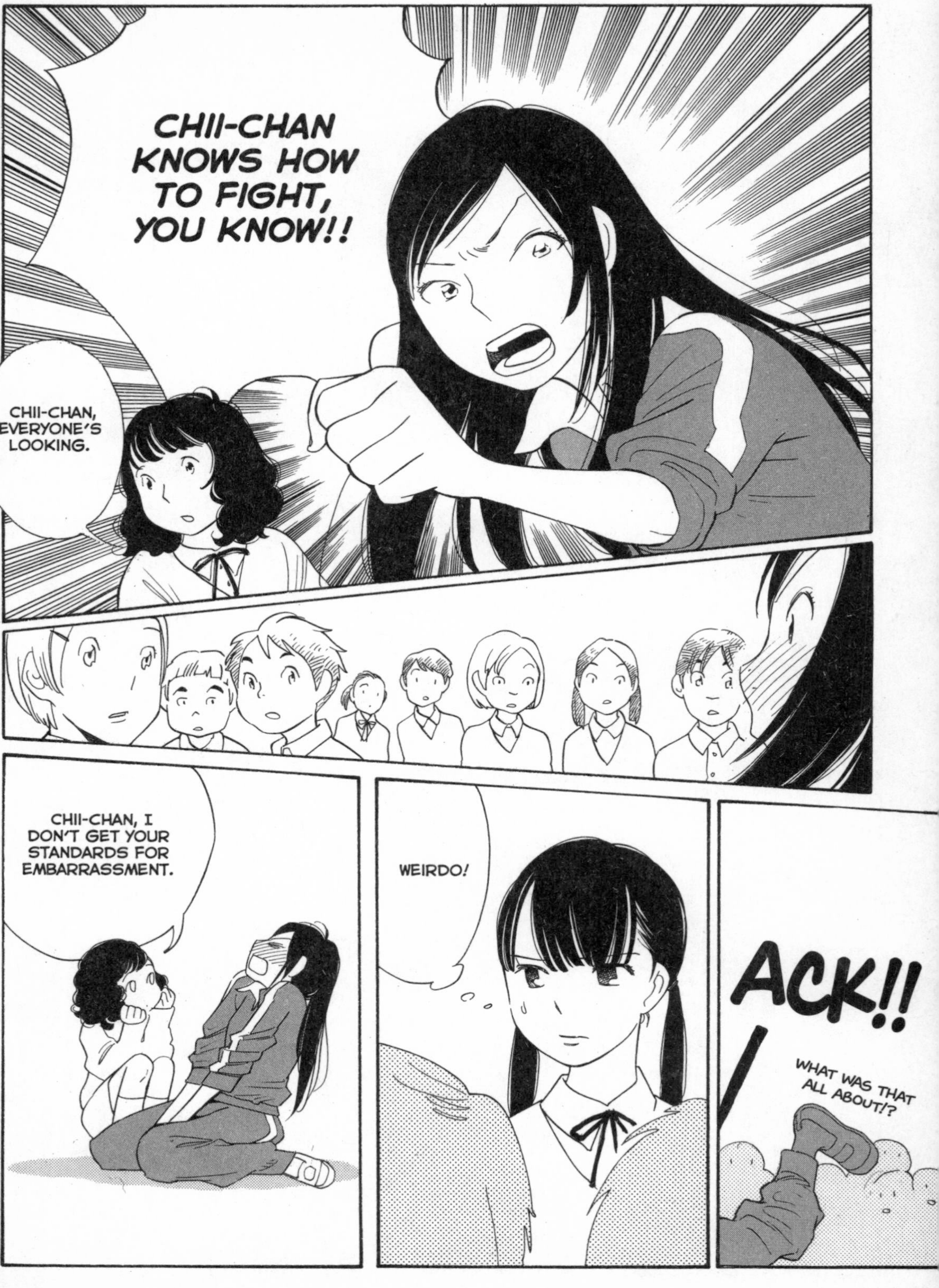
CHII-CHAN KNOWS HOW TO FIGHT, YOU KNOW!!
CHII-CHAN, EVERYONE'S LOOKING.
ACK!!
WHAT WAS THAT ALL ABOUT!?
WEIRDO!
CHII-CHAN, I DON'T GET YOUR STANDARDS FOR EMBARRASSMENT.

35

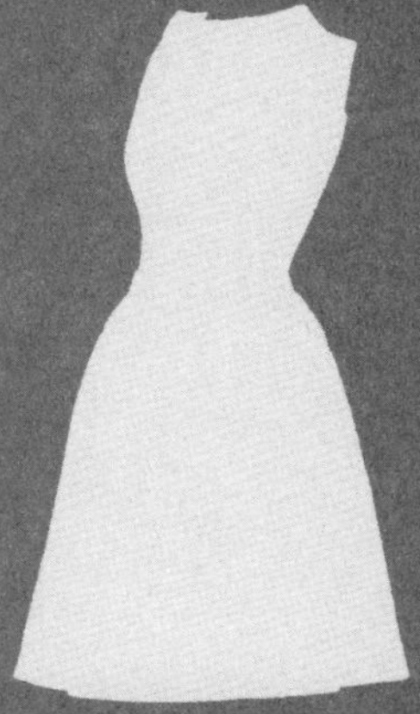

The Fresh-Faced Class Number Three

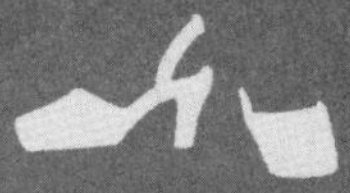

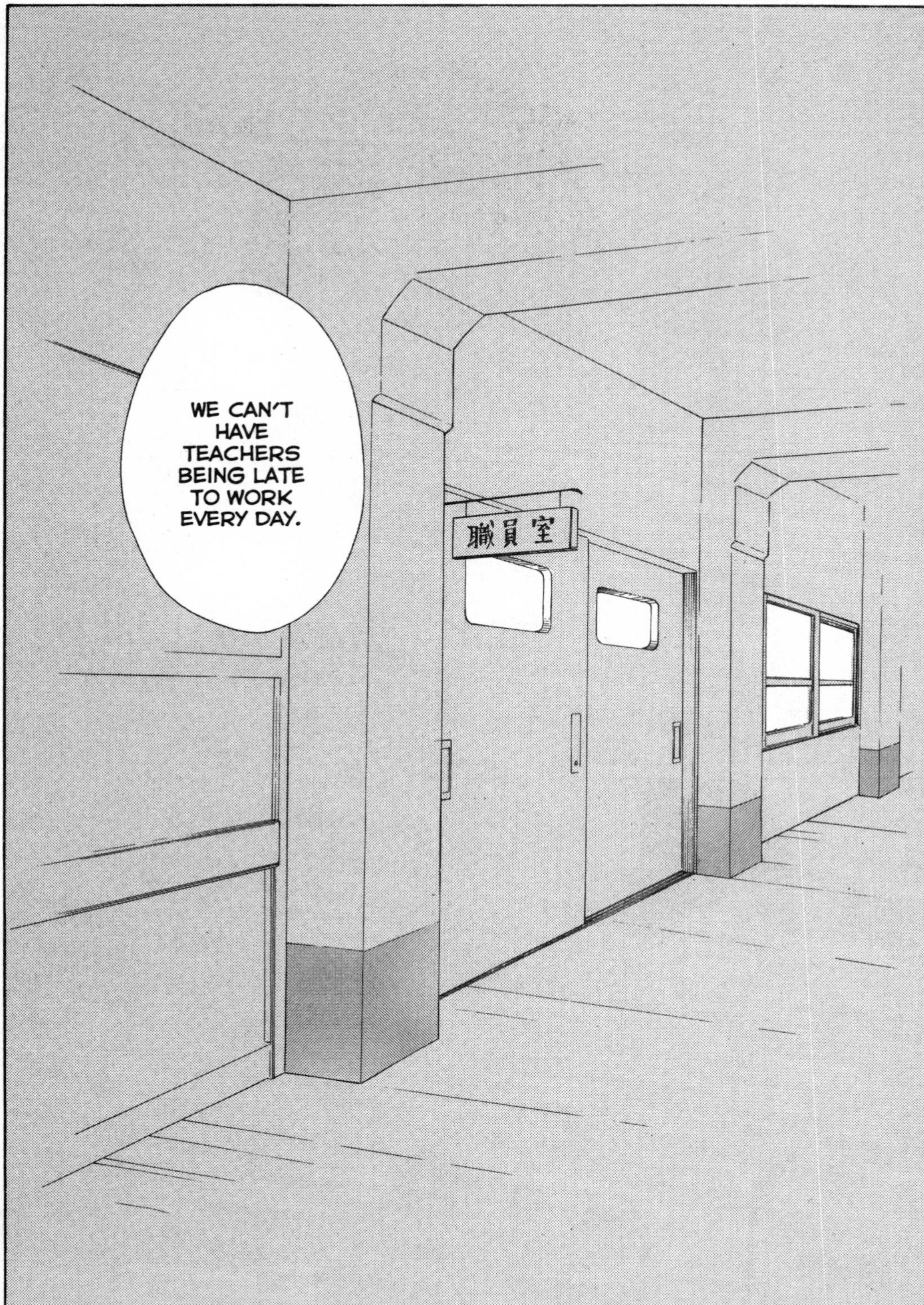
WE CAN'T HAVE TEACHERS BEING LATE TO WORK EVERY DAY.
職員室

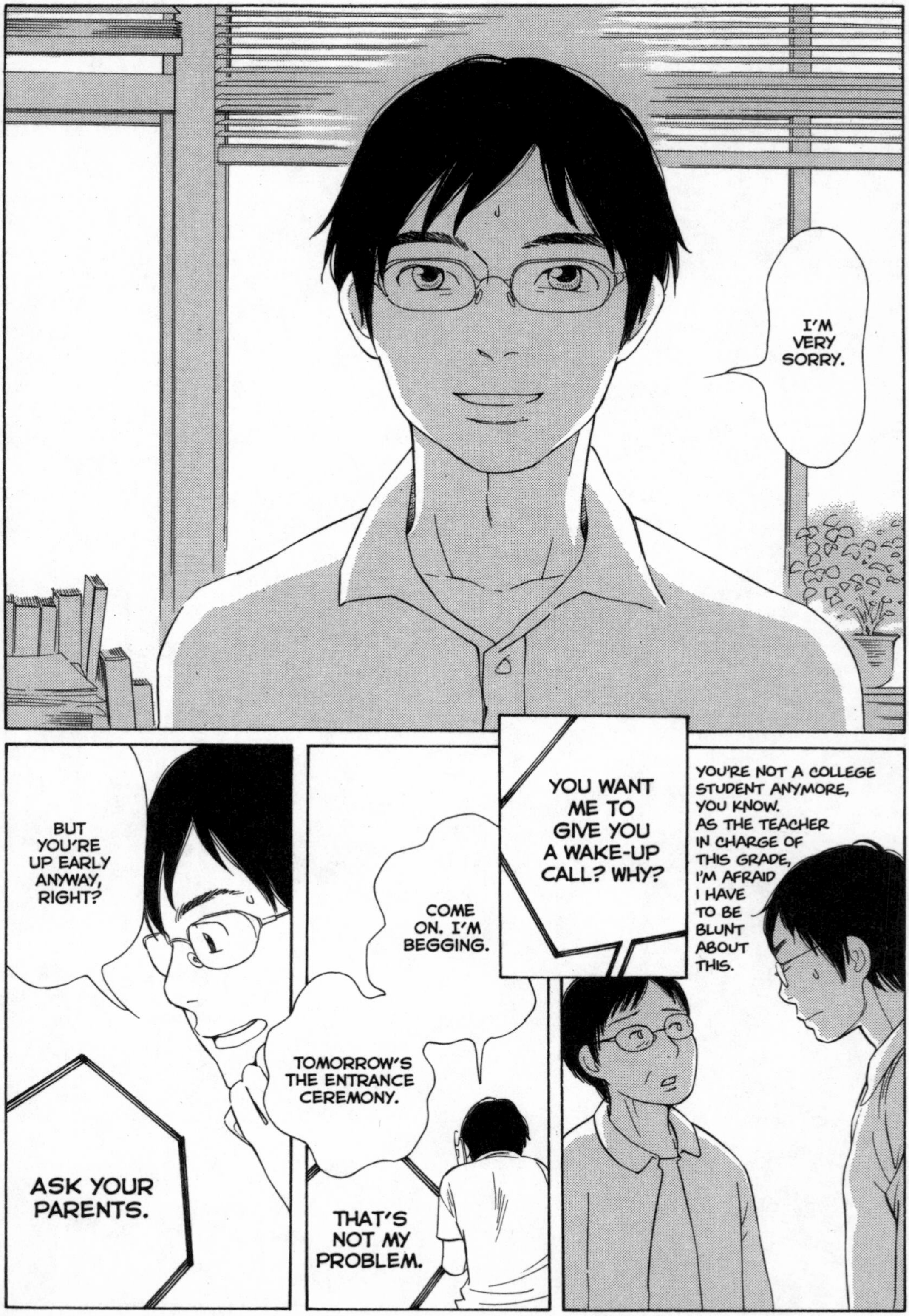
I'M VERY SORRY.
YOU'RE NOT A COLLEGE STUDENT ANYMORE, YOU KNOW. AS THE TEACHER IN CHARGE OF THIS GRADE, I'M AFRAID I HAVE TO BE BLUNT ABOUT THIS.
YOU WANT ME TO GIVE YOU A WAKE-UP CALL? WHY?
COME ON. I'M BEGGING.
TOMORROW'S THE ENTRANCE CEREMONY.
THAT'S NOT MY PROBLEM.
BUT YOU'RE UP EARLY ANYWAY, RIGHT?
ASK YOUR PARENTS.

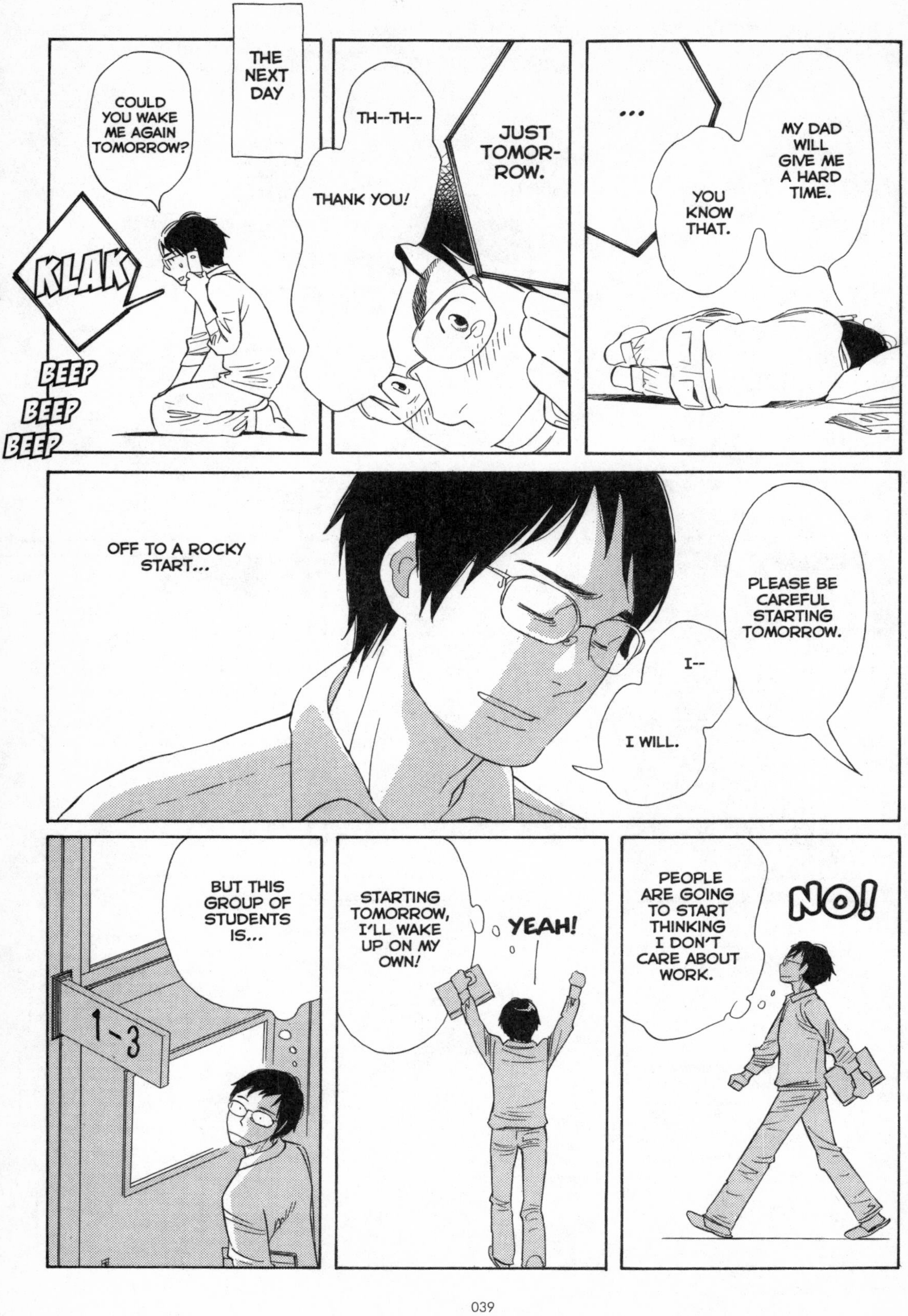

MY DAD WILL GIVE ME A HARD TIME.
YOU KNOW THAT.
...
JUST TOMORROW.
TH--TH--
THANK YOU!
THE NEXT DAY
COULD YOU WAKE ME AGAIN TOMORROW?
KLAK
BEEP BEEP BEEP
PLEASE BE CAREFUL STARTING TOMORROW.
I--
I WILL.
OFF TO A ROCKY START...
NO!
PEOPLE ARE GOING TO START THINKING I DON'T CARE ABOUT WORK.
YEAH!
STARTING TOMORROW, I'LL WAKE UP ON MY OWN!
BUT THIS GROUP OF STUDENTS IS...
1-3

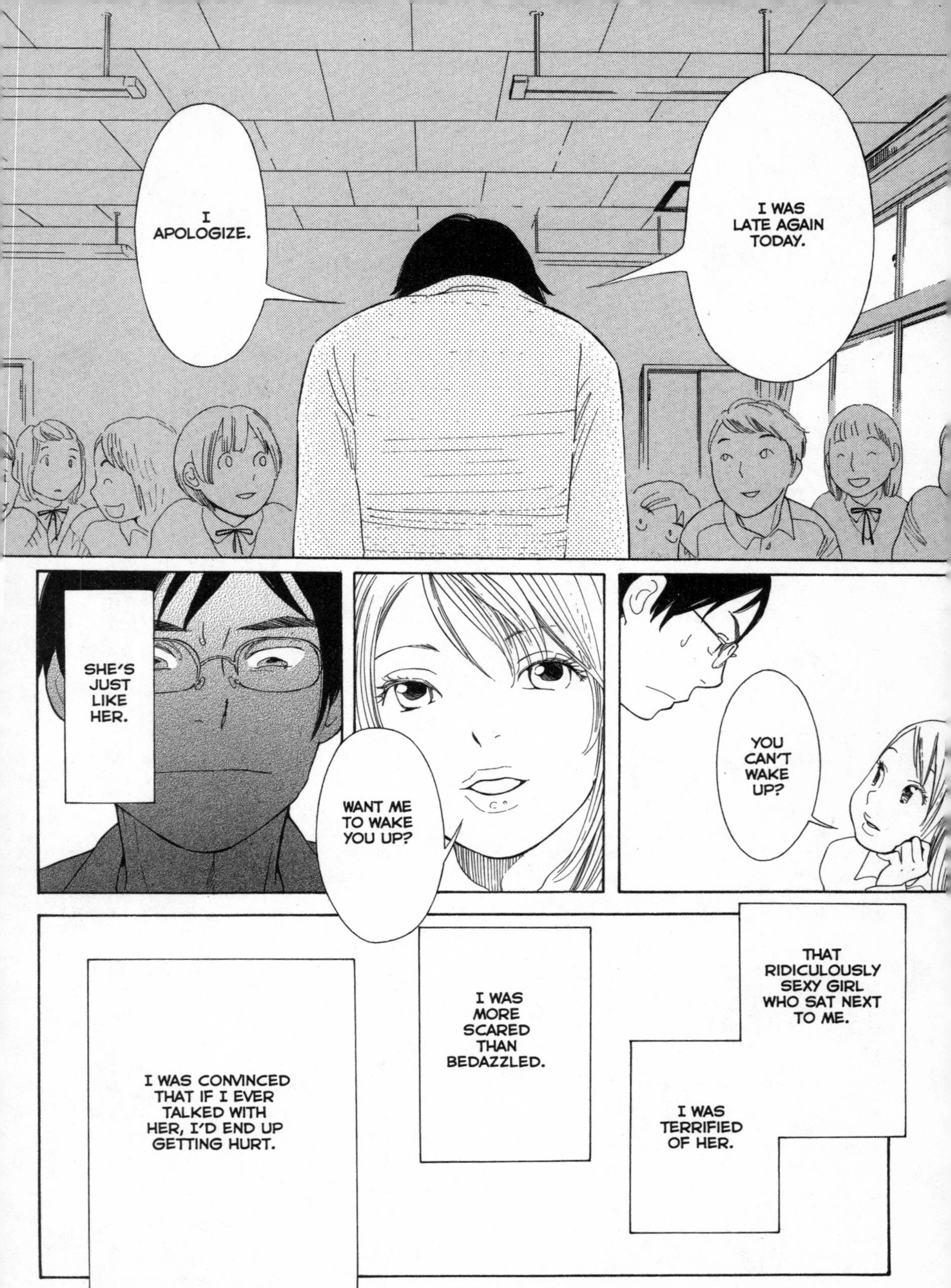

I WAS LATE AGAIN TODAY.
I APOLOGIZE.
YOU CAN'T WAKE UP?
WANT ME TO WAKE YOU UP?
SHE'S JUST LIKE HER.
THAT RIDICULOUSLY SEXY GIRL WHO SAT NEXT TO ME.
I WAS TERRIFIED OF HER.
I WAS MORE SCARED THAN BEDAZZLED.
I WAS CONVINCED THAT IF I EVER TALKED WITH HER, I'D END UP GETTING HURT.

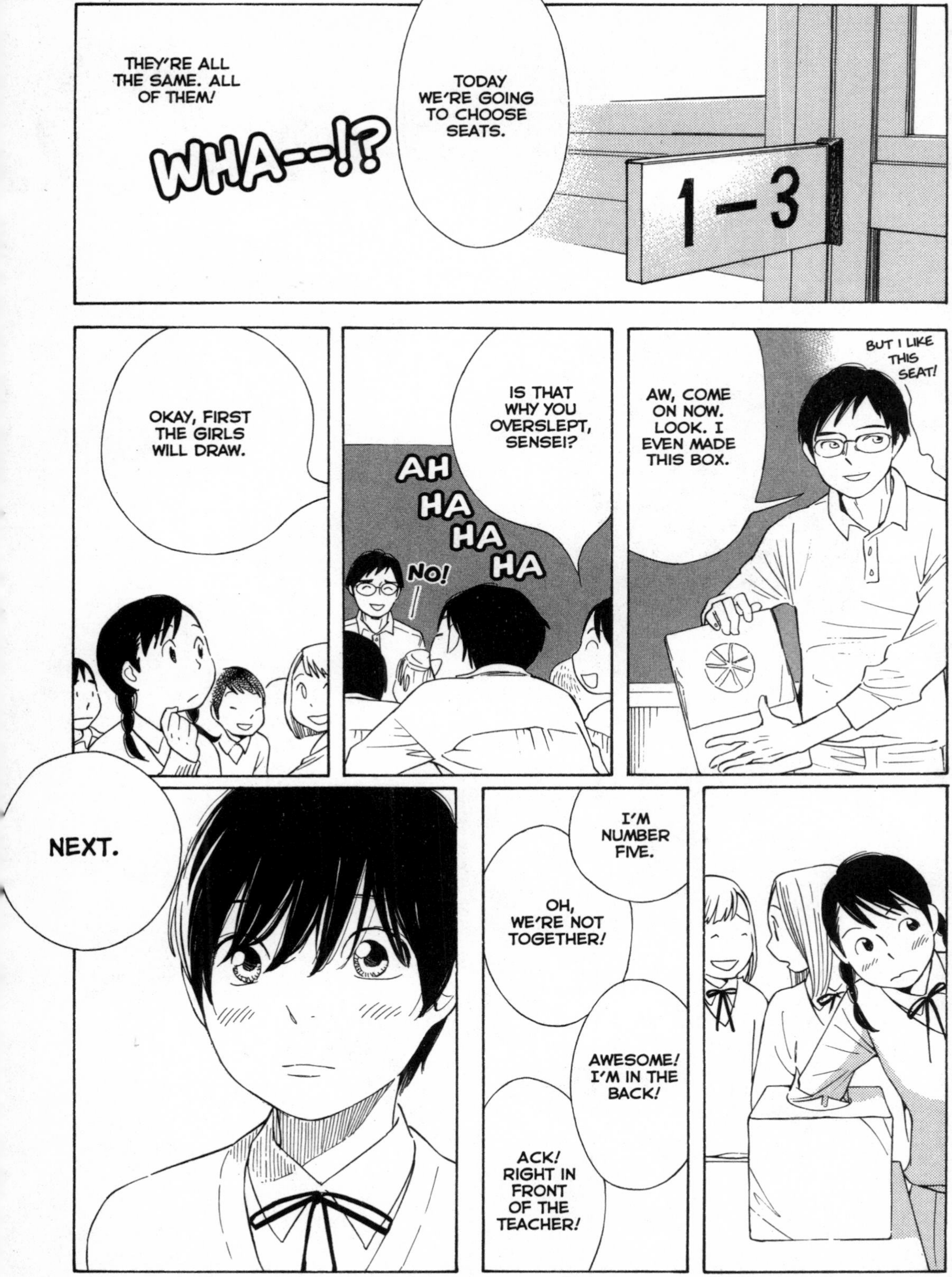
1–3
TODAY WE'RE GOING TO CHOOSE SEATS.
THEY'RE ALL THE SAME. ALL OF THEM!
WHA--!?
BUT I LIKE THIS SEAT!
AW, COME ON NOW. LOOK. I EVEN MADE THIS BOX.
IS THAT WHY YOU OVERSLEPT, SENSEI?
AH HA HA HA HA
NO!
OKAY, FIRST THE GIRLS WILL DRAW.
I'M NUMBER FIVE.
OH, WE'RE NOT TOGETHER!
AWESOME! I'M IN THE BACK!
ACK! RIGHT IN FRONT OF THE TEACHER!
NEXT.

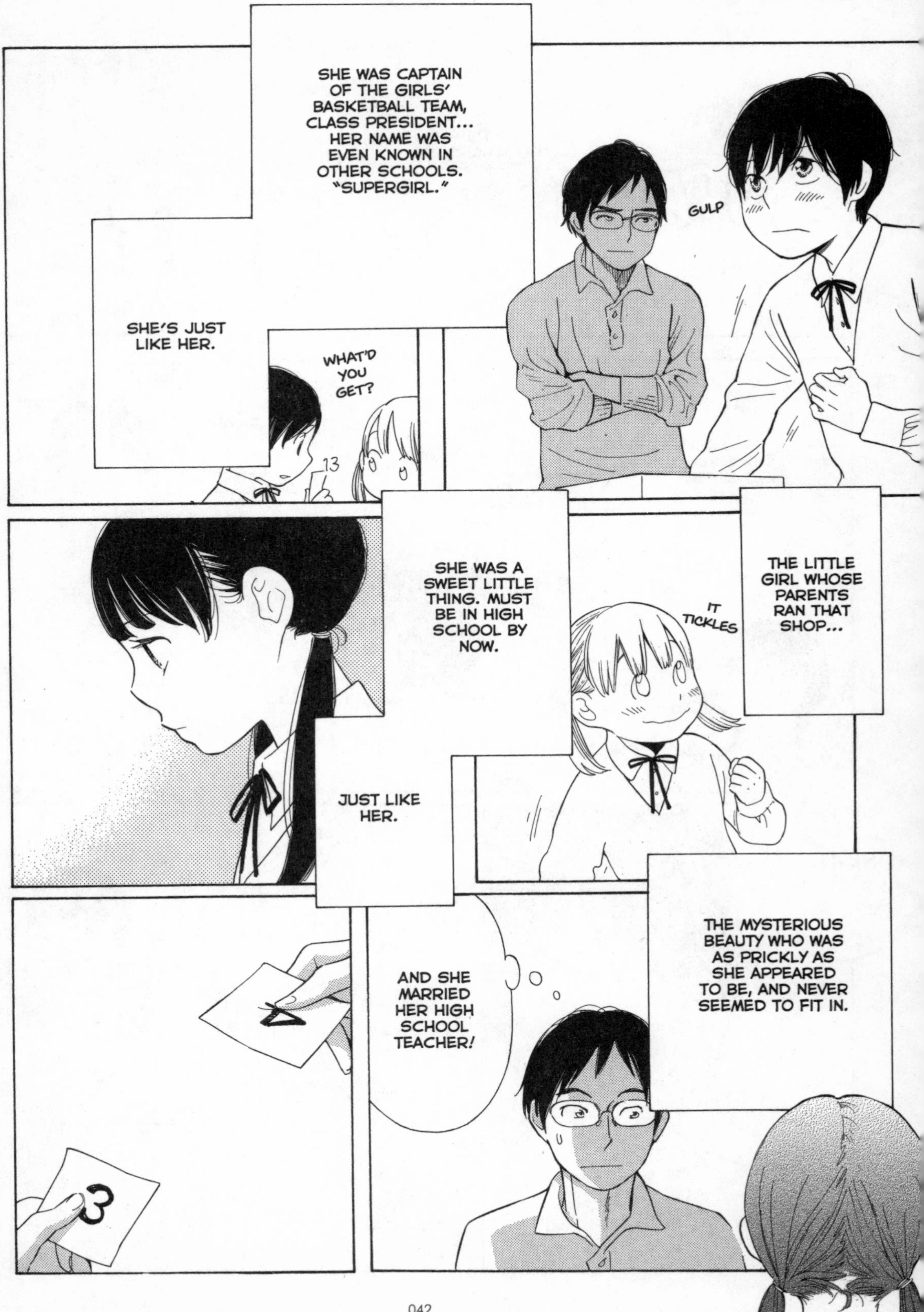
SHE WAS CAPTAIN OF THE GIRLS' BASKETBALL TEAM, CLASS PRESIDENT... HER NAME WAS EVEN KNOWN IN OTHER SCHOOLS. "SUPERGIRL."
GULP
WHAT'D YOU GET?
13
SHE'S JUST LIKE HER.
THE LITTLE GIRL WHOSE PARENTS RAN THAT SHOP...
IT TICKLES
SHE WAS A SWEET LITTLE THING. MUST BE IN HIGH SCHOOL BY NOW.
JUST LIKE HER.
THE MYSTERIOUS BEAUTY WHO WAS AS PRICKLY AS SHE APPEARED TO BE, AND NEVER SEEMED TO FIT IN.
AND SHE MARRIED HER HIGH SCHOOL TEACHER!
3

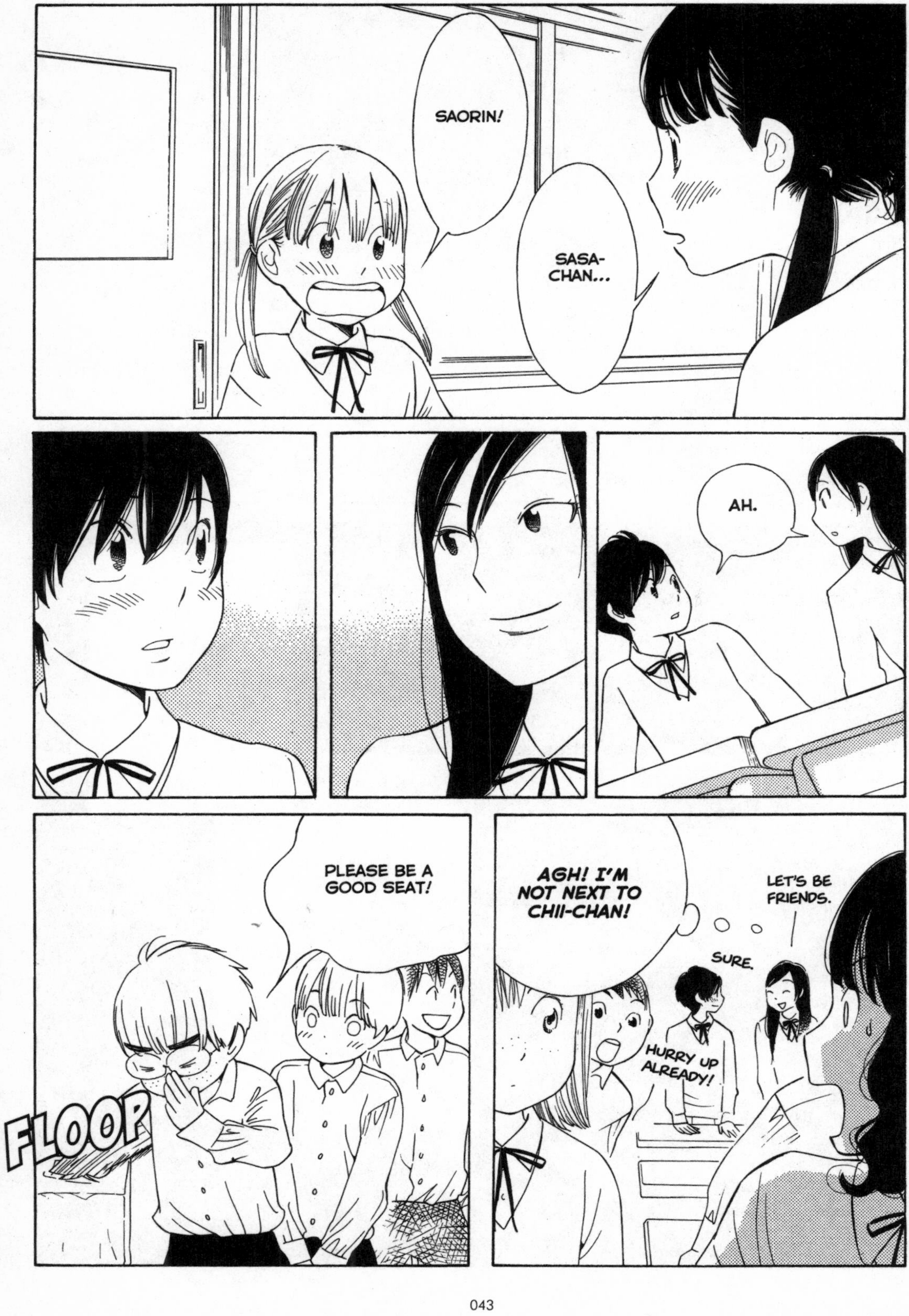
SAORIN!
SASA-CHAN...
AH.
LET'S BE FRIENDS.
AGH! I'M NOT NEXT TO CHII-CHAN!
SURE.
HURRY UP ALREADY!
PLEASE BE A GOOD SEAT!
FLOOP

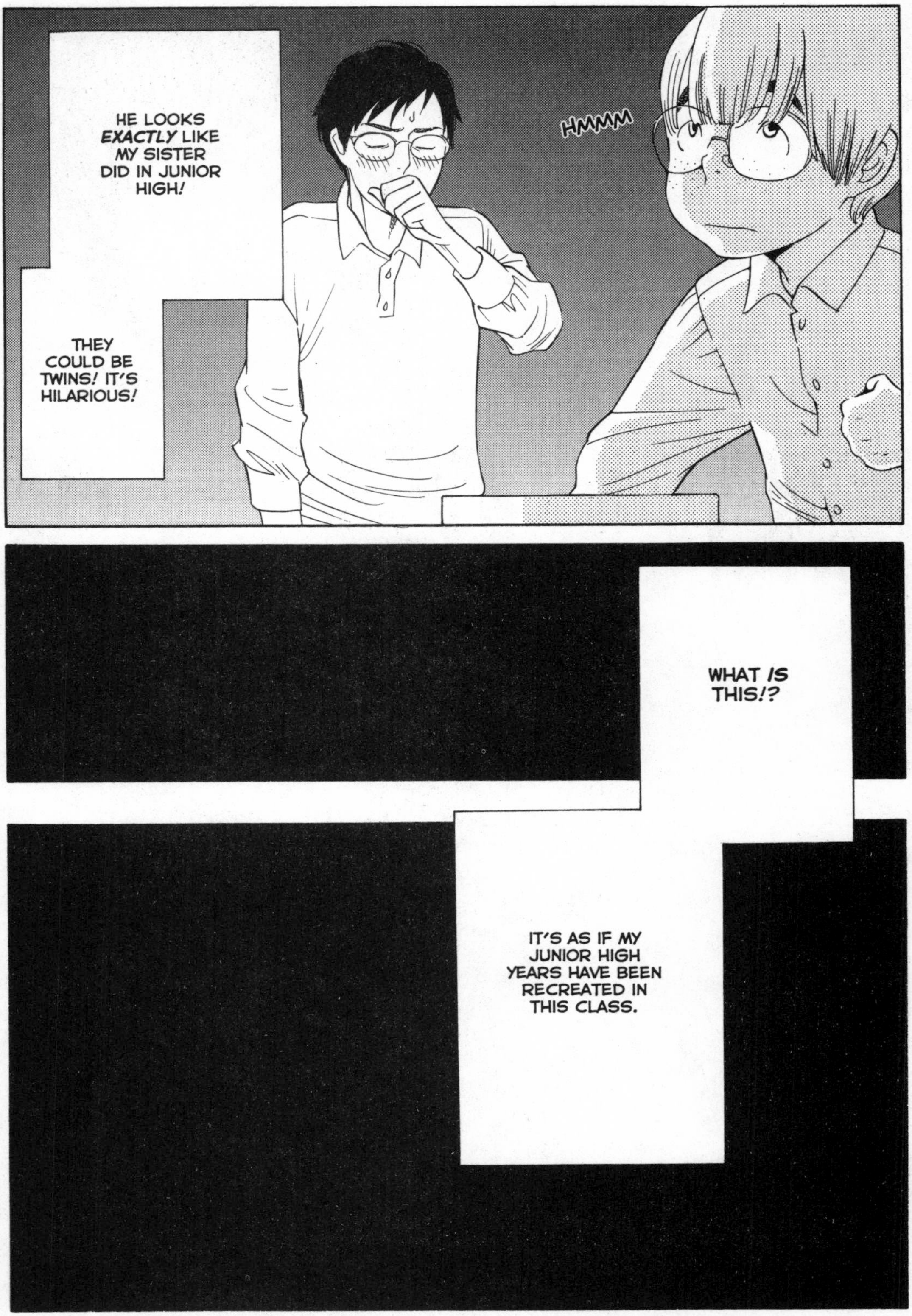
HMMM
HE LOOKS *EXACTLY* LIKE MY SISTER DID IN JUNIOR HIGH!
THEY COULD BE TWINS! IT'S HILARIOUS!
WHAT *IS* THIS!?
IT'S AS IF MY JUNIOR HIGH YEARS HAVE BEEN RECREATED IN THIS CLASS.

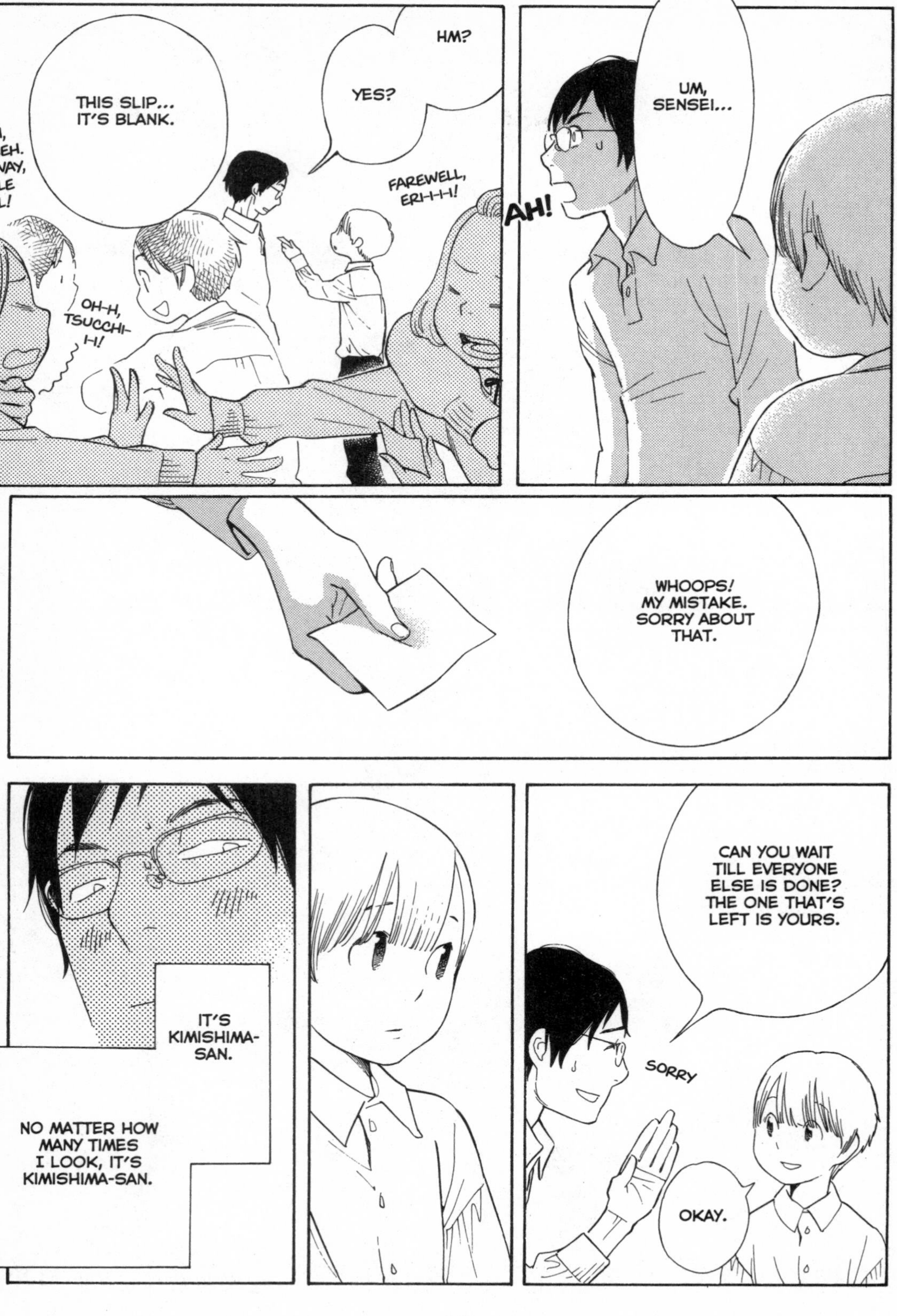
UM, SENSEI...
AH!
HM?
YES?
THIS SLIP... IT'S BLANK.
FAREWELL, ERI-I-I-I!
HEH, HEH, HEH. THIS WAY, LITTLE GIRL!
OH-H, TSUCCHI-I!
WHOOPS! MY MISTAKE. SORRY ABOUT THAT.
CAN YOU WAIT TILL EVERYONE ELSE IS DONE? THE ONE THAT'S LEFT IS YOURS.
SORRY
OKAY.
IT'S KIMISHIMA-SAN.
NO MATTER HOW MANY TIMES I LOOK, IT'S KIMISHIMA-SAN.

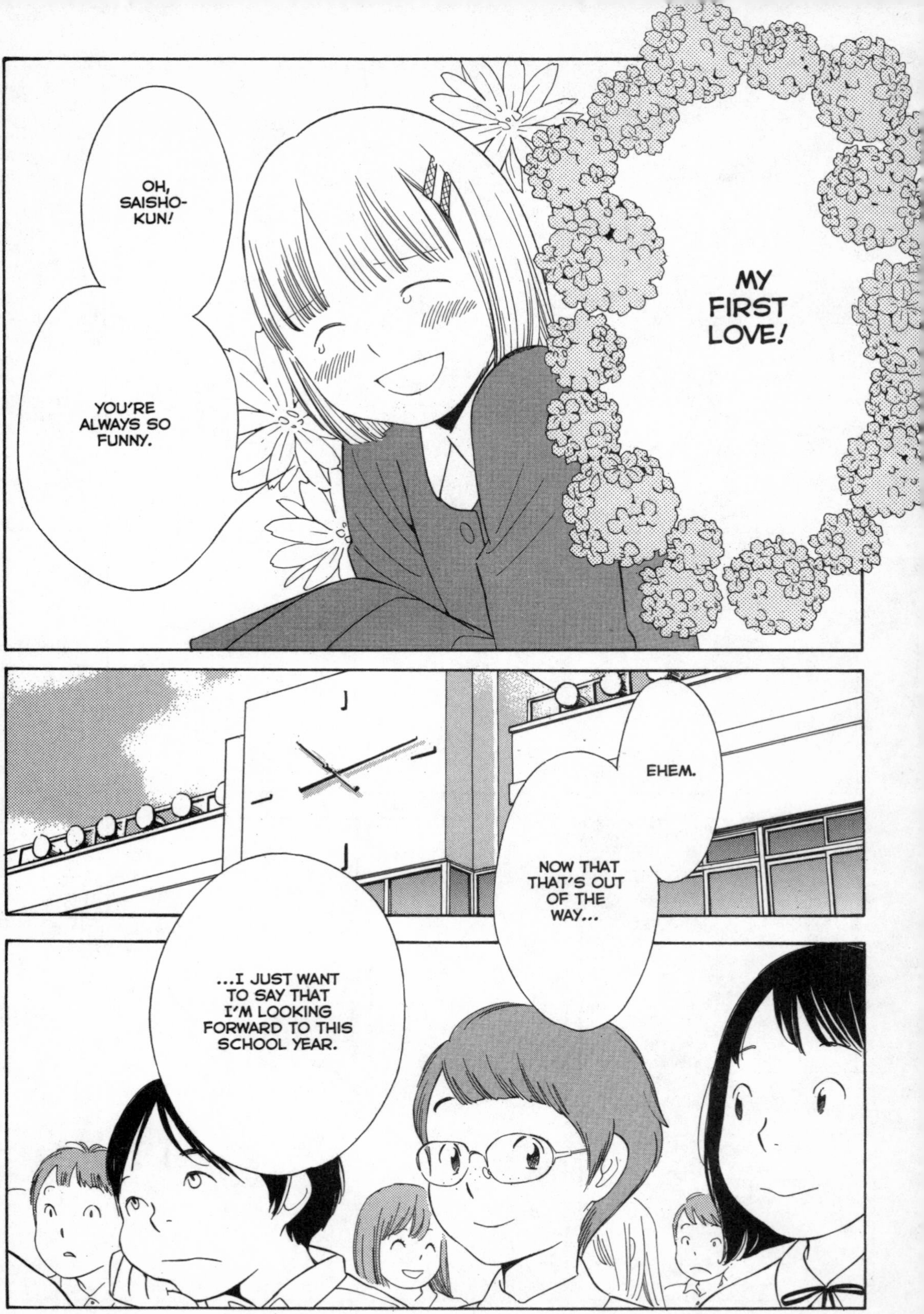
OH, SAISHO-KUN!
YOU'RE ALWAYS SO FUNNY.
MY FIRST LOVE!
EHEM.
NOW THAT THAT'S OUT OF THE WAY...
...I JUST WANT TO SAY THAT I'M LOOKING FORWARD TO THIS SCHOOL YEAR.

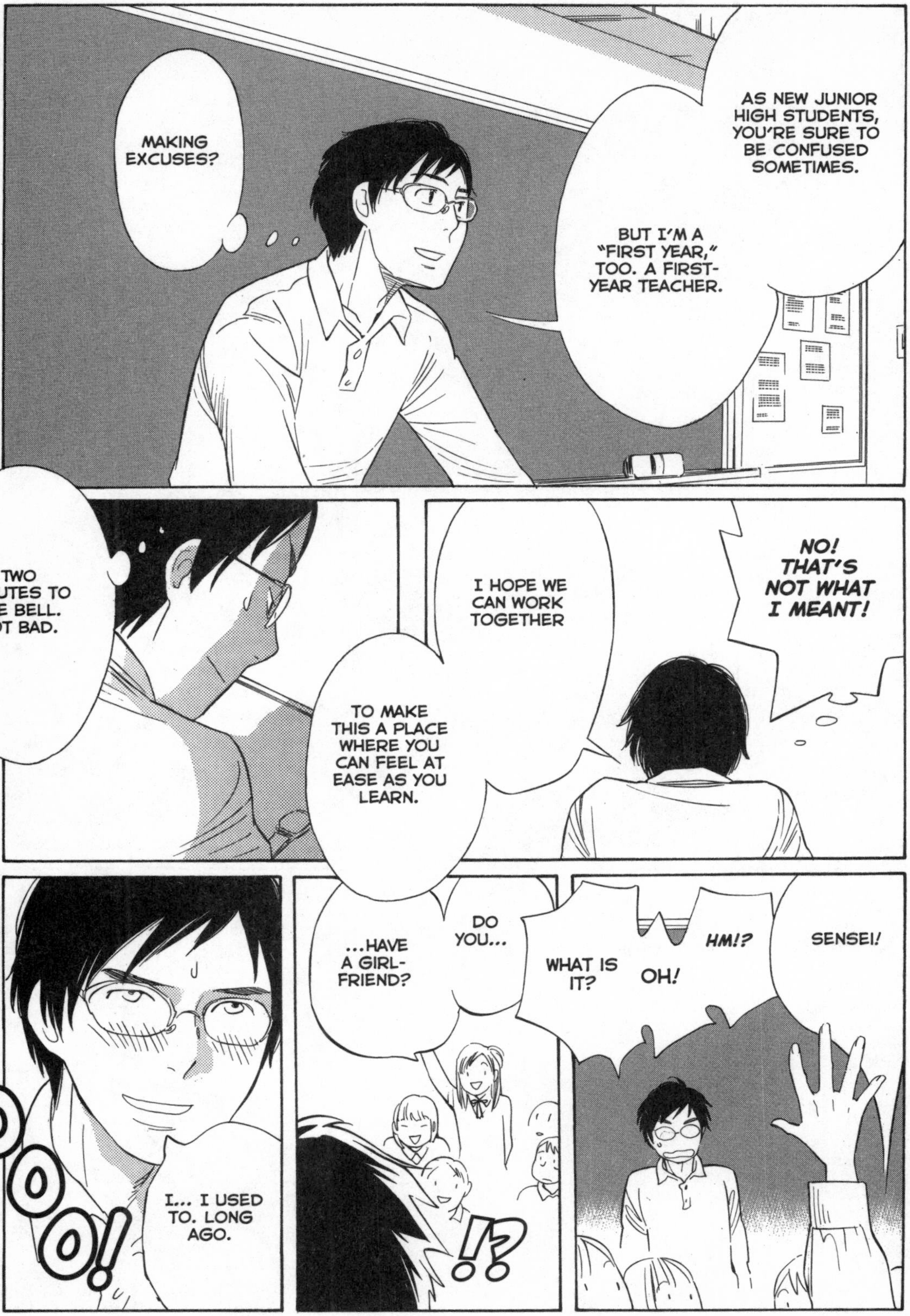
AS NEW JUNIOR HIGH STUDENTS, YOU'RE SURE TO BE CONFUSED SOMETIMES.
BUT I'M A "FIRST YEAR," TOO. A FIRST-YEAR TEACHER.
MAKING EXCUSES?
NO! THAT'S NOT WHAT I MEANT!
I HOPE WE CAN WORK TOGETHER
TO MAKE THIS A PLACE WHERE YOU CAN FEEL AT EASE AS YOU LEARN.
TWO MINUTES TO THE BELL. NOT BAD.
SENSEI!
HM!?
OH!
WHAT IS IT?
DO YOU...
...HAVE A GIRL-FRIEND?
!?
OOO!
I... I USED TO. LONG AGO.

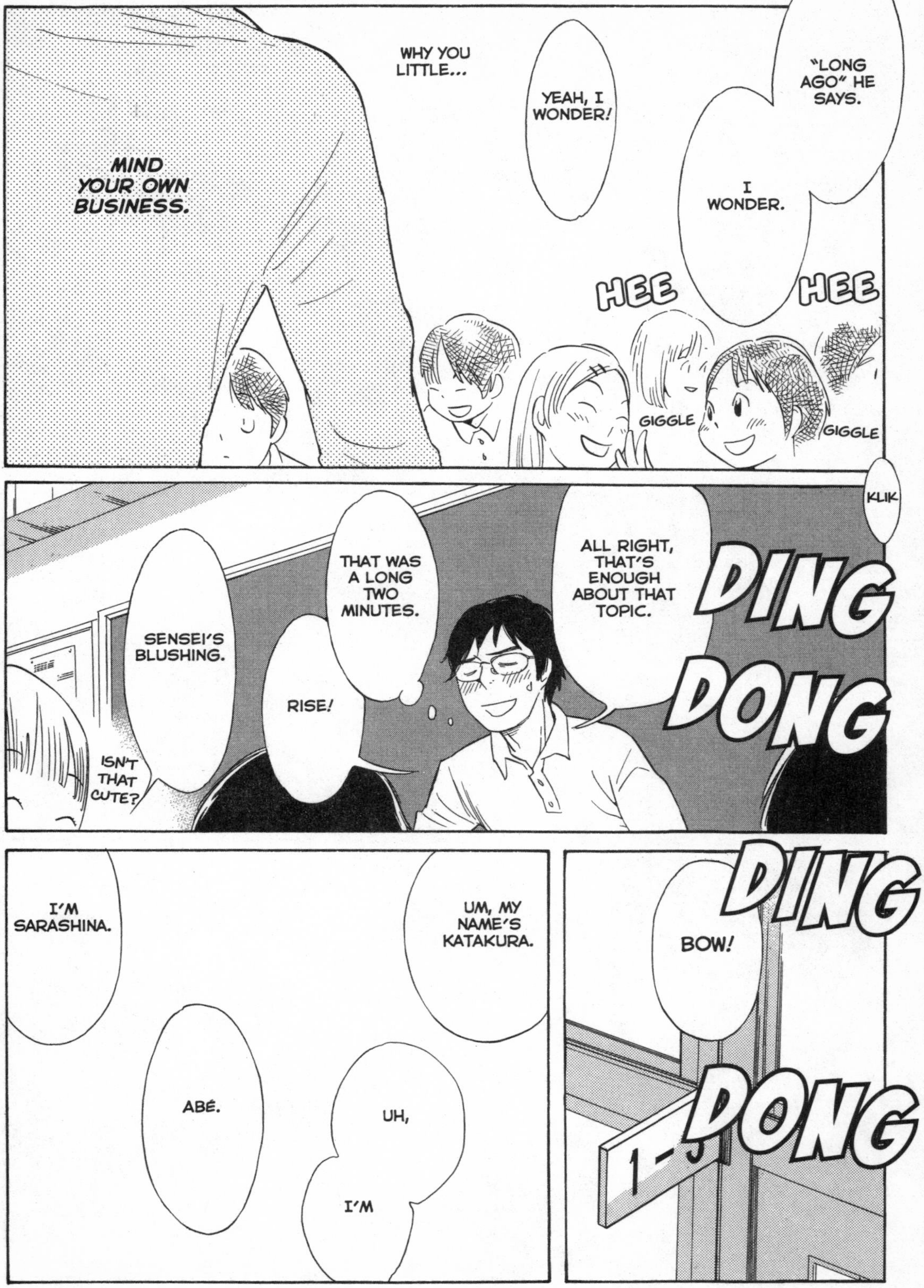
"LONG AGO" HE SAYS.
I WONDER.
YEAH, I WONDER!
WHY YOU LITTLE...
MIND YOUR OWN BUSINESS.
HEE
HEE
GIGGLE
GIGGLE
KLIK
DING DONG
ALL RIGHT, THAT'S ENOUGH ABOUT THAT TOPIC.
THAT WAS A LONG TWO MINUTES.
SENSEI'S BLUSHING.
RISE!
ISN'T THAT CUTE?
DING DONG
BOW!
UM, MY NAME'S KATAKURA.
I'M SARASHINA.
UH,
I'M
ABÉ.

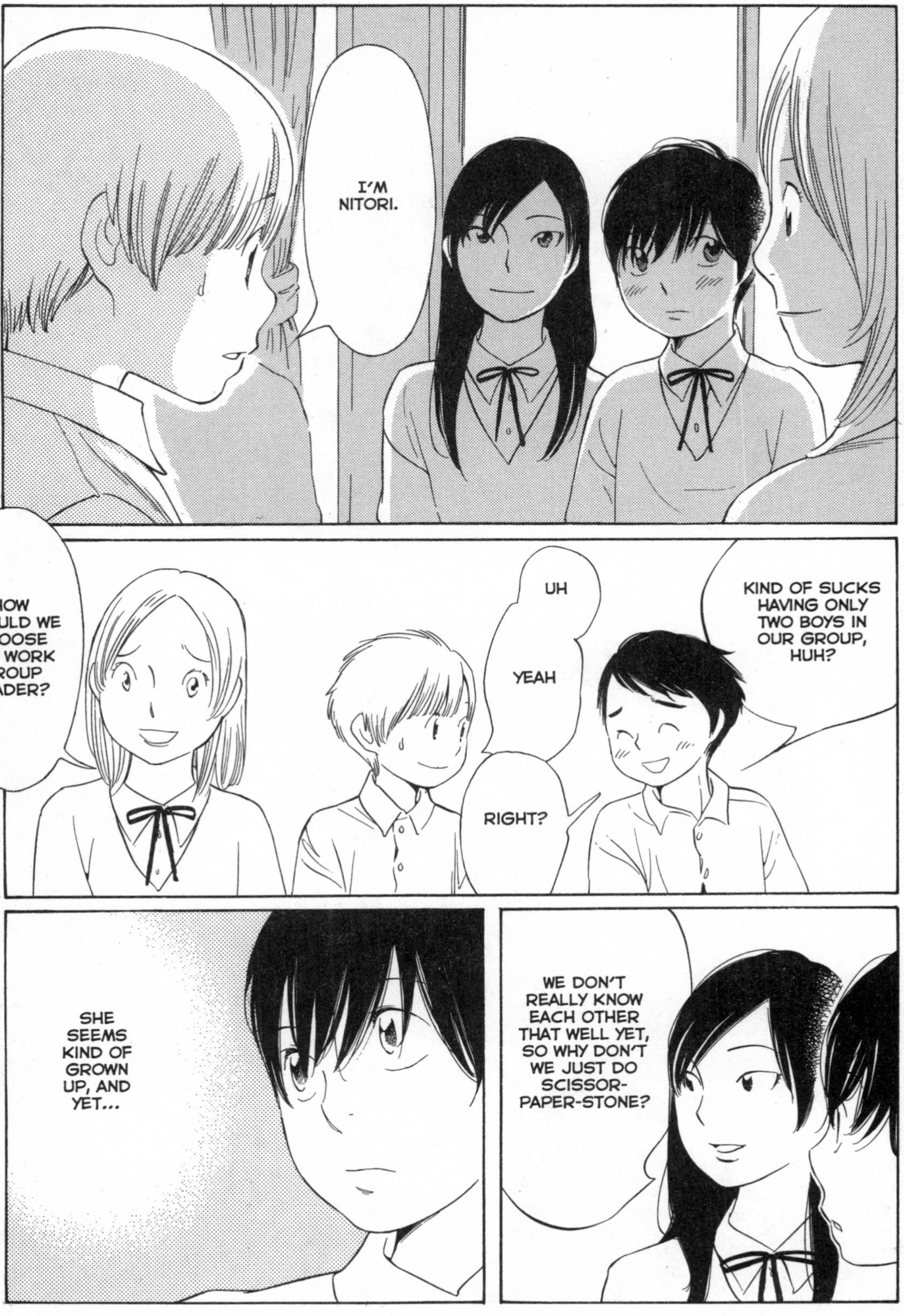
I'M NITORI.
KIND OF SUCKS HAVING ONLY TWO BOYS IN OUR GROUP, HUH?
UH
YEAH
RIGHT?
HOW SHOULD WE CHOOSE THE WORK GROUP LEADER?
WE DON'T REALLY KNOW EACH OTHER THAT WELL YET, SO WHY DON'T WE JUST DO SCISSOR-PAPER-STONE?
SHE SEEMS KIND OF GROWN UP, AND YET...

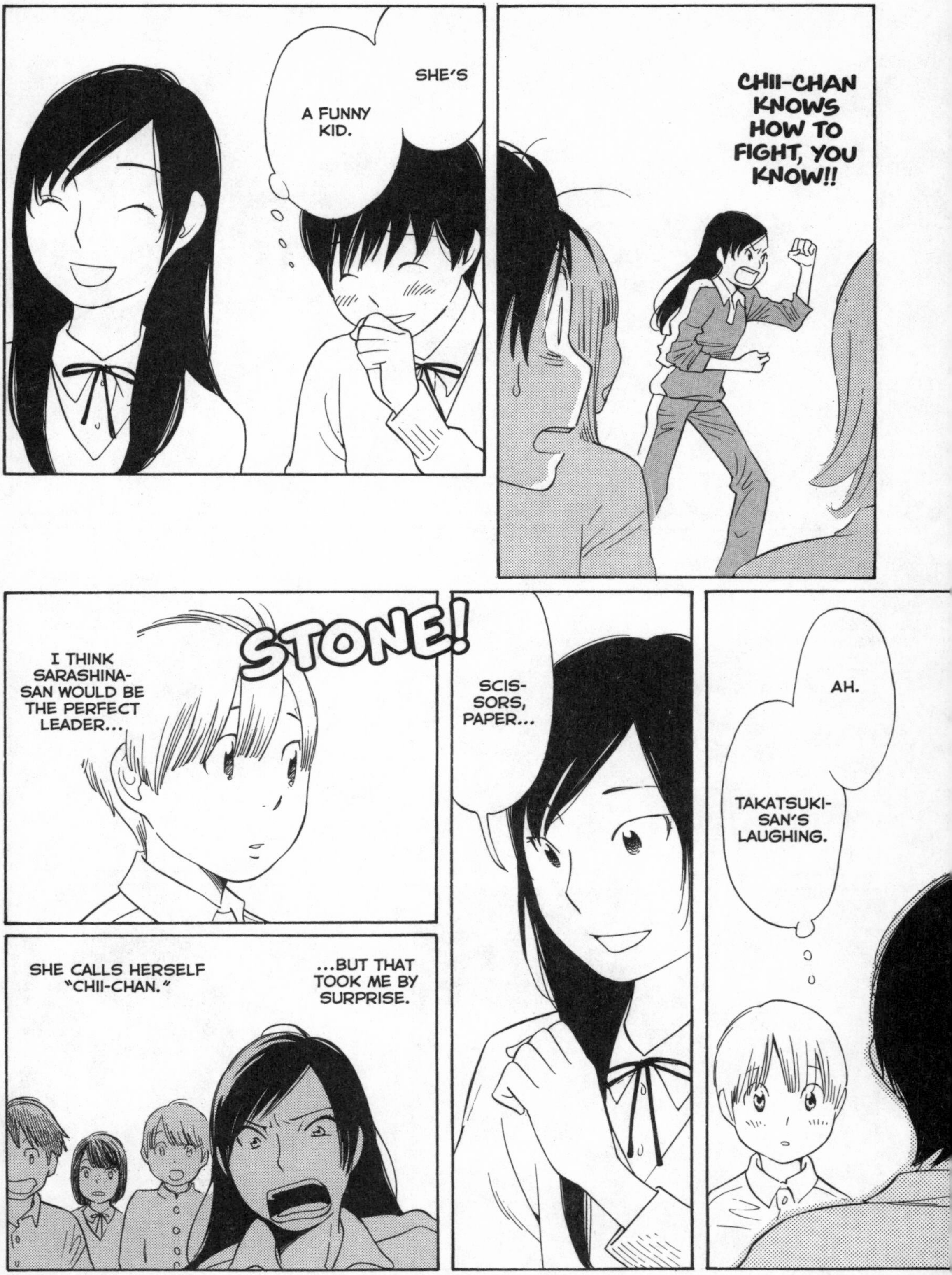
CHII-CHAN KNOWS HOW TO FIGHT, YOU KNOW!!
SHE'S A FUNNY KID.
AH. TAKATSUKI-SAN'S LAUGHING.
SCIS-SORS, PAPER...
STONE!
I THINK SARASHINA-SAN WOULD BE THE PERFECT LEADER...
SHE CALLS HERSELF "CHII-CHAN."
...BUT THAT TOOK ME BY SURPRISE.

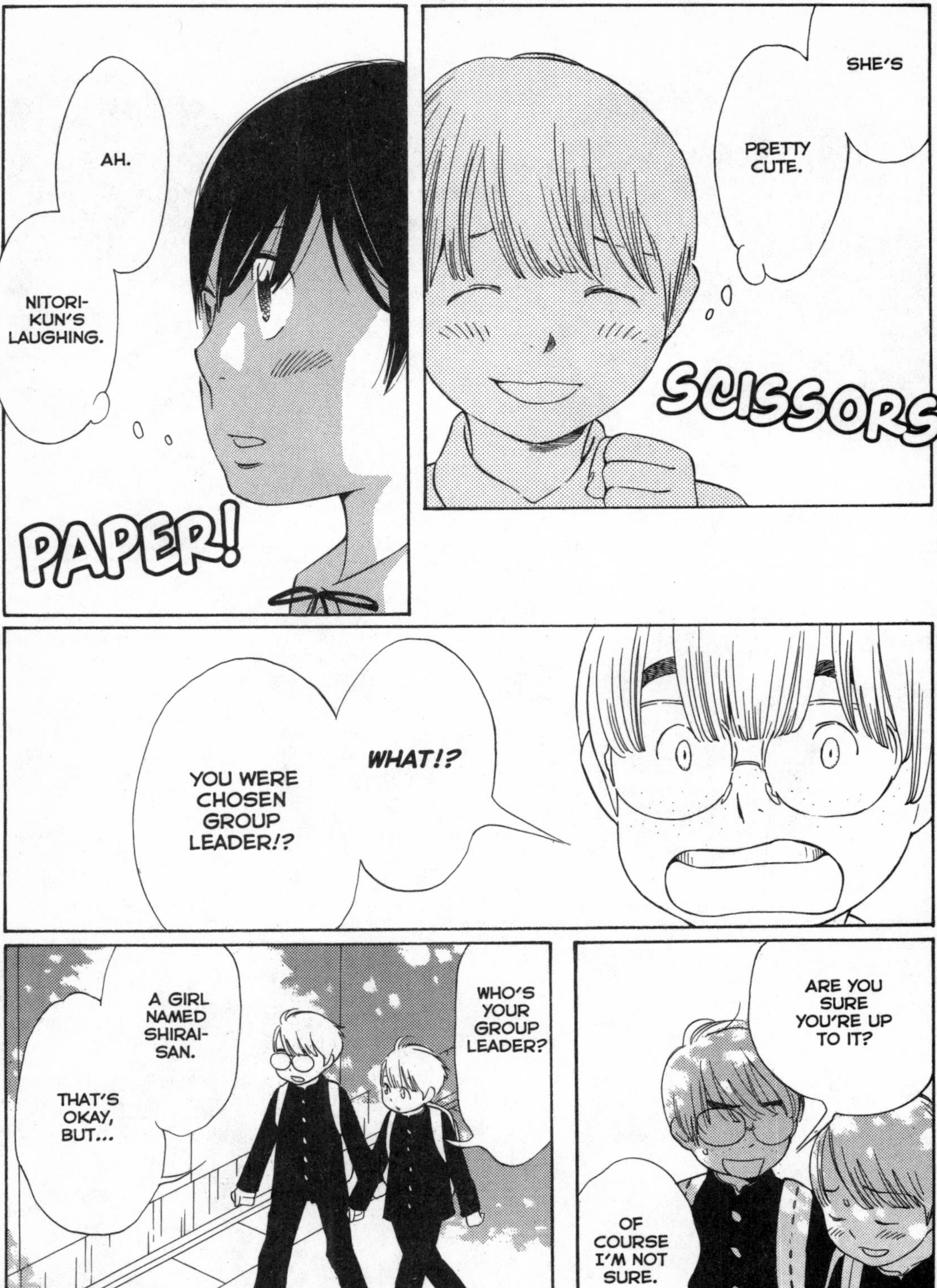
SHE'S PRETTY CUTE.
SCISSORS!
AH.
NITORI-KUN'S LAUGHING.
PAPER!
WHAT!?
YOU WERE CHOSEN GROUP LEADER!?
ARE YOU SURE YOU'RE UP TO IT?
OF COURSE I'M NOT SURE.
WHO'S YOUR GROUP LEADER?
A GIRL NAMED SHIRAI-SAN.
THAT'S OKAY, BUT...

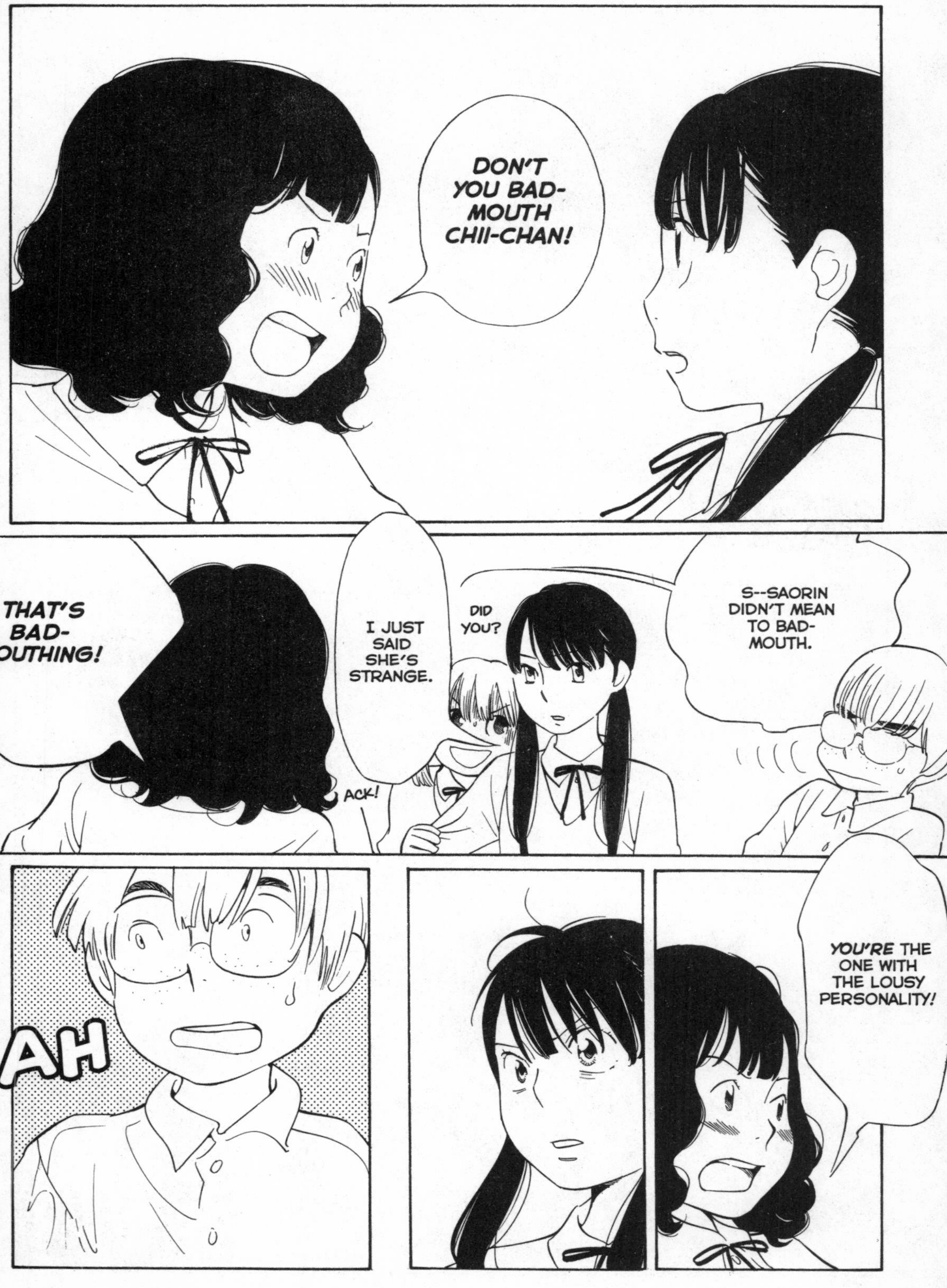
DON'T YOU BAD-MOUTH CHII-CHAN!
S--SAORIN DIDN'T MEAN TO BAD-MOUTH.
DID YOU?
I JUST SAID SHE'S STRANGE.
ACK!
THAT'S BAD-MOUTHING!
YOU'RE THE ONE WITH THE LOUSY PERSONALITY!
AH

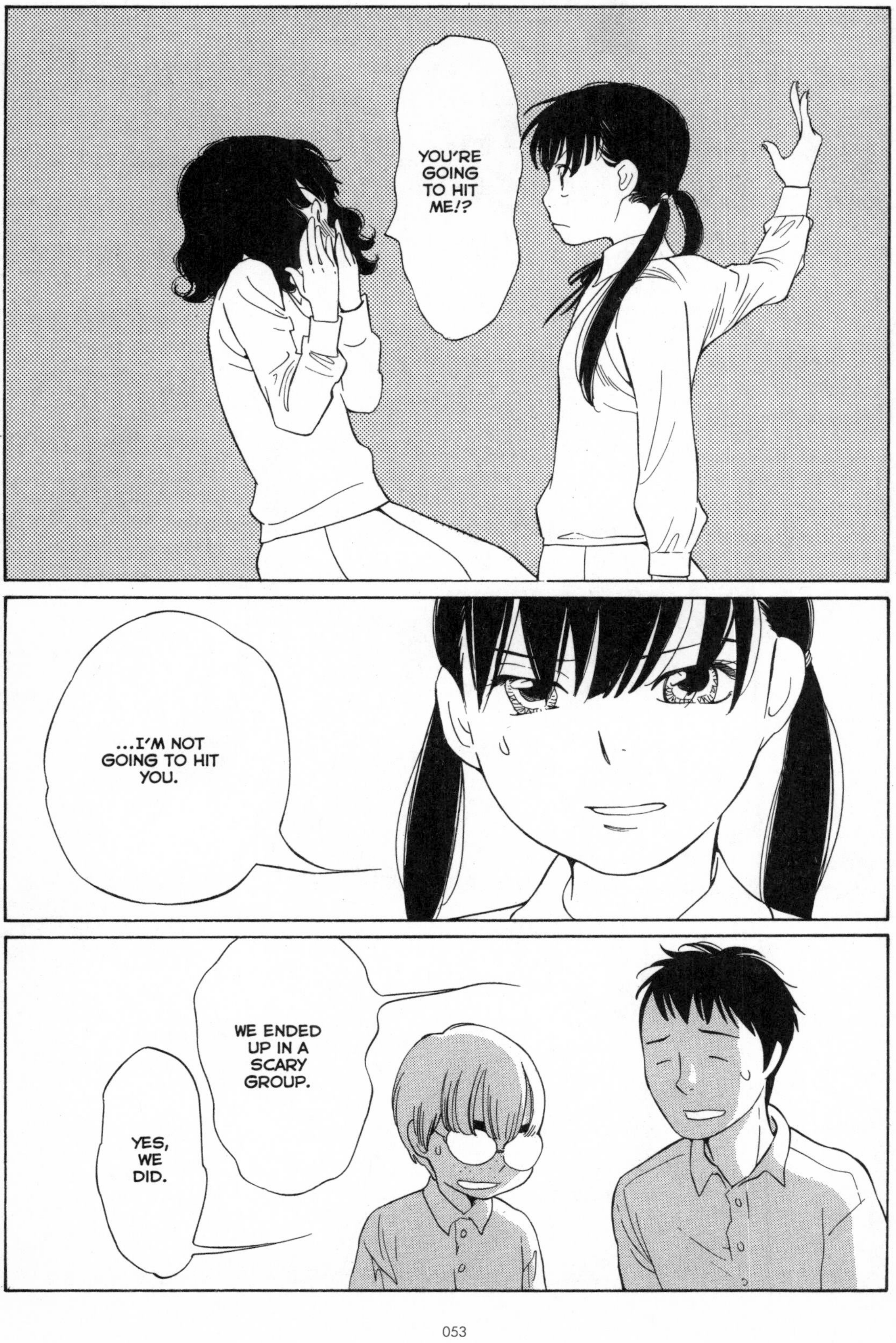
YOU'RE GOING TO HIT ME!?
...I'M NOT GOING TO HIT YOU.
WE ENDED UP IN A SCARY GROUP.
YES, WE DID.

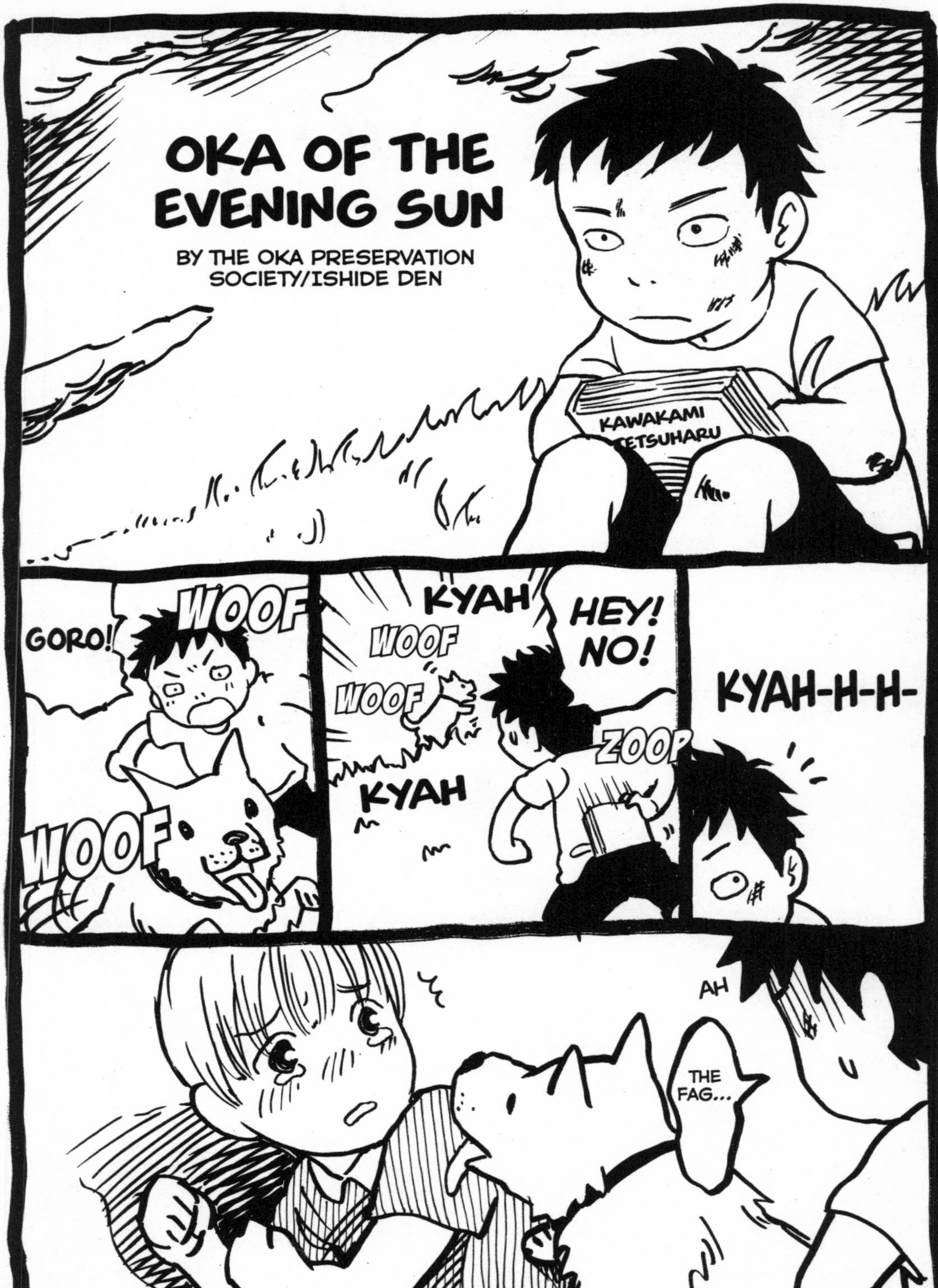
OKA OF THE EVENING SUN
BY THE OKA PRESERVATION SOCIETY//ISHIDE DEN
KAWAKAMI TETSUHARU
KYAH-H-H-
HEY! NO!
ZOOP
KYAH
WOOF
WOOF
KYAH
GORO!
WOOF
WOOF
AH
THE FAG...

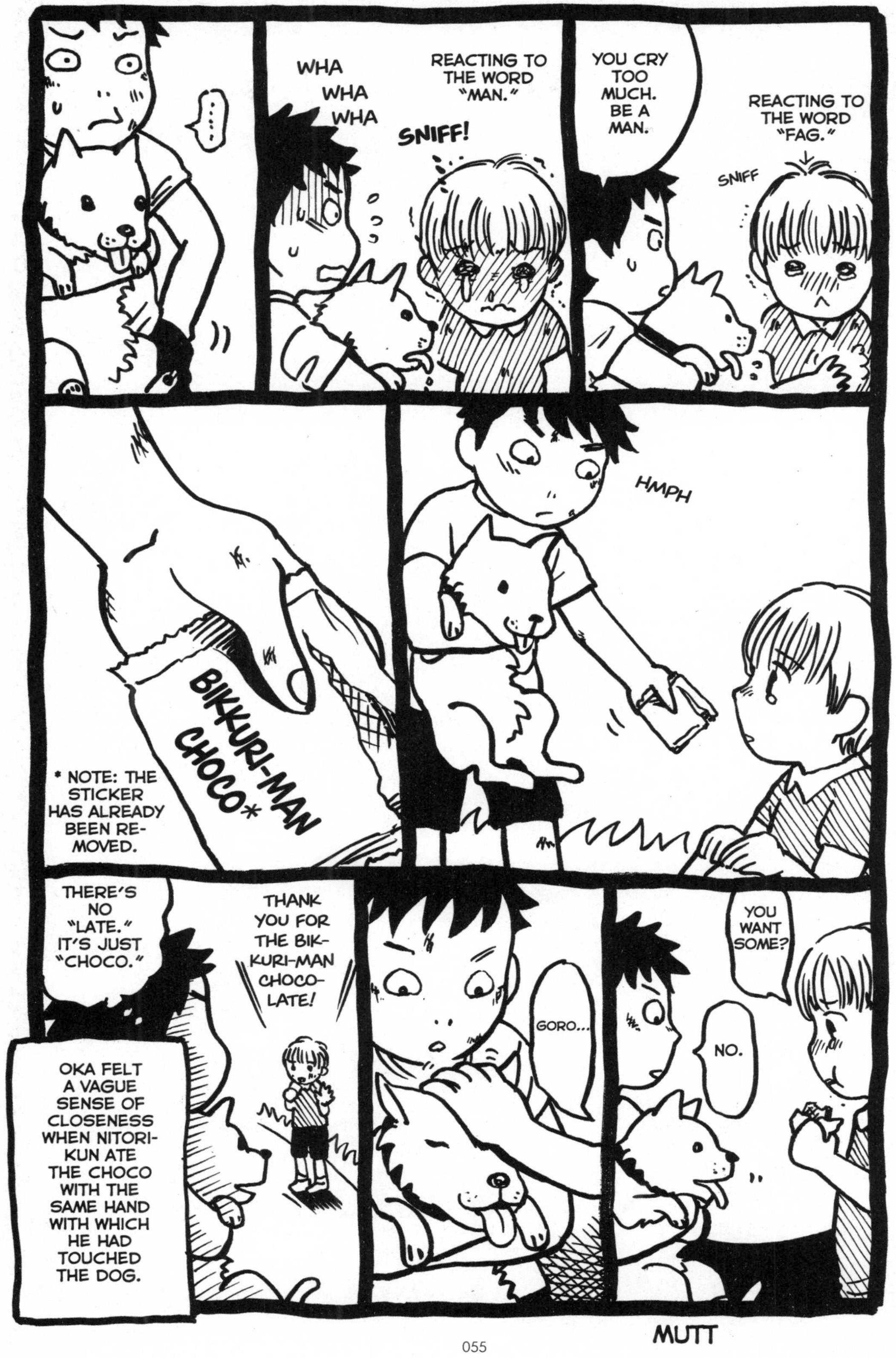
YOU CRY TOO MUCH. BE A MAN.
REACTING TO THE WORD "FAG."
SNIFF
REACTING TO THE WORD "MAN."
WHA WHA WHA
SNIFF!
.....
HMPH
BIKKURI-MAN CHOCO*
* NOTE: THE STICKER HAS ALREADY BEEN RE-MOVED.
YOU WANT SOME?
NO.
GORO...
THANK YOU FOR THE BIK-KURI-MAN CHOCO-LATE!
THERE'S NO "LATE." IT'S JUST "CHOCO."
OKA FELT A VAGUE SENSE OF CLOSENESS WHEN NITORI-KUN ATE THE CHOCO WITH THE SAME HAND WITH WHICH HE HAD TOUCHED THE DOG.

MUTT

"OKA OF THE EVENING SUN" WAS DRAWN BY ISHIDE DEN-SAN, WHO ALWAYS CAME RUNNING TO HELP ME WITH MY WORK ON RAINY DAYS AND STORMY DAYS AND EVEN DAYS WHEN SHE HAD A COLD. SHE MADE HER PROFESSIONAL DEBUT IN *MONTHLY IKKI*, AND IS CURRENTLY DRAWING THE MANGA *REAL WORLD* FOR THAT MAGAZINE. SHE IS A GREAT BIG LUMP OF "GUTS" AND "FRESHNESS."

SHE TOLD ME, "GO AHEAD AND PLUG ME ALL YOU LIKE!" SO THIS WAS MY PLUG.

36

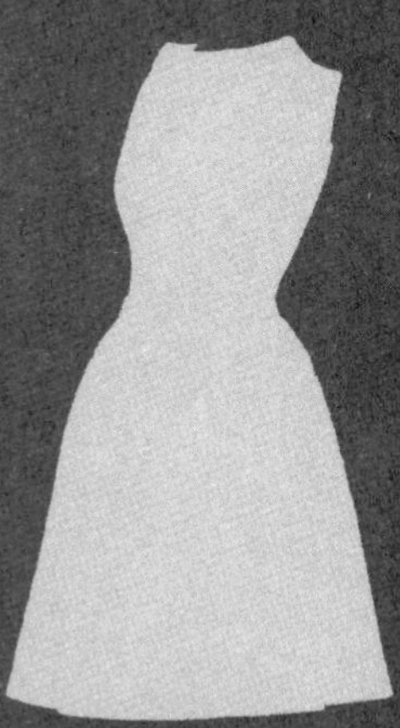

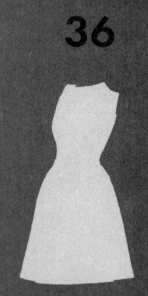

We're All Friends in This Class

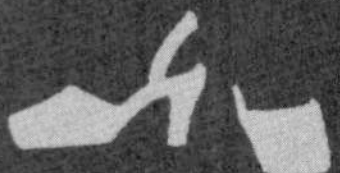

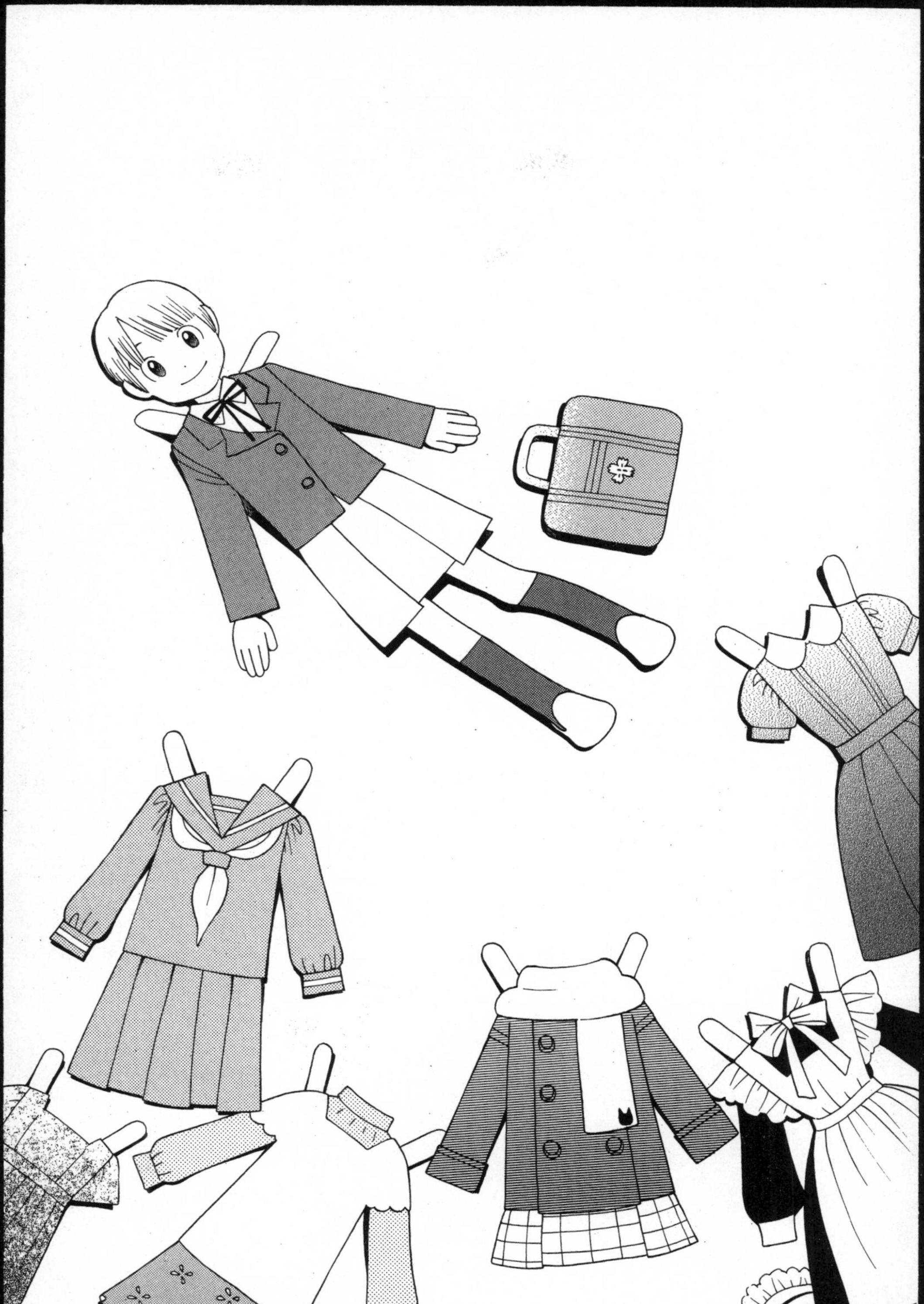

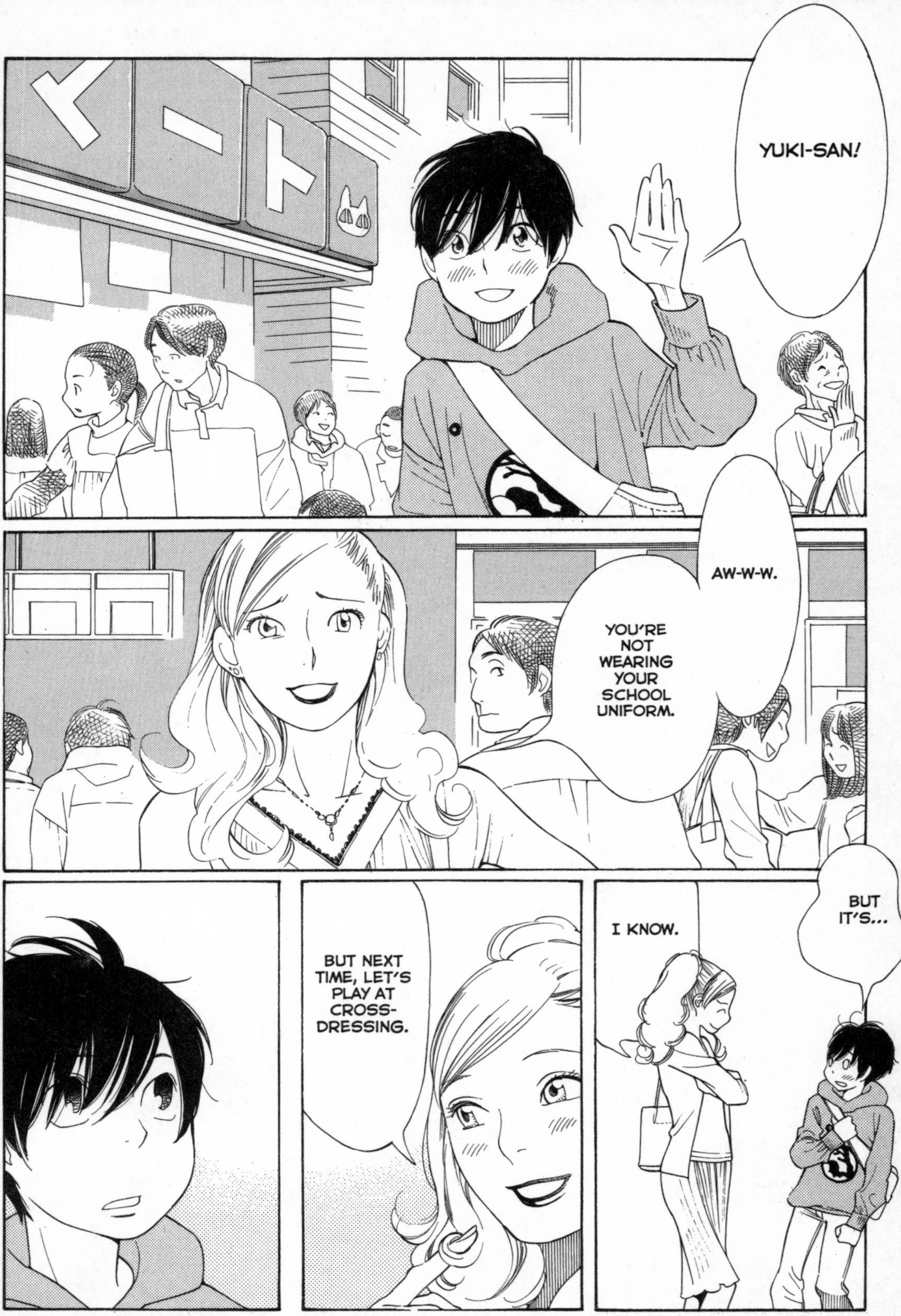
YUKI-SAN!
AW-W-W.
YOU'RE NOT WEARING YOUR SCHOOL UNIFORM.
BUT IT'S...
I KNOW.
BUT NEXT TIME, LET'S PLAY AT CROSS-DRESSING.

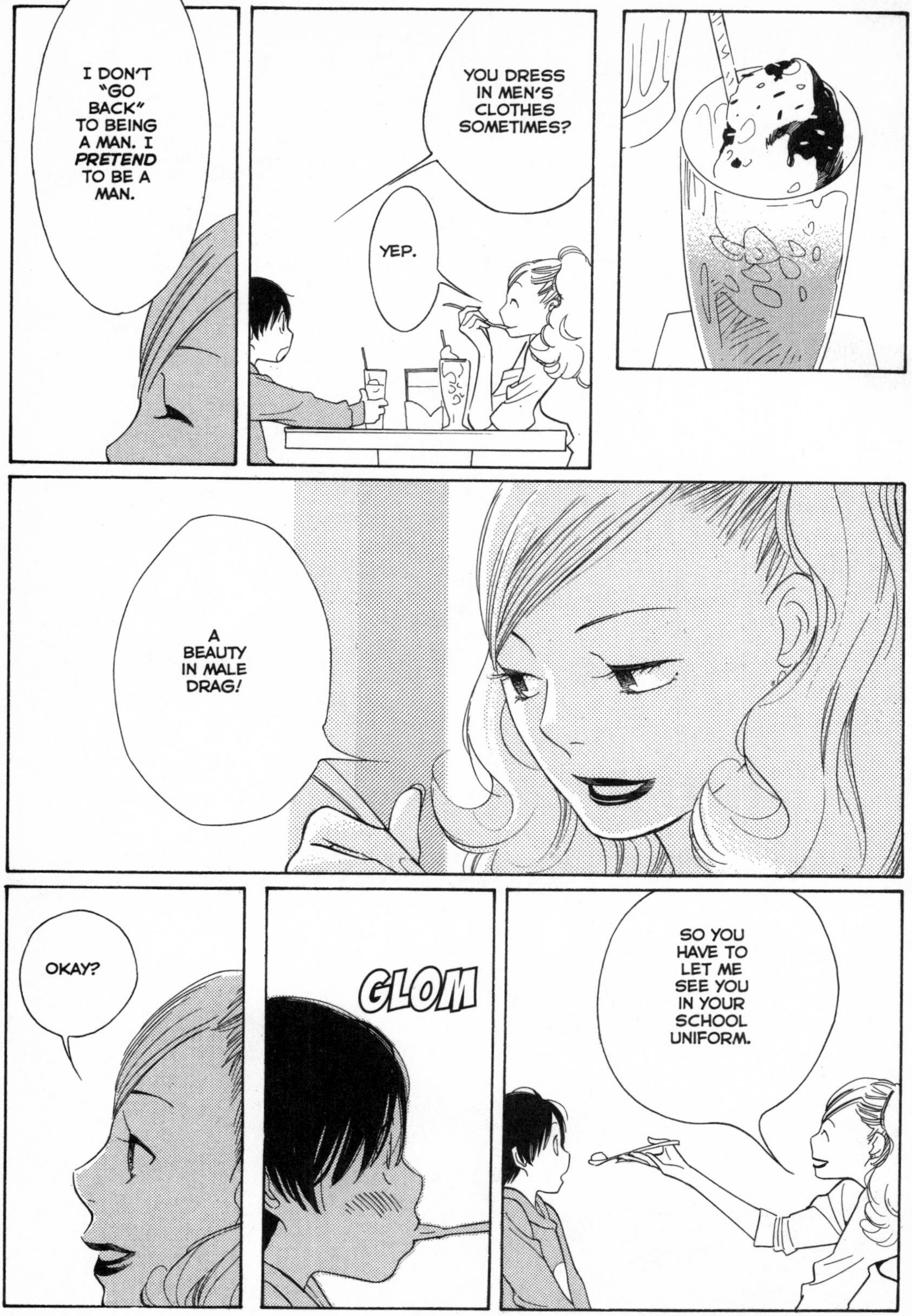
YOU DRESS IN MEN'S CLOTHES SOMETIMES?
YEP.
I DON'T "GO BACK" TO BEING A MAN. I *PRETEND* TO BE A MAN.
A BEAUTY IN MALE DRAG!
SO YOU HAVE TO LET ME SEE YOU IN YOUR SCHOOL UNIFORM.
GLOM
OKAY?

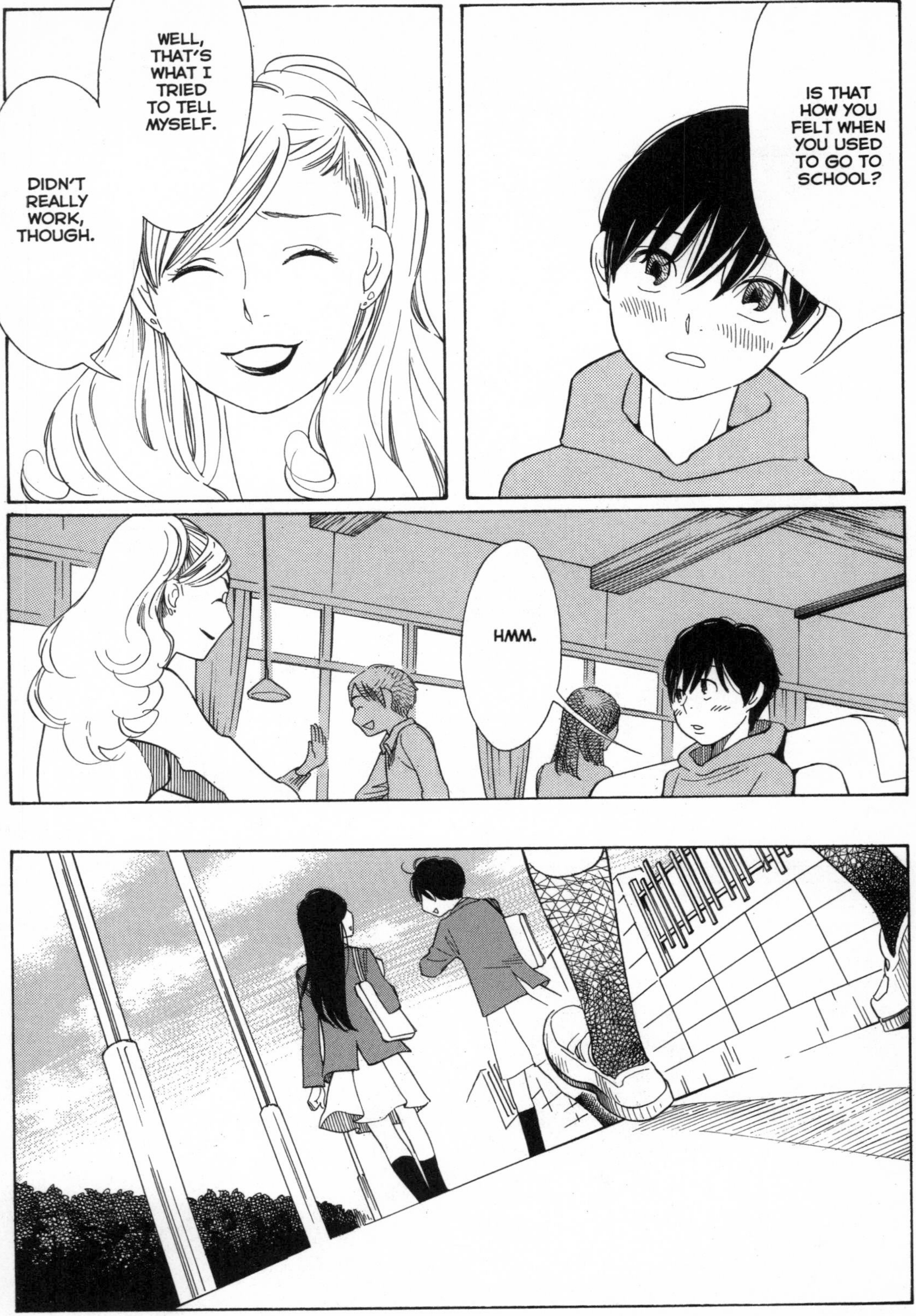
IS THAT HOW YOU FELT WHEN YOU USED TO GO TO SCHOOL?
WELL, THAT'S WHAT I TRIED TO TELL MYSELF.
DIDN'T REALLY WORK, THOUGH.
HMM.

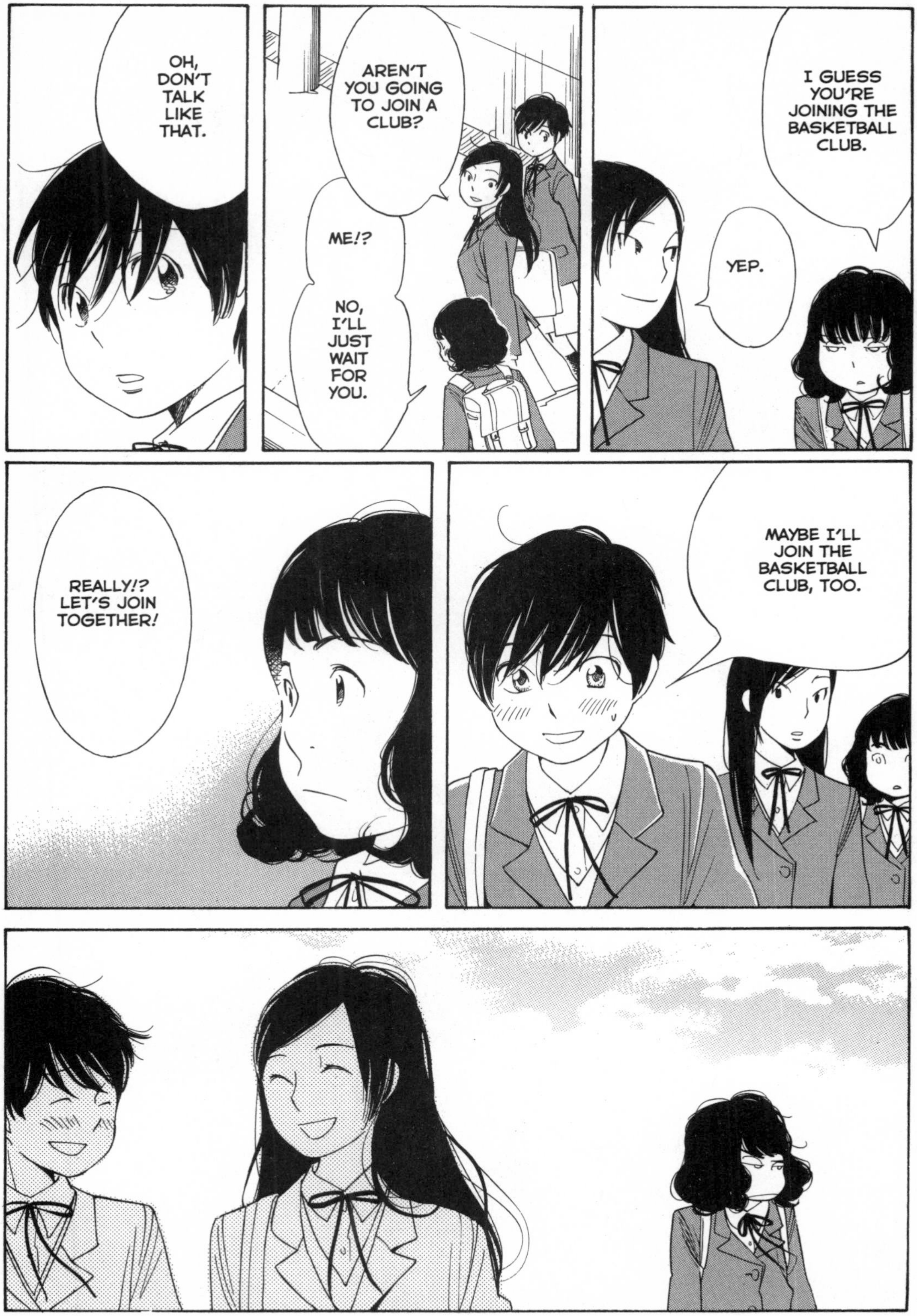
I GUESS YOU'RE JOINING THE BASKETBALL CLUB.
YEP.
AREN'T YOU GOING TO JOIN A CLUB?
ME!?
NO, I'LL JUST WAIT FOR YOU.
OH, DON'T TALK LIKE THAT.
MAYBE I'LL JOIN THE BASKETBALL CLUB, TOO.
REALLY!? LET'S JOIN TOGETHER!

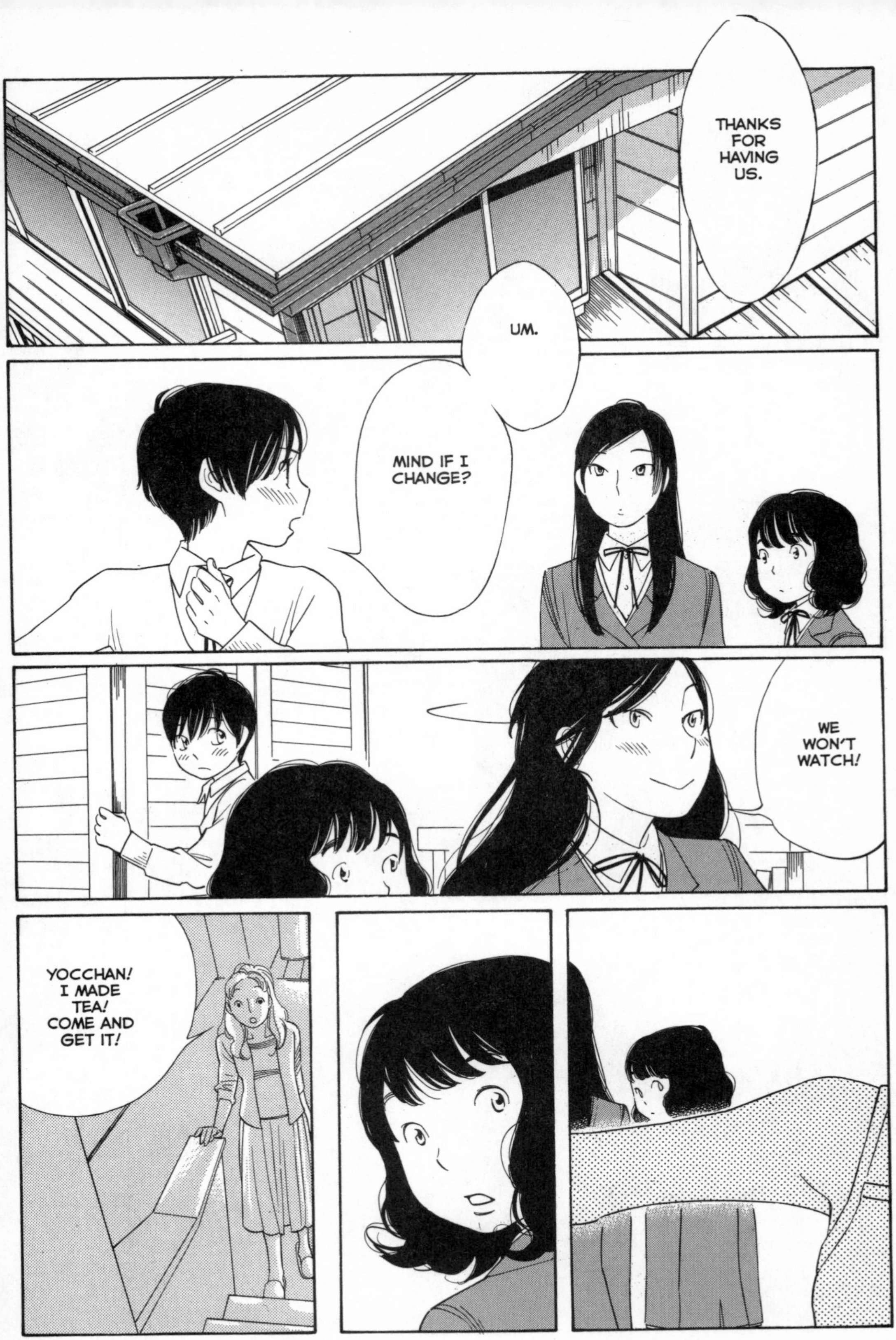
THANKS FOR HAVING US.
UM.
MIND IF I CHANGE?
WE WON'T WATCH!
YOCCHAN! I MADE TEA! COME AND GET IT!

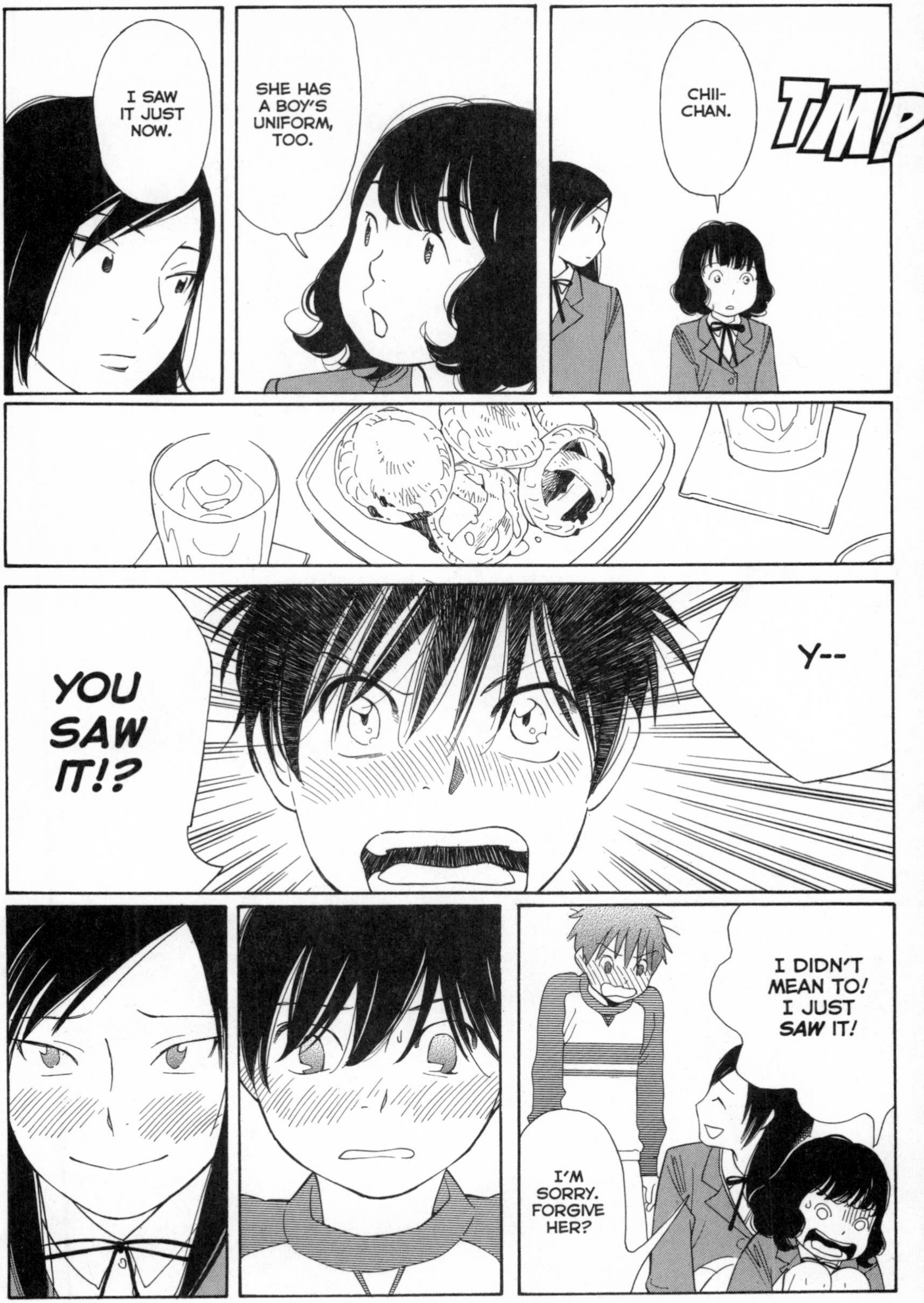
TMP
CHII-CHAN.
SHE HAS A BOY'S UNIFORM, TOO.
I SAW IT JUST NOW.
Y--
YOU SAW IT!?
I DIDN'T MEAN TO! I JUST SAW IT!
I'M SORRY. FORGIVE HER?

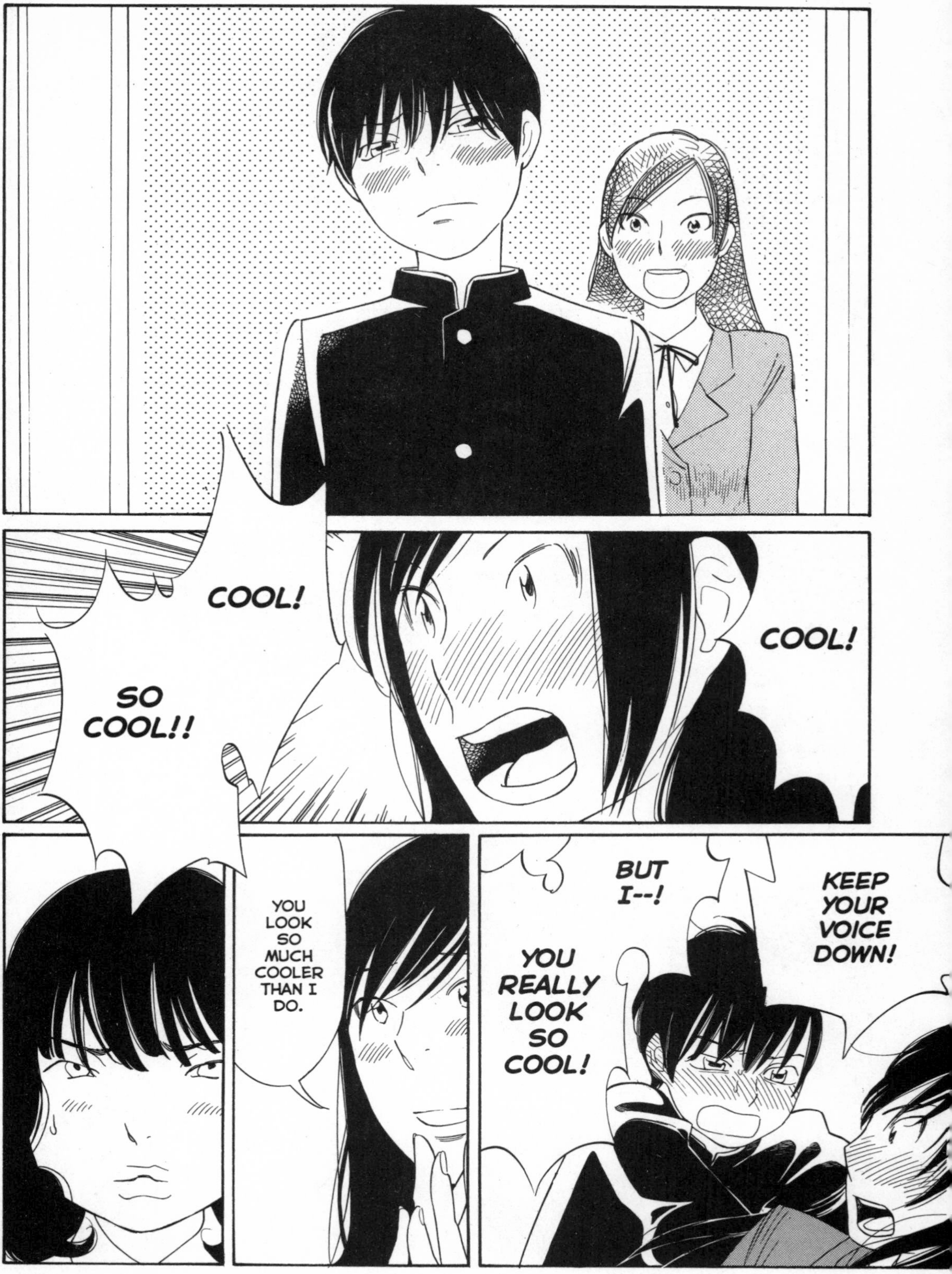
COOL!
COOL!
SO COOL!!
KEEP YOUR VOICE DOWN!
BUT I--!
YOU REALLY LOOK SO COOL!
YOU LOOK SO MUCH COOLER THAN I DO.

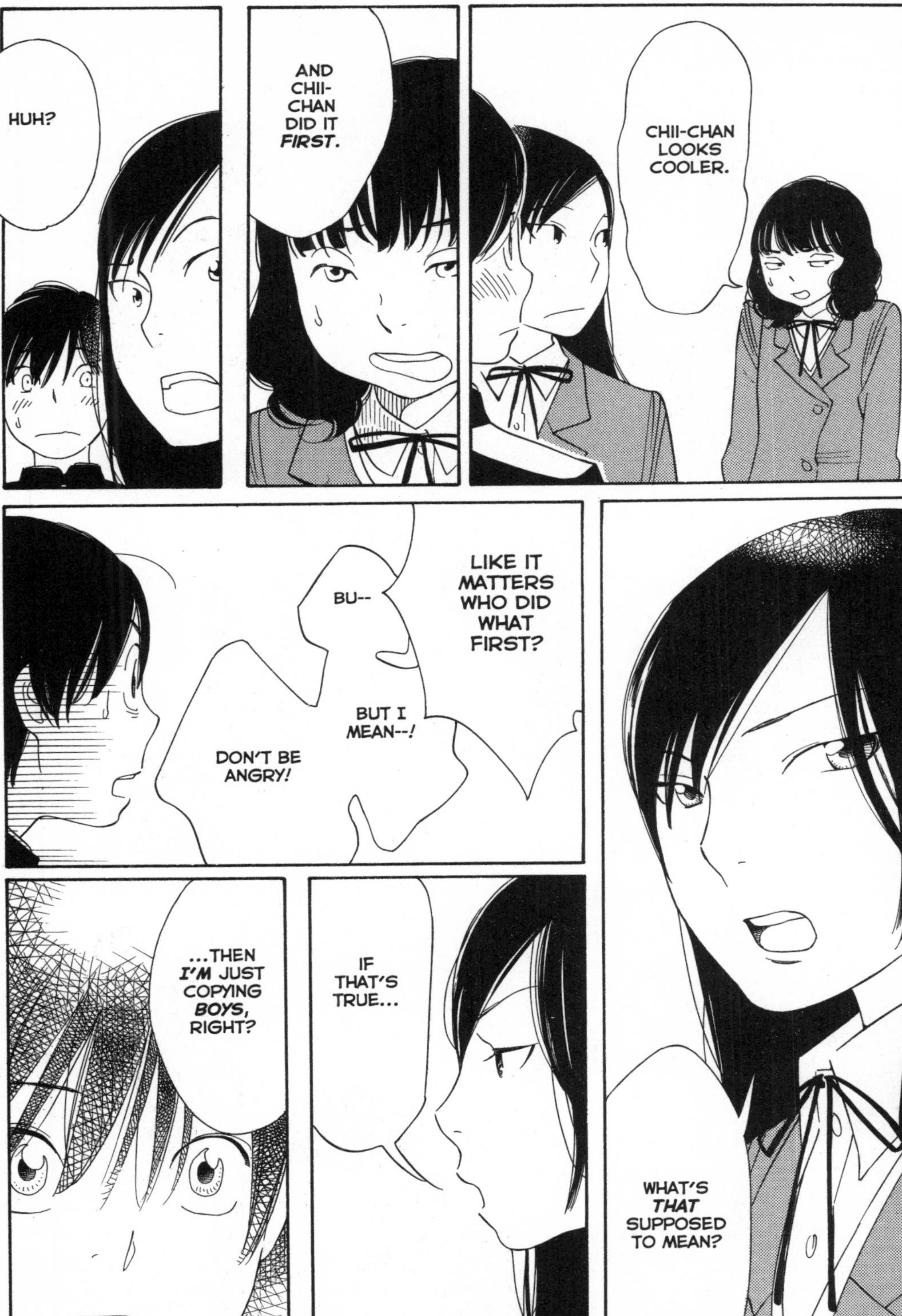
CHII-CHAN LOOKS COOLER.
AND CHII-CHAN DID IT *FIRST*.
HUH?
WHAT'S *THAT* SUPPOSED TO MEAN?
LIKE IT MATTERS WHO DID WHAT FIRST?
BU--
BUT I MEAN--!
DON'T BE ANGRY!
IF THAT'S TRUE...
...THEN *I'M* JUST COPYING *BOYS*, RIGHT?

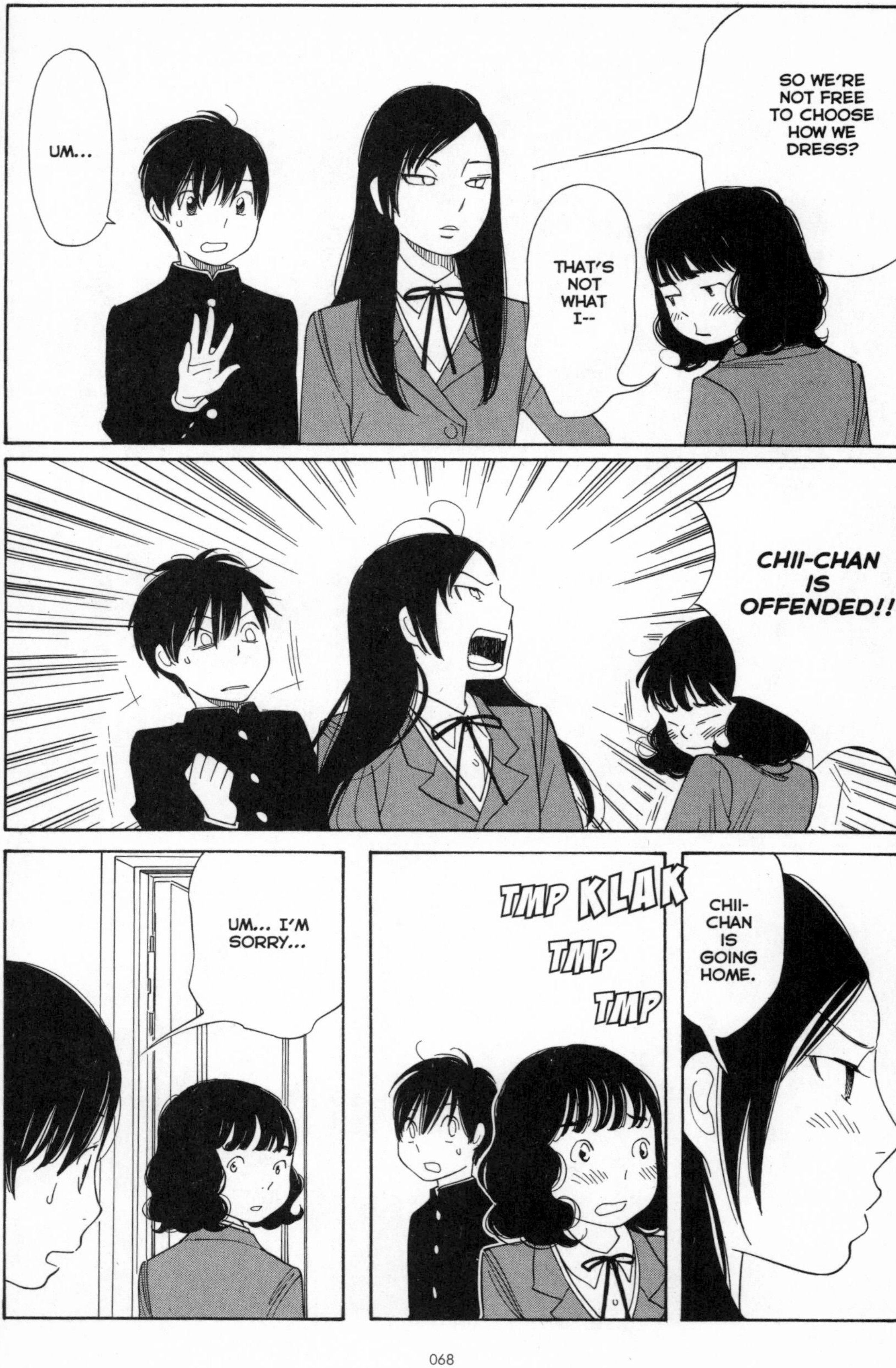
SO WE'RE NOT FREE TO CHOOSE HOW WE DRESS?
THAT'S NOT WHAT I--
UM...
CHII-CHAN IS OFFENDED!!
CHII-CHAN IS GOING HOME.
TMP KLAK
TMP
TMP
UM... I'M SORRY...

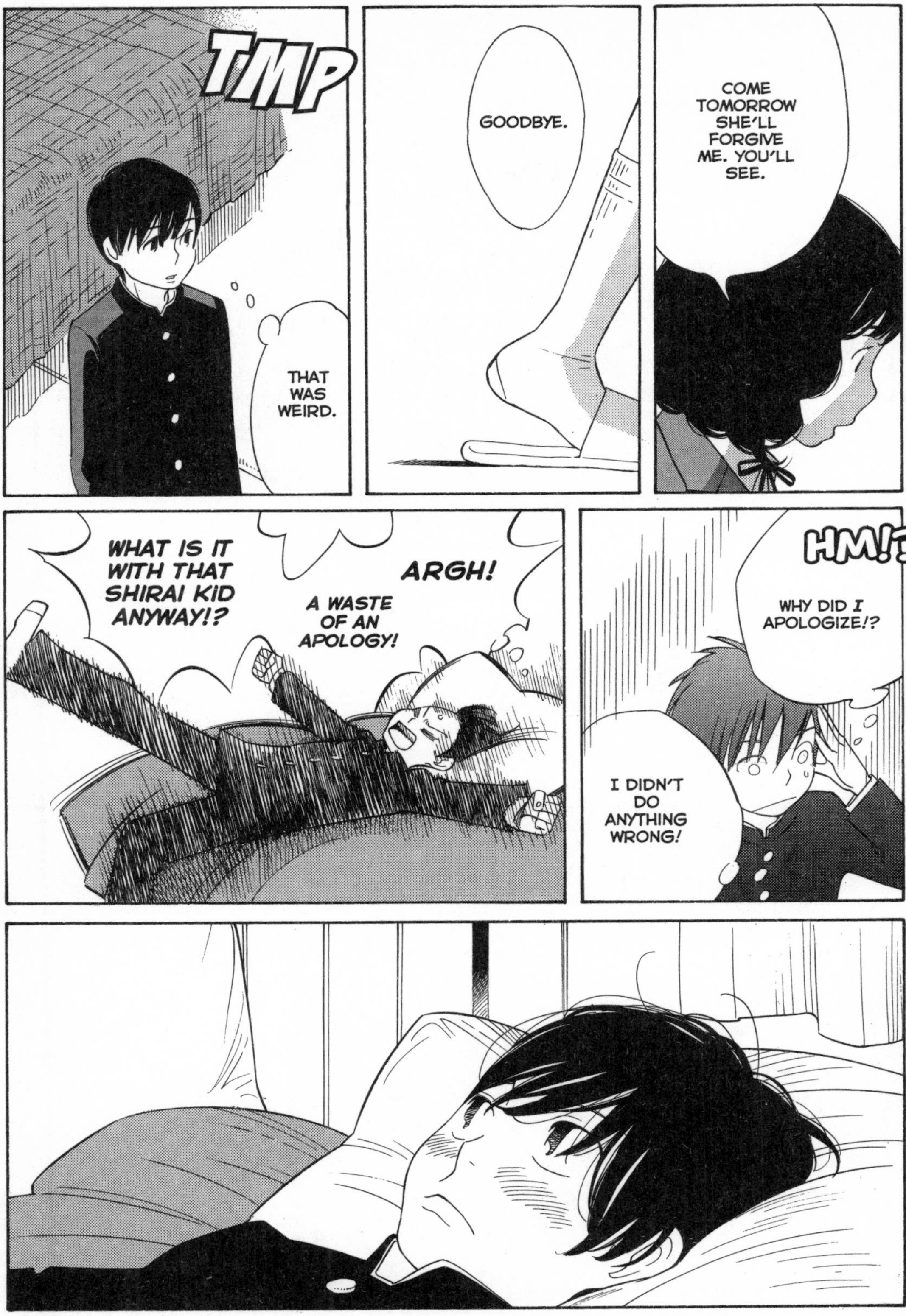
COME TOMORROW SHE'LL FORGIVE ME. YOU'LL SEE.
GOODBYE.
TMP
THAT WAS WEIRD.
HM!?
WHY DID I APOLOGIZE!?
I DIDN'T DO ANYTHING WRONG!
ARGH!
A WASTE OF AN APOLOGY!
WHAT IS IT WITH THAT SHIRAI KID ANYWAY!?

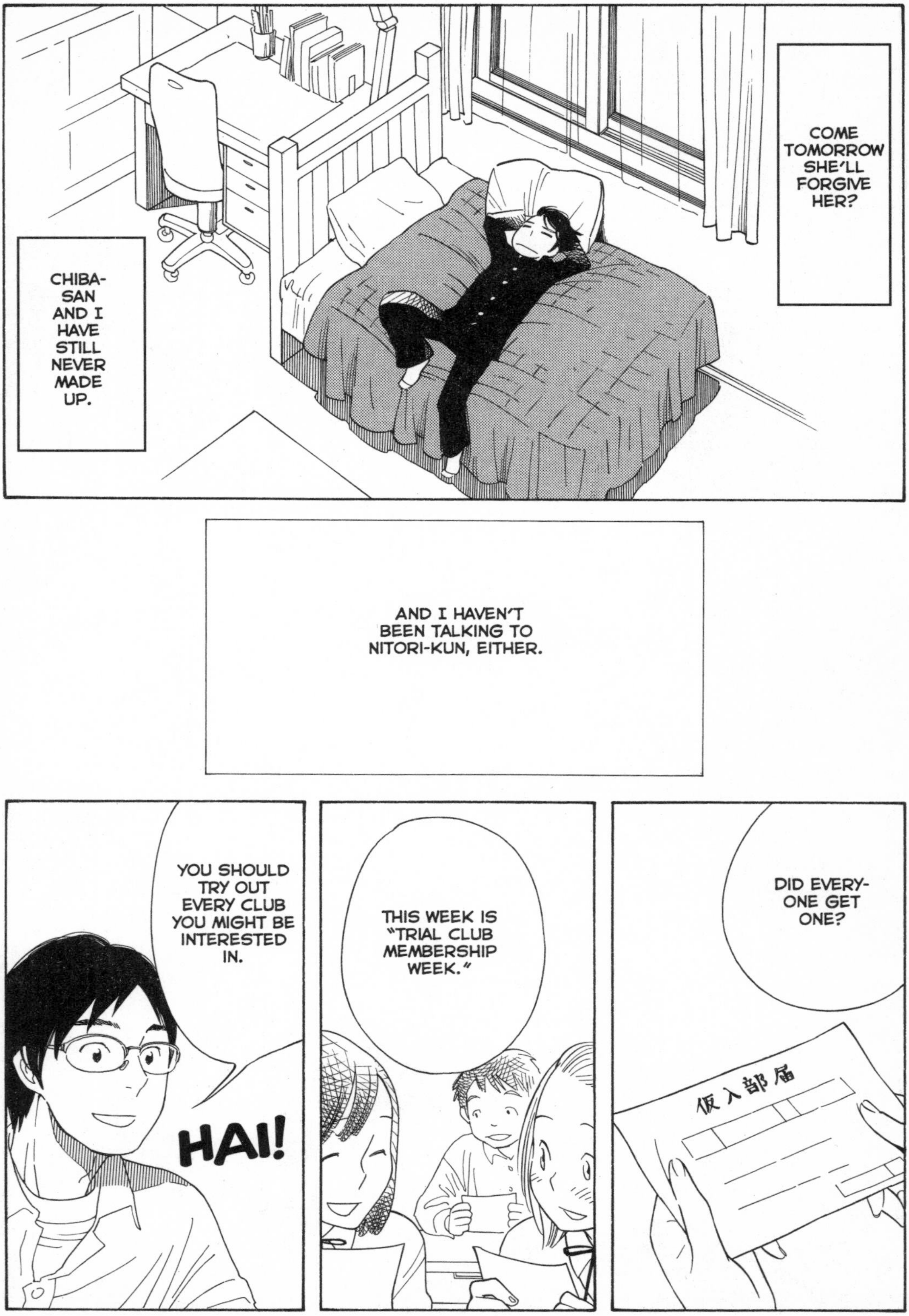
COME TOMORROW SHE'LL FORGIVE HER?
CHIBA-SAN AND I HAVE STILL NEVER MADE UP.
AND I HAVEN'T BEEN TALKING TO NITORI-KUN, EITHER.
DID EVERY-ONE GET ONE?
仮入部届
THIS WEEK IS "TRIAL CLUB MEMBERSHIP WEEK."
YOU SHOULD TRY OUT EVERY CLUB YOU MIGHT BE INTERESTED IN.
HAI!

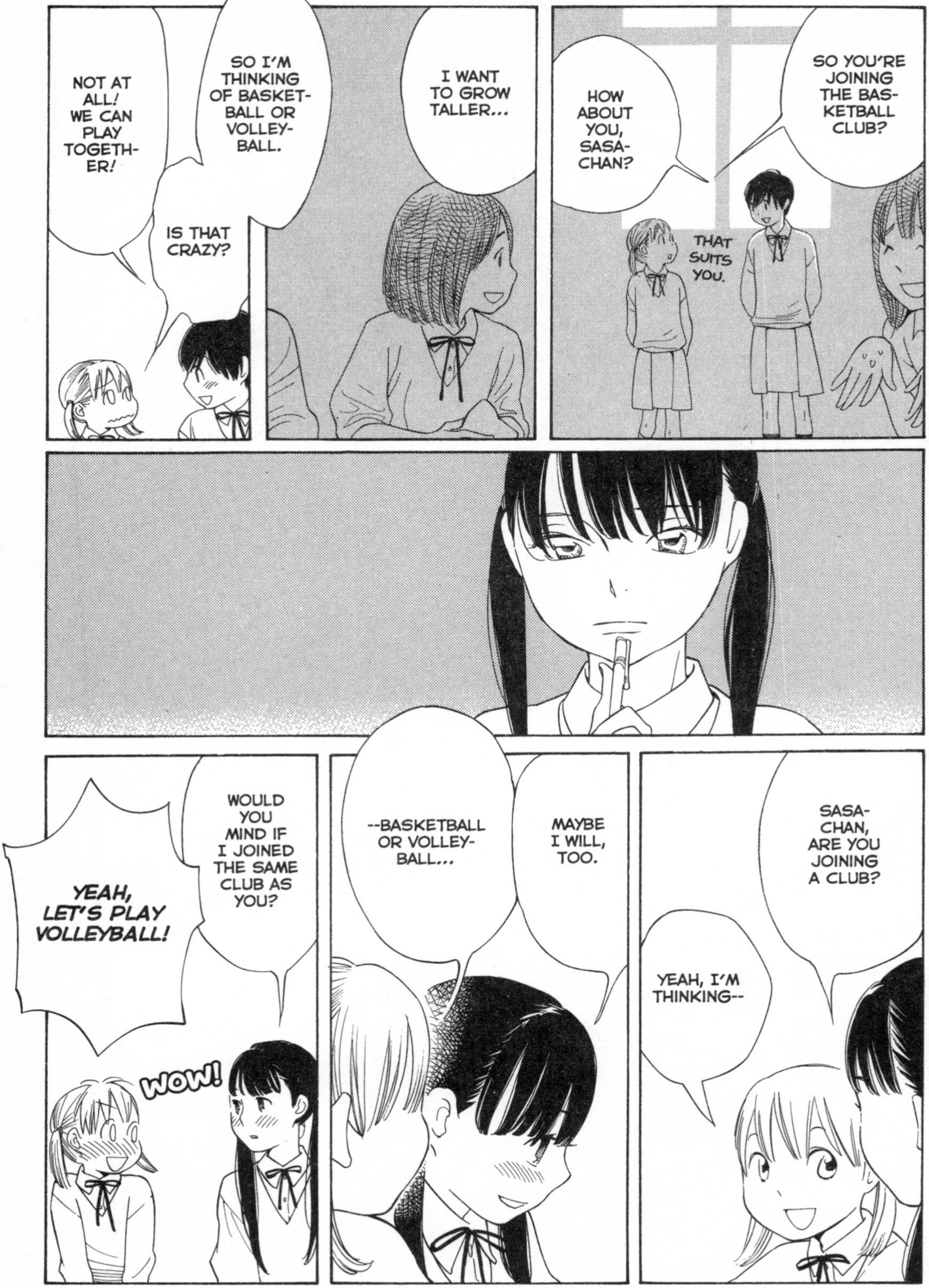
SO YOU'RE JOINING THE BASKETBALL CLUB?
HOW ABOUT YOU, SASA-CHAN?
THAT SUITS YOU.
I WANT TO GROW TALLER...
SO I'M THINKING OF BASKETBALL OR VOLLEYBALL.
IS THAT CRAZY?
NOT AT ALL! WE CAN PLAY TOGETHER!
SASA-CHAN, ARE YOU JOINING A CLUB?
YEAH, I'M THINKING--
--BASKETBALL OR VOLLEYBALL...
MAYBE I WILL, TOO.
WOULD YOU MIND IF I JOINED THE SAME CLUB AS YOU?
YEAH, LET'S PLAY VOLLEYBALL!
WOW!

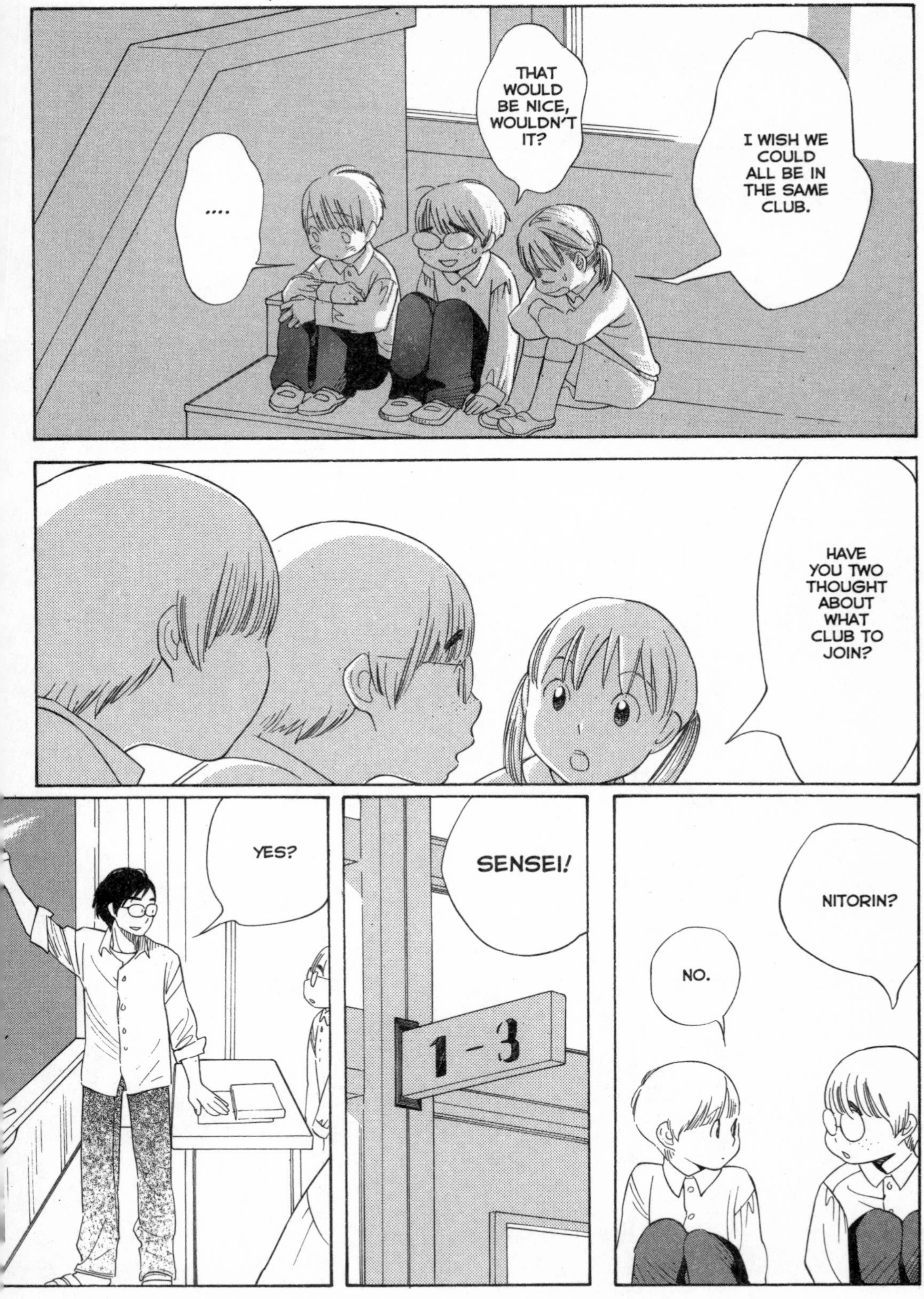
I WISH WE COULD ALL BE IN THE SAME CLUB.
THAT WOULD BE NICE, WOULDN'T IT?
....
HAVE YOU TWO THOUGHT ABOUT WHAT CLUB TO JOIN?
NITORIN?
NO.
SENSEI!
YES?

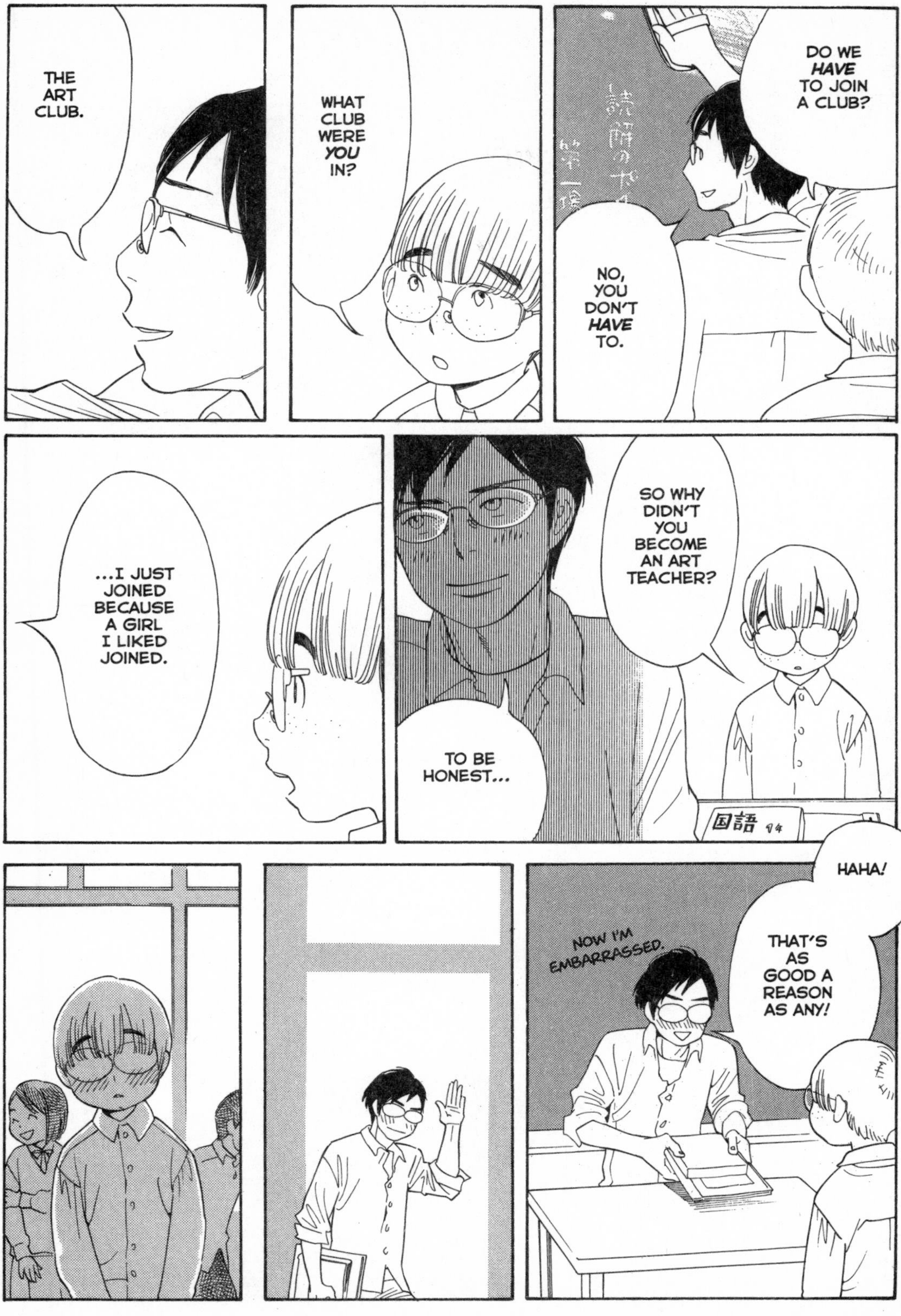
DO WE *HAVE* TO JOIN A CLUB?
NO, YOU DON'T *HAVE* TO.
WHAT CLUB WERE *YOU* IN?
THE ART CLUB.
SO WHY DIDN'T YOU BECOME AN ART TEACHER?
TO BE HONEST...
国語
...I JUST JOINED BECAUSE A GIRL I LIKED JOINED.
HAHA!
THAT'S AS GOOD A REASON AS ANY!
NOW I'M EMBARRASSED.

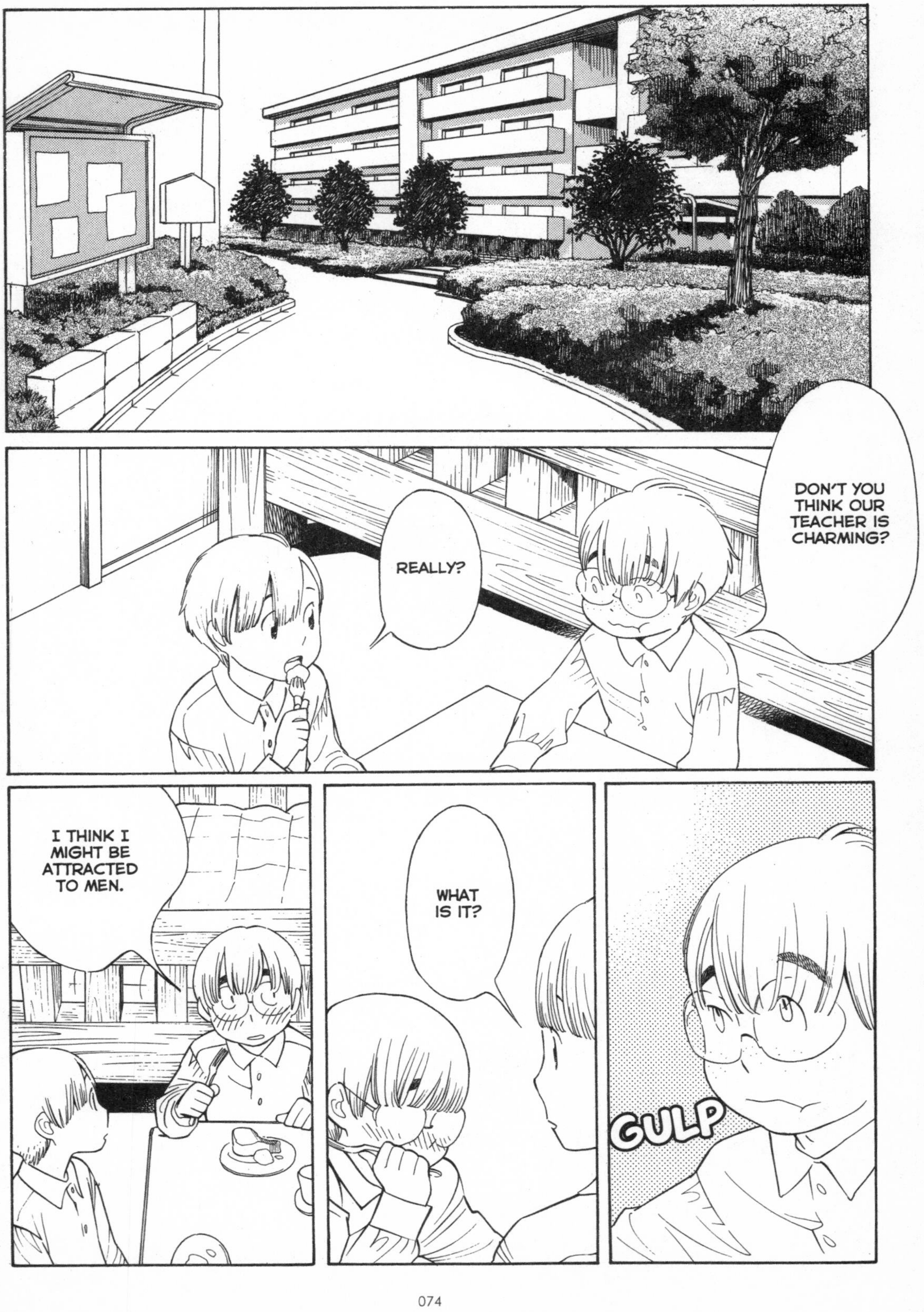
DON'T YOU THINK OUR TEACHER IS CHARMING?
REALLY?
GULP
WHAT IS IT?
I THINK I MIGHT BE ATTRACTED TO MEN.

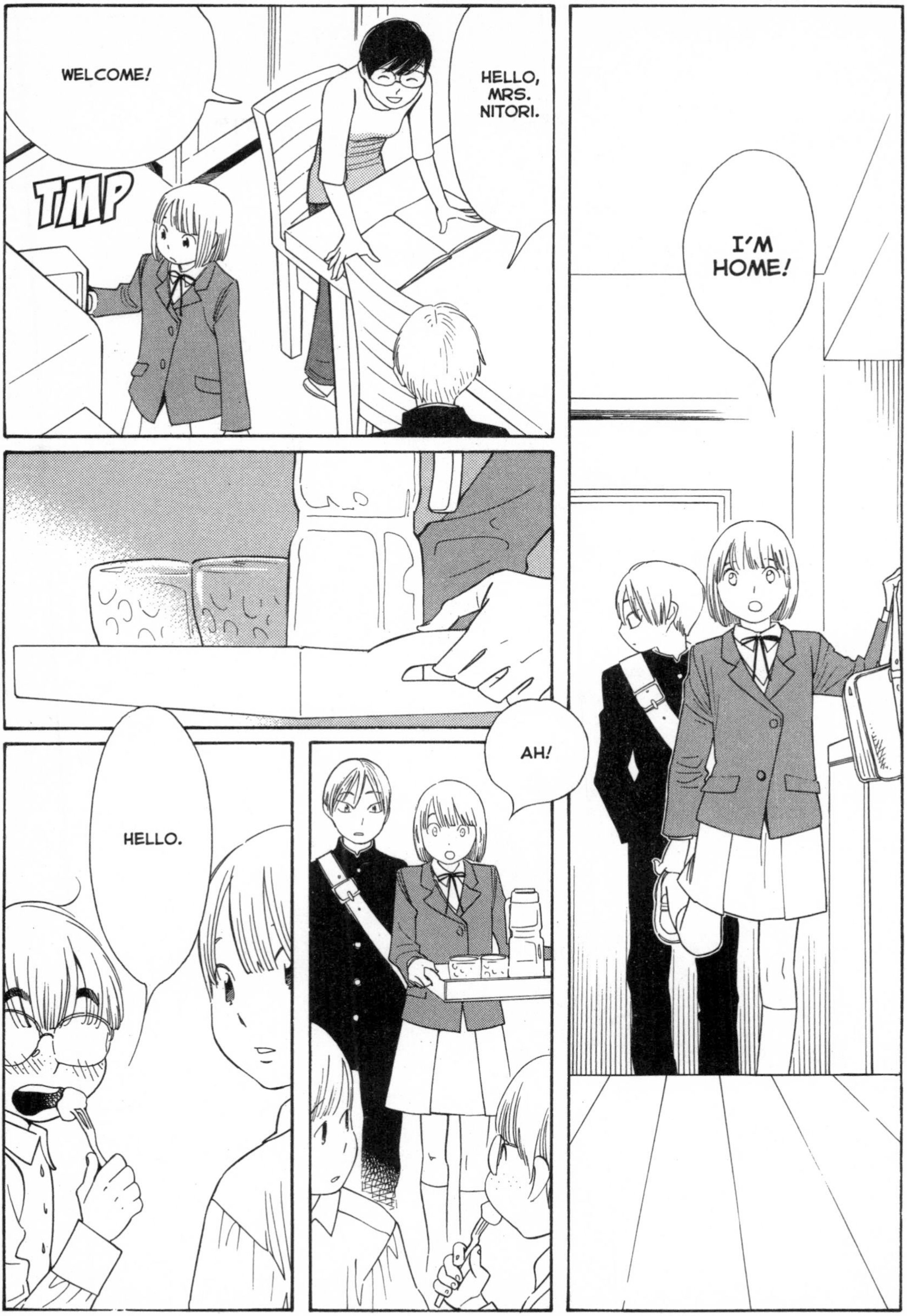
I'M HOME!
HELLO, MRS. NITORI.
WELCOME!
TMP
AH!
HELLO.

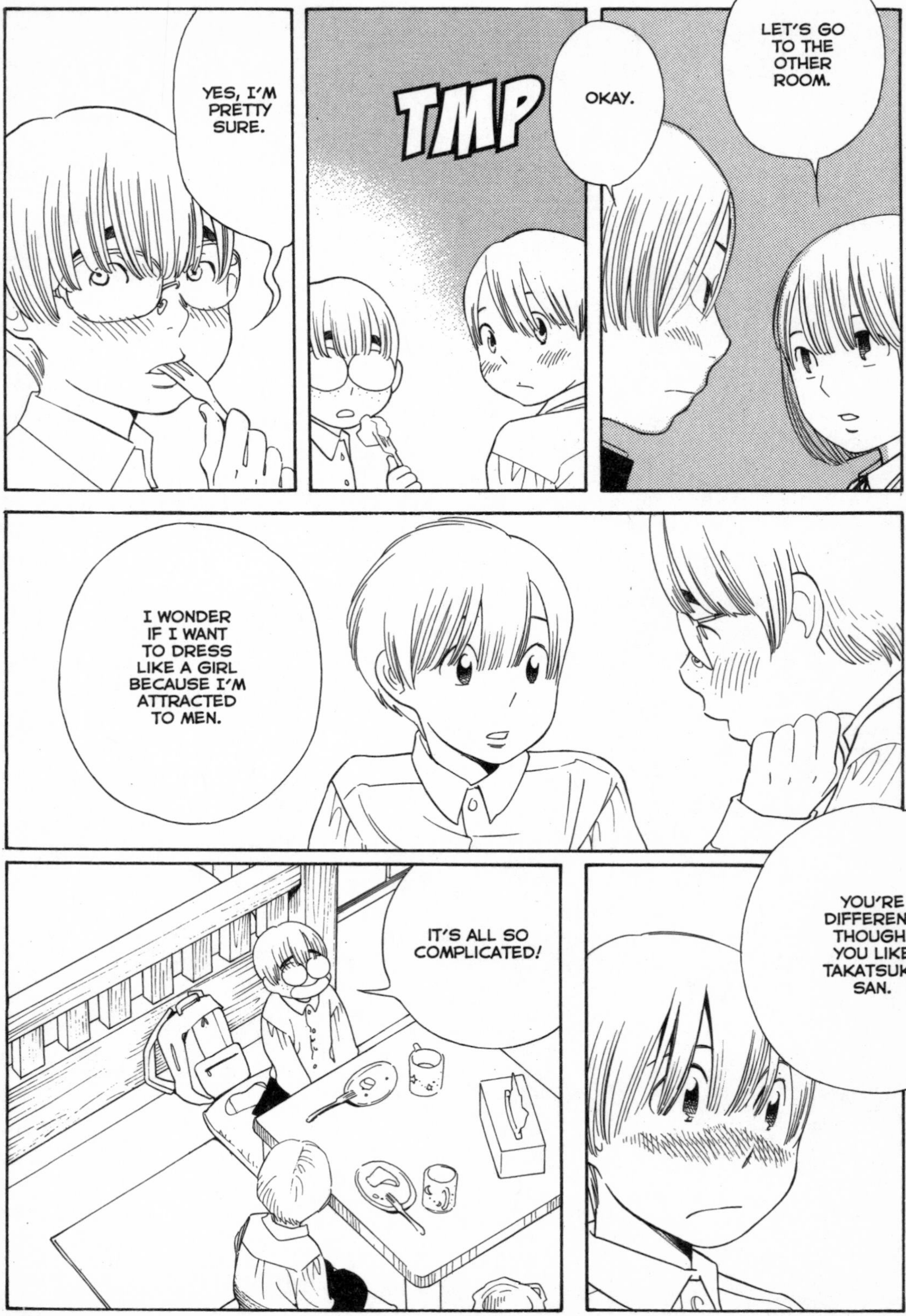
LET'S GO TO THE OTHER ROOM.
OKAY.
TMP
YES, I'M PRETTY SURE.
I WONDER IF I WANT TO DRESS LIKE A GIRL BECAUSE I'M ATTRACTED TO MEN.
YOU'RE DIFFERENT, THOUGH. YOU LIKE TAKATSUKI-SAN.
IT'S ALL SO COMPLICATED!

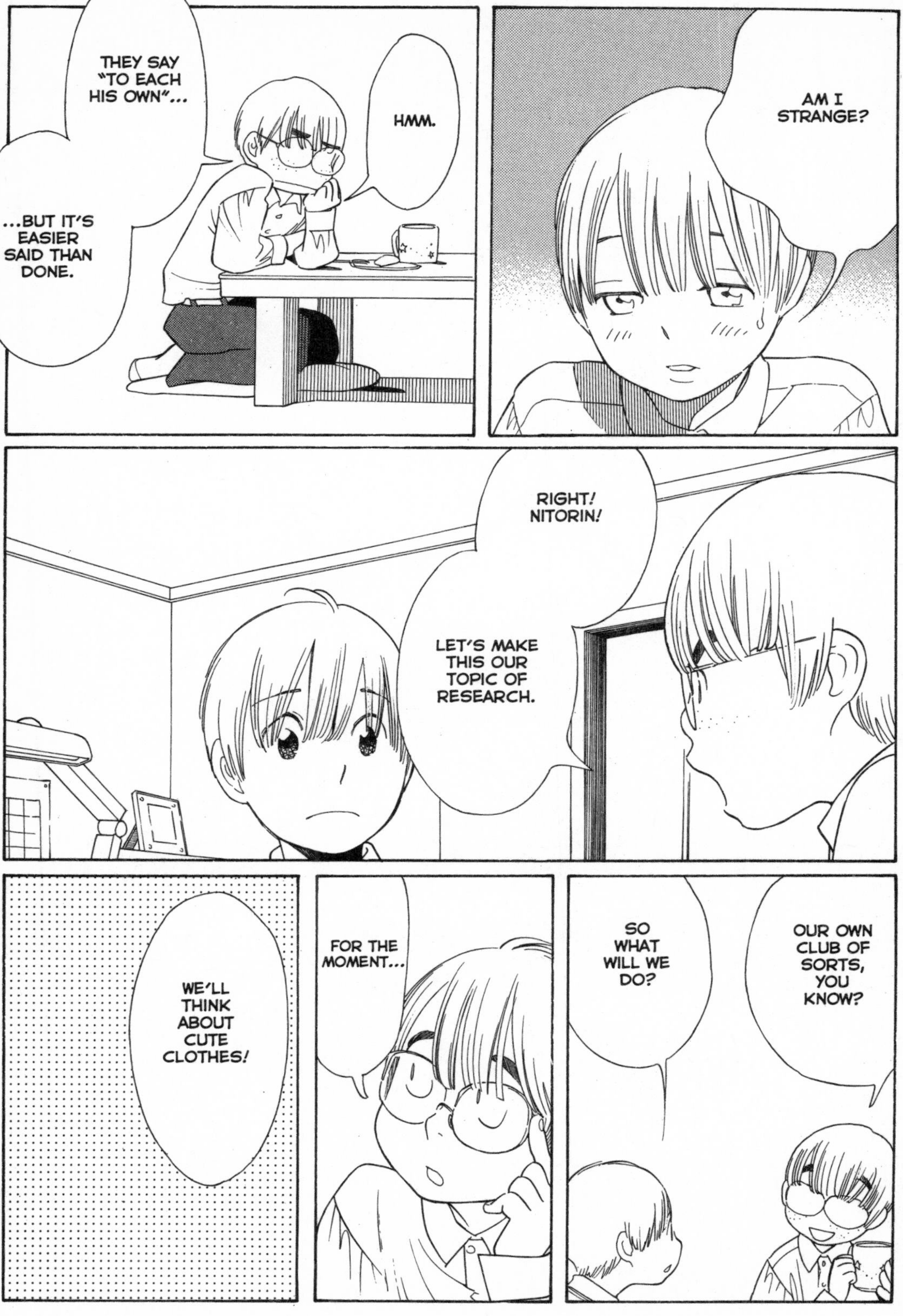
AM I STRANGE?
HMM.
THEY SAY "TO EACH HIS OWN"...
...BUT IT'S EASIER SAID THAN DONE.
RIGHT! NITORIN!
LET'S MAKE THIS OUR TOPIC OF RESEARCH.
OUR OWN CLUB OF SORTS, YOU KNOW?
SO WHAT WILL WE DO?
FOR THE MOMENT...
WE'LL THINK ABOUT CUTE CLOTHES!

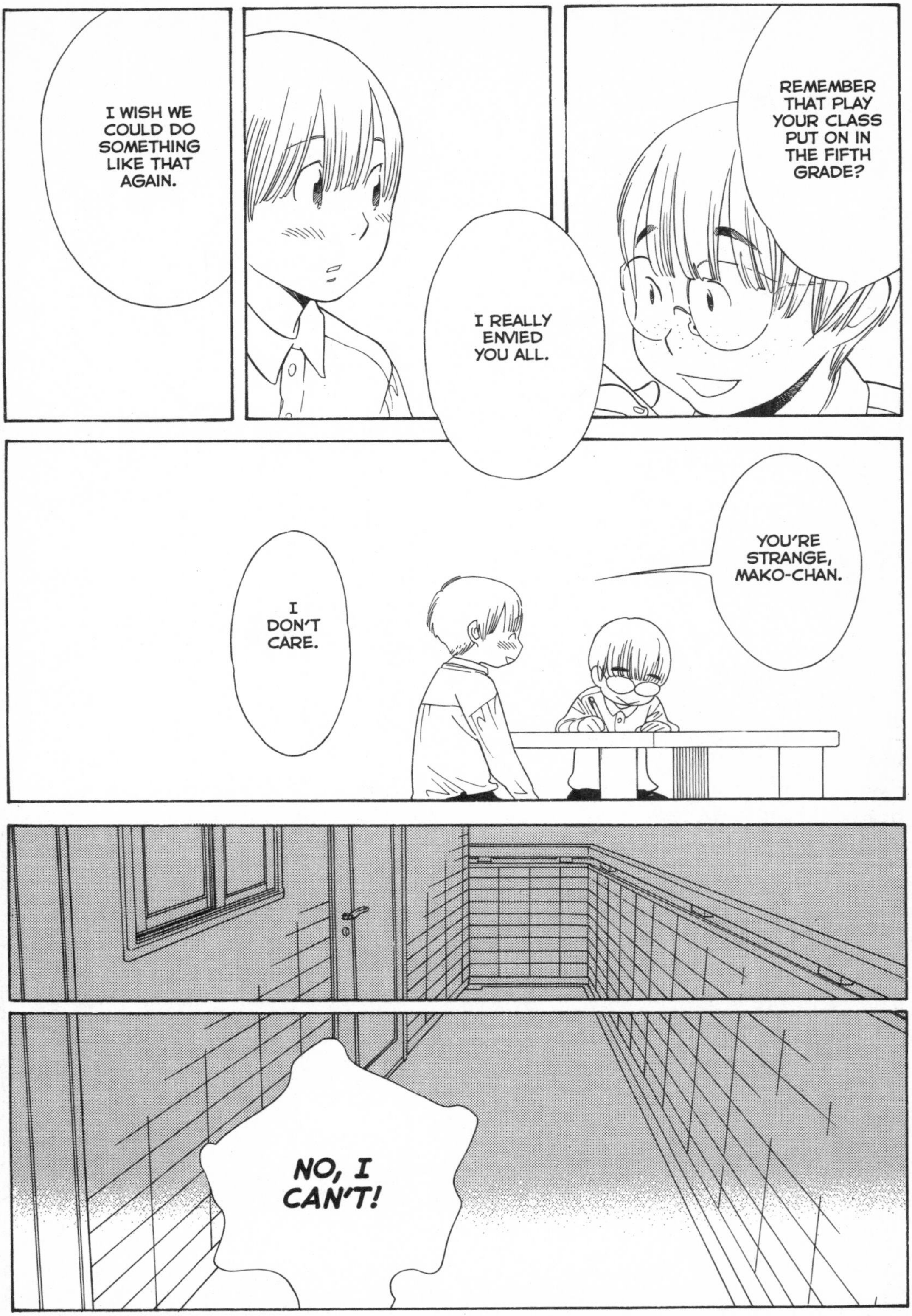
REMEMBER THAT PLAY YOUR CLASS PUT ON IN THE FIFTH GRADE?
I REALLY ENVIED YOU ALL.
I WISH WE COULD DO SOMETHING LIKE THAT AGAIN.
YOU'RE STRANGE, MAKO-CHAN.
I DON'T CARE.
NO, I CAN'T!

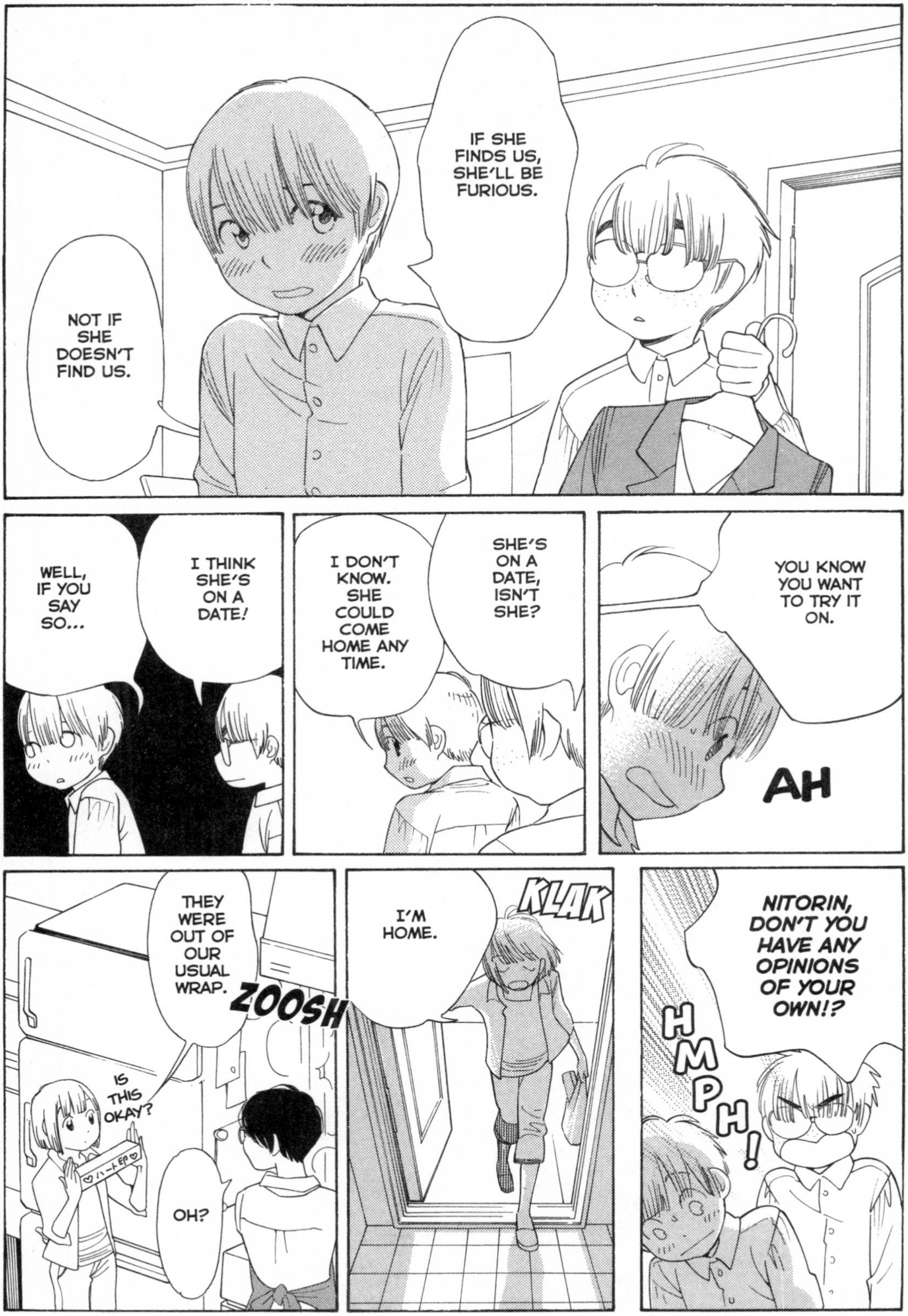
IF SHE FINDS US, SHE'LL BE FURIOUS.
NOT IF SHE DOESN'T FIND US.
YOU KNOW YOU WANT TO TRY IT ON.
AH
SHE'S ON A DATE, ISN'T SHE?
I DON'T KNOW. SHE COULD COME HOME ANY TIME.
I THINK SHE'S ON A DATE!
WELL, IF YOU SAY SO...
NITORIN, DON'T YOU HAVE ANY OPINIONS OF YOUR OWN!?
HMPH!
KLAK
I'M HOME.
THEY WERE OUT OF OUR USUAL WRAP.
ZOOSH
IS THIS OKAY?
OH?

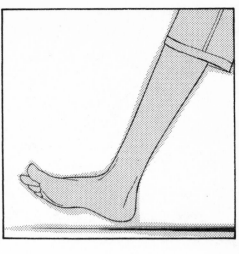

WHY DON'T

I--I'M SORRY.

THE NEXT TIME YOU PUT ON MY UNIFORM I'LL *KILL* YOU!!

YOU JUST

GRAB

I MADE HIM DO IT! I'M SORRY!

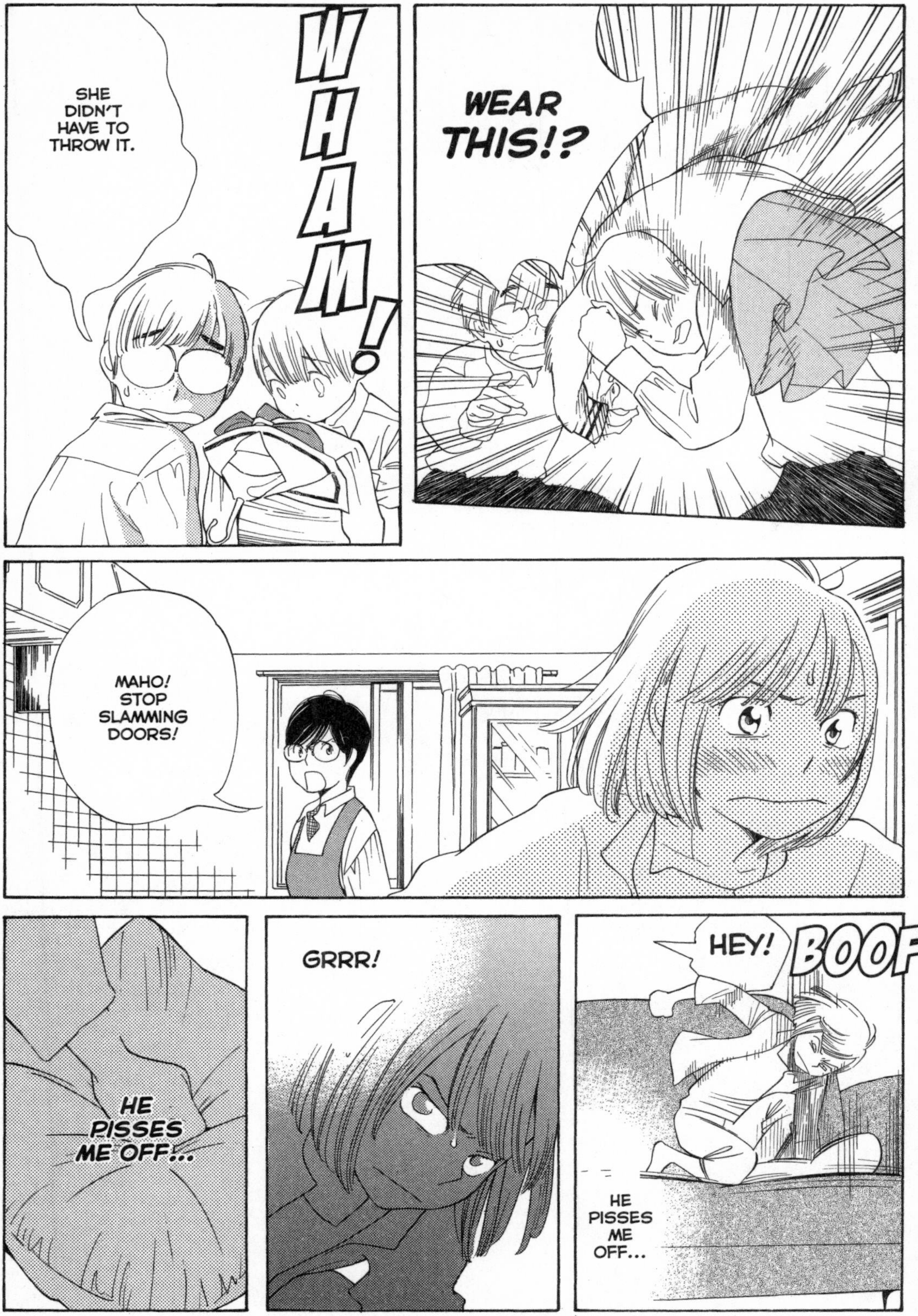
WEAR THIS!?
WHAM!
SHE DIDN'T HAVE TO THROW IT.
MAHO! STOP SLAMMING DOORS!
BOOF
HEY!
HE PISSES ME OFF...
GRRR!
HE PISSES ME OFF...

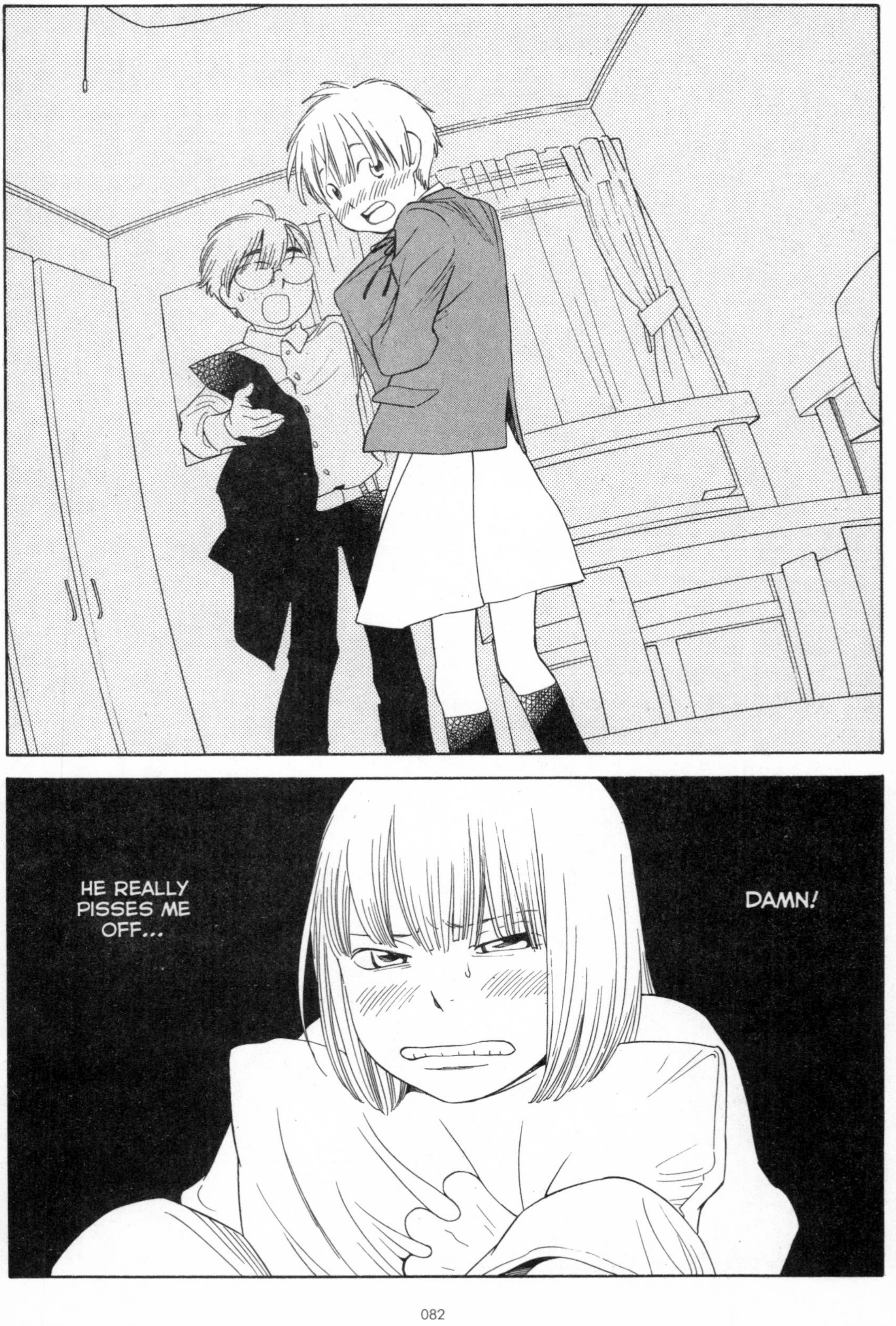
DAMN!
HE REALLY PISSES ME OFF...

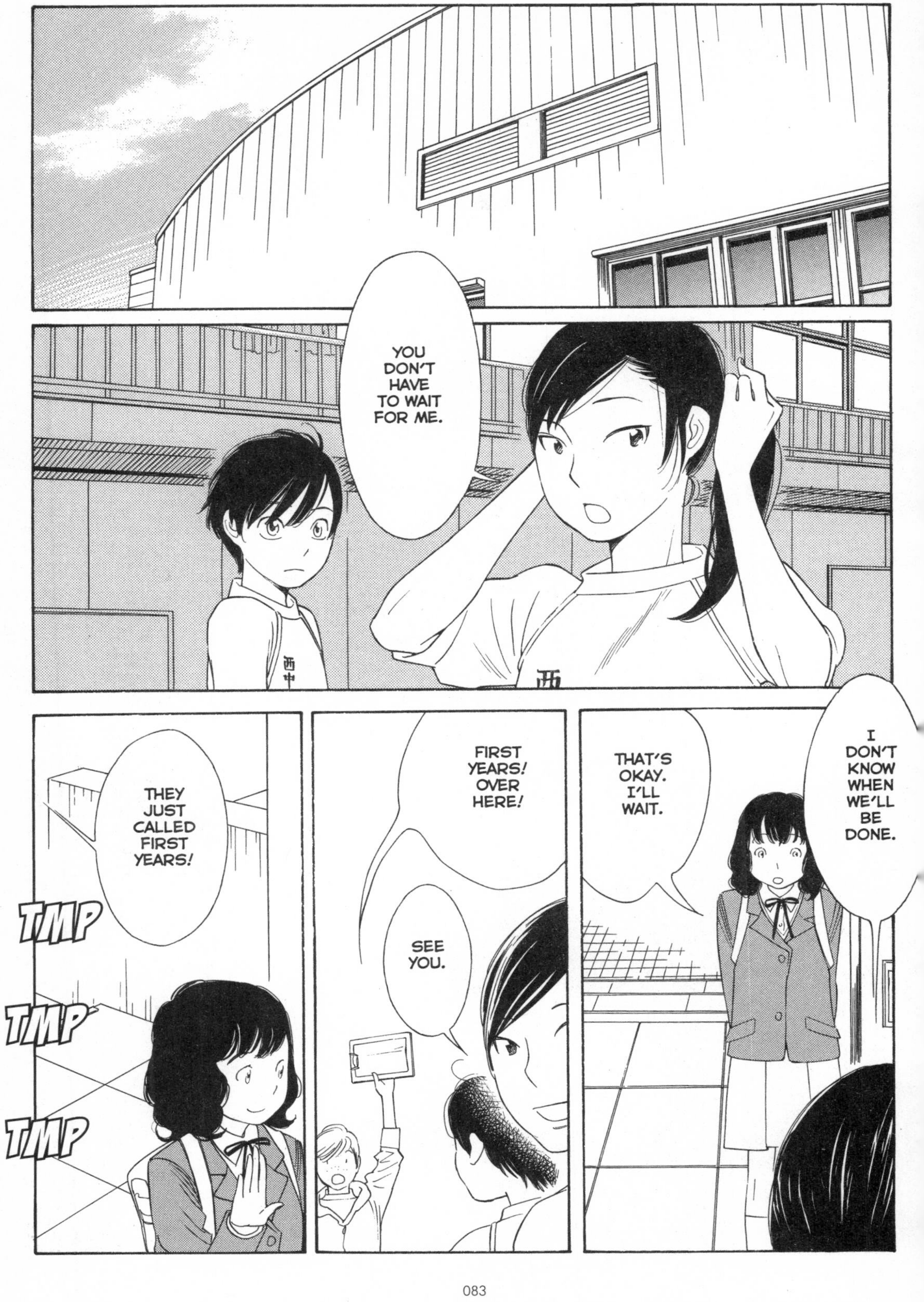
YOU DON'T HAVE TO WAIT FOR ME.
I DON'T KNOW WHEN WE'LL BE DONE.
THAT'S OKAY. I'LL WAIT.
FIRST YEARS! OVER HERE!
SEE YOU.
THEY JUST CALLED FIRST YEARS!
TMP
TMP
TMP

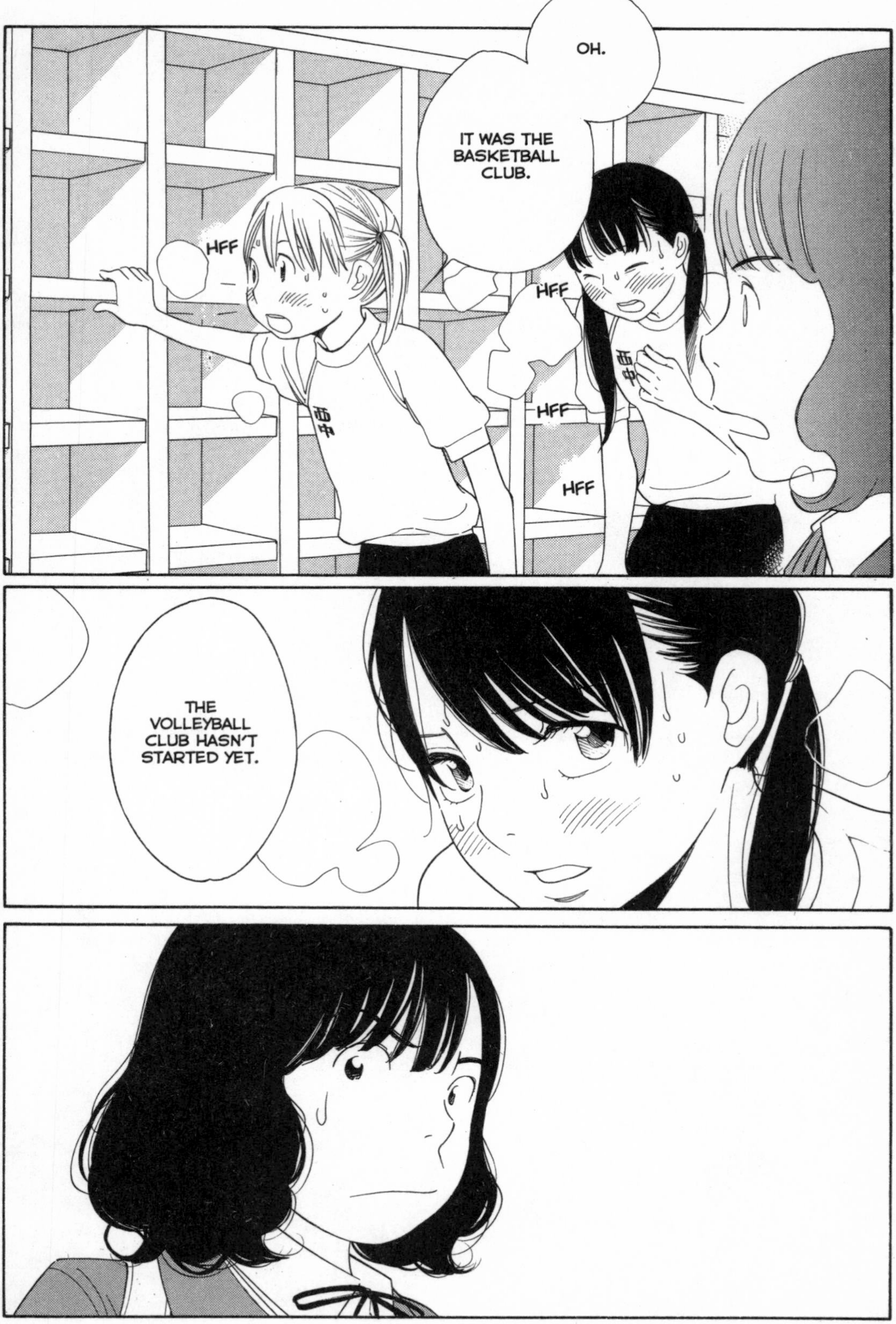
OH.
IT WAS THE BASKETBALL CLUB.
HFF
HFF
HFF
HFF
THE VOLLEYBALL CLUB HASN'T STARTED YET.

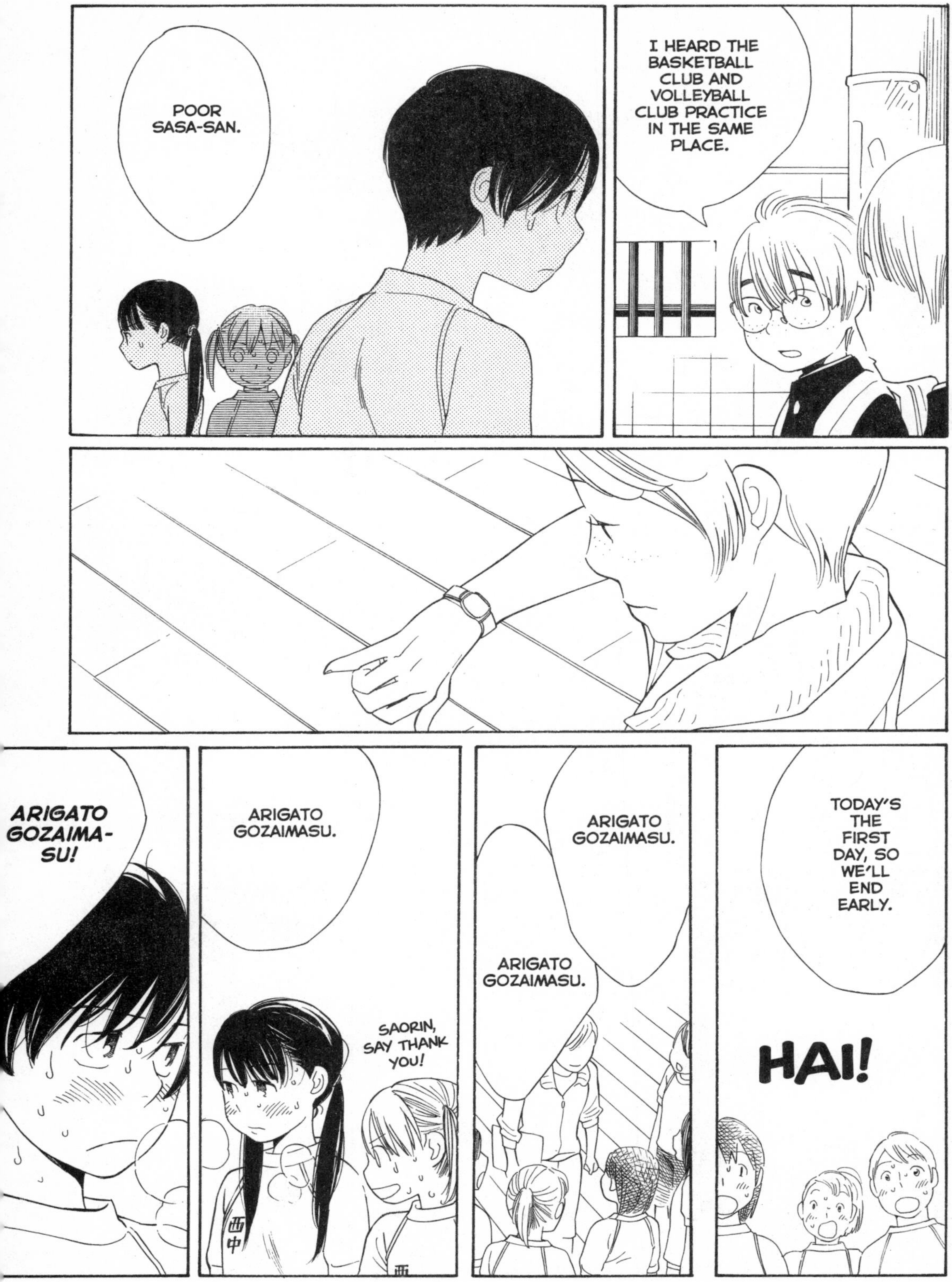
I HEARD THE BASKETBALL CLUB AND VOLLEYBALL CLUB PRACTICE IN THE SAME PLACE.
POOR SASA-SAN.
TODAY'S THE FIRST DAY, SO WE'LL END EARLY.
HAI!
ARIGATO GOZAIMASU.
ARIGATO GOZAIMASU.
ARIGATO GOZAIMASU.
SAORIN, SAY THANK YOU!
ARIGATO GOZAIMA-SU!

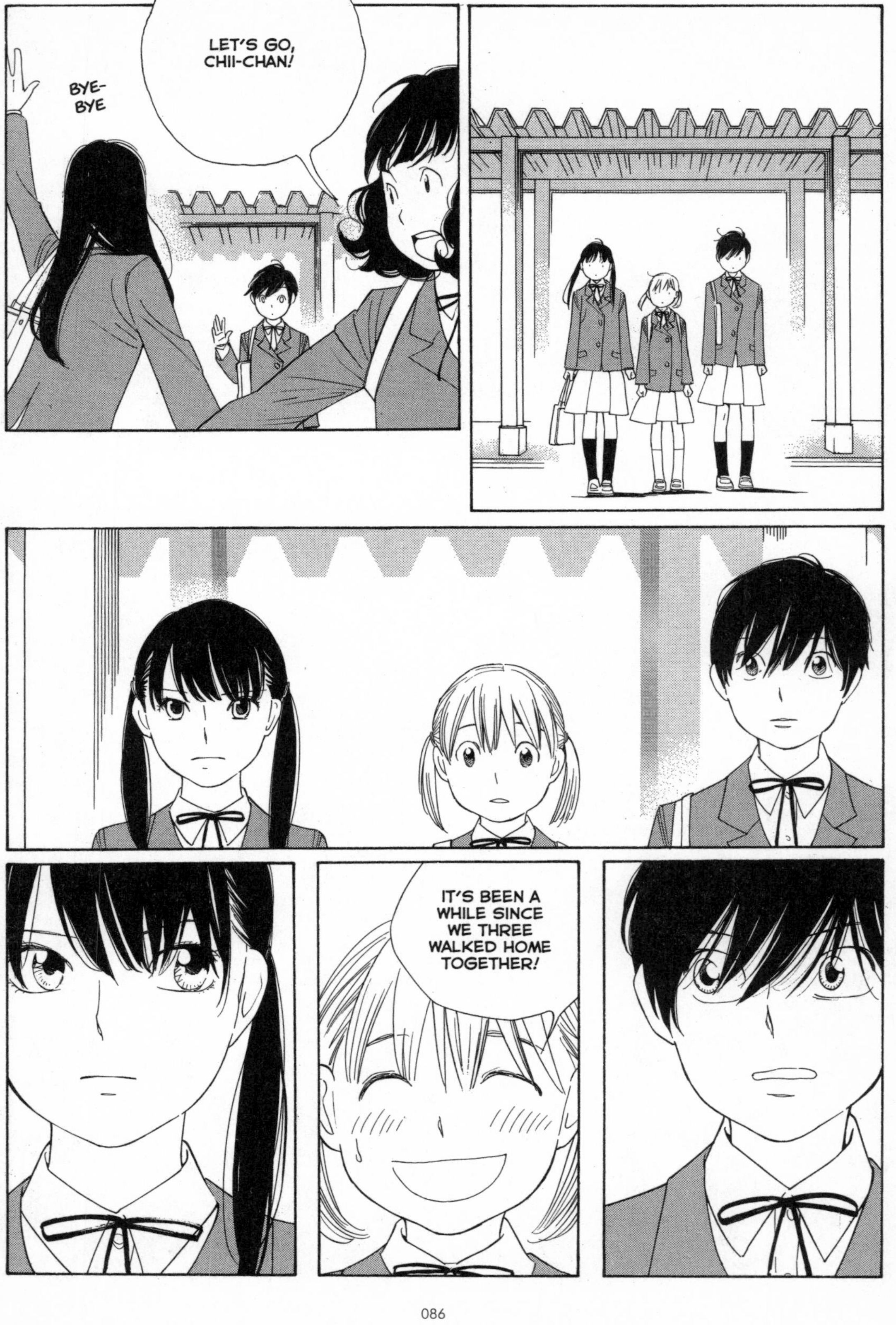
LET'S GO, CHII-CHAN!
BYE-BYE
IT'S BEEN A WHILE SINCE WE THREE WALKED HOME TOGETHER!

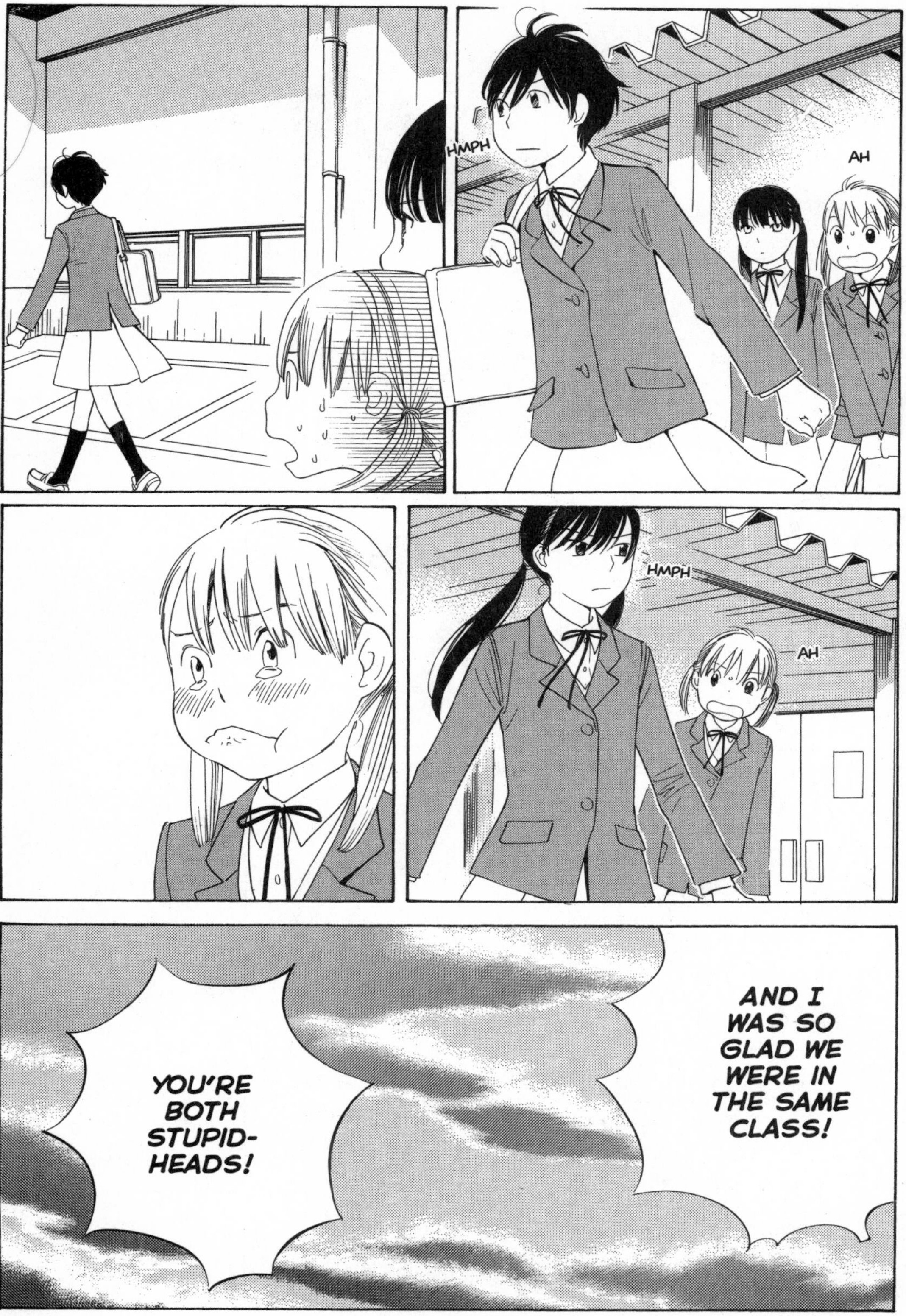
HMPH
AH
HMPH
AH
AND I WAS SO GLAD WE WERE IN THE SAME CLASS!
YOU'RE BOTH STUPID-HEADS!

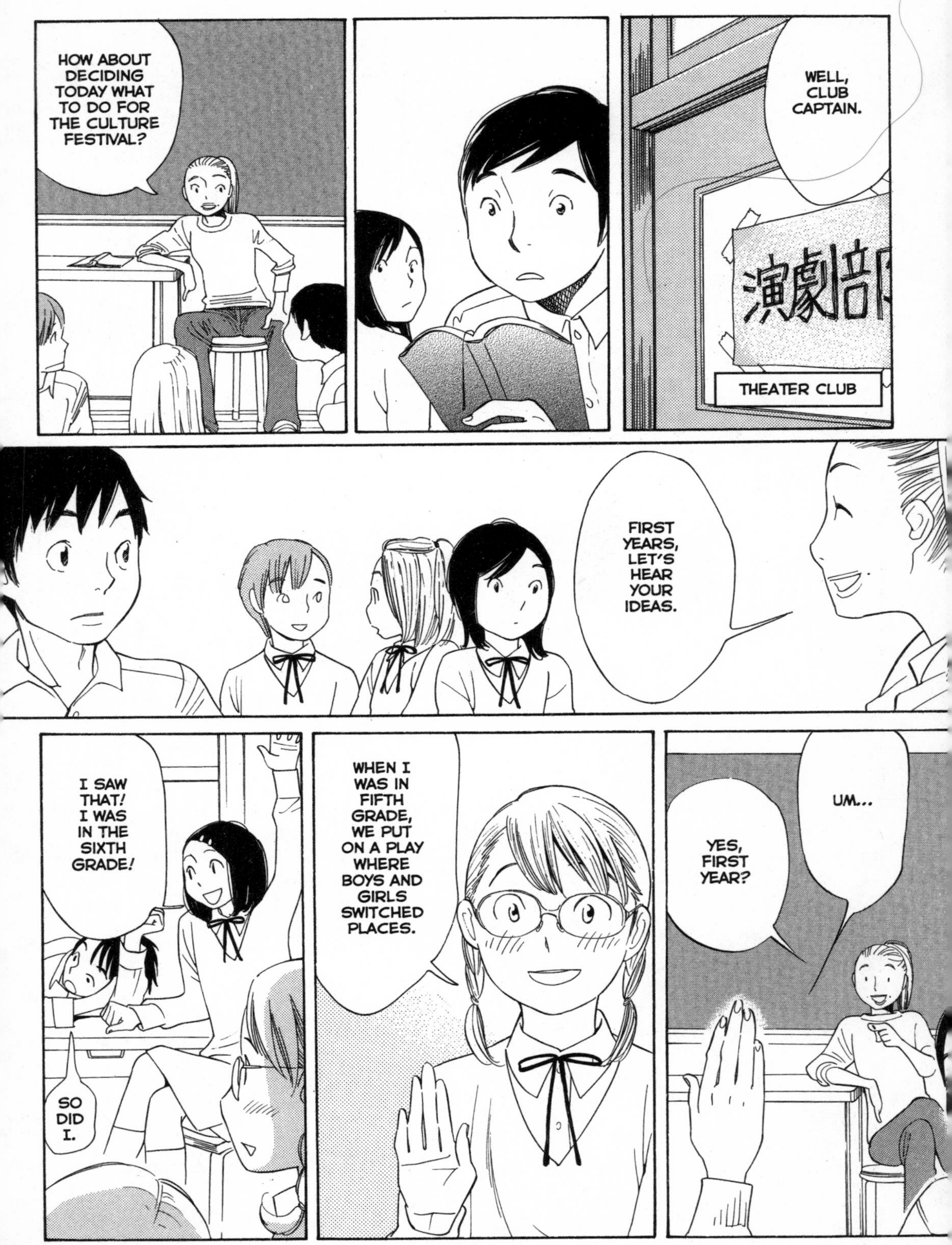
WELL, CLUB CAPTAIN.
THEATER CLUB
HOW ABOUT DECIDING TODAY WHAT TO DO FOR THE CULTURE FESTIVAL?
FIRST YEARS, LET'S HEAR YOUR IDEAS.
UM...
YES, FIRST YEAR?
WHEN I WAS IN FIFTH GRADE, WE PUT ON A PLAY WHERE BOYS AND GIRLS SWITCHED PLACES.
I SAW THAT! I WAS IN THE SIXTH GRADE!
SO DID I.

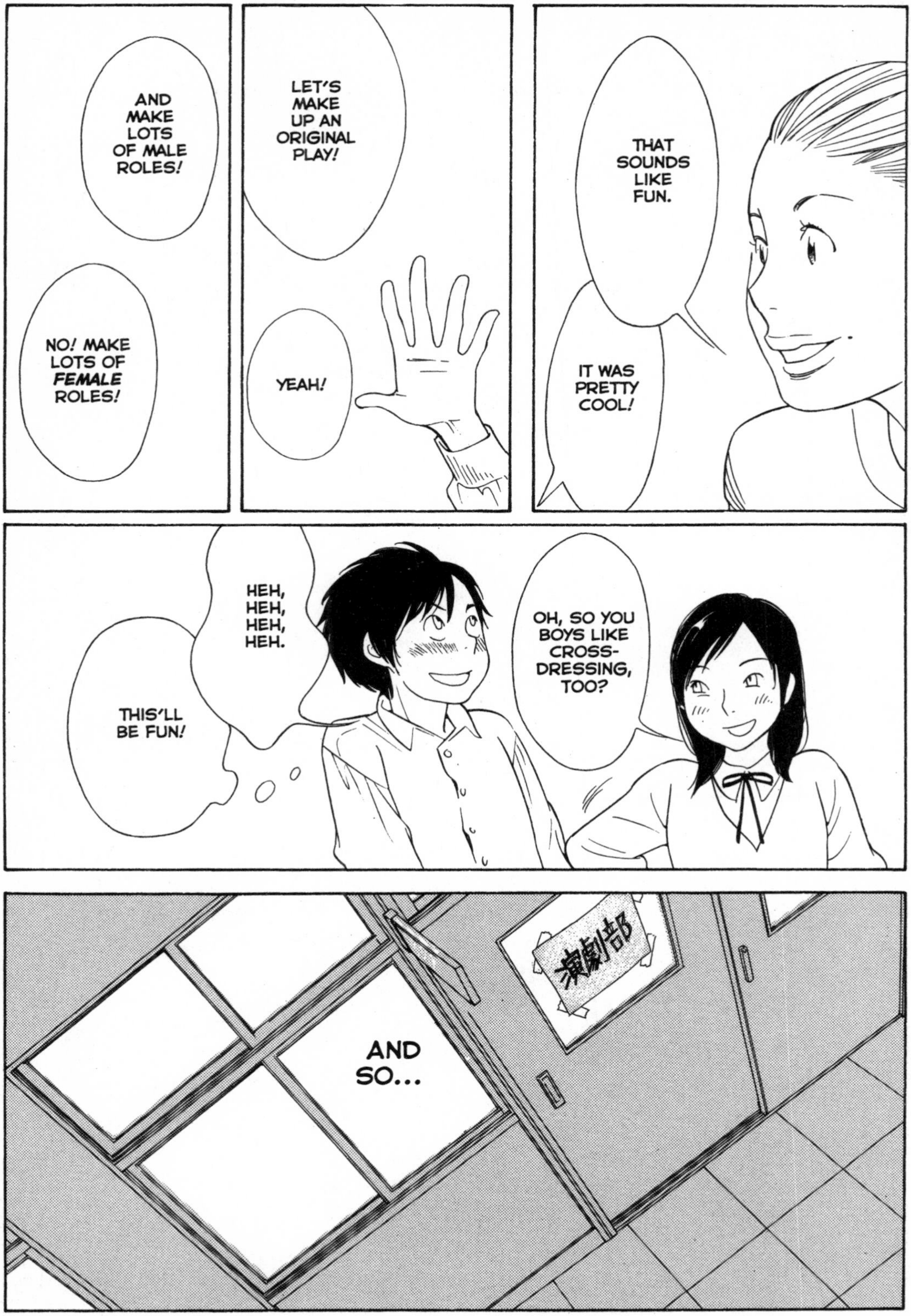
THAT SOUNDS LIKE FUN.
IT WAS PRETTY COOL!
LET'S MAKE UP AN ORIGINAL PLAY!
YEAH!
AND MAKE LOTS OF MALE ROLES!
NO! MAKE LOTS OF *FEMALE* ROLES!
OH, SO YOU BOYS LIKE CROSS-DRESSING, TOO?
HEH, HEH, HEH, HEH.
THIS'LL BE FUN!
演劇部
AND SO...

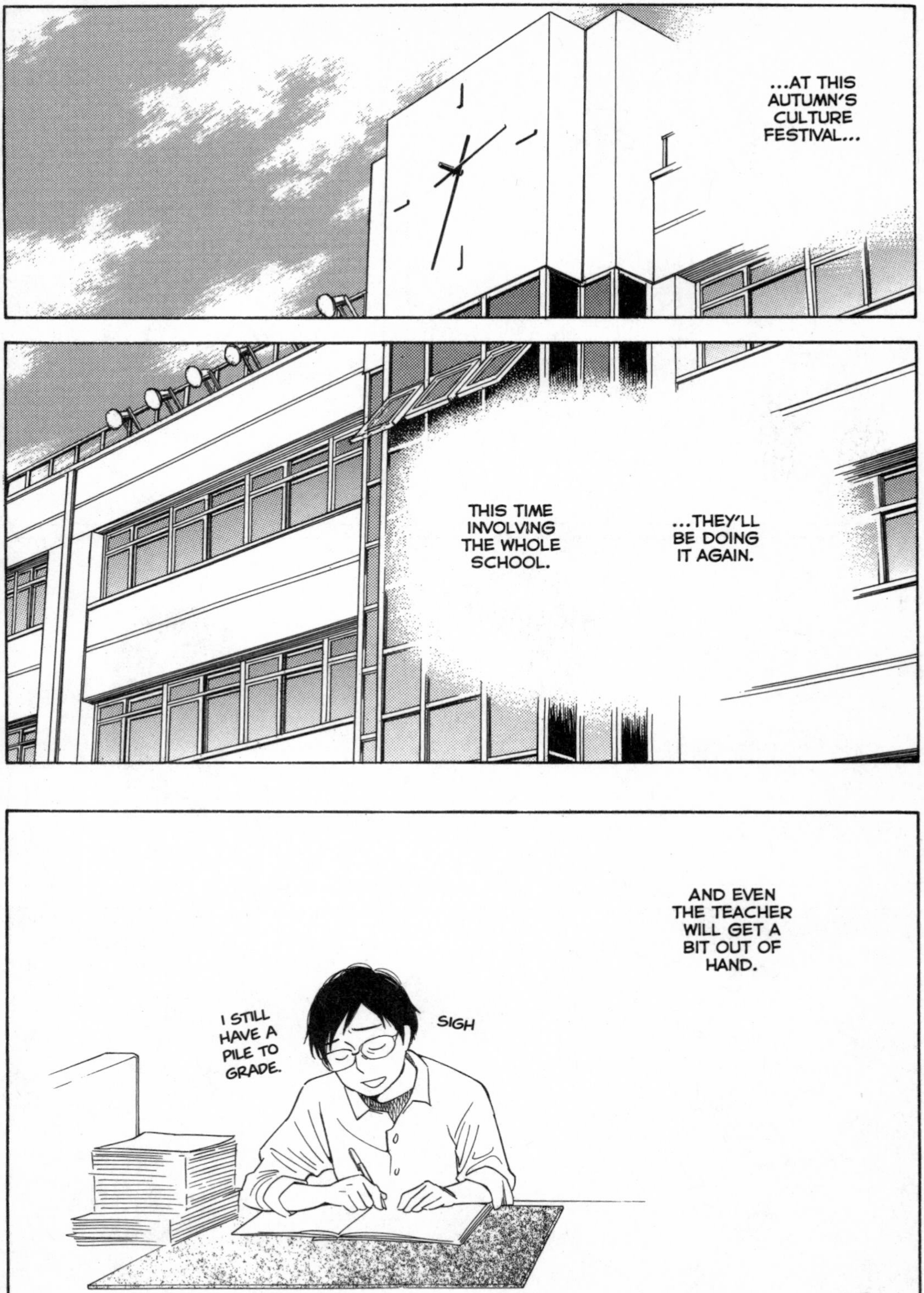
...AT THIS AUTUMN'S CULTURE FESTIVAL...
...THEY'LL BE DOING IT AGAIN.
THIS TIME INVOLVING THE WHOLE SCHOOL.
AND EVEN THE TEACHER WILL GET A BIT OUT OF HAND.
SIGH
I STILL HAVE A PILE TO GRADE.

37

Beautiful Monday

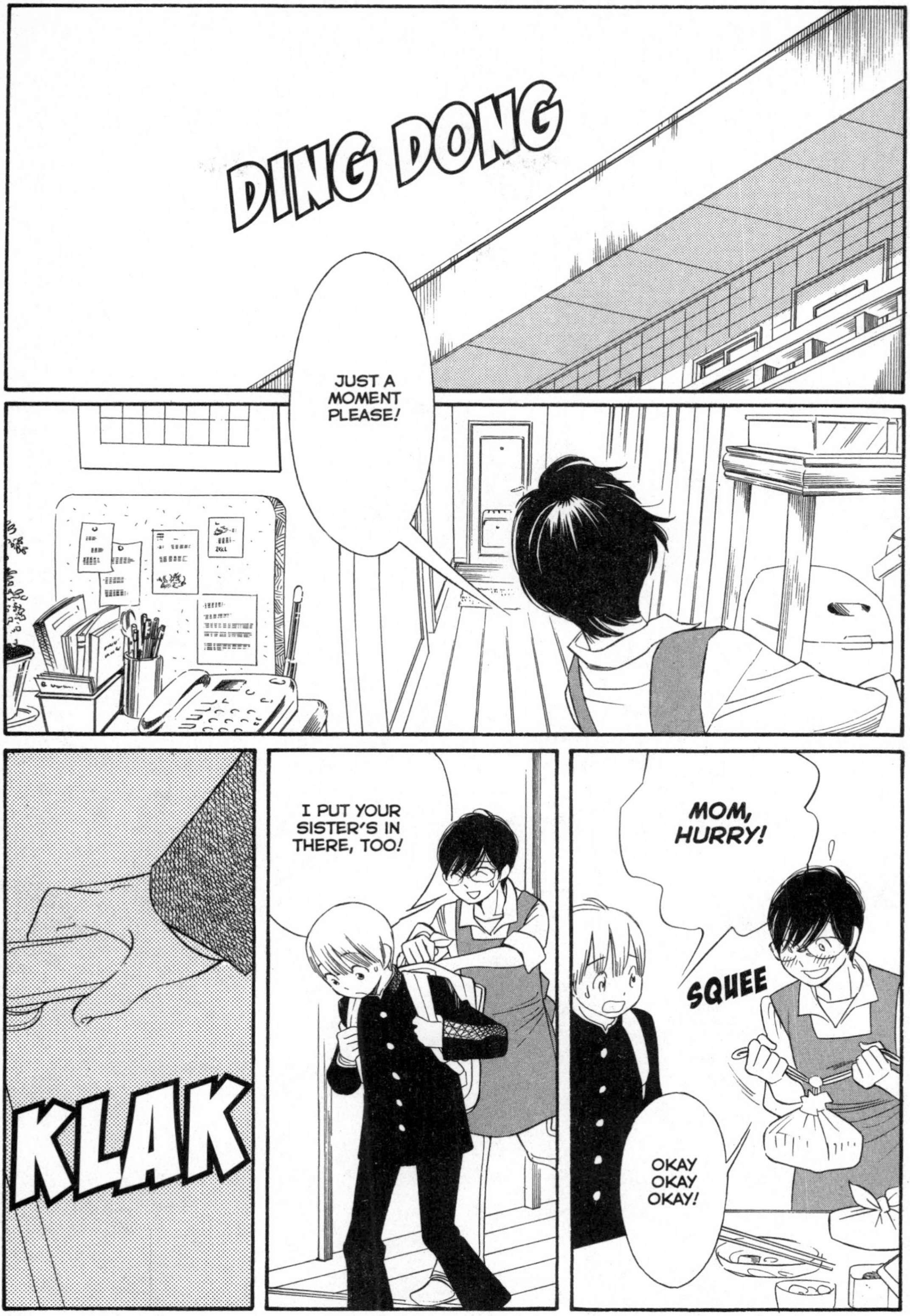
DING DONG
JUST A MOMENT PLEASE!
MOM, HURRY!
SQUEE
OKAY OKAY OKAY!
I PUT YOUR SISTER'S IN THERE, TOO!
KLAK

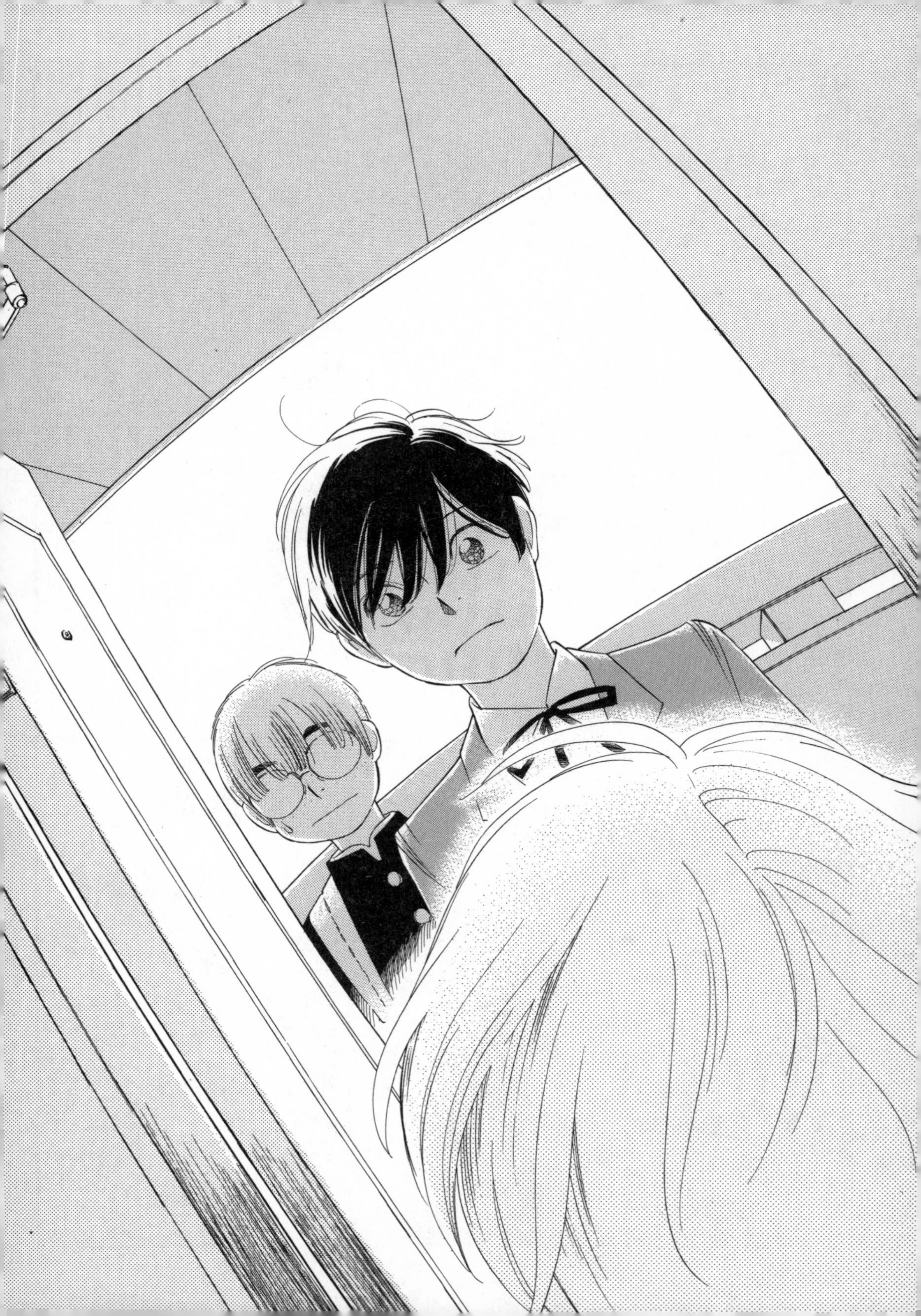

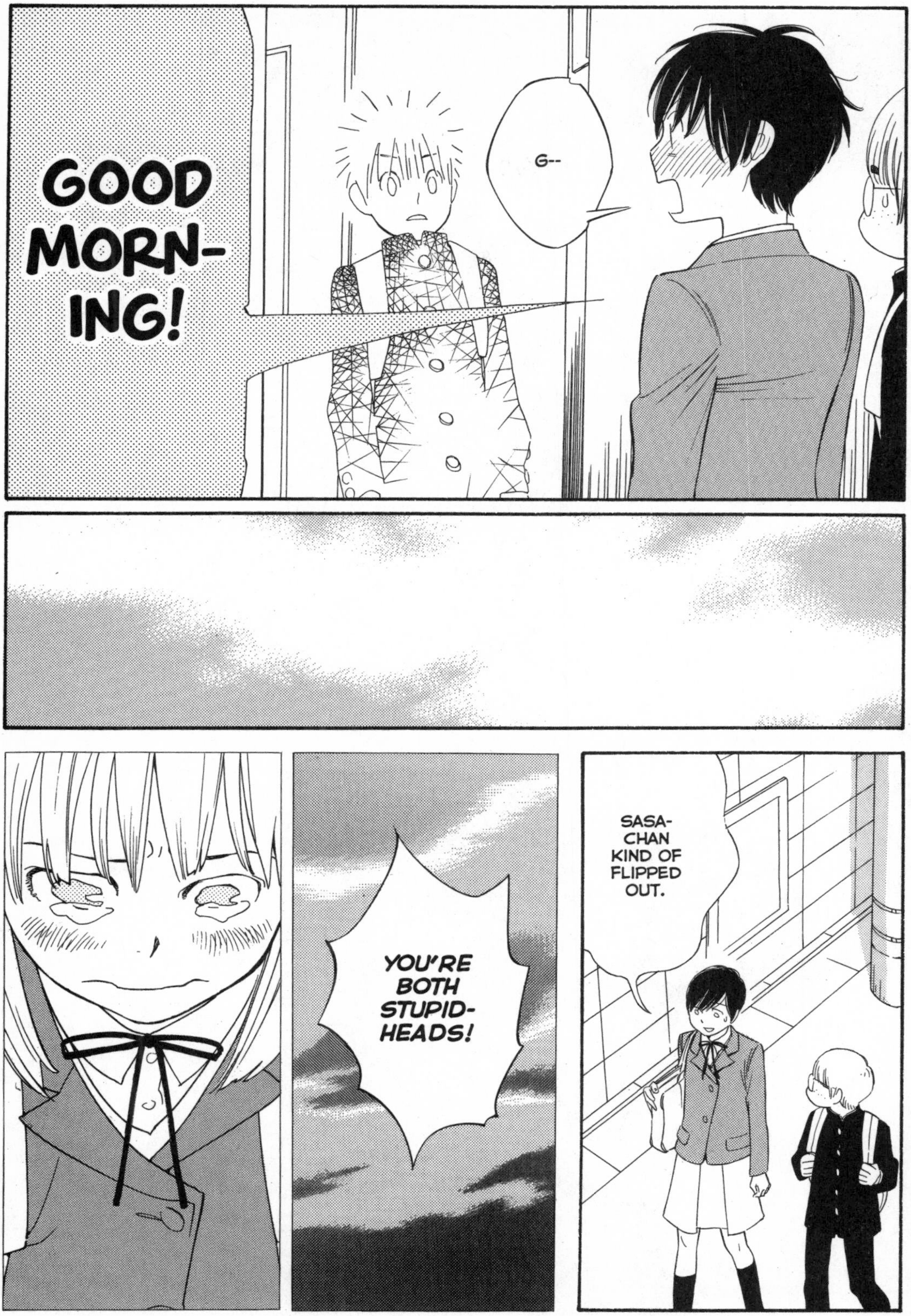
G--
GOOD MORN-ING!
SASA-CHAN KIND OF FLIPPED OUT.
YOU'RE BOTH STUPID-HEADS!

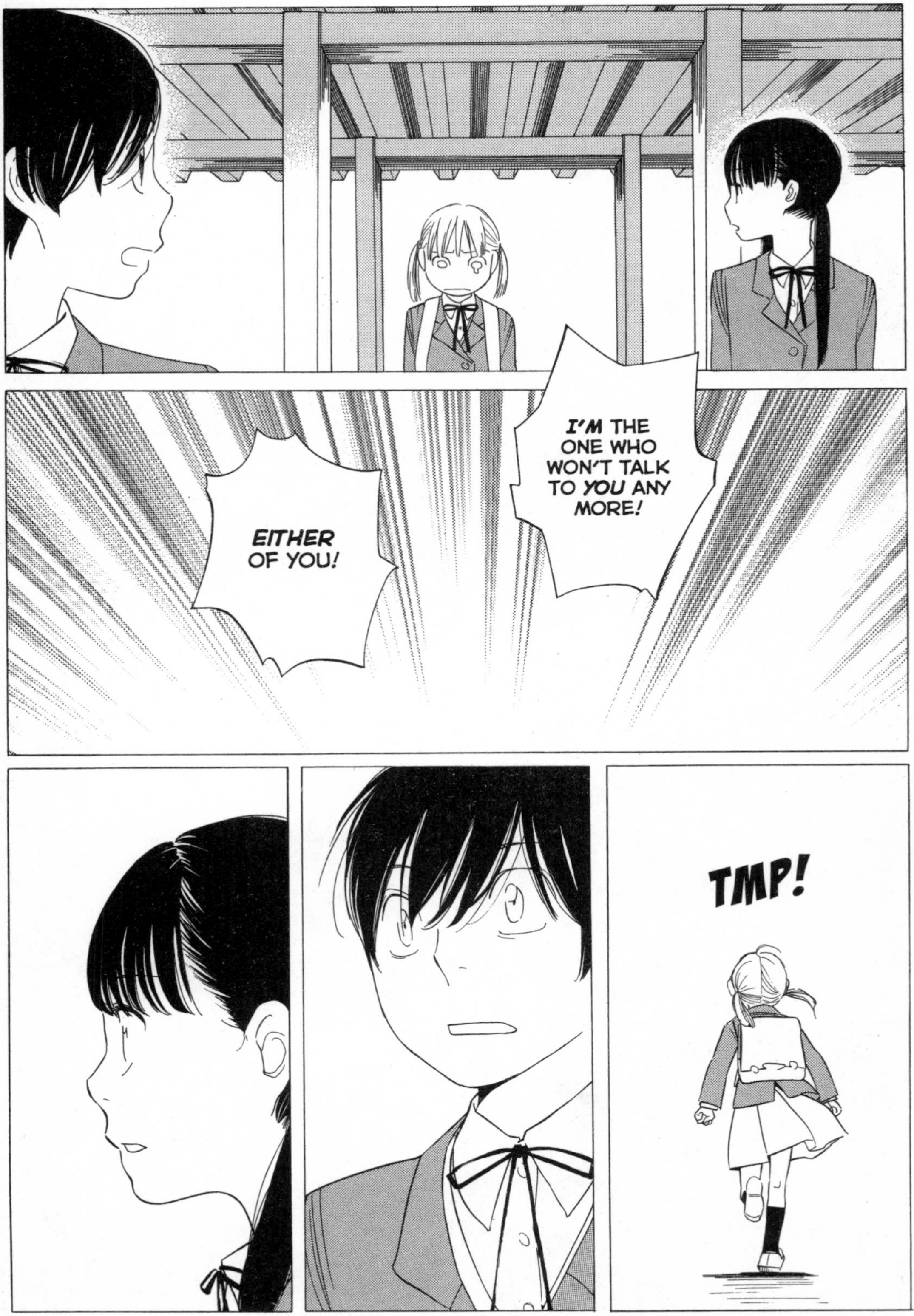
I'M THE ONE WHO WON'T TALK TO *YOU* ANY MORE!
EITHER OF YOU!
TMP!

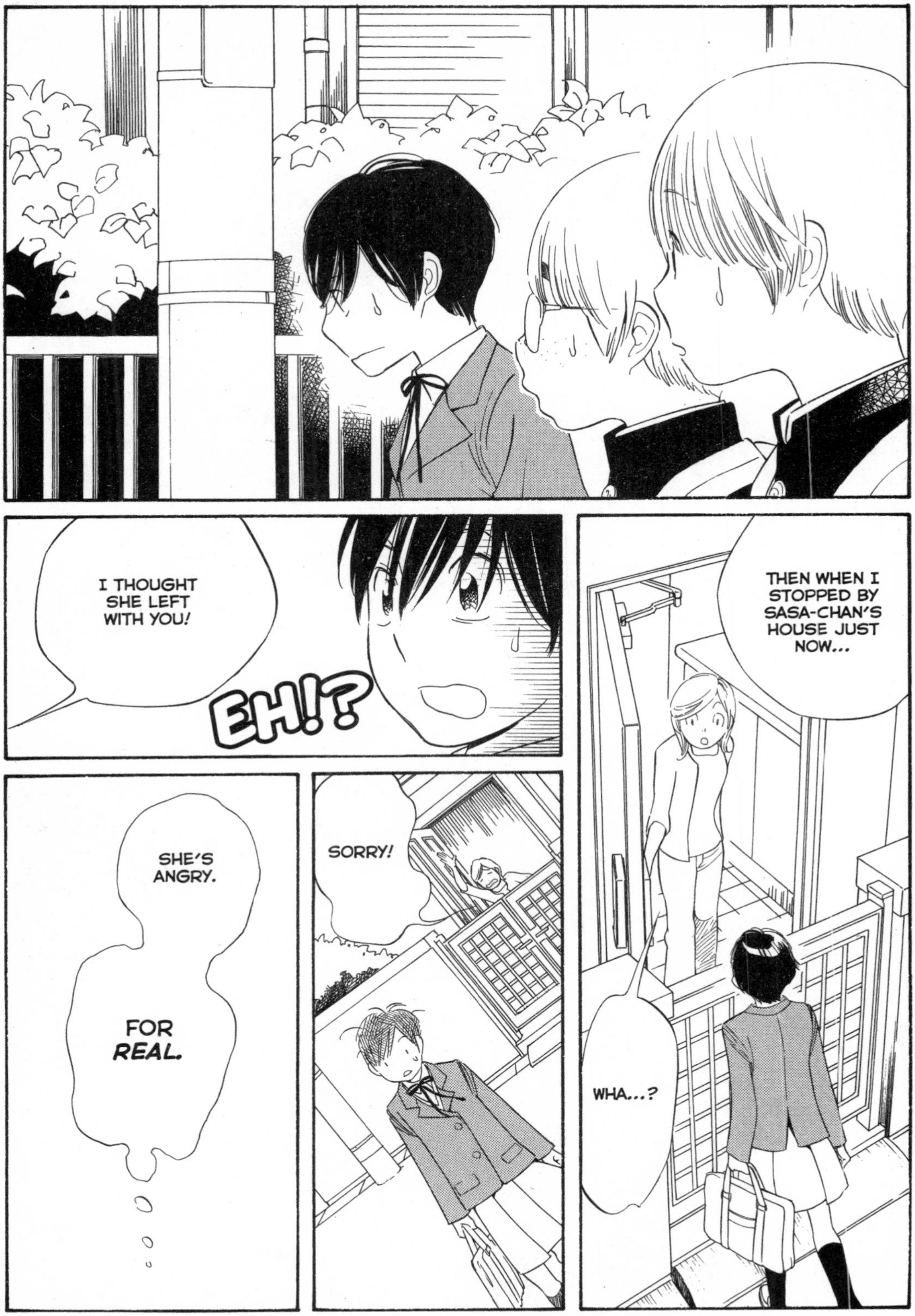
THEN WHEN I STOPPED BY SASA-CHAN'S HOUSE JUST NOW...
WHA...?
I THOUGHT SHE LEFT WITH YOU!
EH!?
SORRY!
SHE'S ANGRY.
FOR *REAL.*

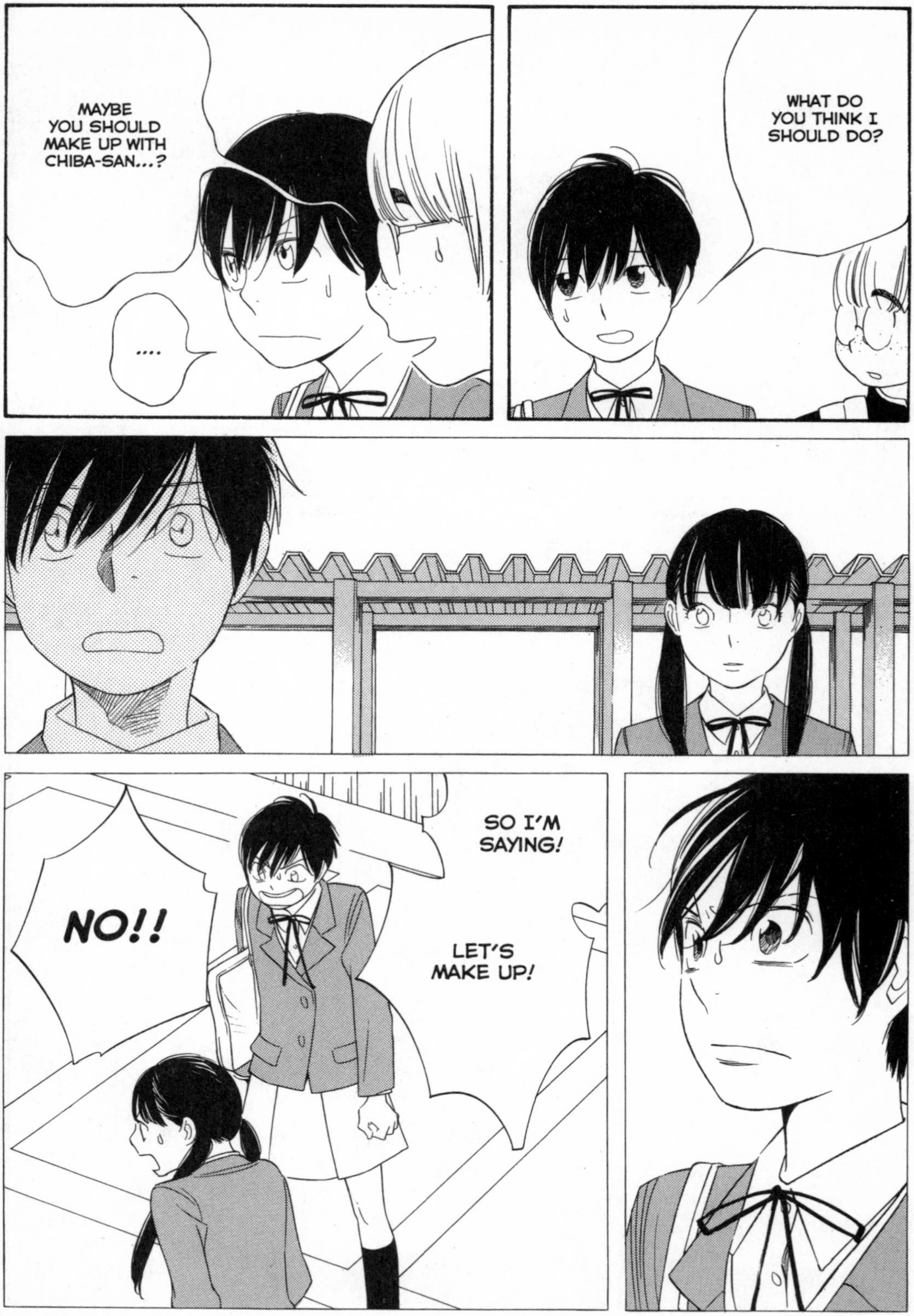
WHAT DO YOU THINK I SHOULD DO?
MAYBE YOU SHOULD MAKE UP WITH CHIBA-SAN...?
....
SO I'M SAYING!
LET'S MAKE UP!
NO!!

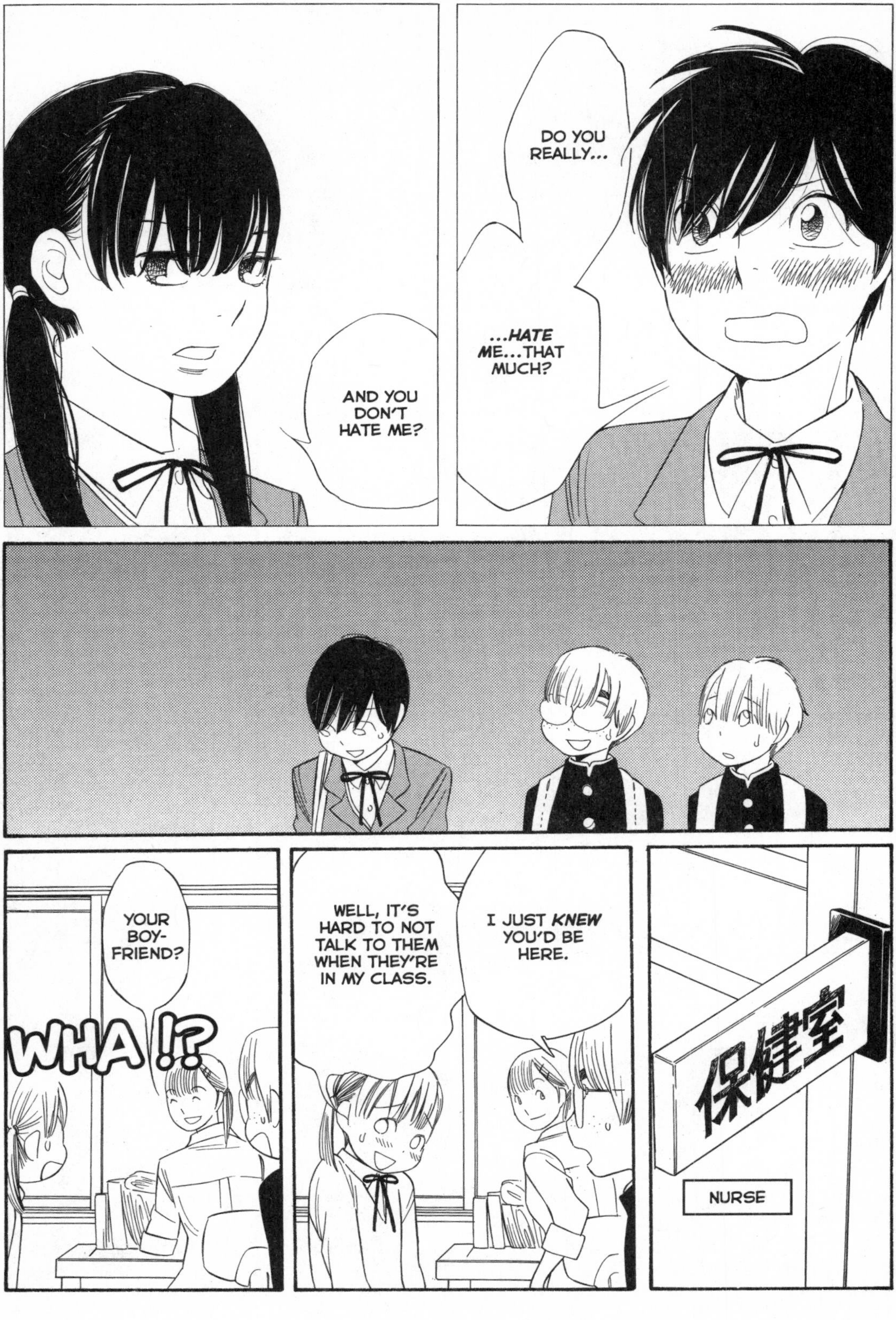
DO YOU REALLY...
...*HATE ME*...THAT MUCH?
AND YOU DON'T HATE ME?
保健室
NURSE
I JUST *KNEW* YOU'D BE HERE.
WELL, IT'S HARD TO NOT TALK TO THEM WHEN THEY'RE IN MY CLASS.
YOUR BOY-FRIEND?
WHA !?

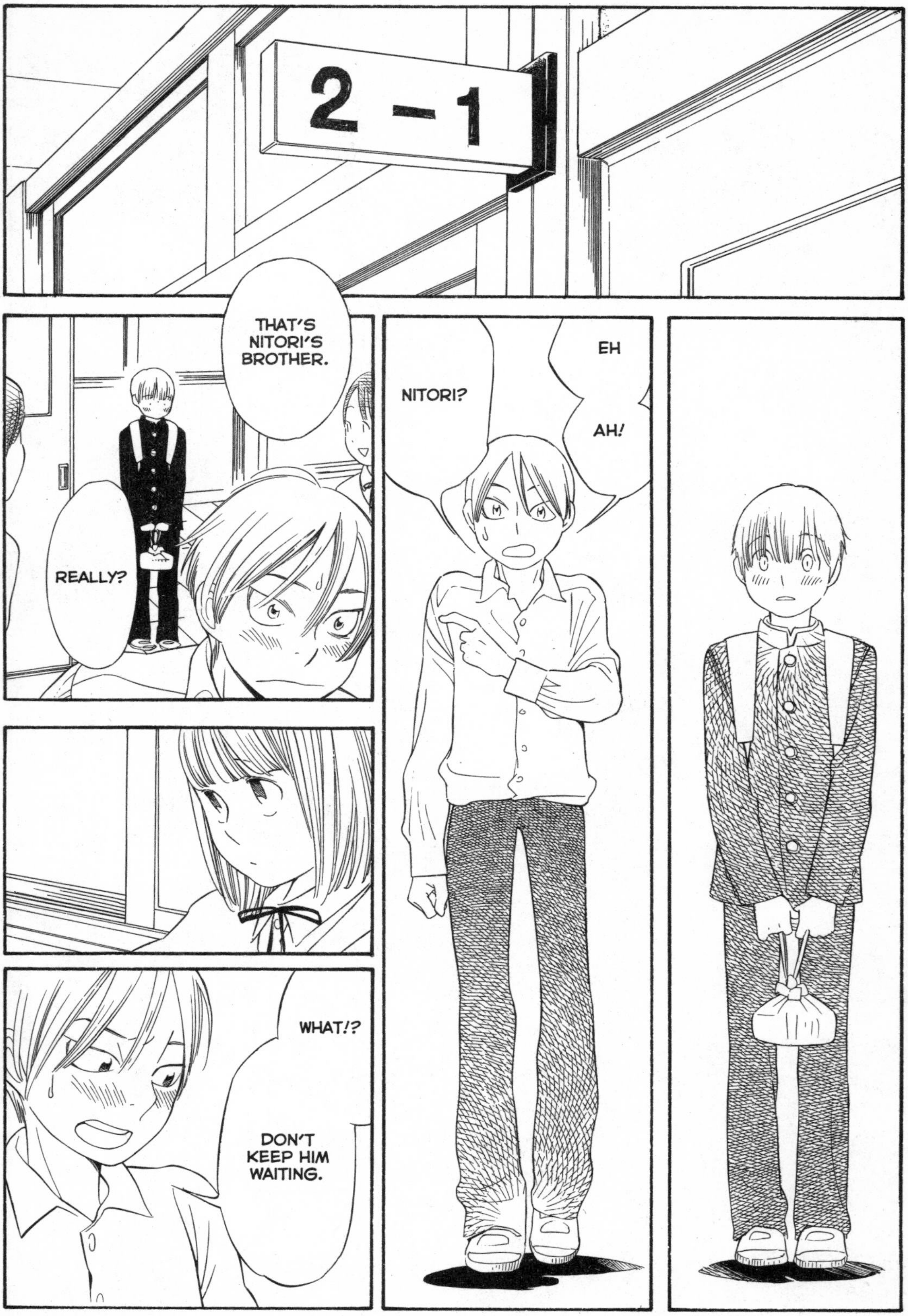
2 - 1
EH
AH!
NITORI?
THAT'S NITORI'S BROTHER.
REALLY?
WHAT!?
DON'T KEEP HIM WAITING.

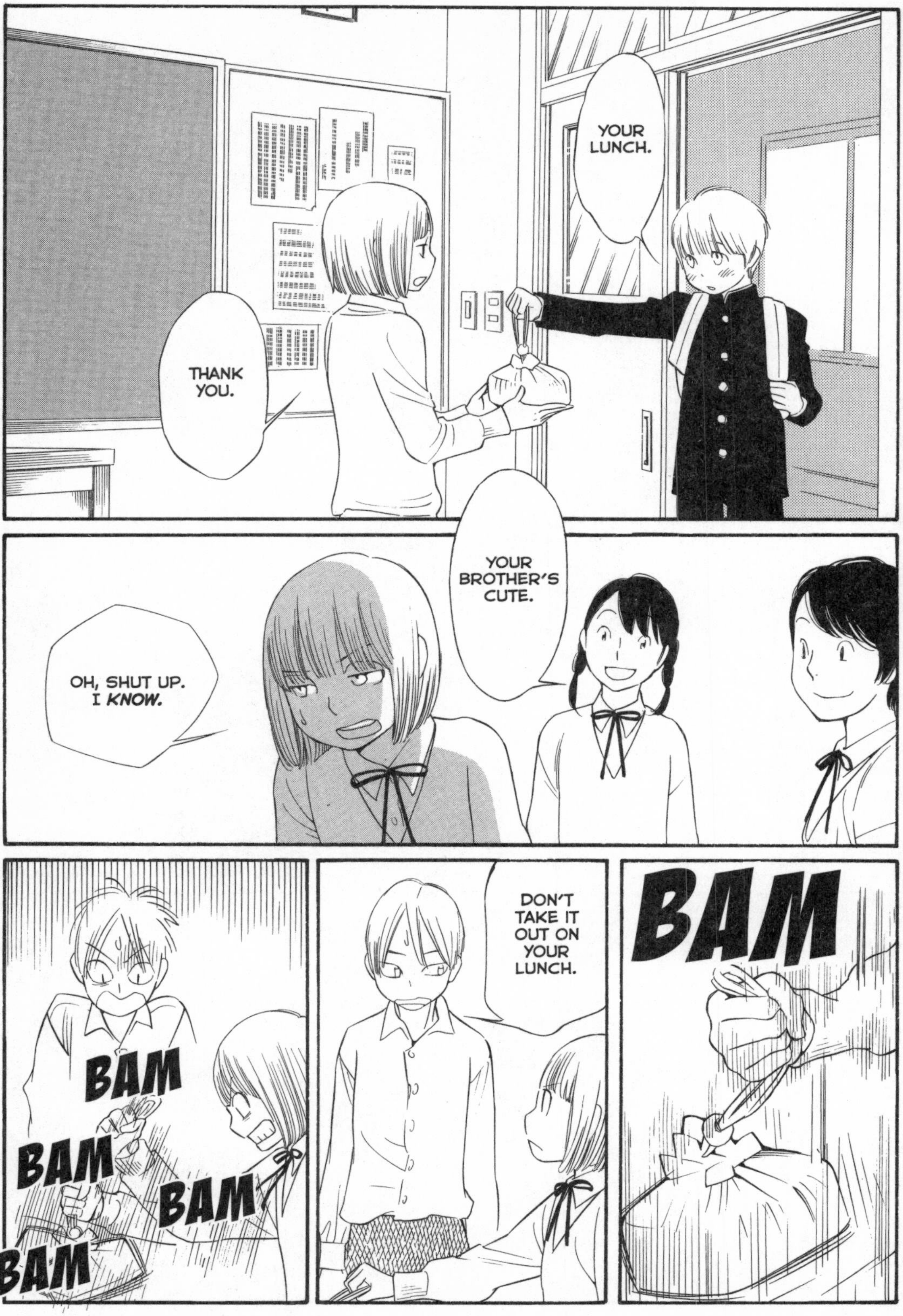
YOUR LUNCH.
THANK YOU.
YOUR BROTHER'S CUTE.
OH, SHUT UP. I *KNOW.*
BAM
DON'T TAKE IT OUT ON YOUR LUNCH.
BAM
BAM
BAM
BAM

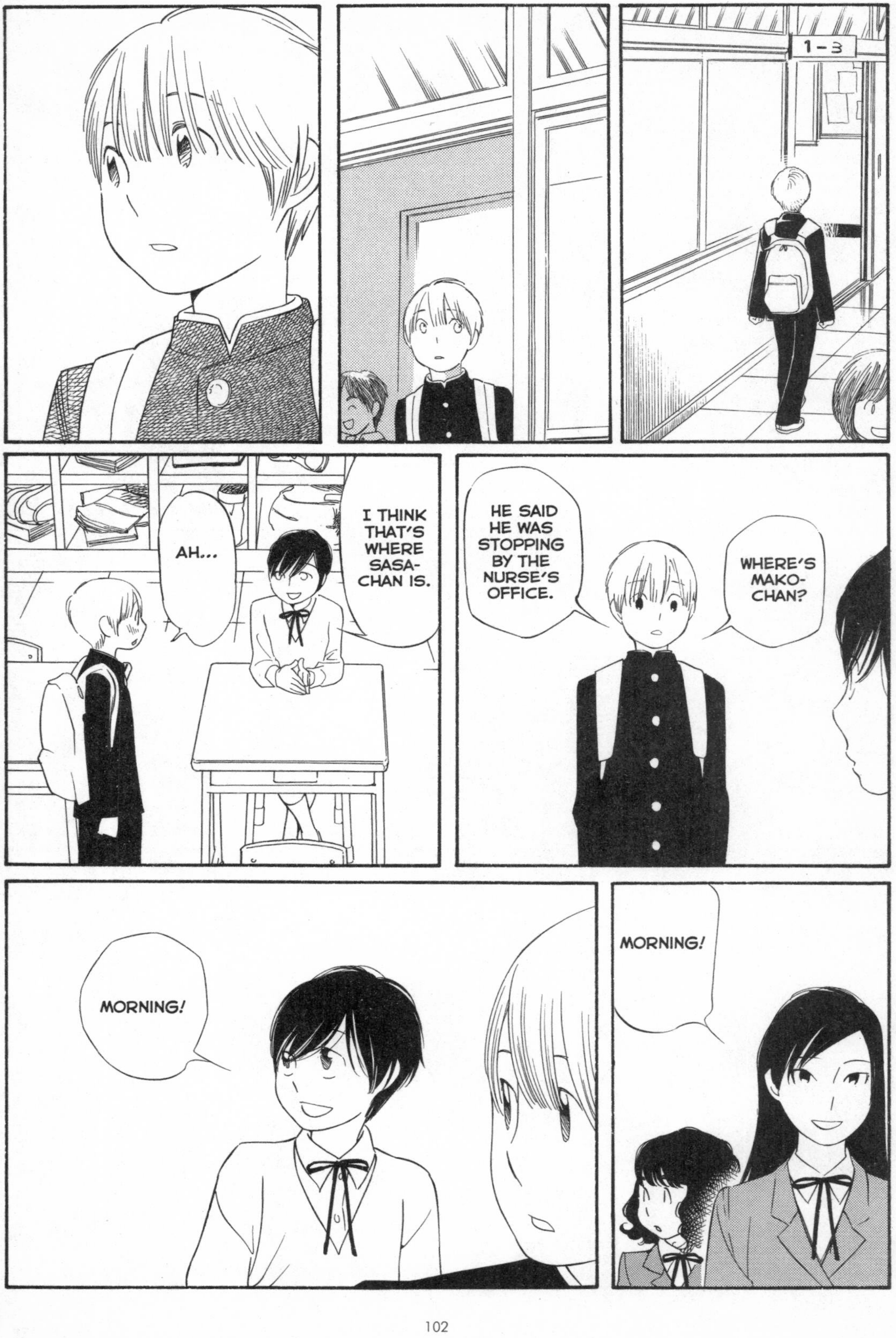
WHERE'S MAKO-CHAN?
HE SAID HE WAS STOPPING BY THE NURSE'S OFFICE.
I THINK THAT'S WHERE SASA-CHAN IS.
AH...
MORNING!
MORNING!

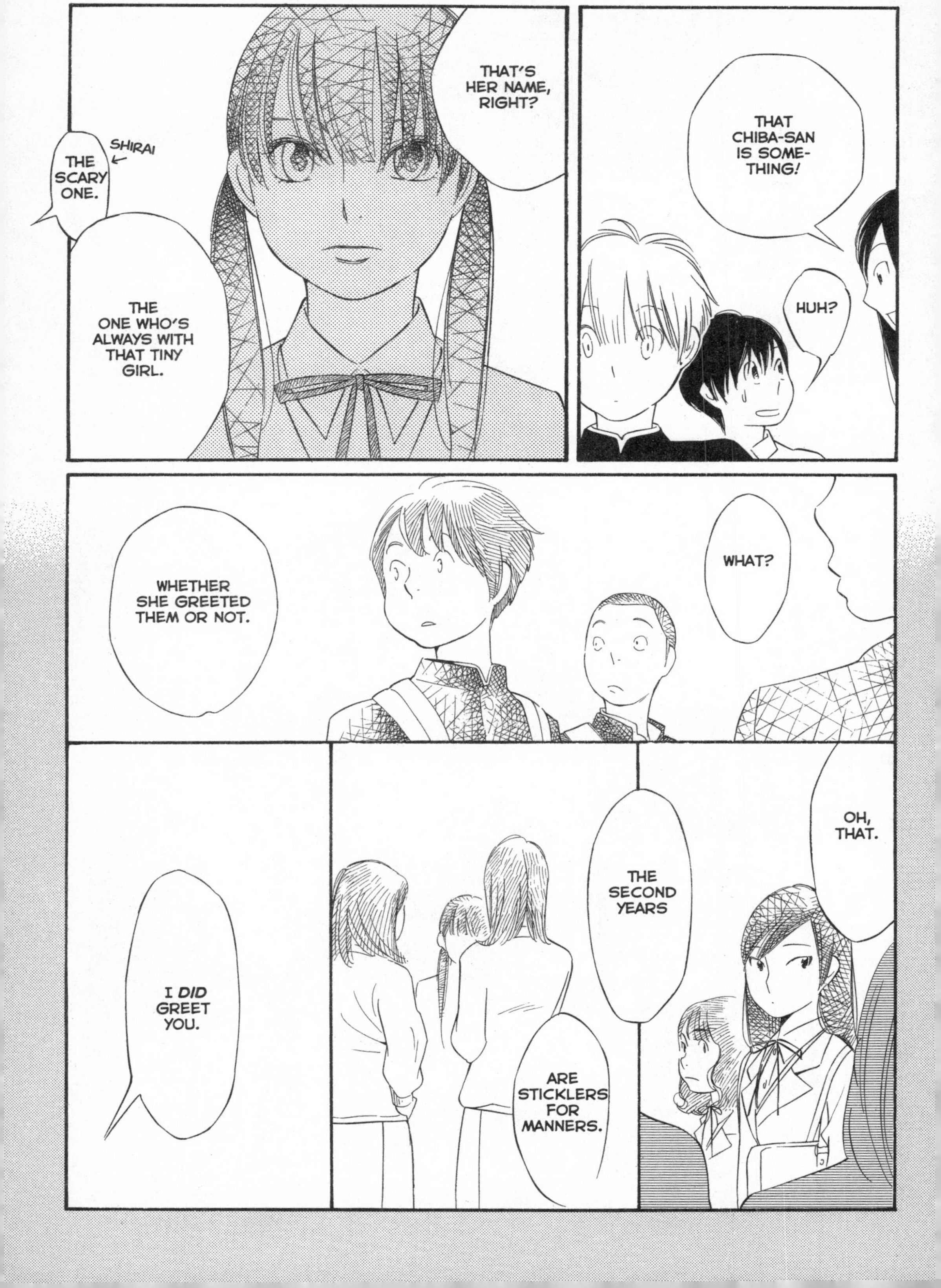
THAT CHIBA-SAN IS SOME-THING!
HUH?
THAT'S HER NAME, RIGHT?
SHIRAI
THE SCARY ONE.
THE ONE WHO'S ALWAYS WITH THAT TINY GIRL.
WHAT?
WHETHER SHE GREETED THEM OR NOT.
OH, THAT.
THE SECOND YEARS
ARE STICKLERS FOR MANNERS.
I *DID* GREET YOU.

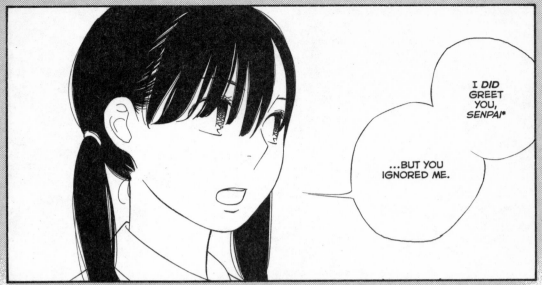

I DID GREET YOU, SENPAI*
...BUT YOU IGNORED ME.
IT WAS LIKE, WHO'S THE SENPAI HERE?
WHY DOES SHE HAVE TO BE LIKE THAT?
ARE YOU STUPID? PICKING FIGHTS WITH SENPAI?

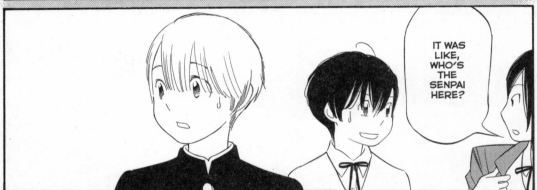

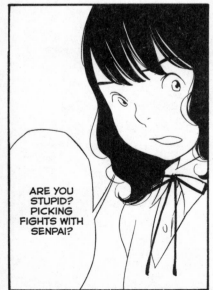

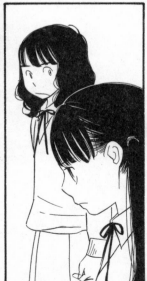

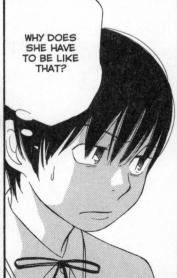

*SENPAI: A SENIOR COLLEAGUE, OR A STUDENT IN A HIGHER GRADE THAN ONESELF.

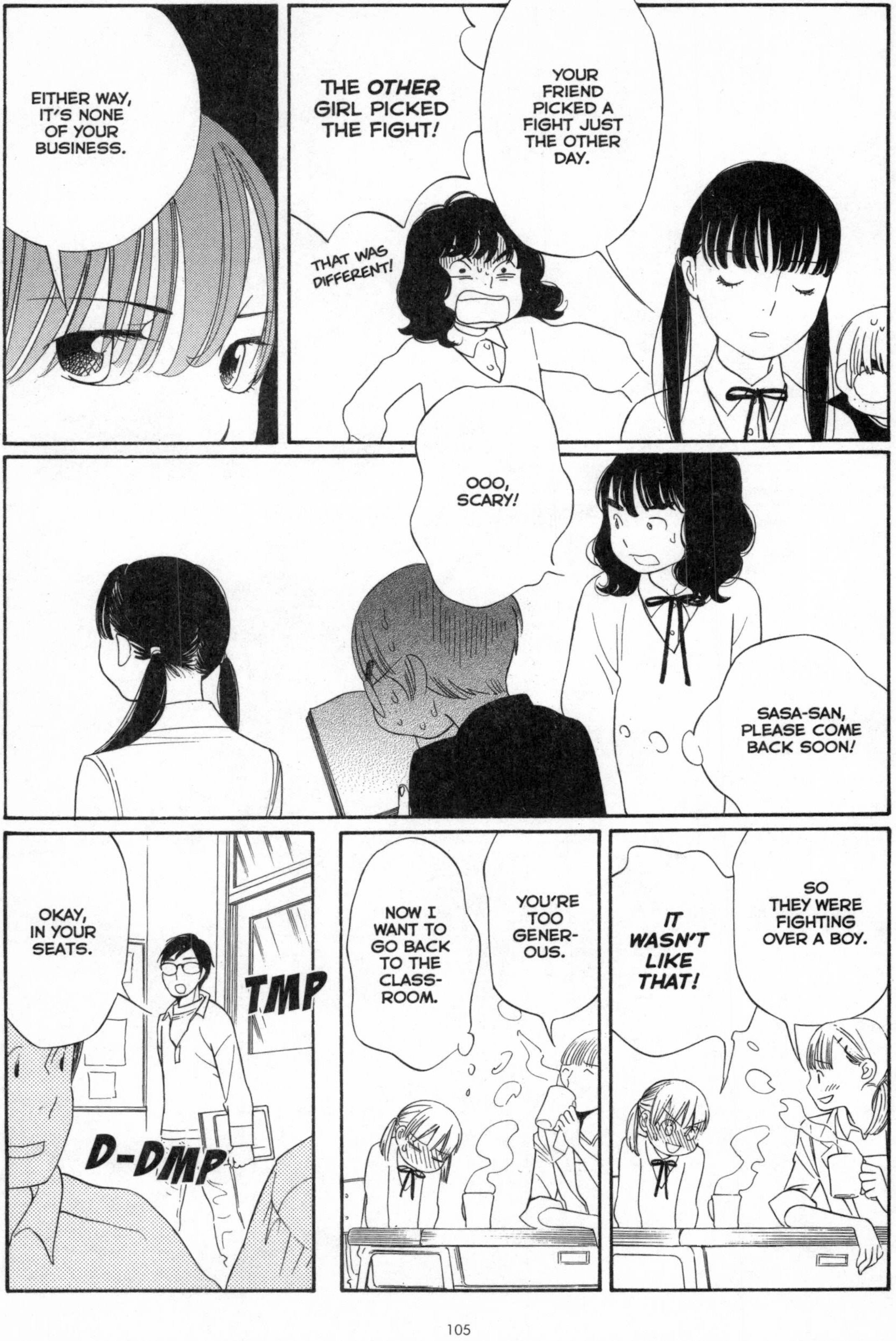
YOUR FRIEND PICKED A FIGHT JUST THE OTHER DAY.
THE OTHER GIRL PICKED THE FIGHT!
THAT WAS DIFFERENT!
EITHER WAY, IT'S NONE OF YOUR BUSINESS.
OOO, SCARY!
SASA-SAN, PLEASE COME BACK SOON!
SO THEY WERE FIGHTING OVER A BOY.
IT WASN'T LIKE THAT!
YOU'RE TOO GENER-OUS.
NOW I WANT TO GO BACK TO THE CLASS-ROOM.
OKAY, IN YOUR SEATS.
TMP
D-DMP

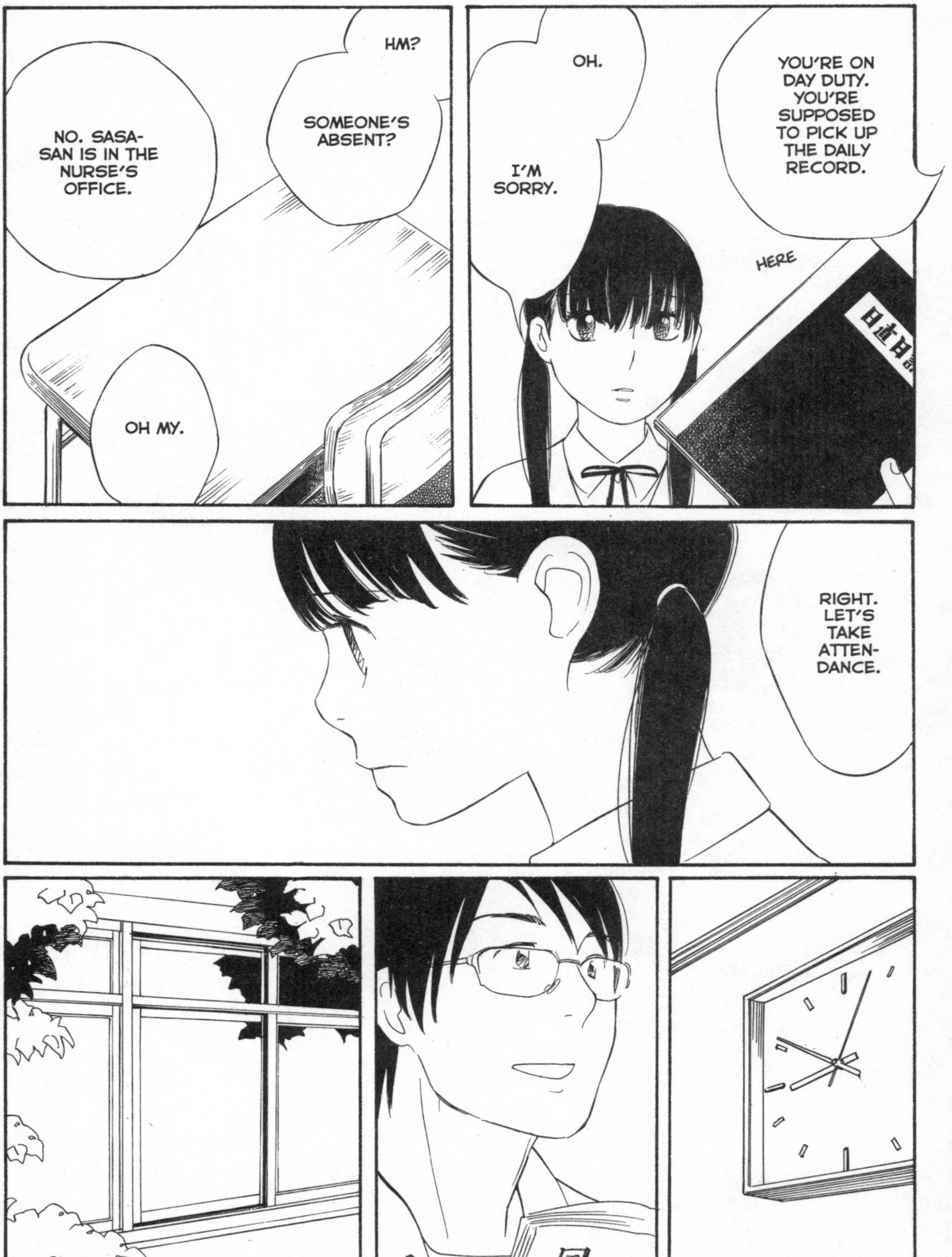
YOU'RE ON DAY DUTY. YOU'RE SUPPOSED TO PICK UP THE DAILY RECORD.
OH.
I'M SORRY.
HERE
HM?
SOMEONE'S ABSENT?
NO. SASA-SAN IS IN THE NURSE'S OFFICE.
OH MY.
RIGHT. LET'S TAKE ATTEN-DANCE.
国語

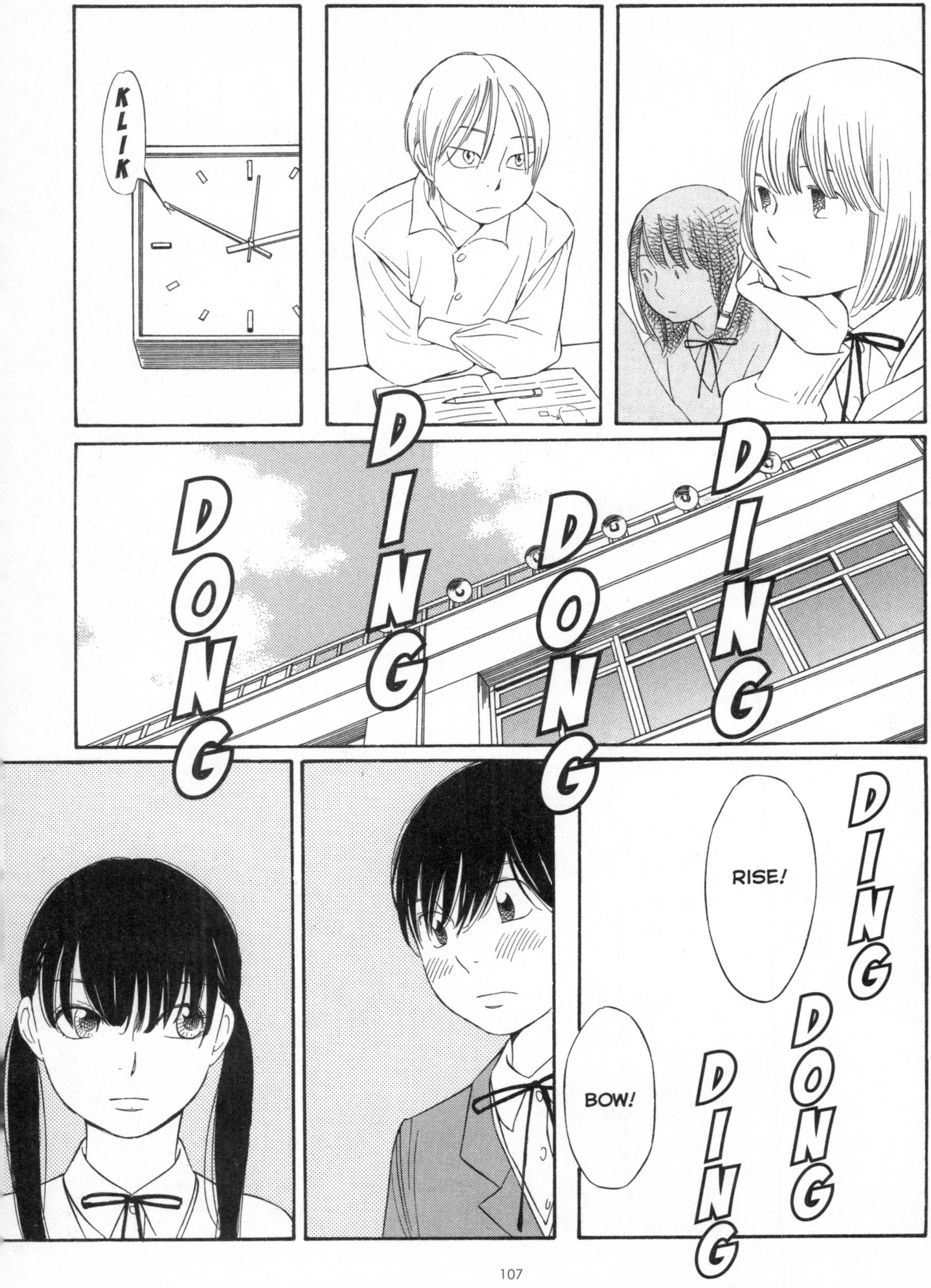
KLIK
DING
DONG
DING
DONG
DING
RISE!
DONG
DING
BOW!

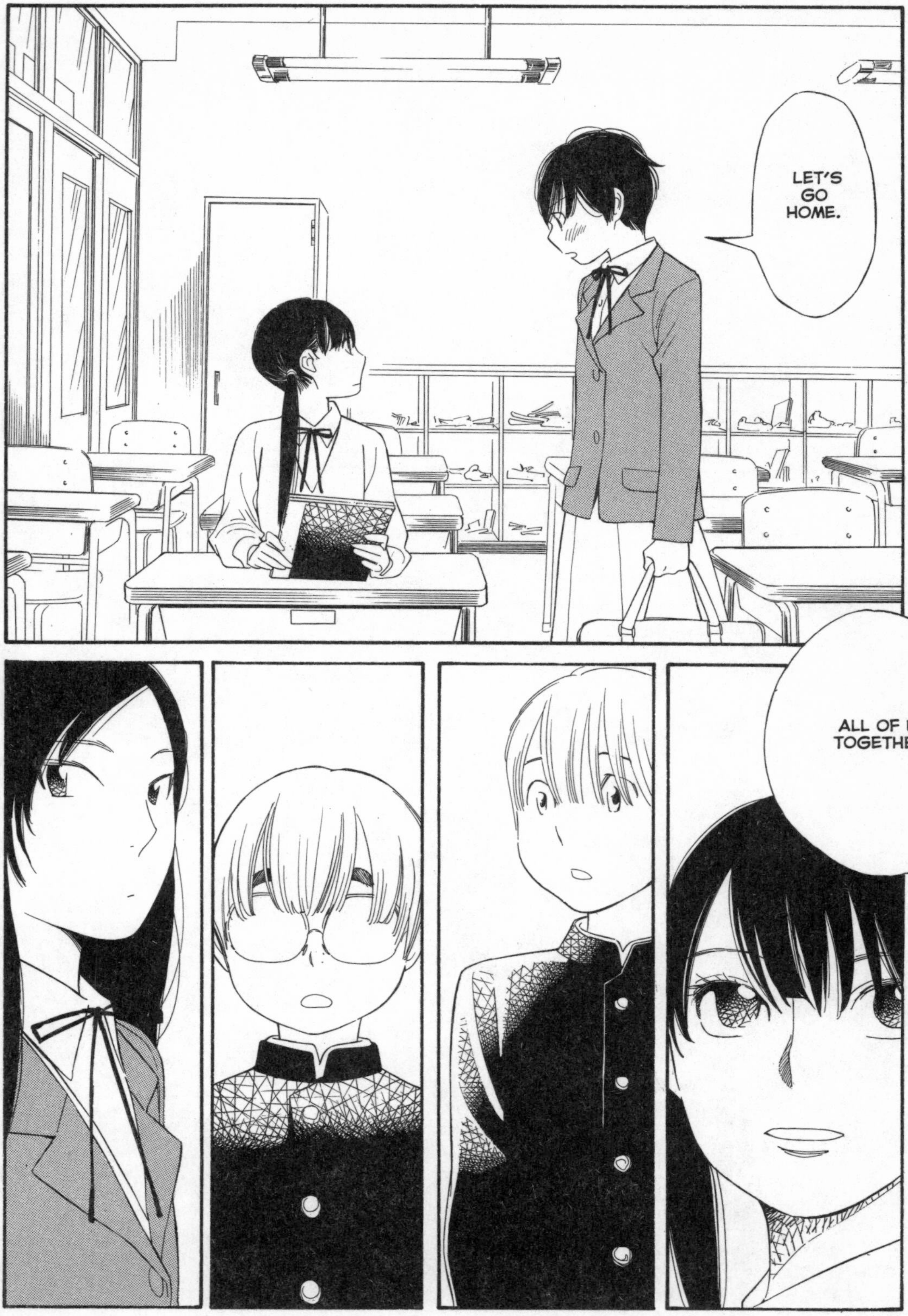
LET'S GO HOME.
ALL OF US, TOGETHER.

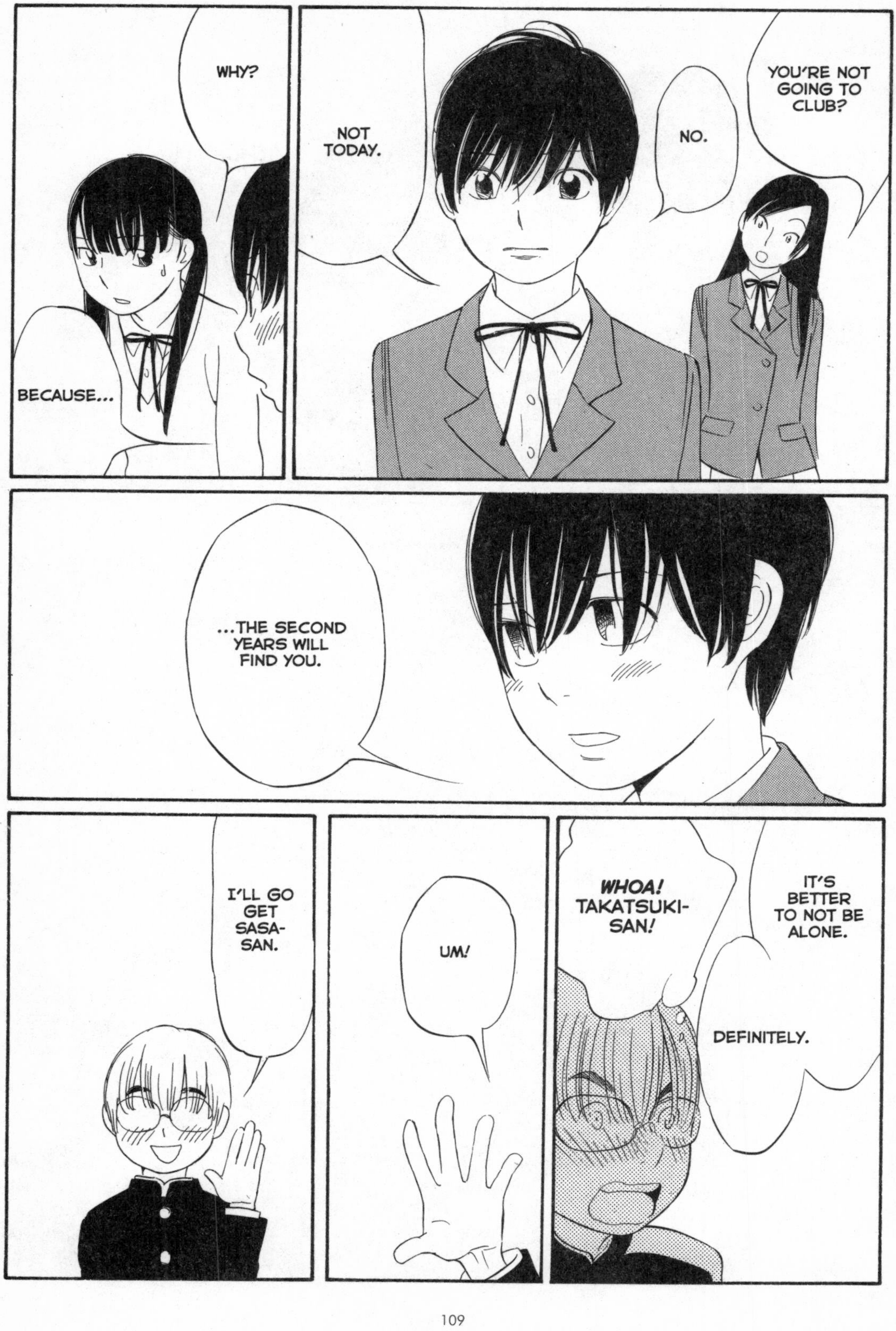
YOU'RE NOT GOING TO CLUB?
NO.
NOT TODAY.
WHY?
BECAUSE...
...THE SECOND YEARS WILL FIND YOU.
IT'S BETTER TO NOT BE ALONE.
WHOA! TAKATSUKI-SAN!
DEFINITELY.
UM!
I'LL GO GET SASA-SAN.

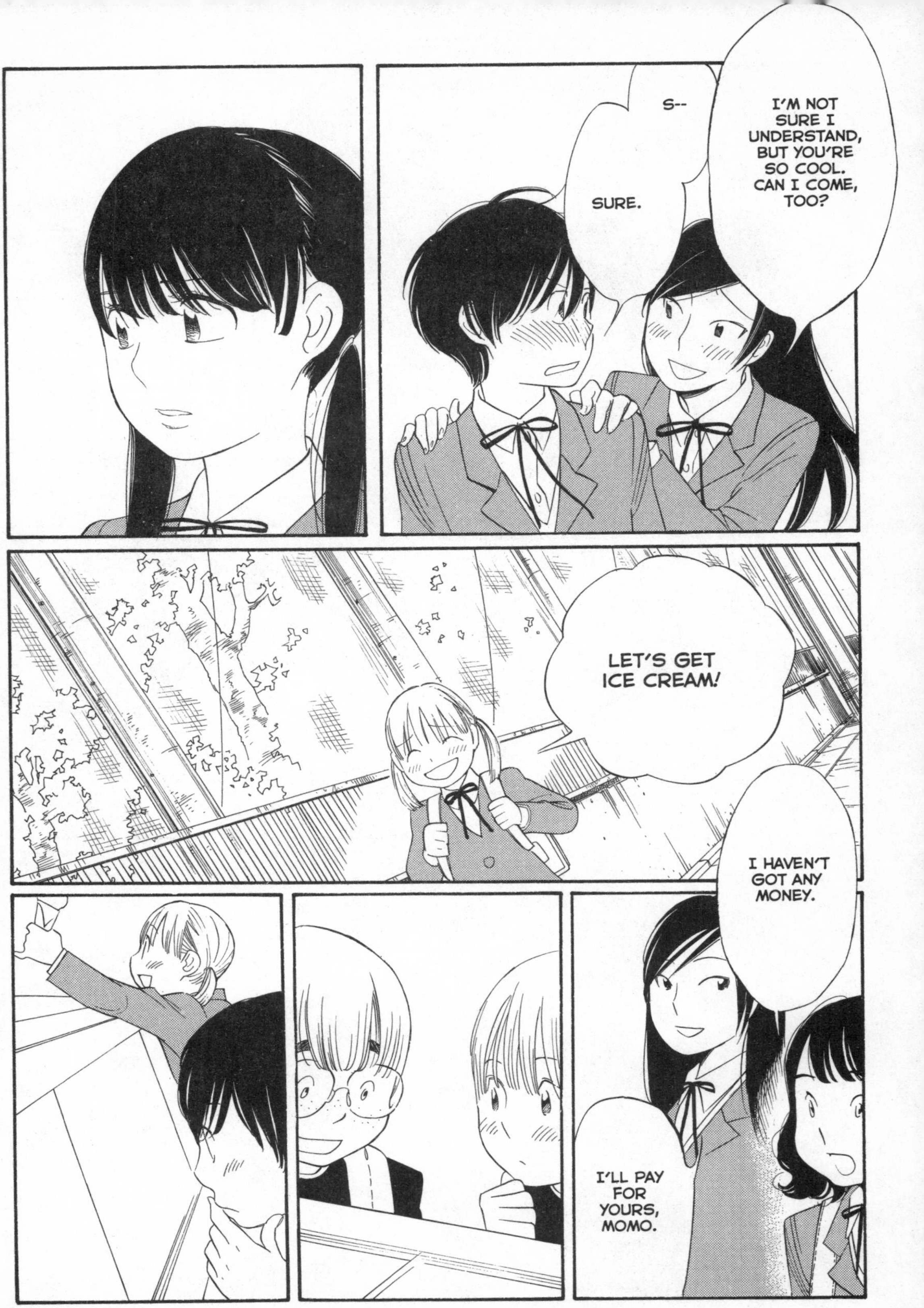
I'M NOT SURE I UNDERSTAND, BUT YOU'RE SO COOL. CAN I COME, TOO?
S--
SURE.
LET'S GET ICE CREAM!
I HAVEN'T GOT ANY MONEY.
I'LL PAY FOR YOURS, MOMO.

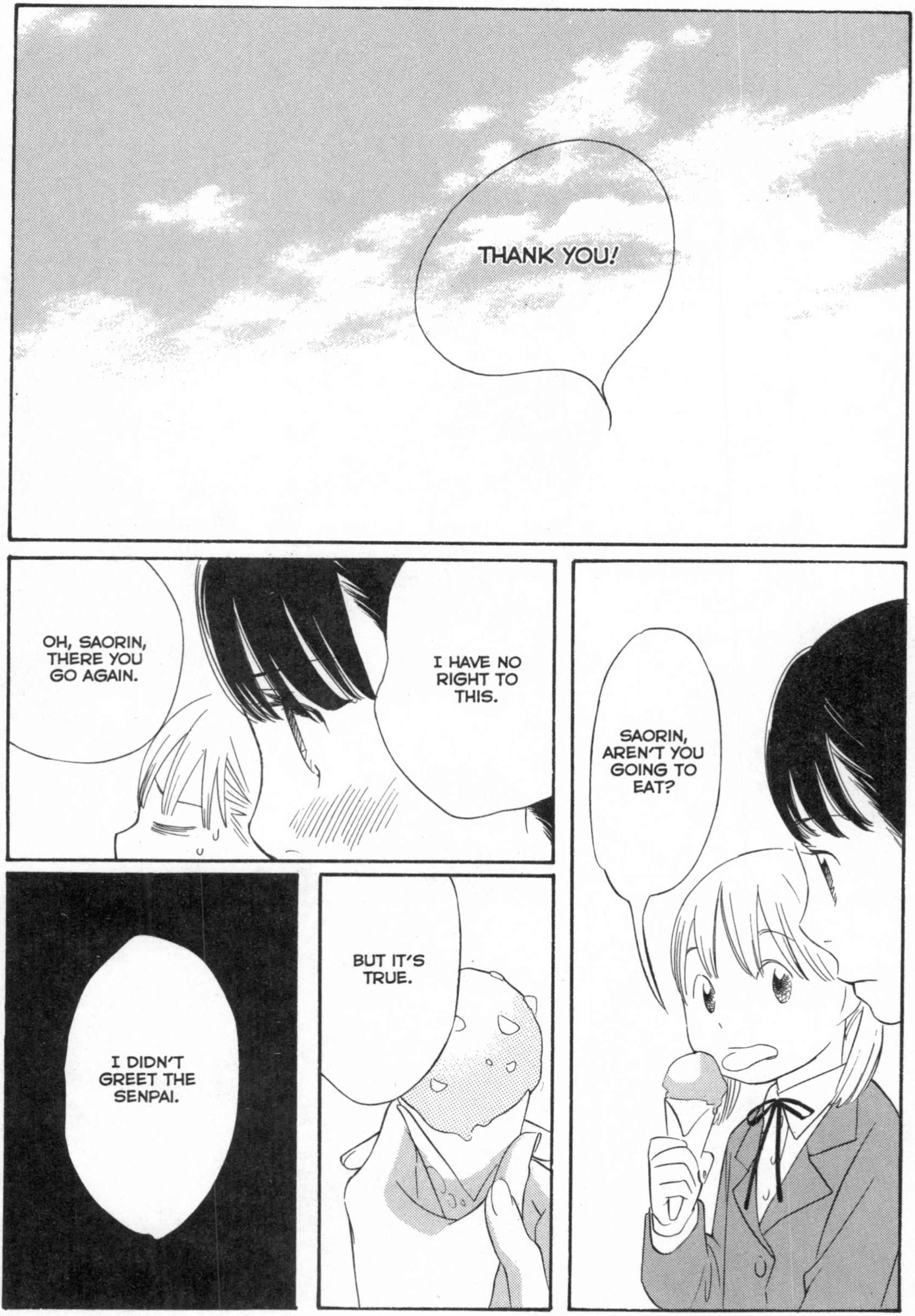
THANK YOU!
SAORIN, AREN'T YOU GOING TO EAT?
I HAVE NO RIGHT TO THIS.
OH, SAORIN, THERE YOU GO AGAIN.
BUT IT'S TRUE.
I DIDN'T GREET THE SENPAI.

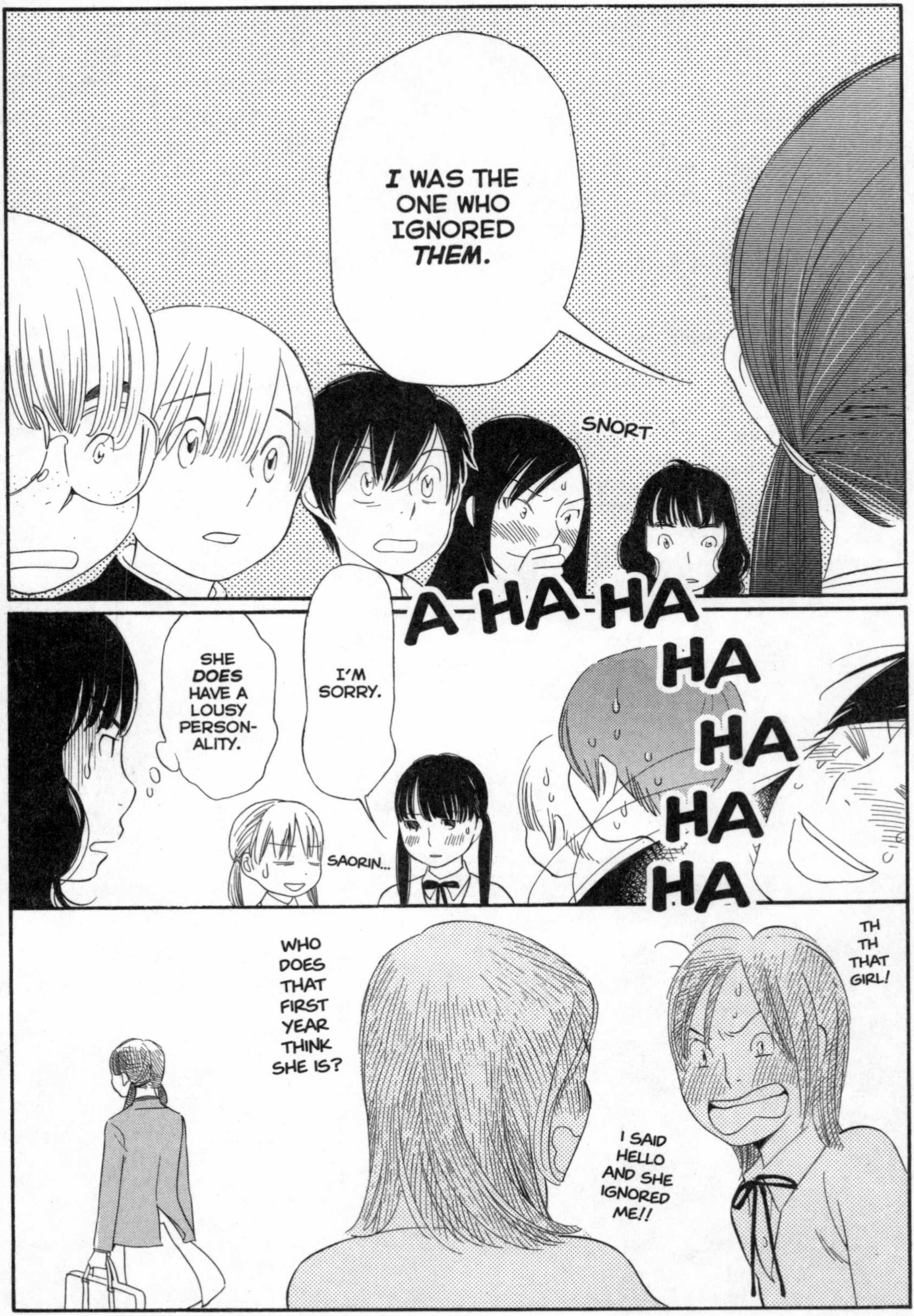
I WAS THE ONE WHO IGNORED THEM.
SNORT
A HA HA HA HA HA HA HA
I'M SORRY.
SHE DOES HAVE A LOUSY PERSONALITY.
SAORIN...
TH TH THAT GIRL!
I SAID HELLO AND SHE IGNORED ME!!
WHO DOES THAT FIRST YEAR THINK SHE IS?

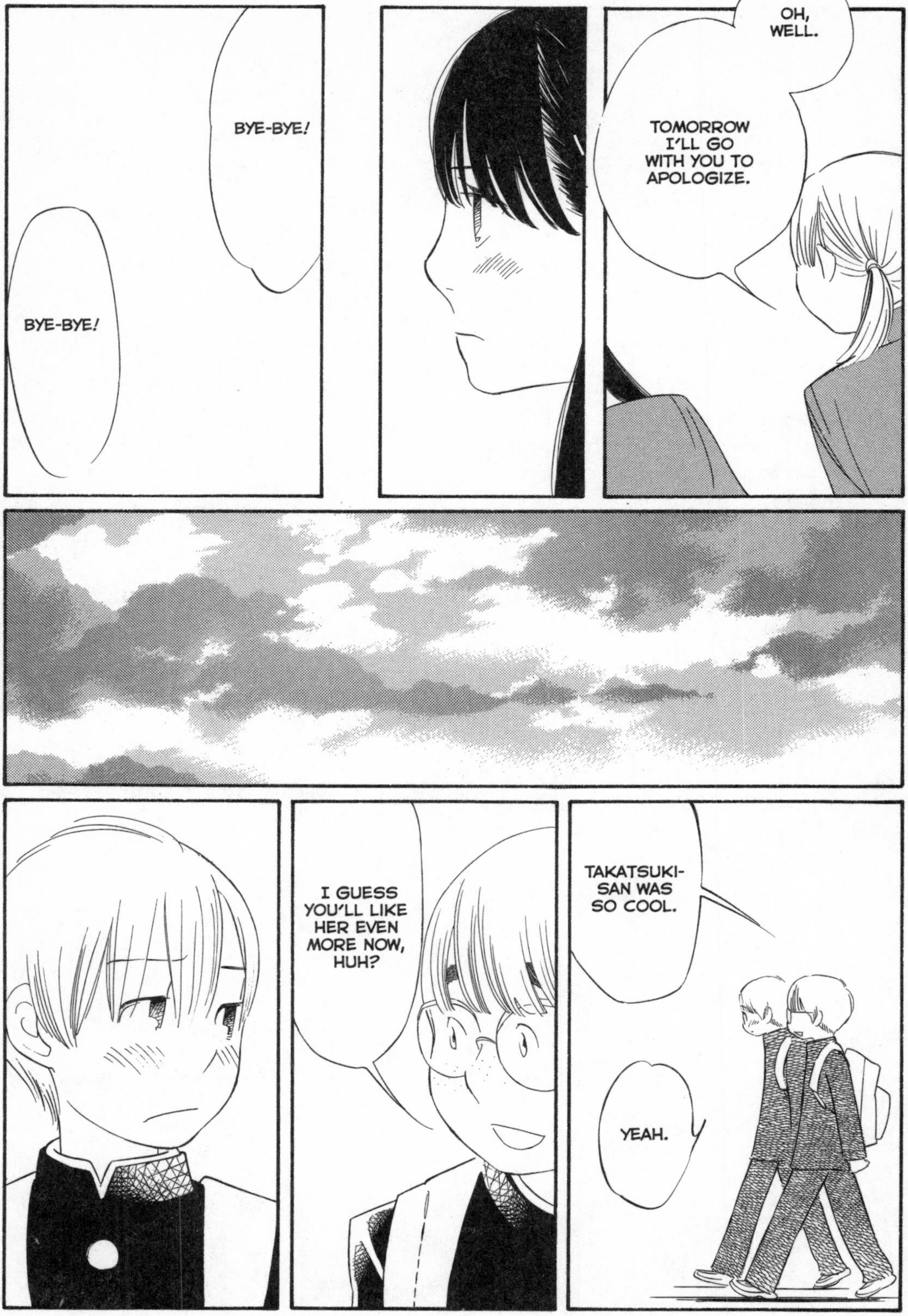
OH, WELL.
TOMORROW I'LL GO WITH YOU TO APOLOGIZE.
BYE-BYE!
BYE-BYE!
TAKATSUKI-SAN WAS SO COOL.
YEAH.
I GUESS YOU'LL LIKE HER EVEN MORE NOW, HUH?

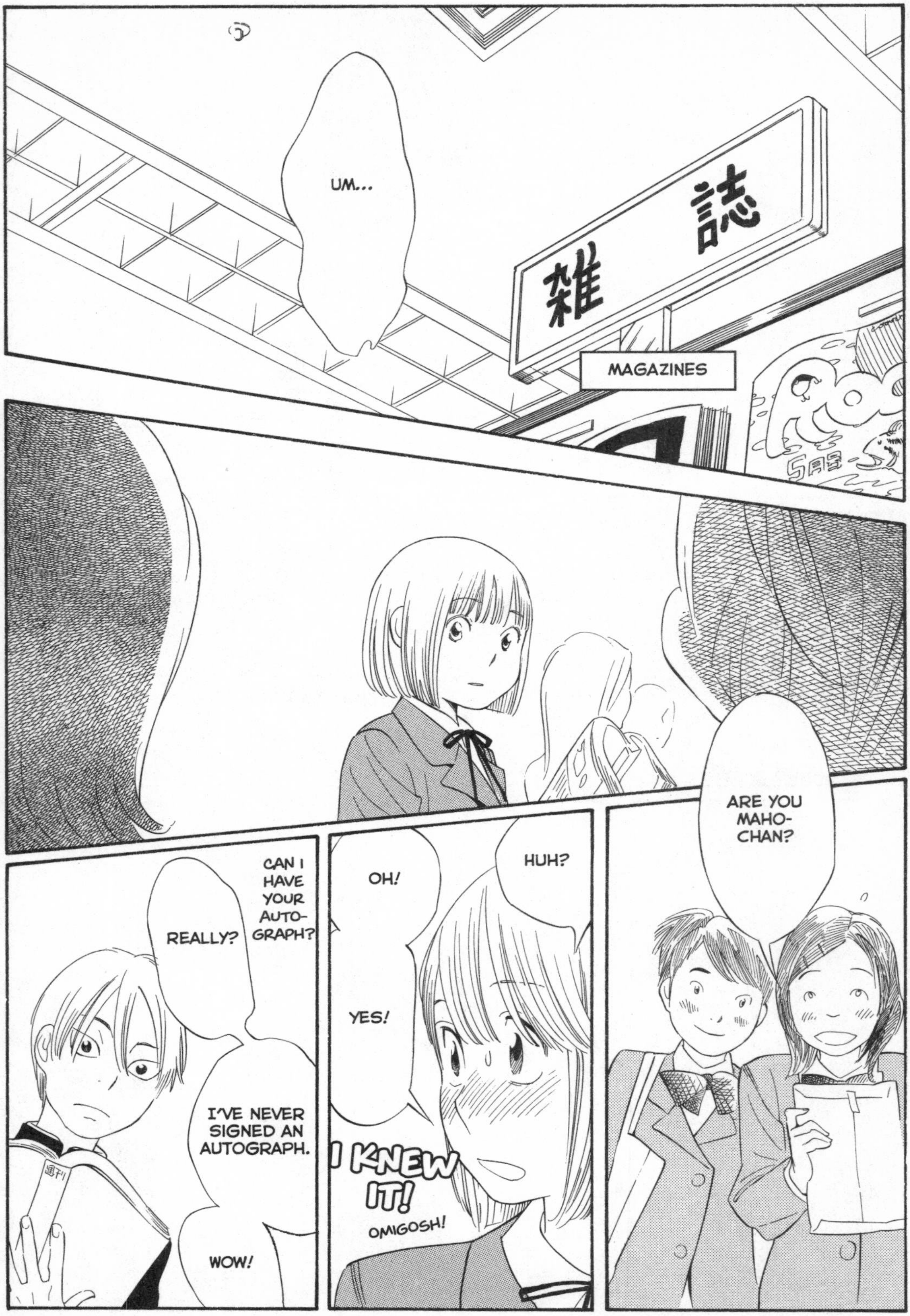
UM...
雑誌
MAGAZINES
ARE YOU MAHO-CHAN?
HUH?
OH!
YES!
I KNEW IT!
OMIGOSH!
CAN I HAVE YOUR AUTOGRAPH?
REALLY?
I'VE NEVER SIGNED AN AUTOGRAPH.
WOW!

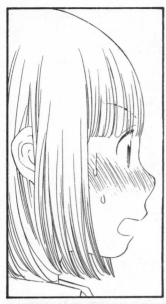

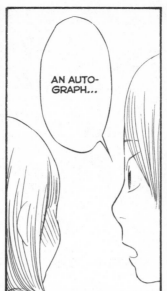

MAHO-CHAN WAS SO NICE!
YEAH!
WHOA.
AN AUTO-GRAPH...
HOLY COW.
SOME-ONE ASKED *ME*
FOR AN *AUTO-GRAPH*.
MAHO.

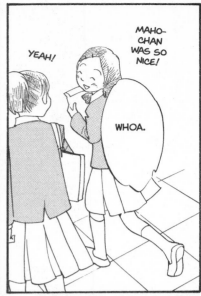

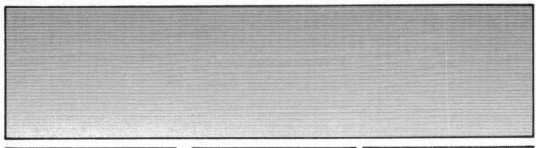

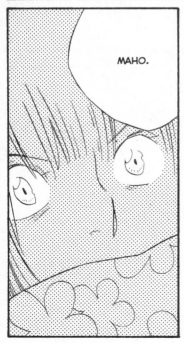

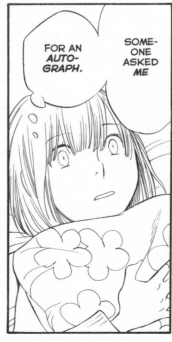

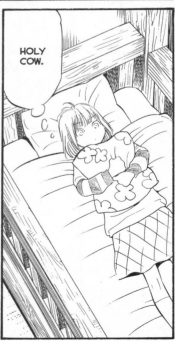

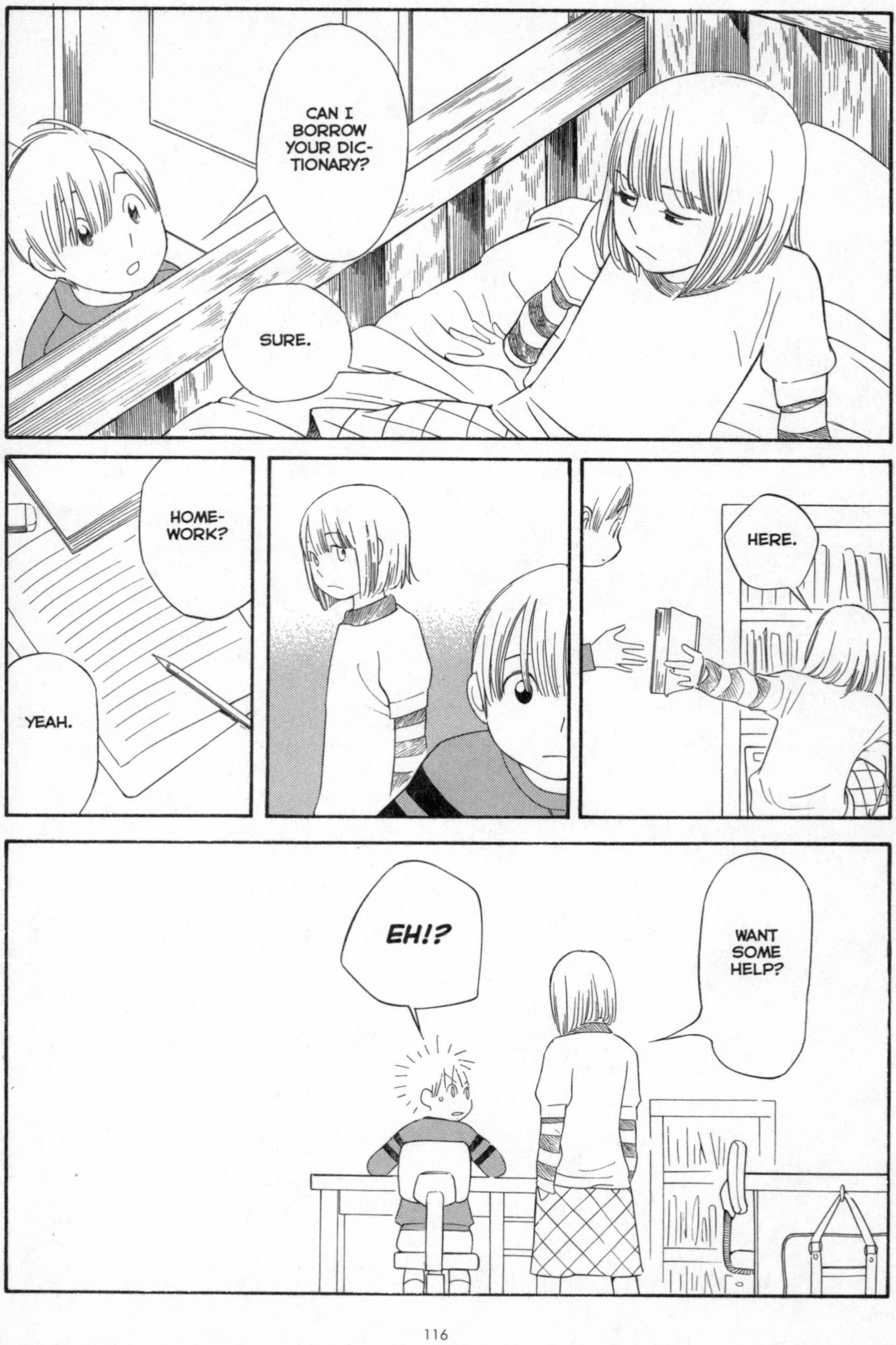
CAN I BORROW YOUR DIC-TIONARY?
SURE.
HERE.
HOME-WORK?
YEAH.
WANT SOME HELP?
EH!?

38

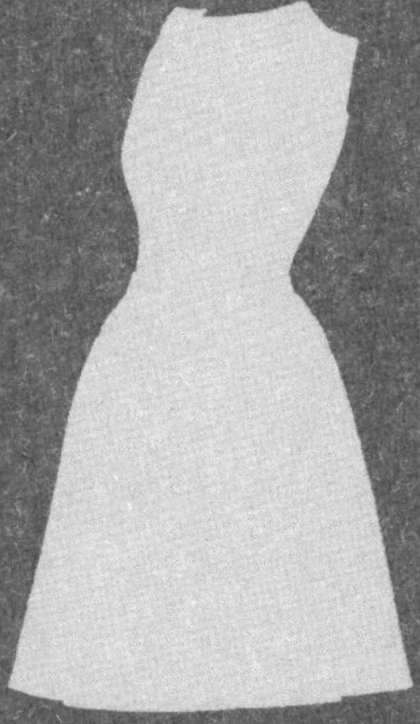

The Teacher Loves a Mystery

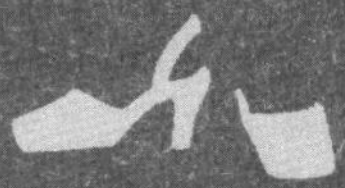

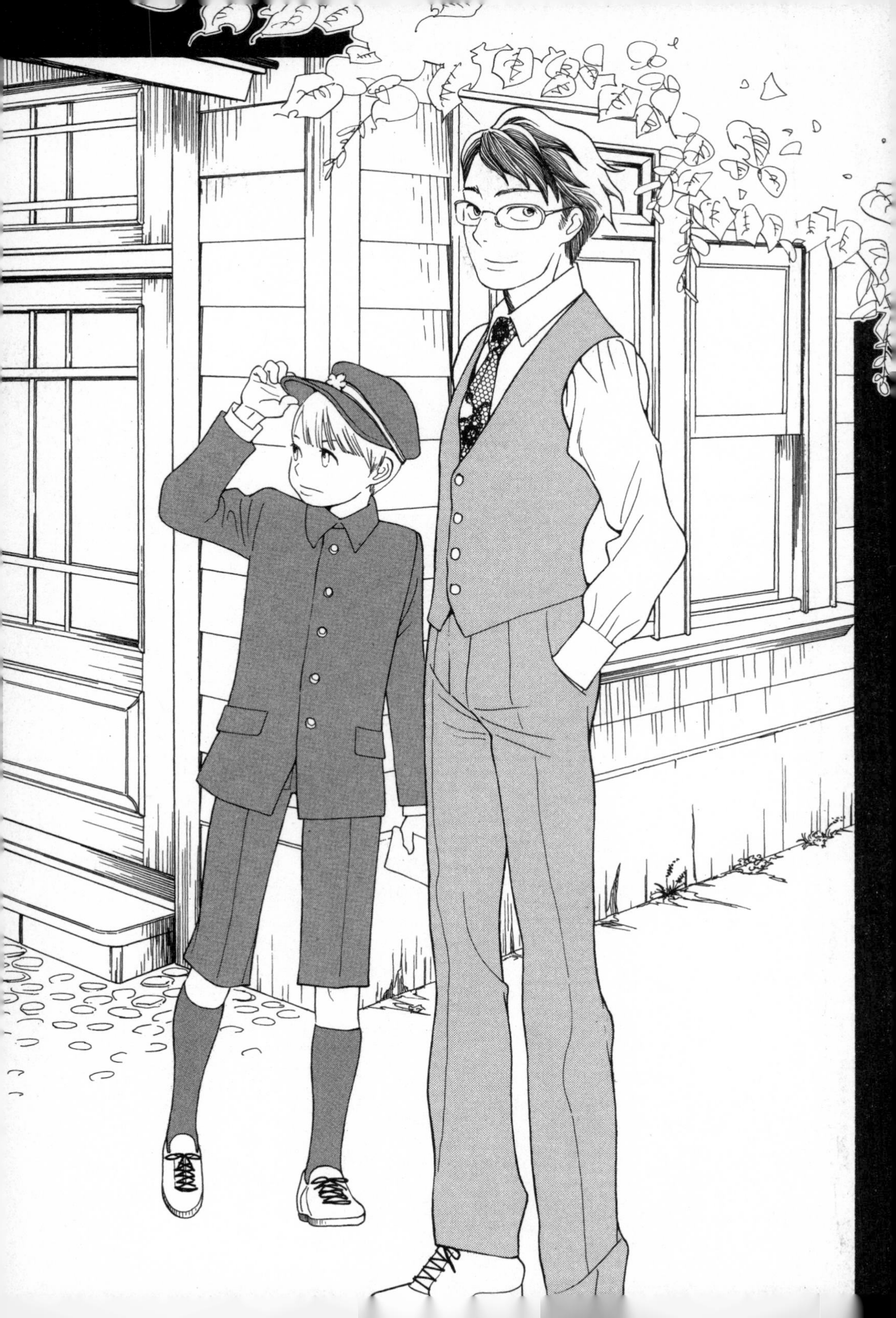

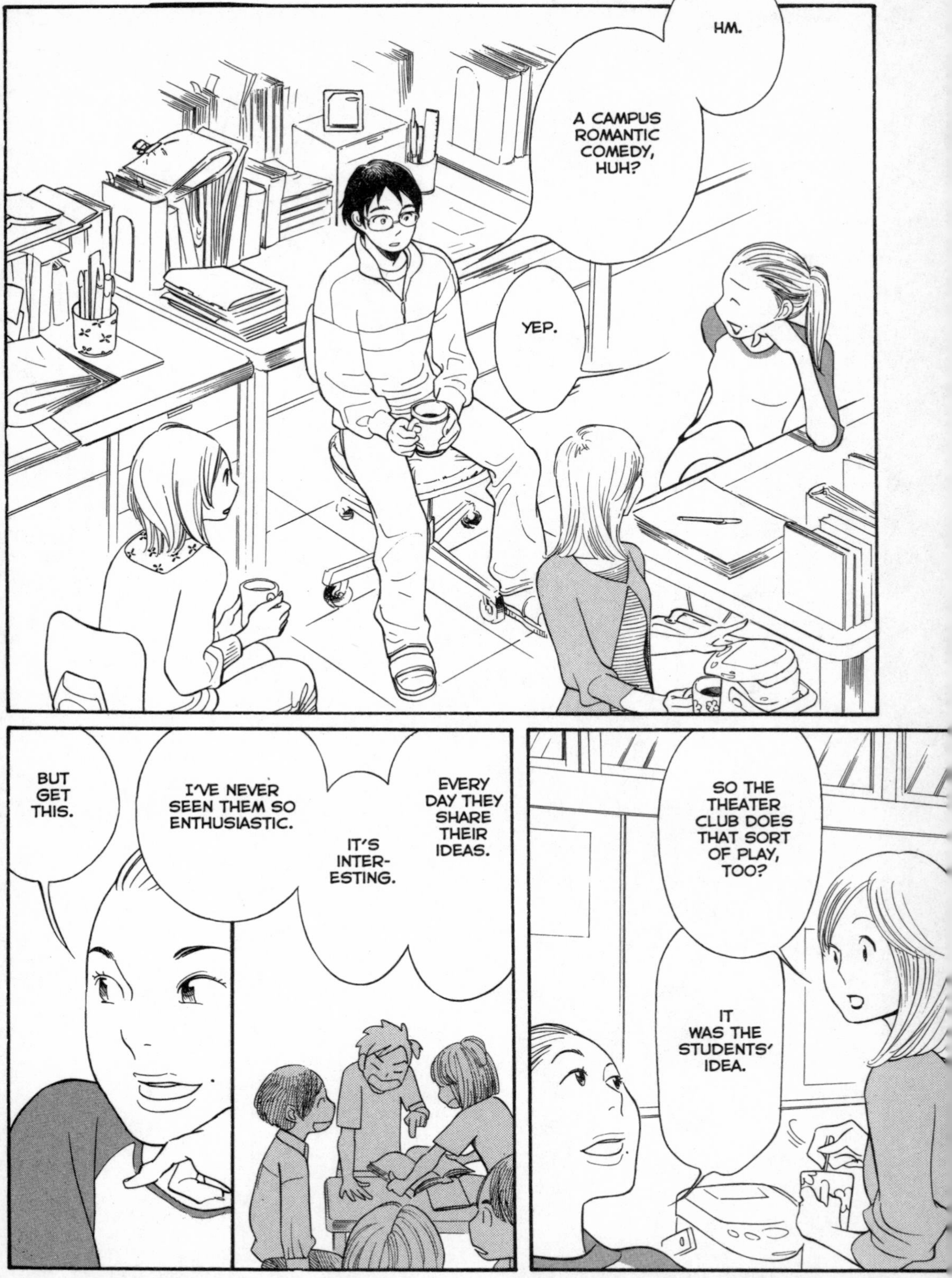
HM.
A CAMPUS ROMANTIC COMEDY, HUH?
YEP.
SO THE THEATER CLUB DOES THAT SORT OF PLAY, TOO?
IT WAS THE STUDENTS' IDEA.
EVERY DAY THEY SHARE THEIR IDEAS.
IT'S INTER-ESTING.
I'VE NEVER SEEN THEM SO ENTHUSIASTIC.
BUT GET THIS.

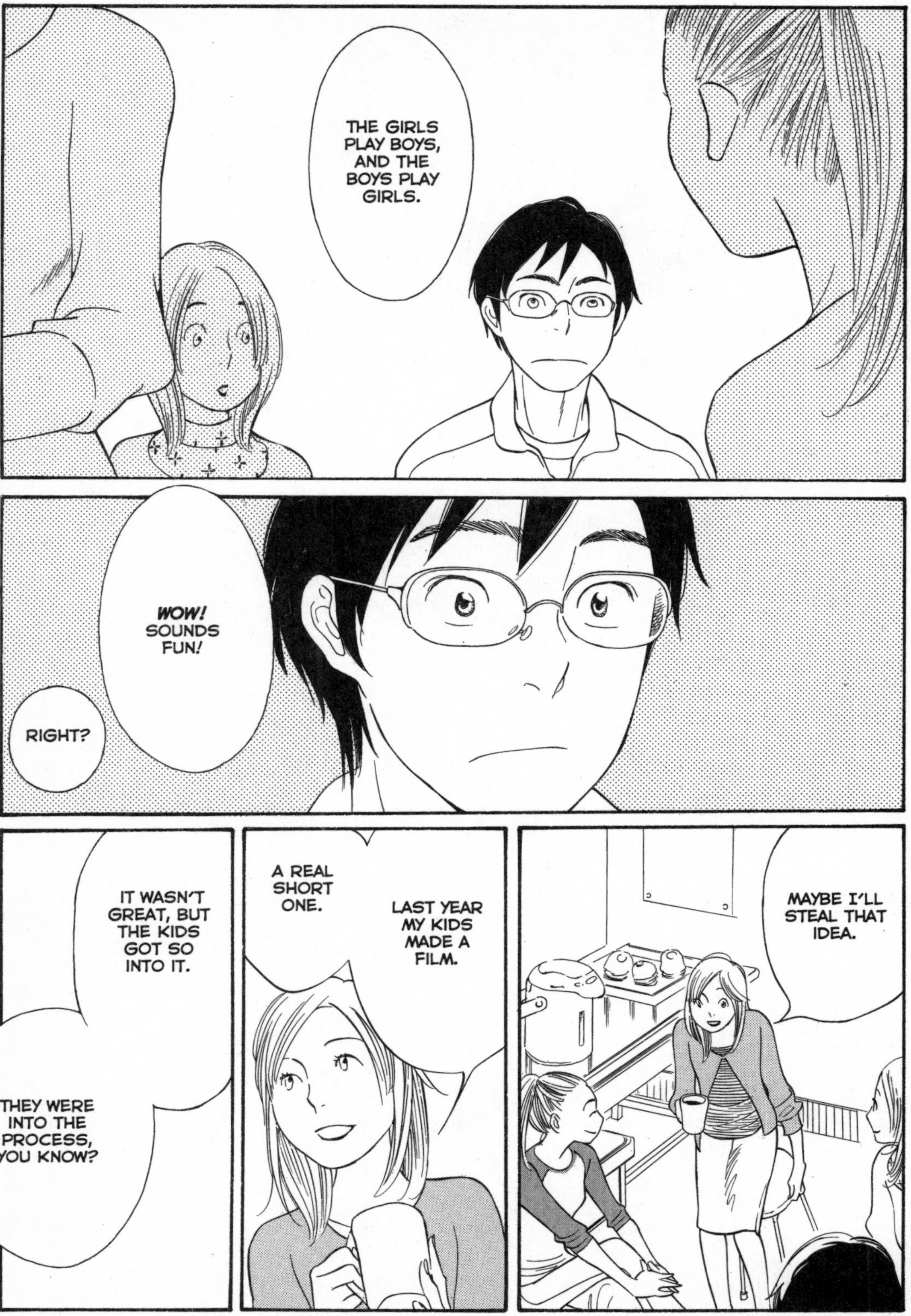
THE GIRLS PLAY BOYS, AND THE BOYS PLAY GIRLS.
WOW! SOUNDS FUN!
RIGHT?
MAYBE I'LL STEAL THAT IDEA.
LAST YEAR MY KIDS MADE A FILM.
A REAL SHORT ONE.
IT WASN'T GREAT, BUT THE KIDS GOT SO INTO IT.
THEY WERE INTO THE PROCESS, YOU KNOW?

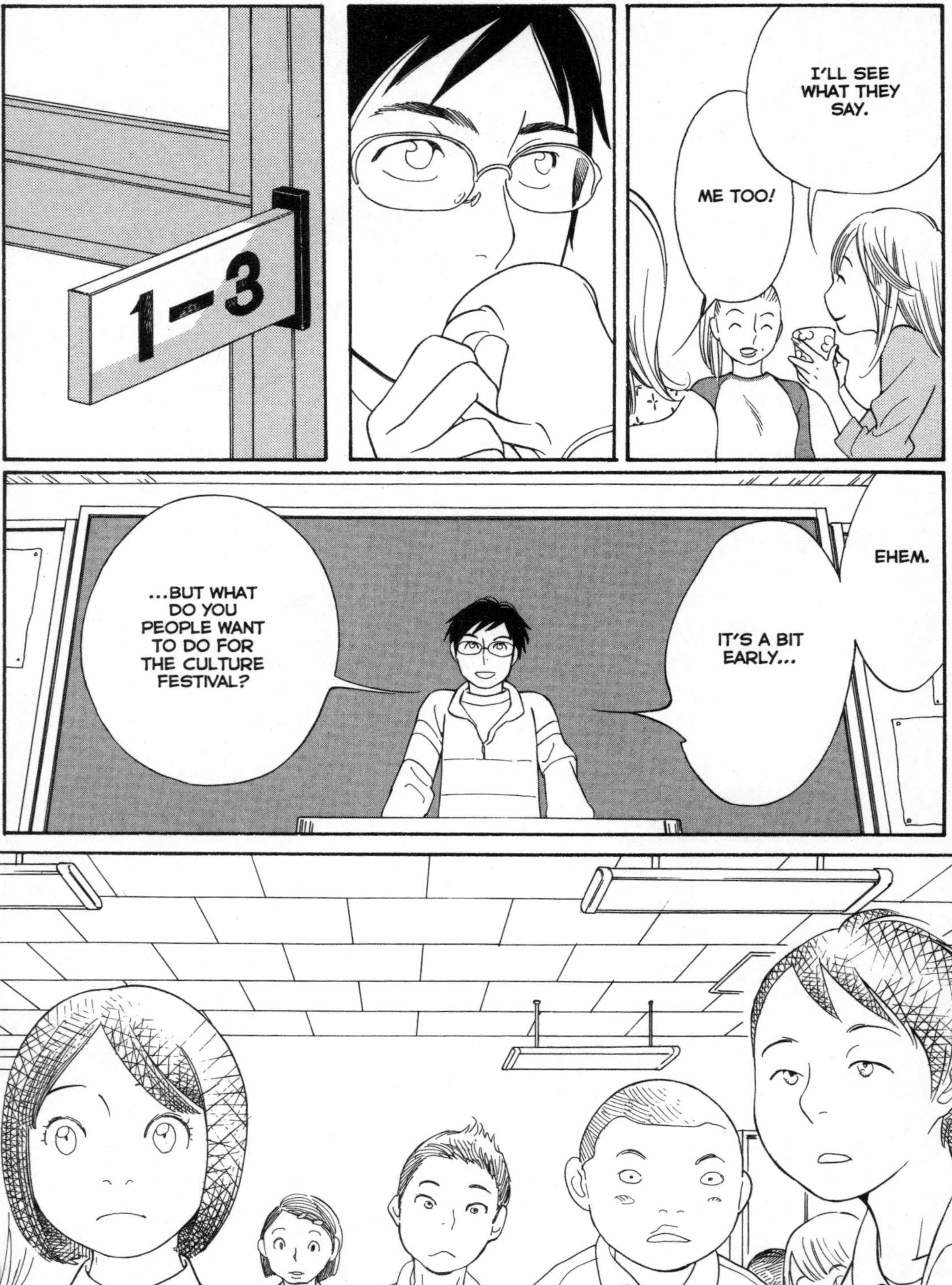
I'LL SEE WHAT THEY SAY.
ME TOO!
1-3
EHEM.
IT'S A BIT EARLY...
...BUT WHAT DO YOU PEOPLE WANT TO DO FOR THE CULTURE FESTIVAL?

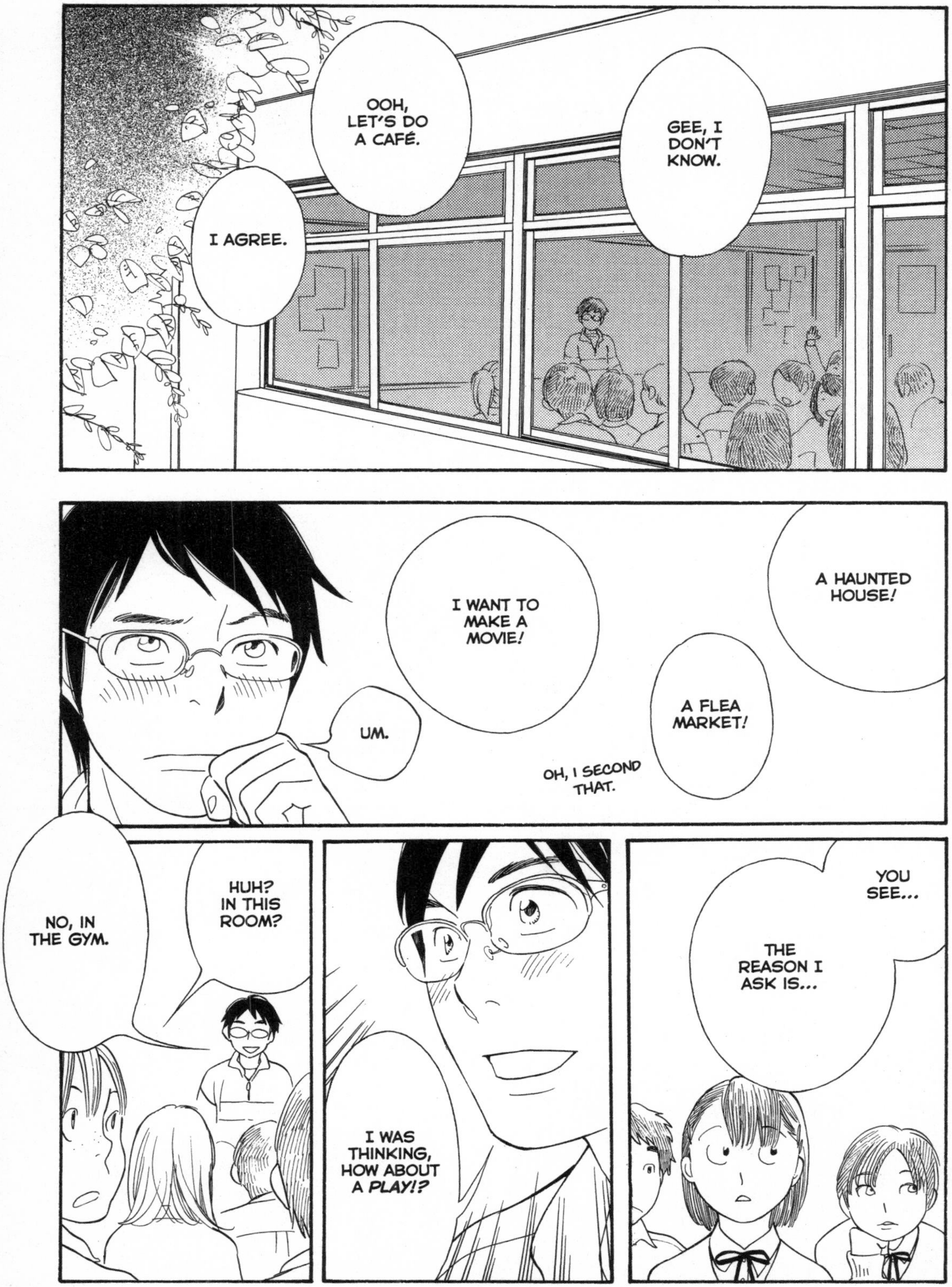
GEE, I DON'T KNOW.
OOH, LET'S DO A CAFÉ.
I AGREE.
A HAUNTED HOUSE!
I WANT TO MAKE A MOVIE!
A FLEA MARKET!
OH, I SECOND THAT.
UM.
YOU SEE...
THE REASON I ASK IS...
I WAS THINKING, HOW ABOUT A *PLAY*!?
HUH? IN THIS ROOM?
NO, IN THE GYM.

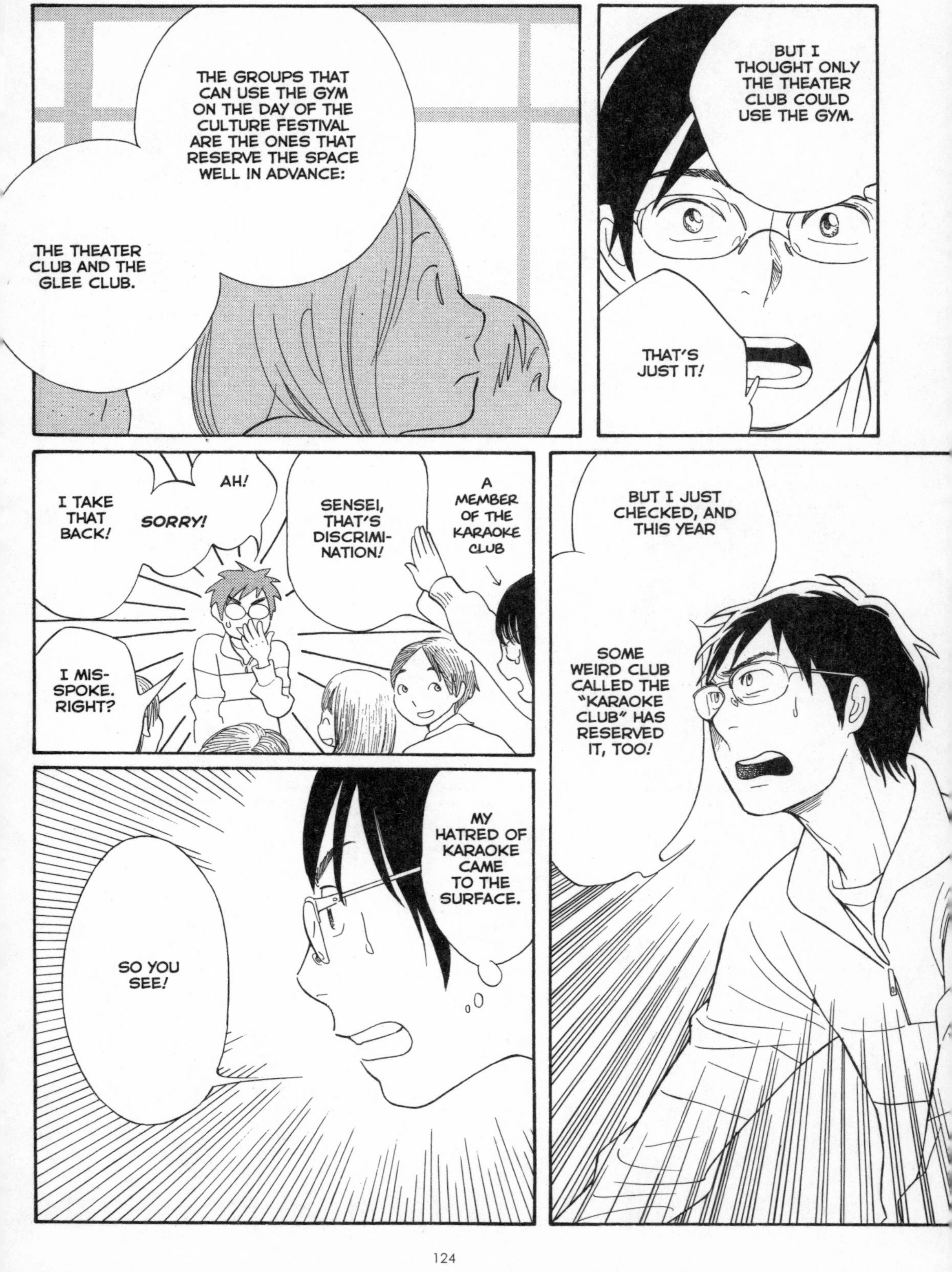
BUT I THOUGHT ONLY THE THEATER CLUB COULD USE THE GYM.
THAT'S JUST IT!
THE GROUPS THAT CAN USE THE GYM ON THE DAY OF THE CULTURE FESTIVAL ARE THE ONES THAT RESERVE THE SPACE WELL IN ADVANCE:
THE THEATER CLUB AND THE GLEE CLUB.
BUT I JUST CHECKED, AND THIS YEAR
SOME WEIRD CLUB CALLED THE "KARAOKE CLUB" HAS RESERVED IT, TOO!
A MEMBER OF THE KARAOKE CLUB
SENSEI, THAT'S DISCRIMINATION!
AH!
SORRY!
I TAKE THAT BACK!
I MISSPOKE. RIGHT?
MY HATRED OF KARAOKE CAME TO THE SURFACE.
SO YOU SEE!

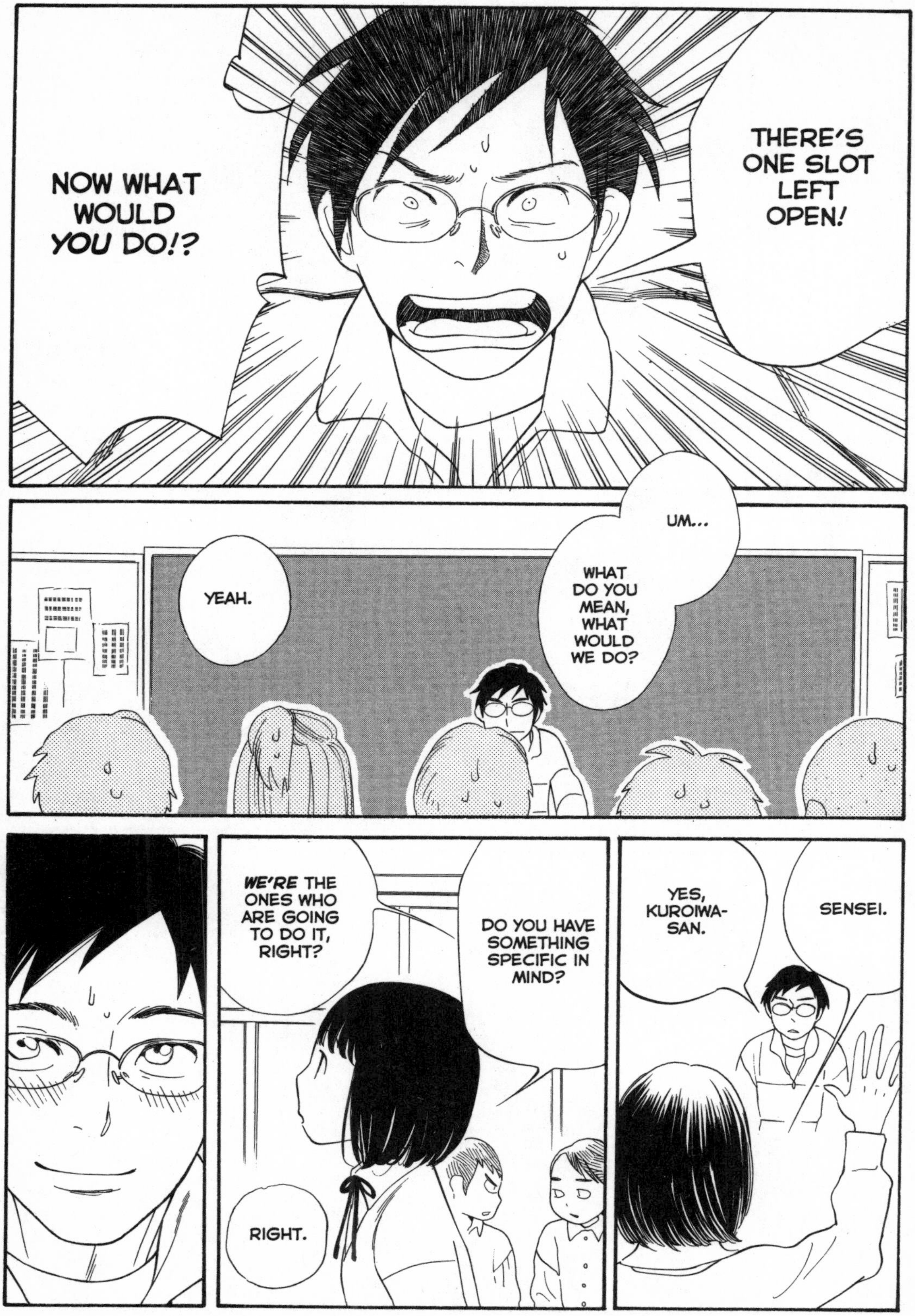
THERE'S ONE SLOT LEFT OPEN!
NOW WHAT WOULD *YOU* DO!?
UM...
WHAT DO YOU MEAN, WHAT WOULD WE DO?
YEAH.
SENSEI.
YES, KUROIWA-SAN.
DO YOU HAVE SOMETHING SPECIFIC IN MIND?
WE'RE THE ONES WHO ARE GOING TO DO IT, RIGHT?
RIGHT.

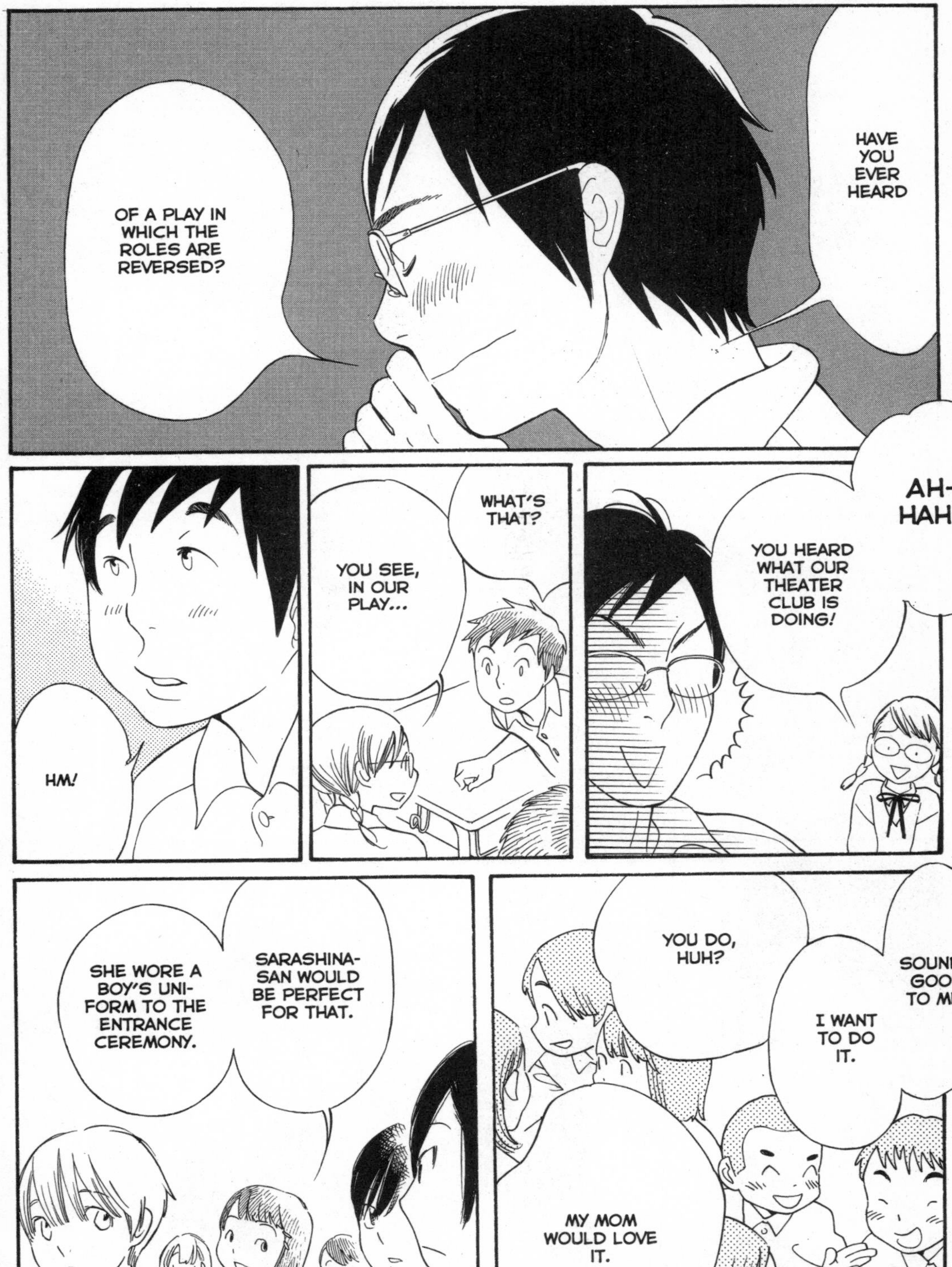
HAVE YOU EVER HEARD
OF A PLAY IN WHICH THE ROLES ARE REVERSED?
AH-HAH!
YOU HEARD WHAT OUR THEATER CLUB IS DOING!
WHAT'S THAT?
YOU SEE, IN OUR PLAY...
HM!
SOUNDS GOOD TO ME.
YOU DO, HUH?
I WANT TO DO IT.
MY MOM WOULD LOVE IT.
SARASHINA-SAN WOULD BE PERFECT FOR THAT.
SHE WORE A BOY'S UNI-FORM TO THE ENTRANCE CEREMONY.

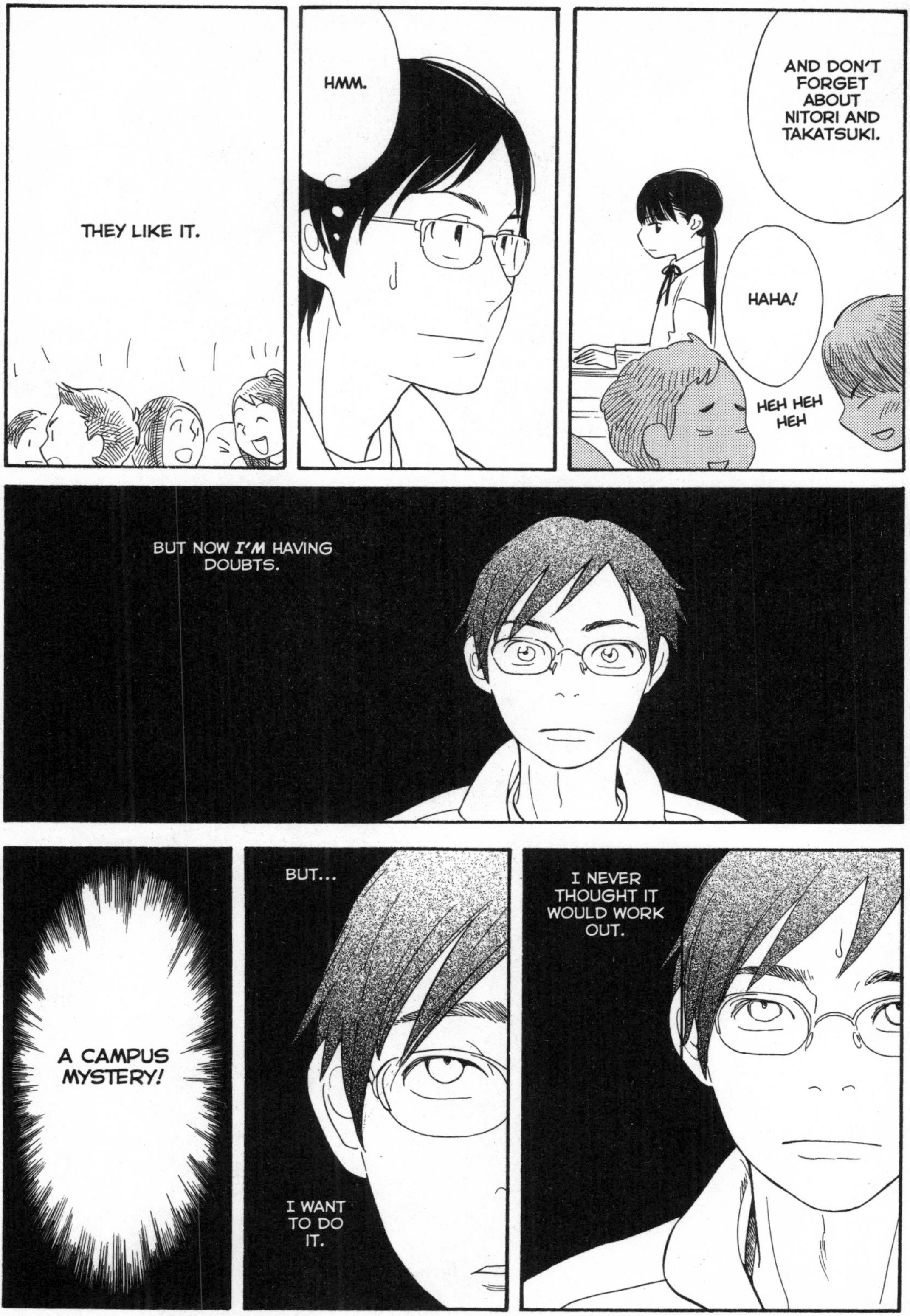
AND DON'T FORGET ABOUT NITORI AND TAKATSUKI.
HAHA!
HEH HEH HEH
HMM.
THEY LIKE IT.
BUT NOW *I'M* HAVING DOUBTS.
I NEVER THOUGHT IT WOULD WORK OUT.
BUT...
I WANT TO DO IT.
A CAMPUS MYSTERY!

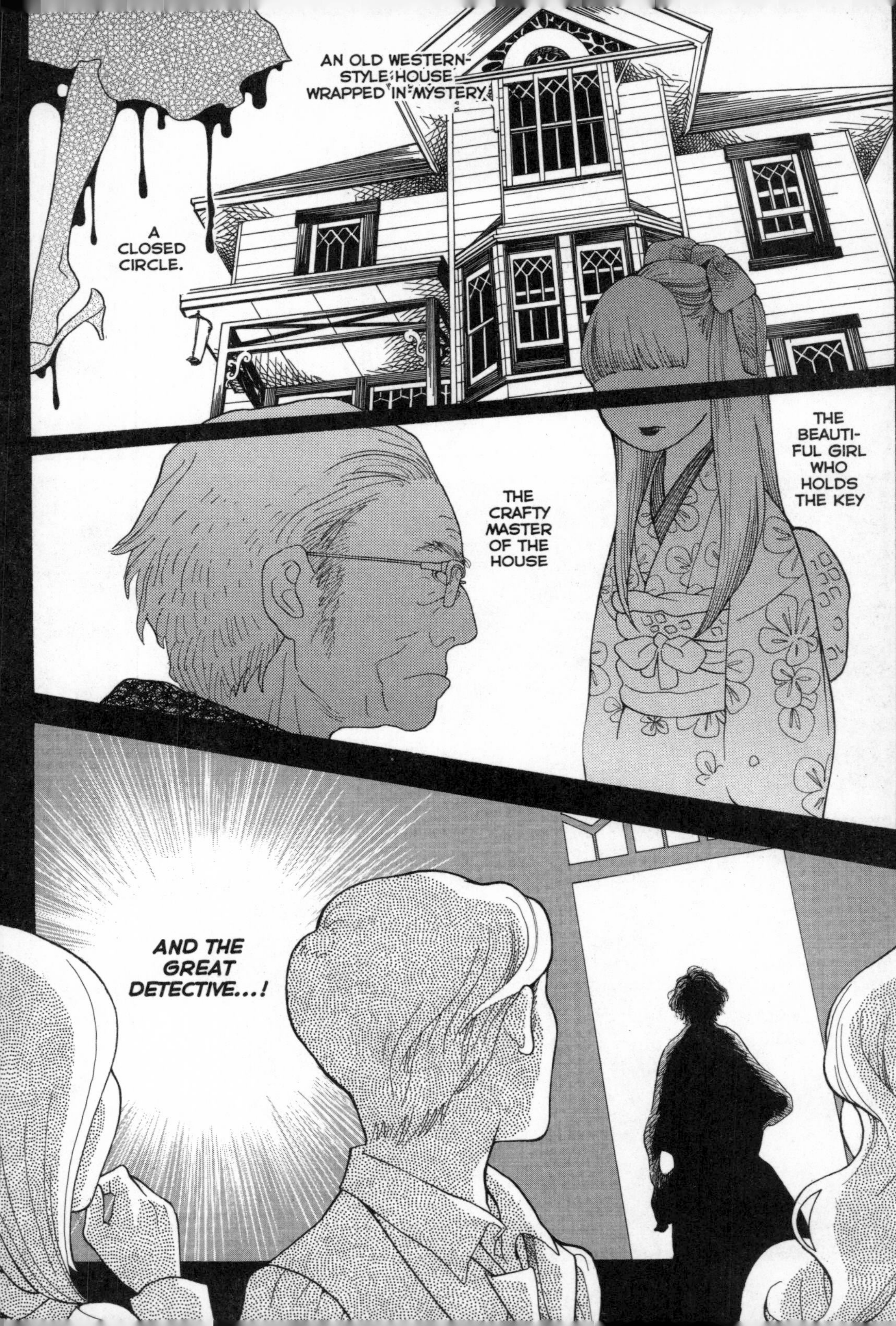
AN OLD WESTERN-STYLE HOUSE WRAPPED IN MYSTERY.
A CLOSED CIRCLE.
THE BEAUTIFUL GIRL WHO HOLDS THE KEY
THE CRAFTY MASTER OF THE HOUSE
AND THE GREAT DETECTIVE...!

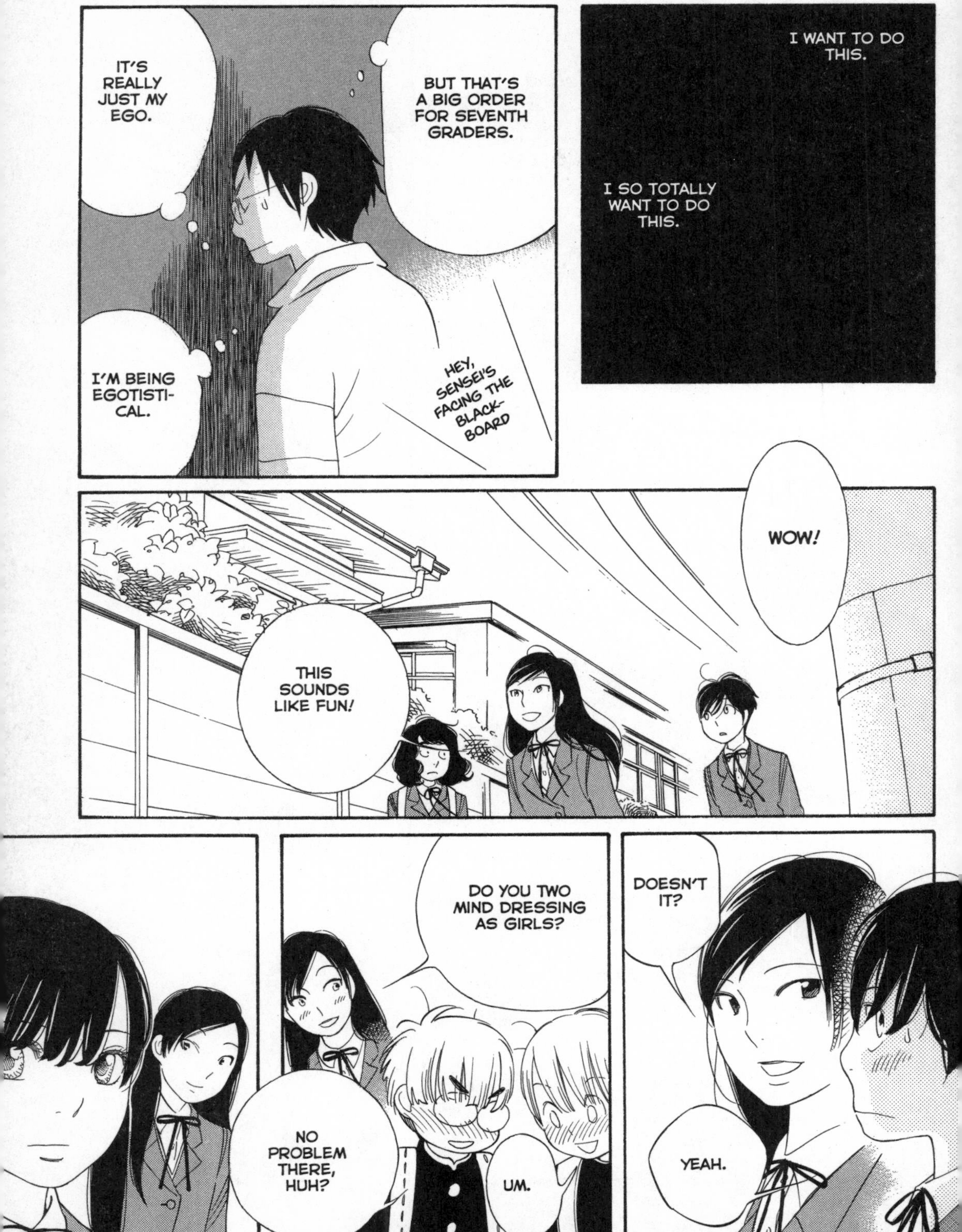
I WANT TO DO THIS.
I SO TOTALLY WANT TO DO THIS.
BUT THAT'S A BIG ORDER FOR SEVENTH GRADERS.
IT'S REALLY JUST MY EGO.
HEY, SENSEI'S FACING THE BLACK-BOARD
I'M BEING EGOTISTI-CAL.
WOW!
THIS SOUNDS LIKE FUN!
DOESN'T IT?
YEAH.
DO YOU TWO MIND DRESSING AS GIRLS?
UM.
NO PROBLEM THERE, HUH?

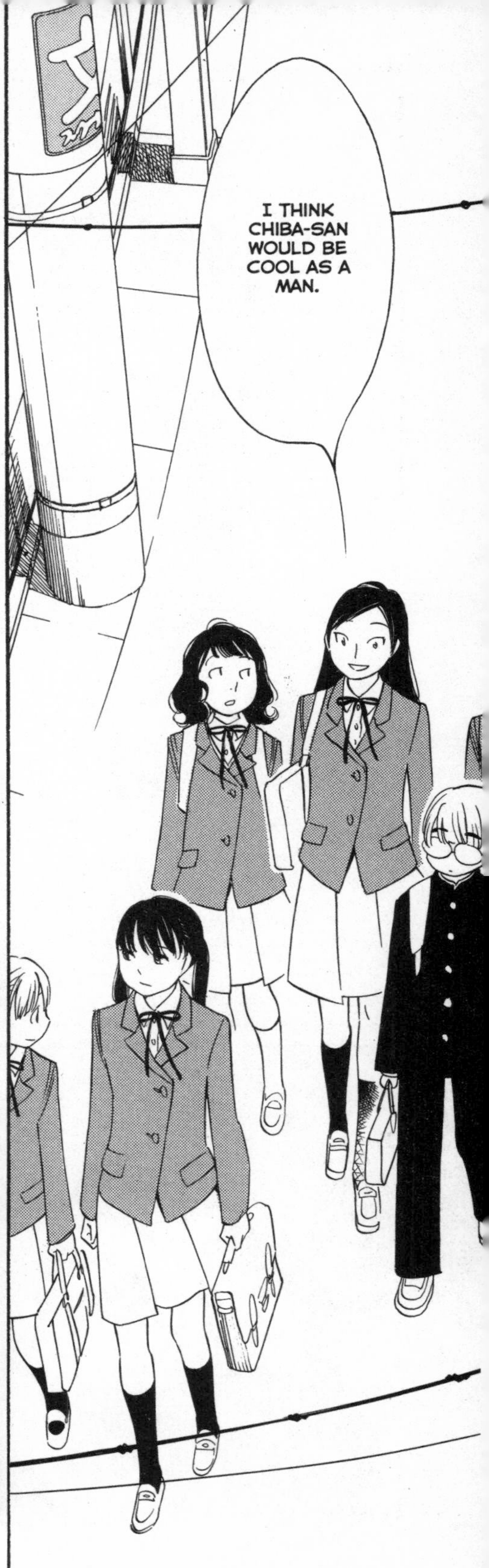
I THINK CHIBA-SAN WOULD BE COOL AS A MAN.

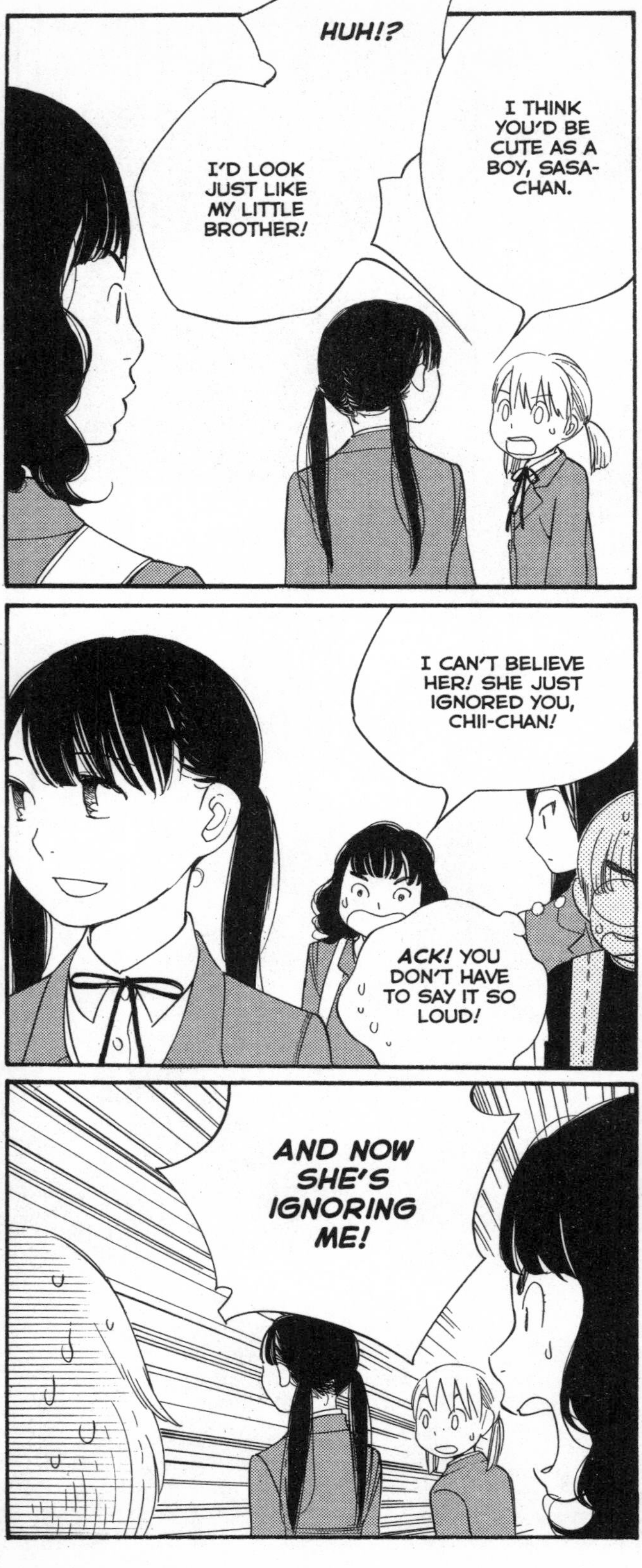
I THINK YOU'D BE CUTE AS A BOY, SASA-CHAN.
HUH!?
I'D LOOK JUST LIKE MY LITTLE BROTHER!
I CAN'T BELIEVE HER! SHE JUST IGNORED YOU, CHII-CHAN!
ACK! YOU DON'T HAVE TO SAY IT SO LOUD!
AND NOW SHE'S IGNORING ME!

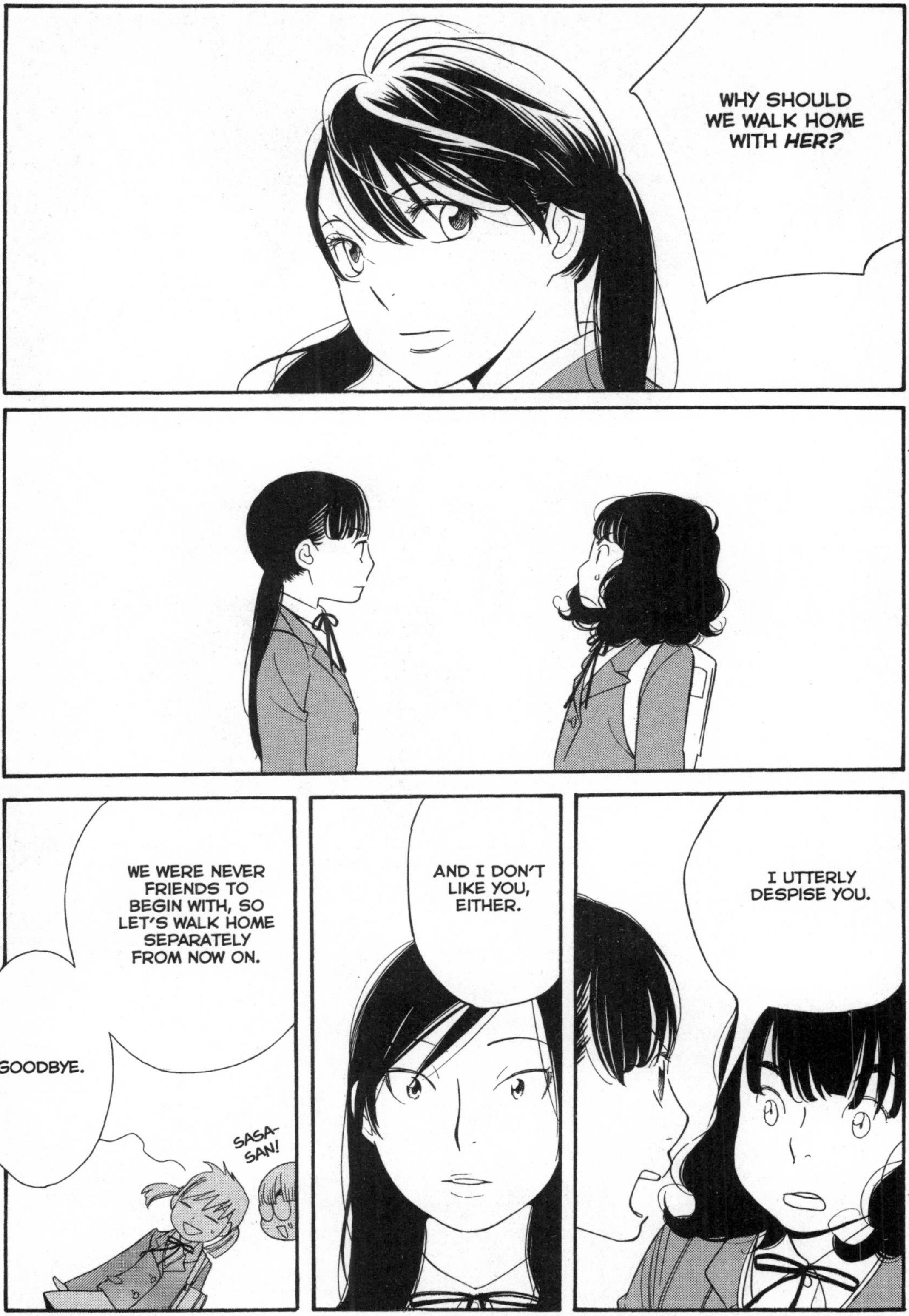
WHY SHOULD WE WALK HOME WITH *HER?*
I UTTERLY DESPISE YOU.
AND I DON'T LIKE YOU, EITHER.
WE WERE NEVER FRIENDS TO BEGIN WITH, SO LET'S WALK HOME SEPARATELY FROM NOW ON.
GOODBYE.
SASA-SAN!

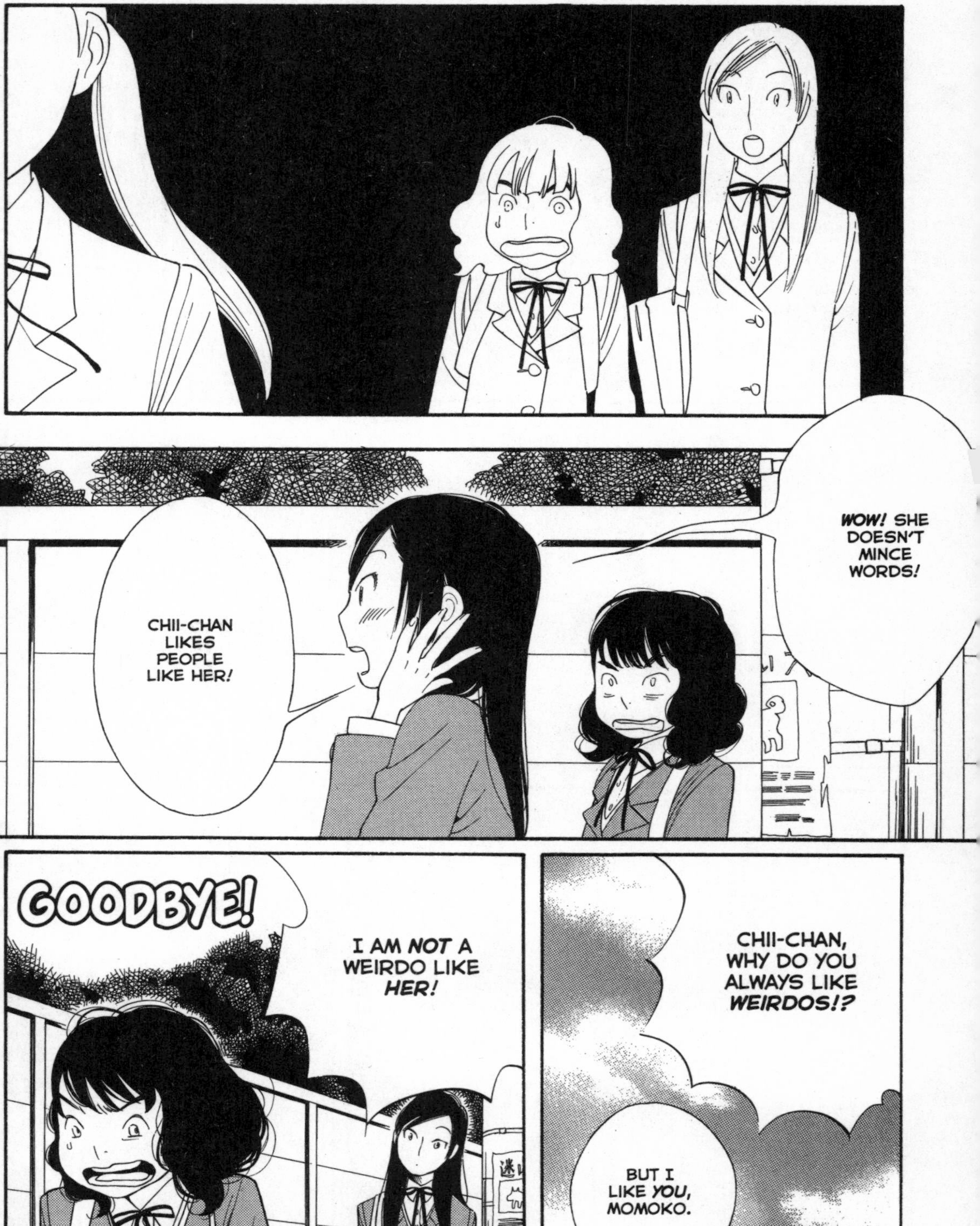
WOW! SHE DOESN'T MINCE WORDS!
CHII-CHAN LIKES PEOPLE LIKE HER!
CHII-CHAN, WHY DO YOU ALWAYS LIKE WEIRDOS!?
BUT I LIKE YOU, MOMOKO.
I AM NOT A WEIRDO LIKE HER!
GOODBYE!

SARASHINA-SAN... YOU'RE PRETTY STRANGE.

REALLY!?

BUT I LIKE YOU, TOO, TAKATSUKI-SAN.

HA HA HA...

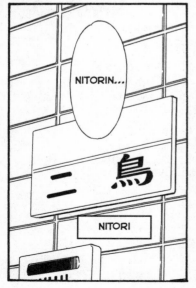

NITORIN...

二鳥

NITORI

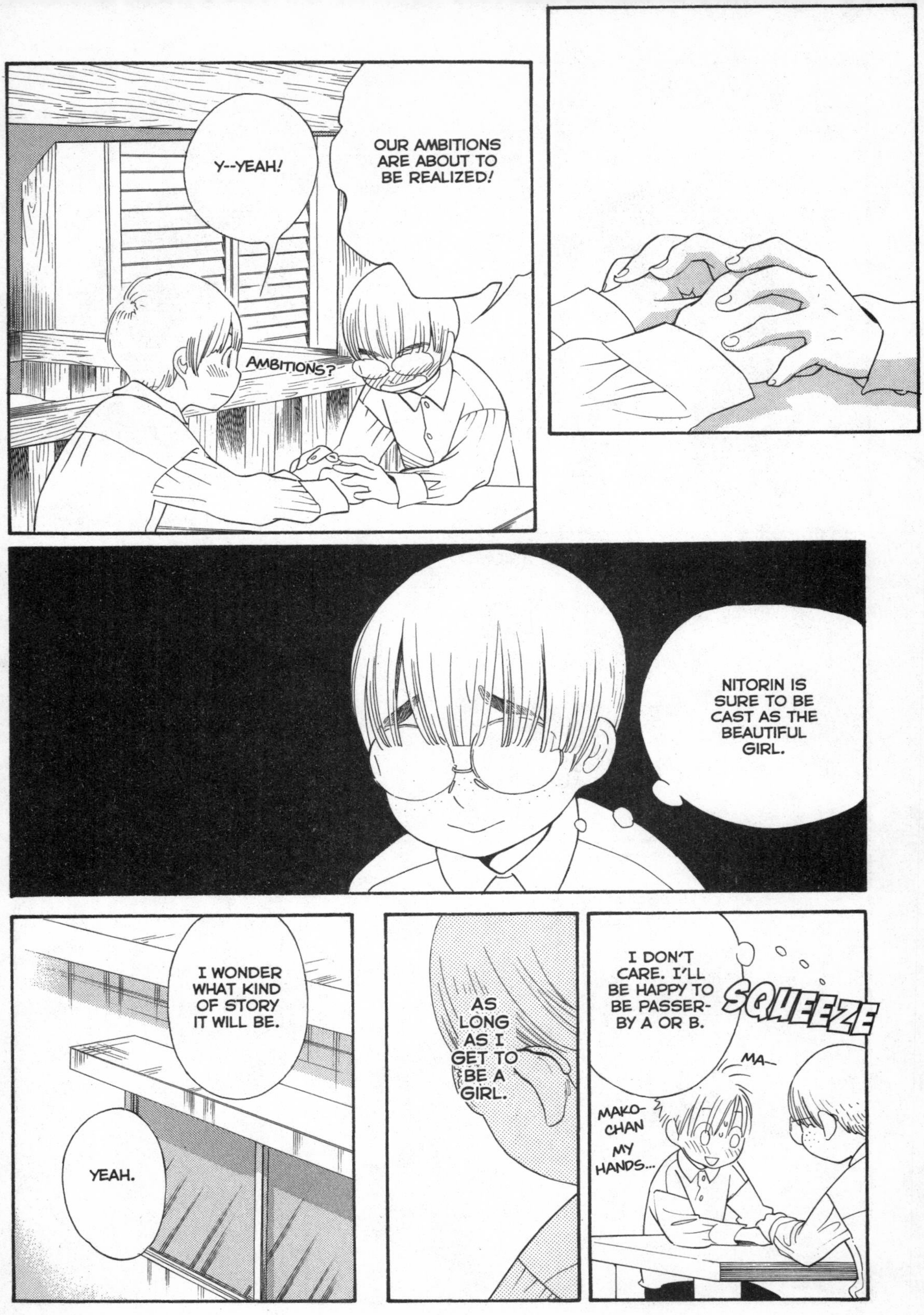
OUR AMBITIONS ARE ABOUT TO BE REALIZED!
Y--YEAH!
AMBITIONS?
NITORIN IS SURE TO BE CAST AS THE BEAUTIFUL GIRL.
I DON'T CARE. I'LL BE HAPPY TO BE PASSER-BY A OR B.
SQUEEZE
MA-
MAKO-CHAN MY HANDS...
AS LONG AS I GET TO BE A GIRL.
I WONDER WHAT KIND OF STORY IT WILL BE.
YEAH.

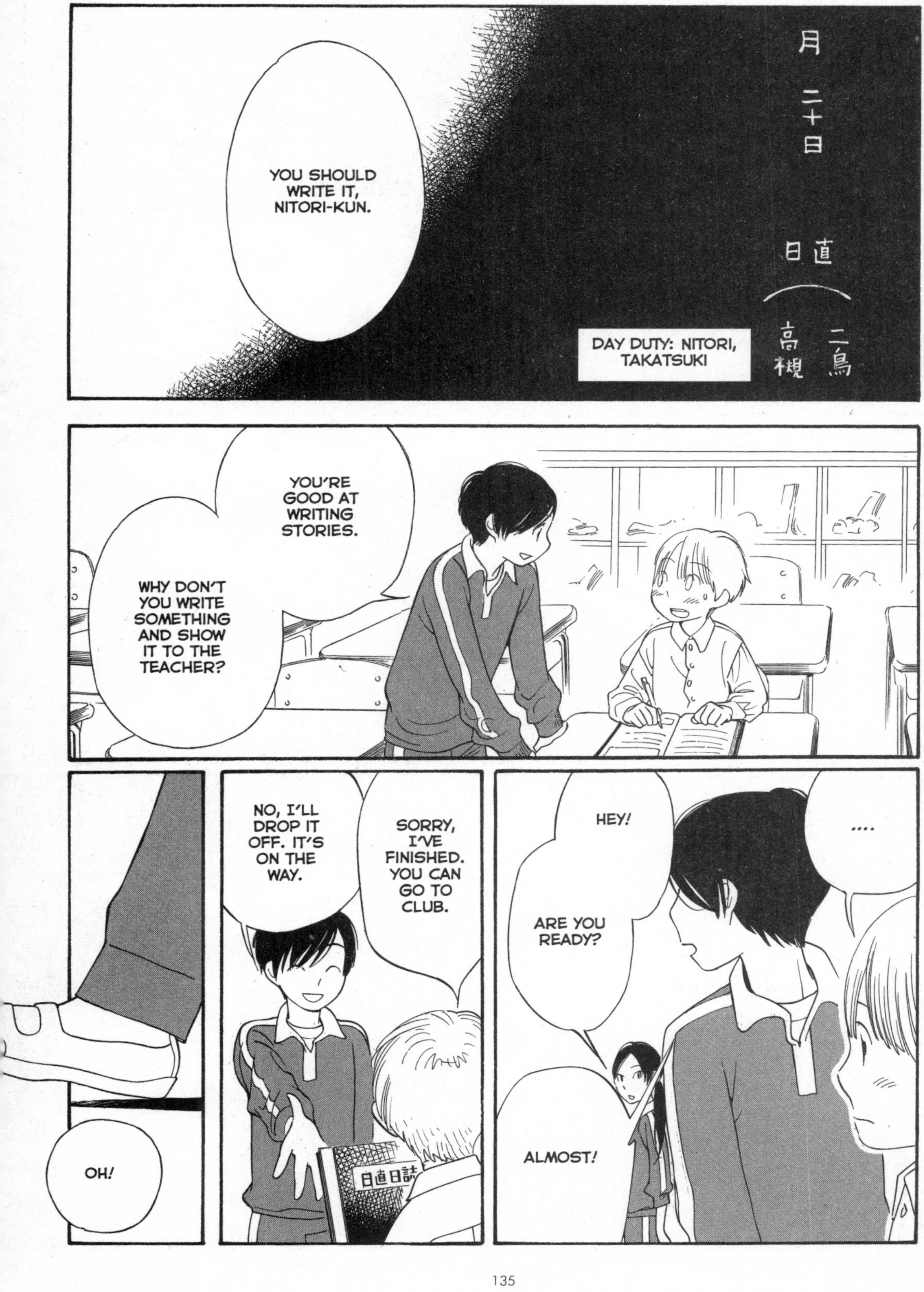

月 二十日
日直 二鳥 高槻
DAY DUTY: NITORI, TAKATSUKI
YOU SHOULD WRITE IT, NITORI-KUN.
YOU'RE GOOD AT WRITING STORIES.
WHY DON'T YOU WRITE SOMETHING AND SHOW IT TO THE TEACHER?
....
HEY!
ARE YOU READY?
ALMOST!
SORRY, I'VE FINISHED. YOU CAN GO TO CLUB.
NO, I'LL DROP IT OFF. IT'S ON THE WAY.
日直日誌
OH!

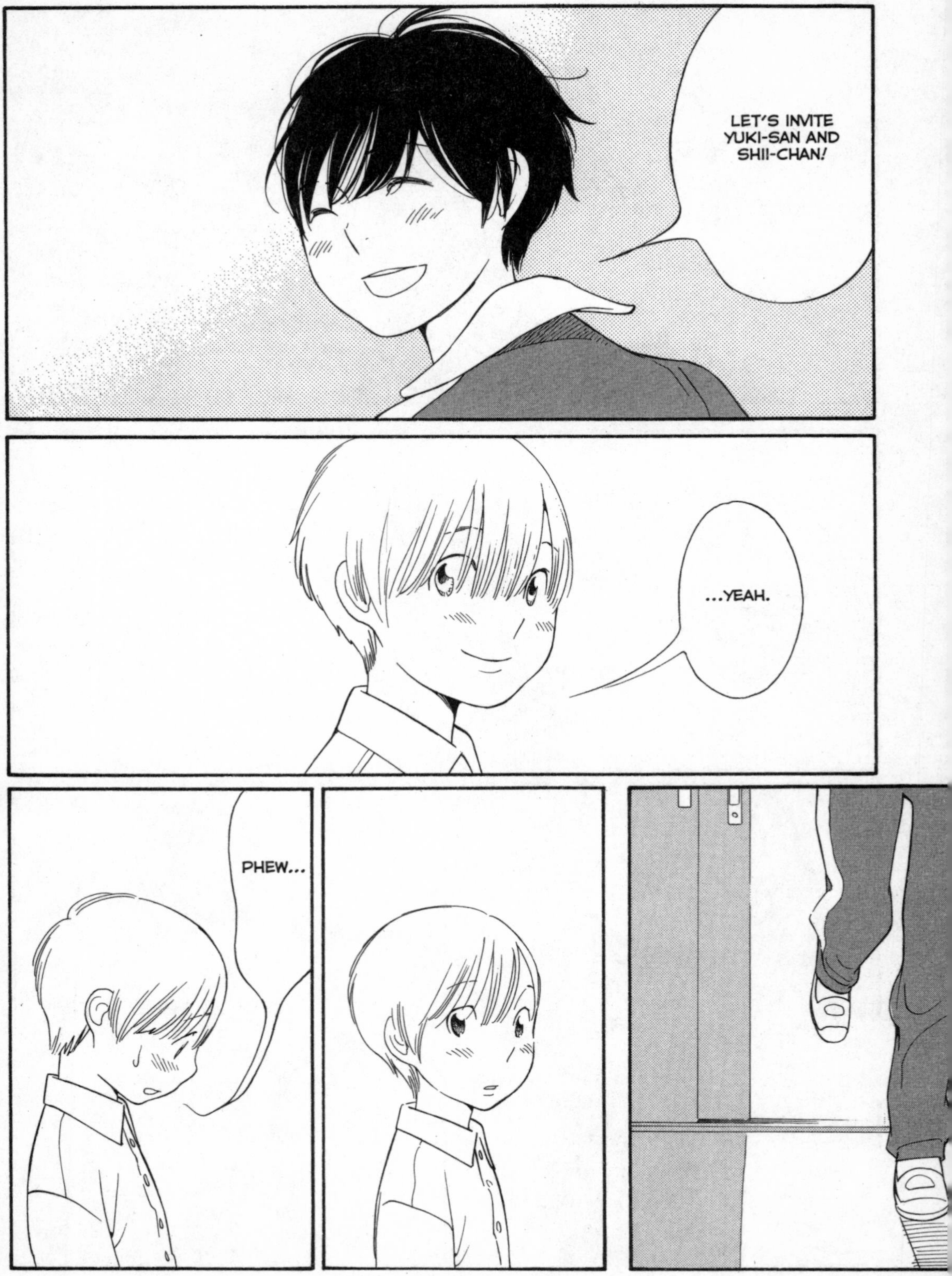
LET'S INVITE YUKI-SAN AND SHII-CHAN!
...YEAH.
PHEW...

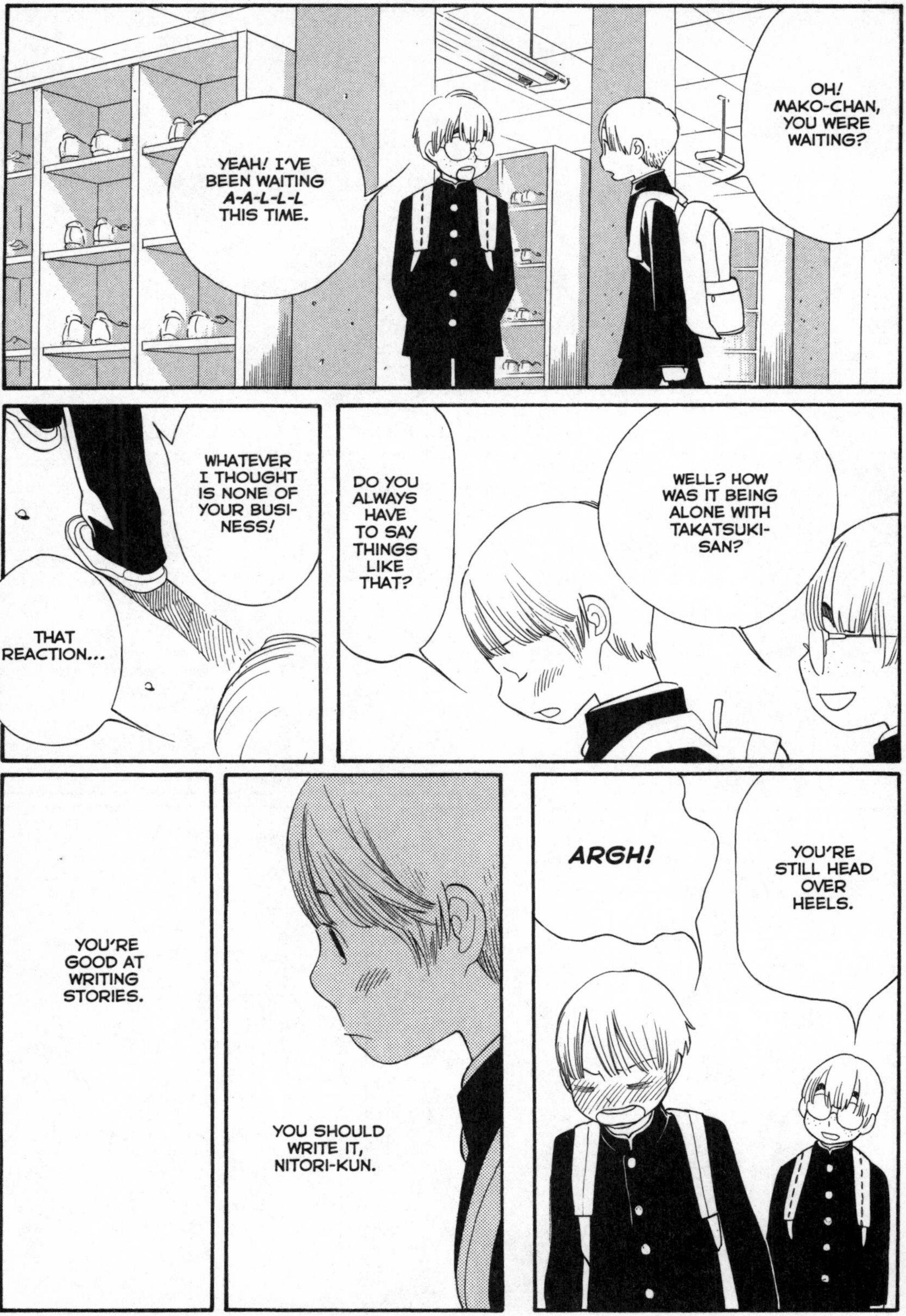
OH! MAKO-CHAN, YOU WERE WAITING?
YEAH! I'VE BEEN WAITING A-A-L-L-L THIS TIME.
WELL? HOW WAS IT BEING ALONE WITH TAKATSUKI-SAN?
DO YOU ALWAYS HAVE TO SAY THINGS LIKE THAT?
WHATEVER I THOUGHT IS NONE OF YOUR BUSINESS!
THAT REACTION...
YOU'RE STILL HEAD OVER HEELS.
ARGH!
YOU SHOULD WRITE IT, NITORI-KUN.
YOU'RE GOOD AT WRITING STORIES.

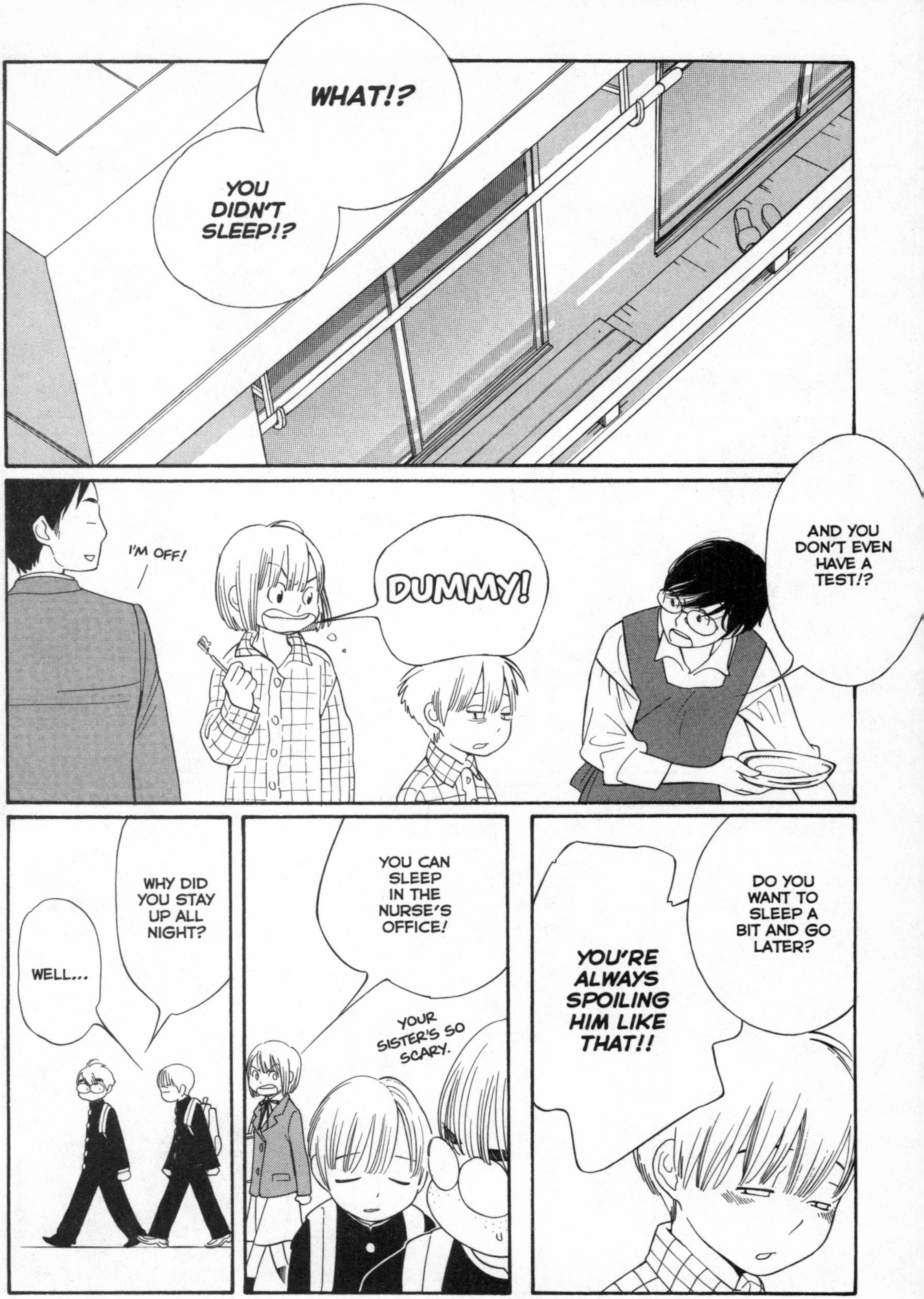
WHAT!?
YOU DIDN'T SLEEP!?
AND YOU DON'T EVEN HAVE A TEST!?
DUMMY!
I'M OFF!
DO YOU WANT TO SLEEP A BIT AND GO LATER?
YOU'RE ALWAYS SPOILING HIM LIKE THAT!!
YOU CAN SLEEP IN THE NURSE'S OFFICE!
YOUR SISTER'S SO SCARY.
WHY DID YOU STAY UP ALL NIGHT?
WELL...

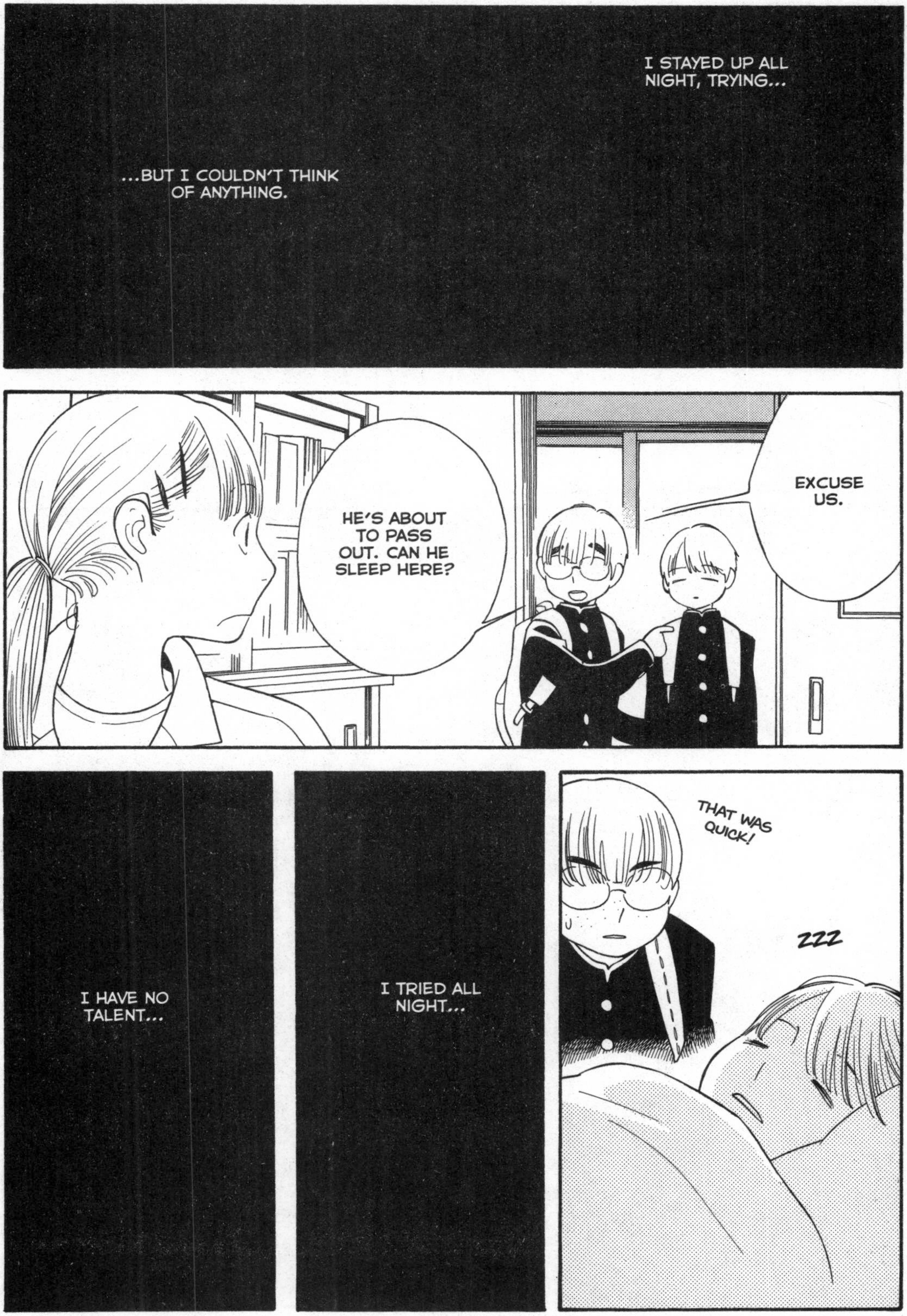
I STAYED UP ALL NIGHT, TRYING...
...BUT I COULDN'T THINK OF ANYTHING.
EXCUSE US.
HE'S ABOUT TO PASS OUT. CAN HE SLEEP HERE?
THAT WAS QUICK!
ZZZ
I TRIED ALL NIGHT...
I HAVE NO TALENT...

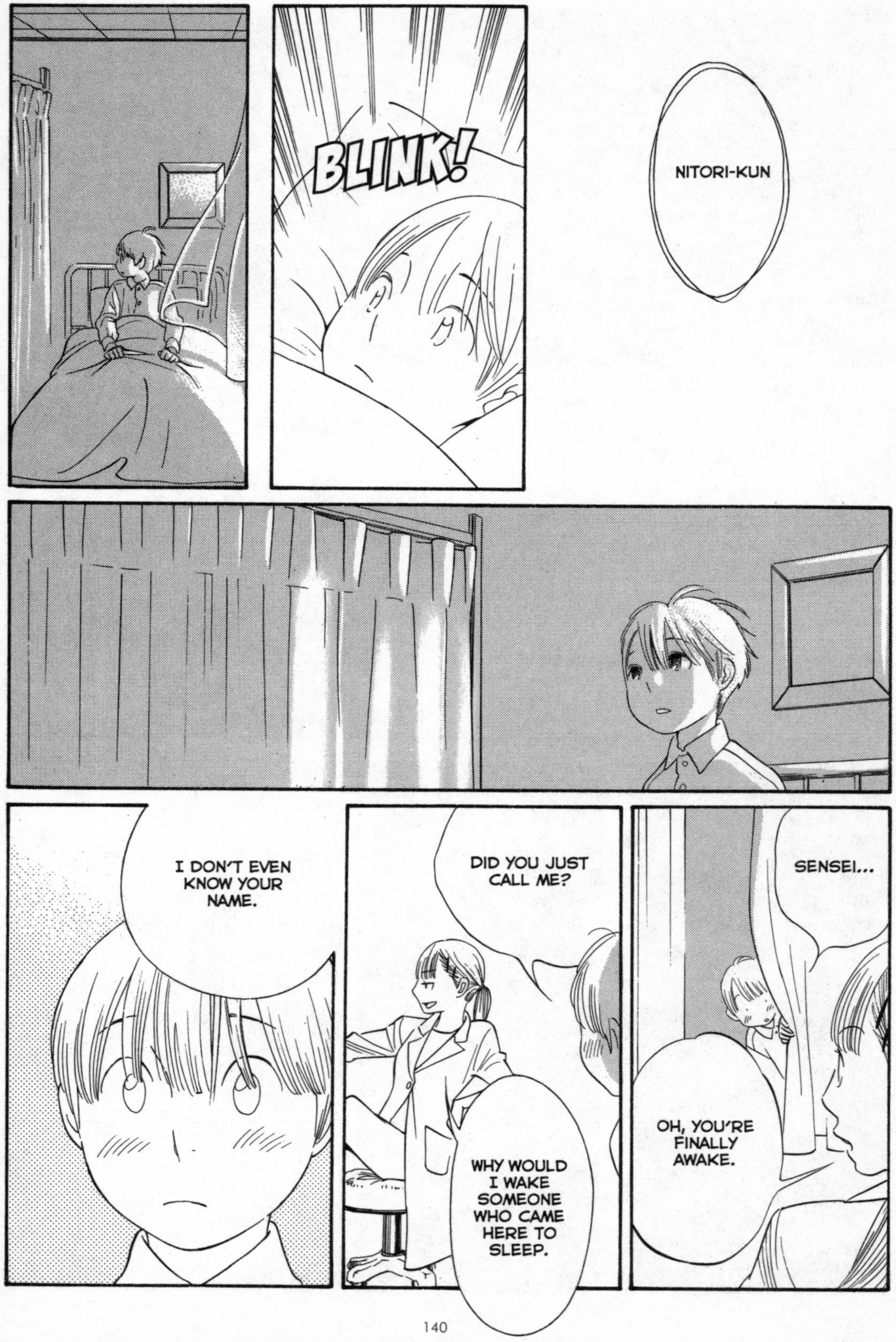
NITORI-KUN
BLINK!
SENSEI...
OH, YOU'RE FINALLY AWAKE.
DID YOU JUST CALL ME?
WHY WOULD I WAKE SOMEONE WHO CAME HERE TO SLEEP.
I DON'T EVEN KNOW YOUR NAME.

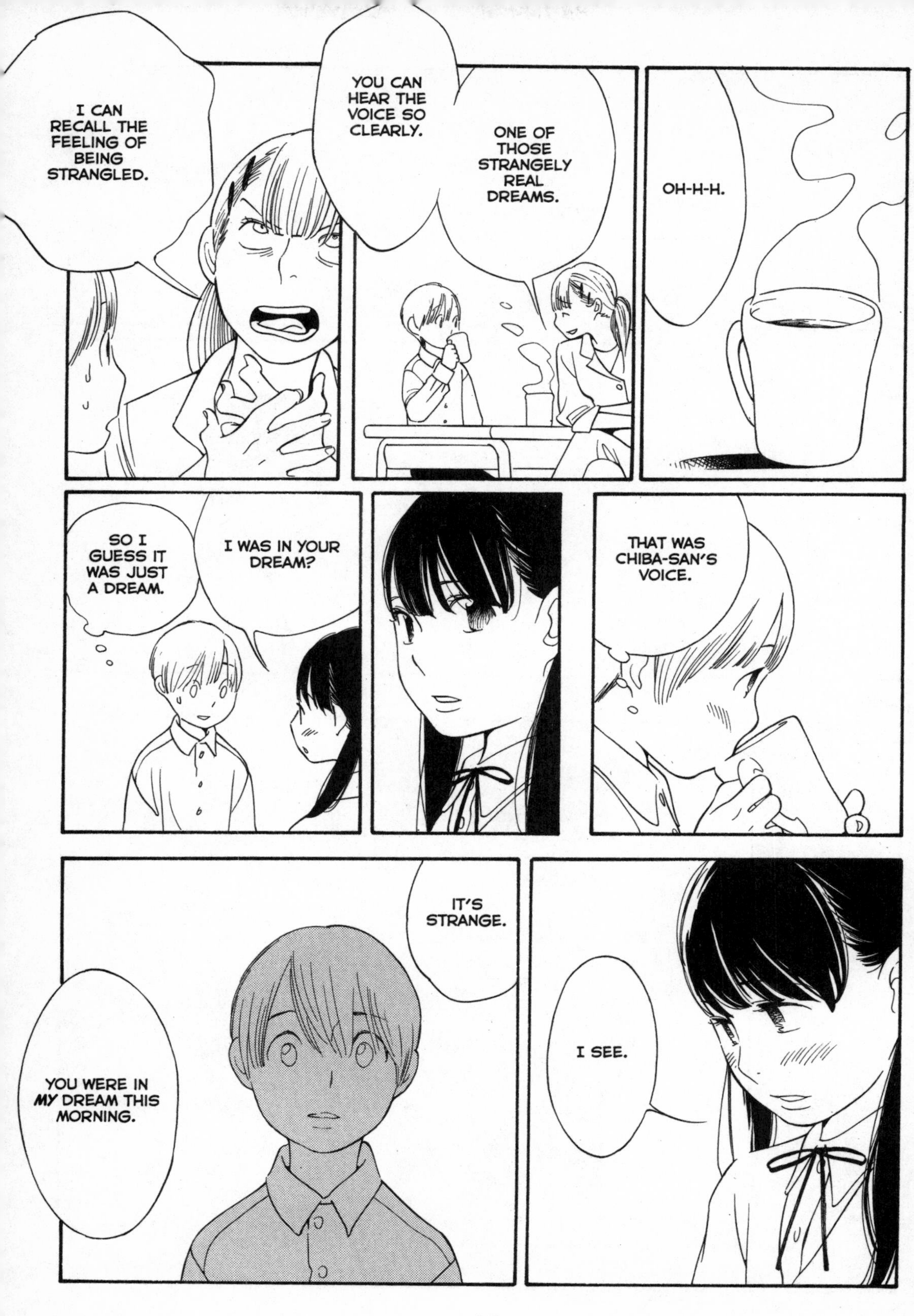
OH-H-H.
ONE OF THOSE STRANGELY REAL DREAMS.
YOU CAN HEAR THE VOICE SO CLEARLY.
I CAN RECALL THE FEELING OF BEING STRANGLED.
THAT WAS CHIBA-SAN'S VOICE.
I WAS IN YOUR DREAM?
SO I GUESS IT WAS JUST A DREAM.
I SEE.
IT'S STRANGE.
YOU WERE IN *MY* DREAM THIS MORNING.

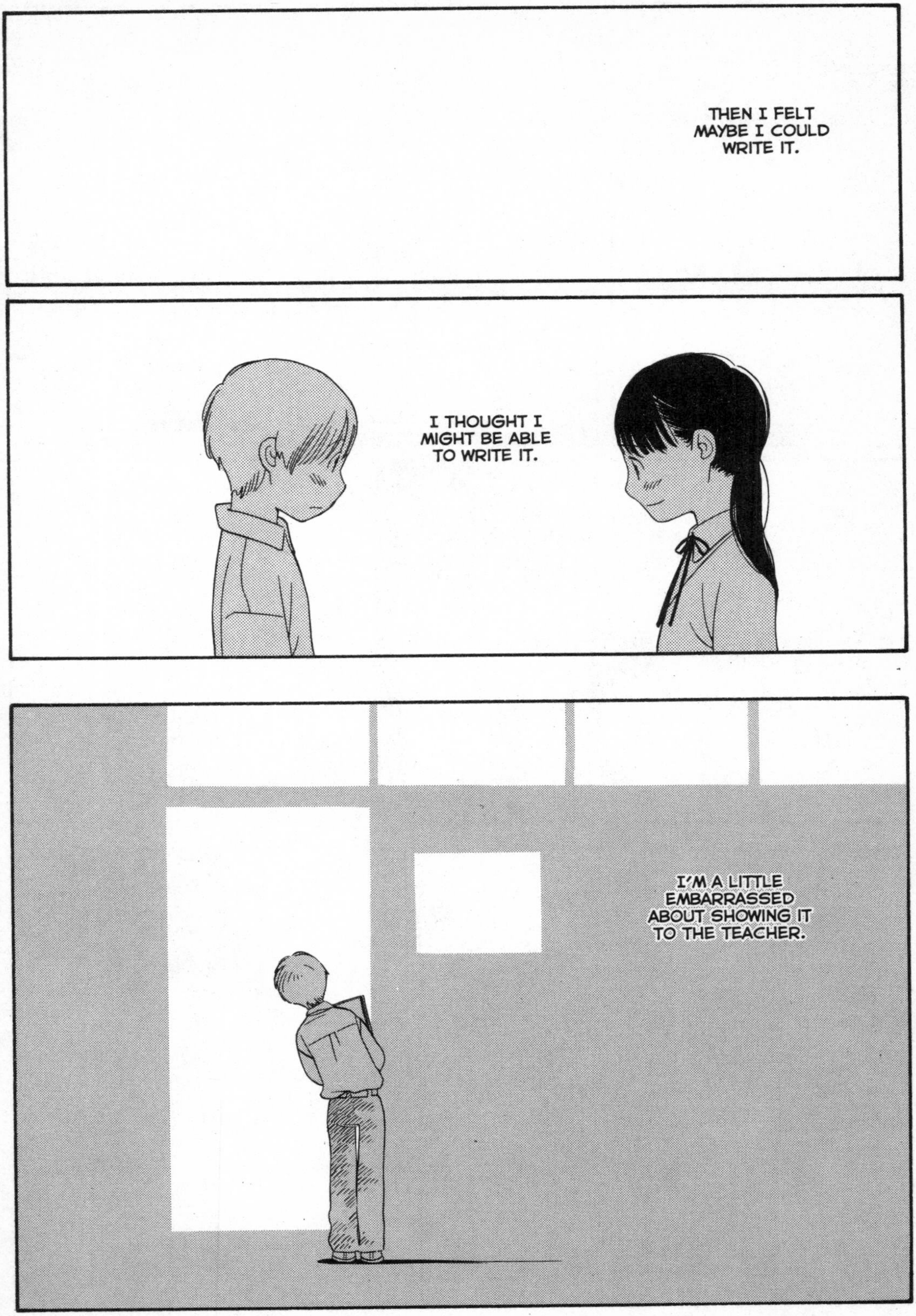
THEN I FELT MAYBE I COULD WRITE IT.
I THOUGHT I MIGHT BE ABLE TO WRITE IT.
I'M A LITTLE EMBARRASSED ABOUT SHOWING IT TO THE TEACHER.

39

Practicing Being Girls

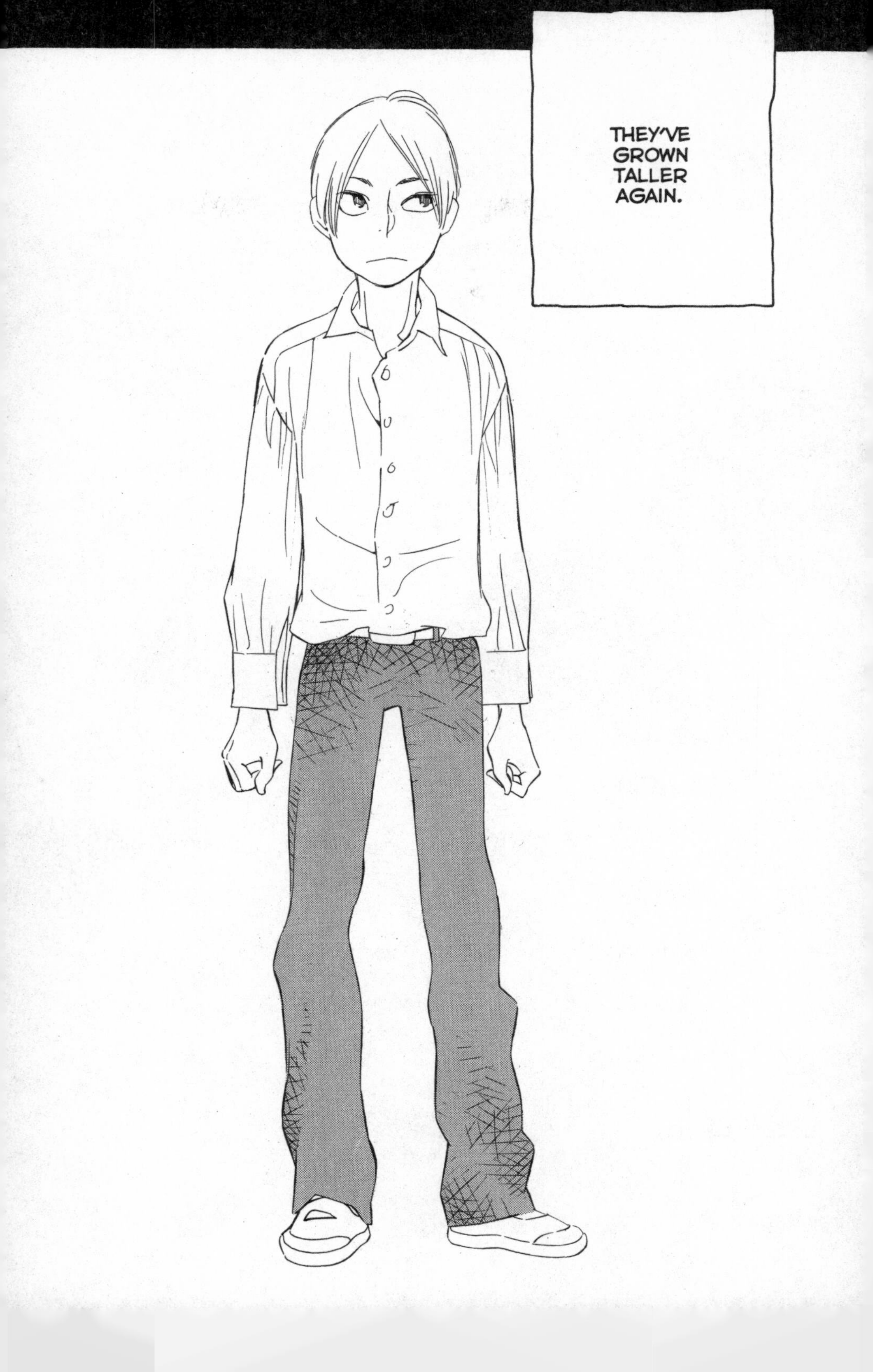
THEY'VE GROWN TALLER AGAIN.

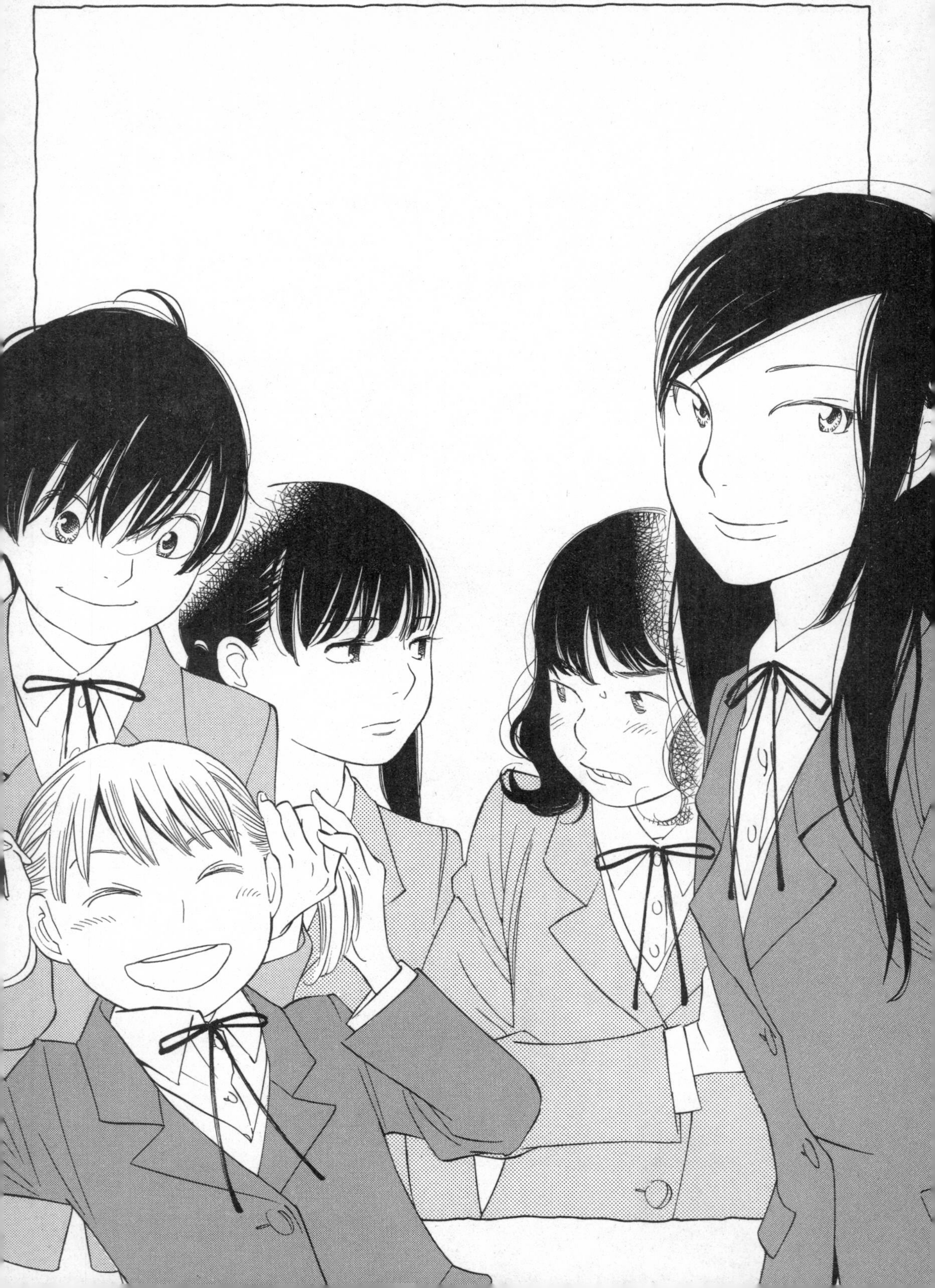

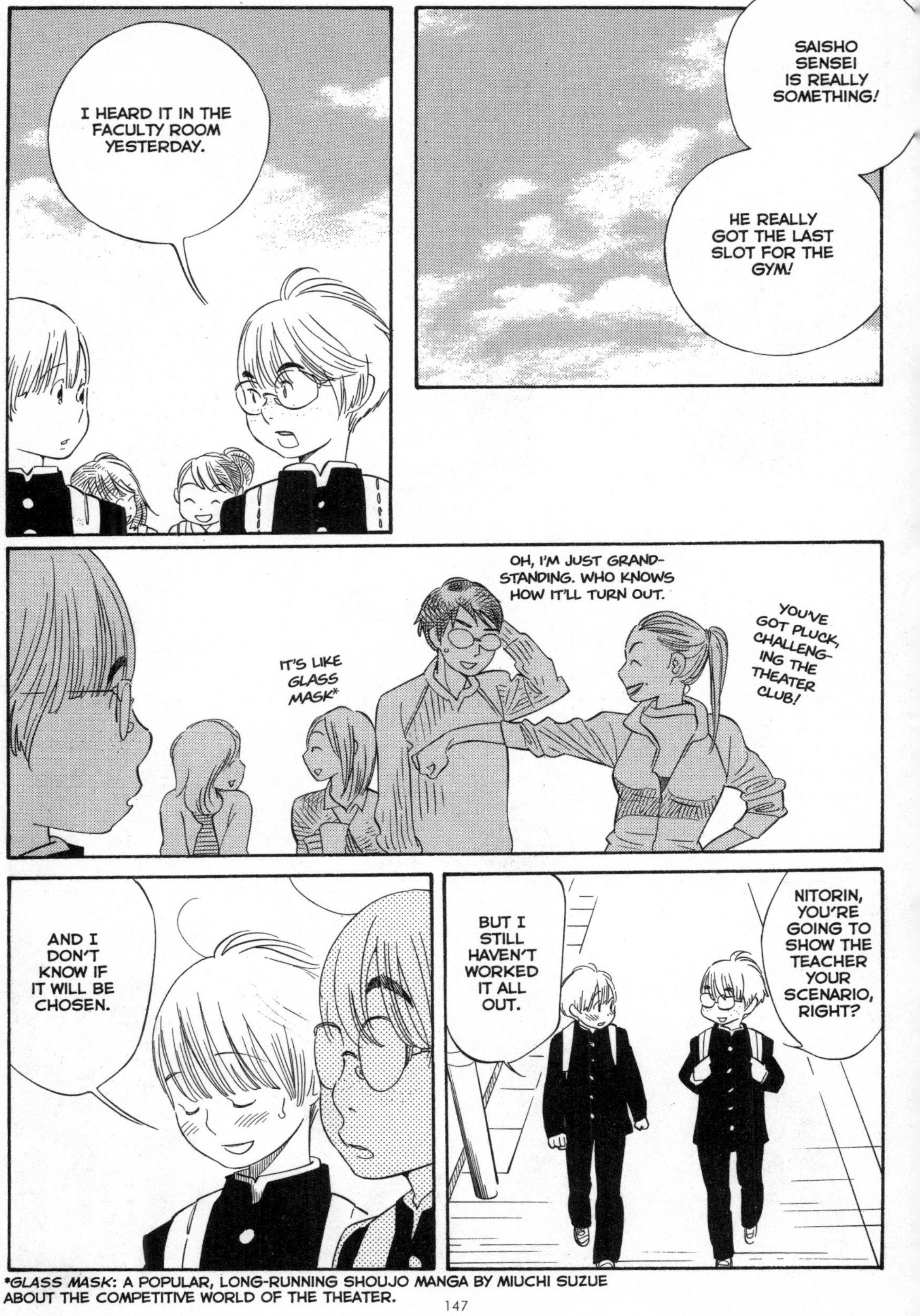
SAISHO SENSEI IS REALLY SOMETHING!
HE REALLY GOT THE LAST SLOT FOR THE GYM!
I HEARD IT IN THE FACULTY ROOM YESTERDAY.
YOU'VE GOT PLUCK, CHALLENGING THE THEATER CLUB!
OH, I'M JUST GRANDSTANDING. WHO KNOWS HOW IT'LL TURN OUT.
IT'S LIKE GLASS MASK*
NITORIN, YOU'RE GOING TO SHOW THE TEACHER YOUR SCENARIO, RIGHT?
BUT I STILL HAVEN'T WORKED IT ALL OUT.
AND I DON'T KNOW IF IT WILL BE CHOSEN.

**GLASS MASK*: A POPULAR, LONG-RUNNING SHOUJO MANGA BY MIUCHI SUZUE ABOUT THE COMPETITIVE WORLD OF THE THEATER.

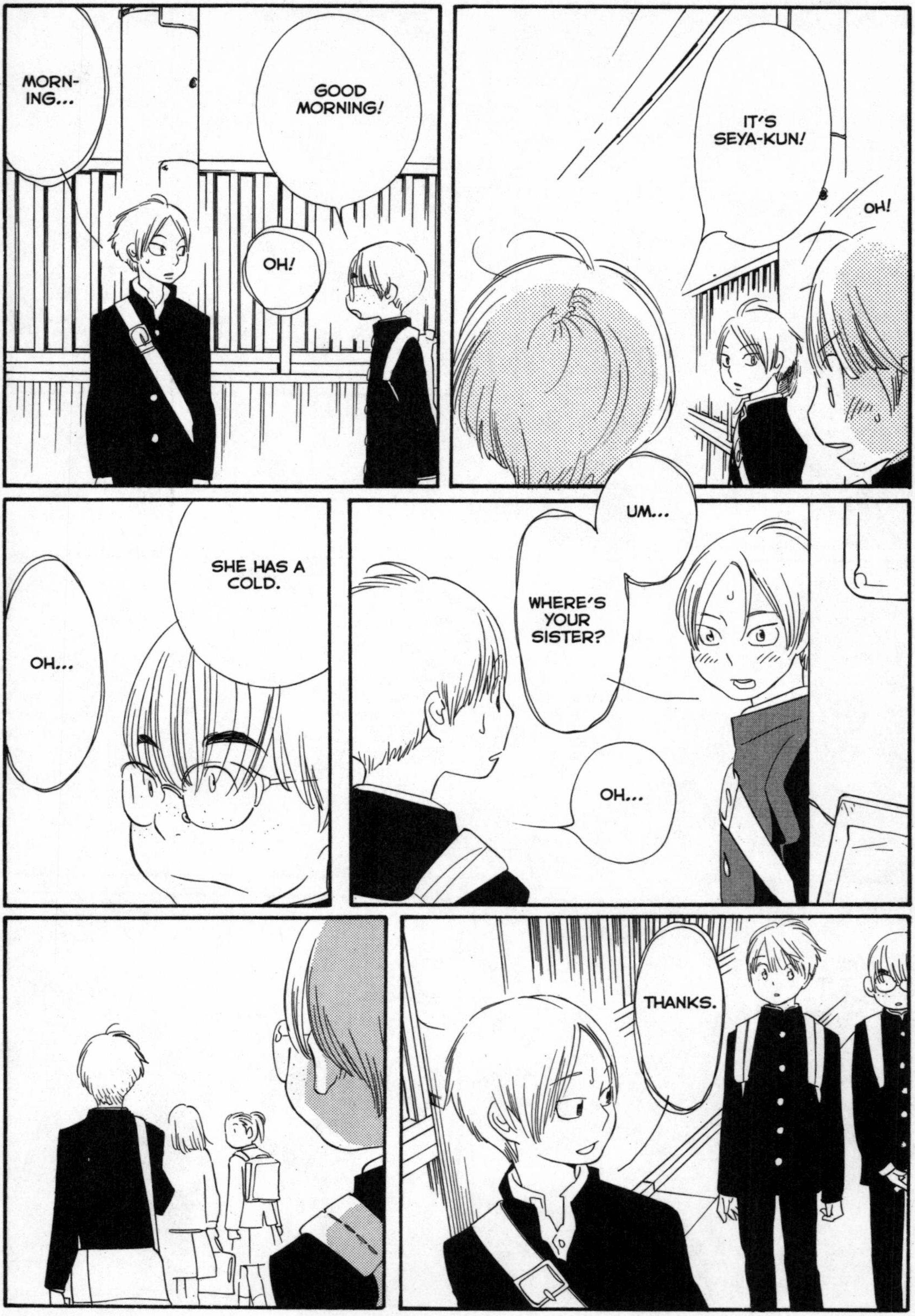
IT'S SEYA-KUN!
OH!
GOOD MORNING!
OH!
MORN-ING...
UM...
WHERE'S YOUR SISTER?
OH...
SHE HAS A COLD.
OH...
THANKS.

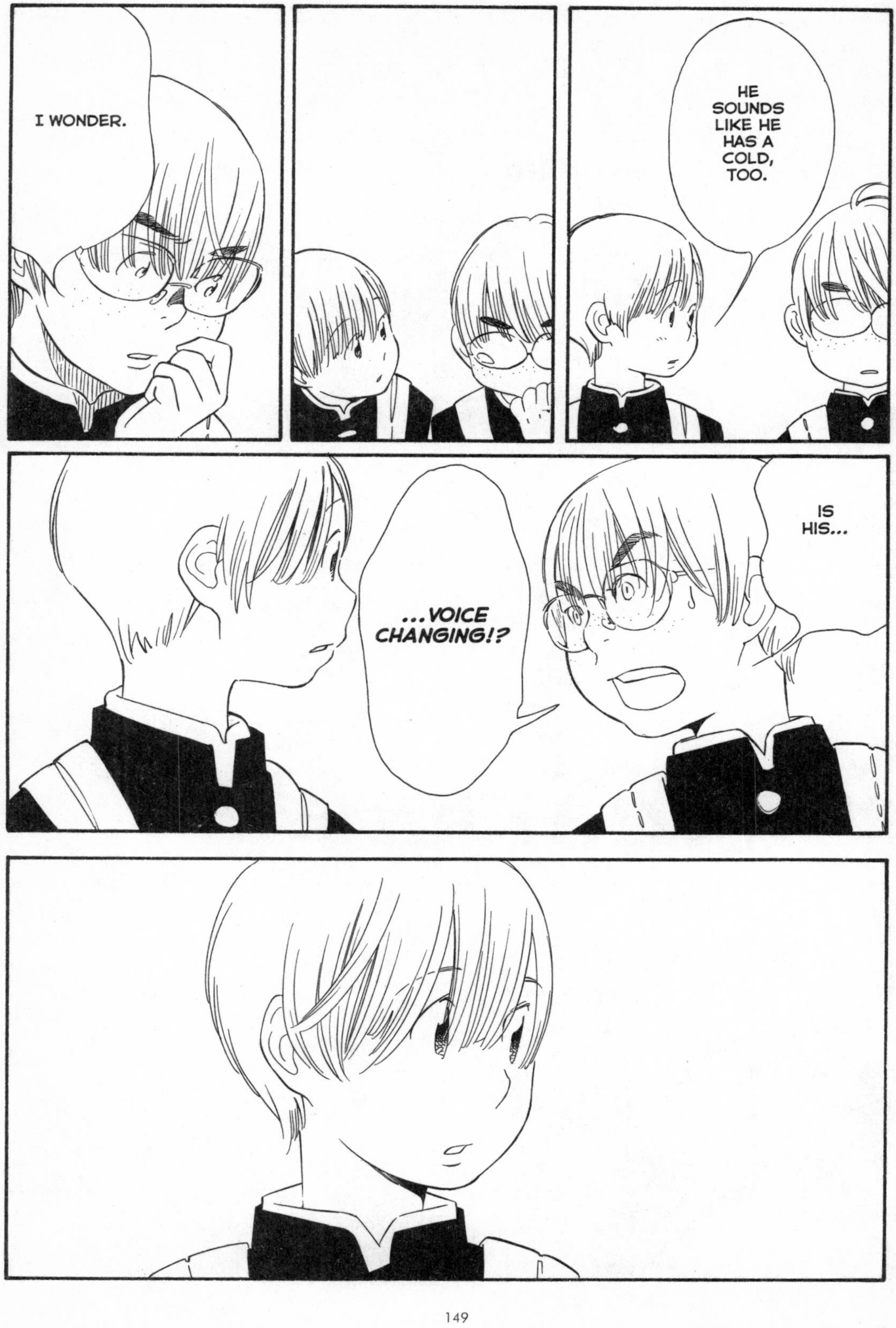
HE SOUNDS LIKE HE HAS A COLD, TOO.
I WONDER.
IS HIS...
...VOICE CHANGING!?

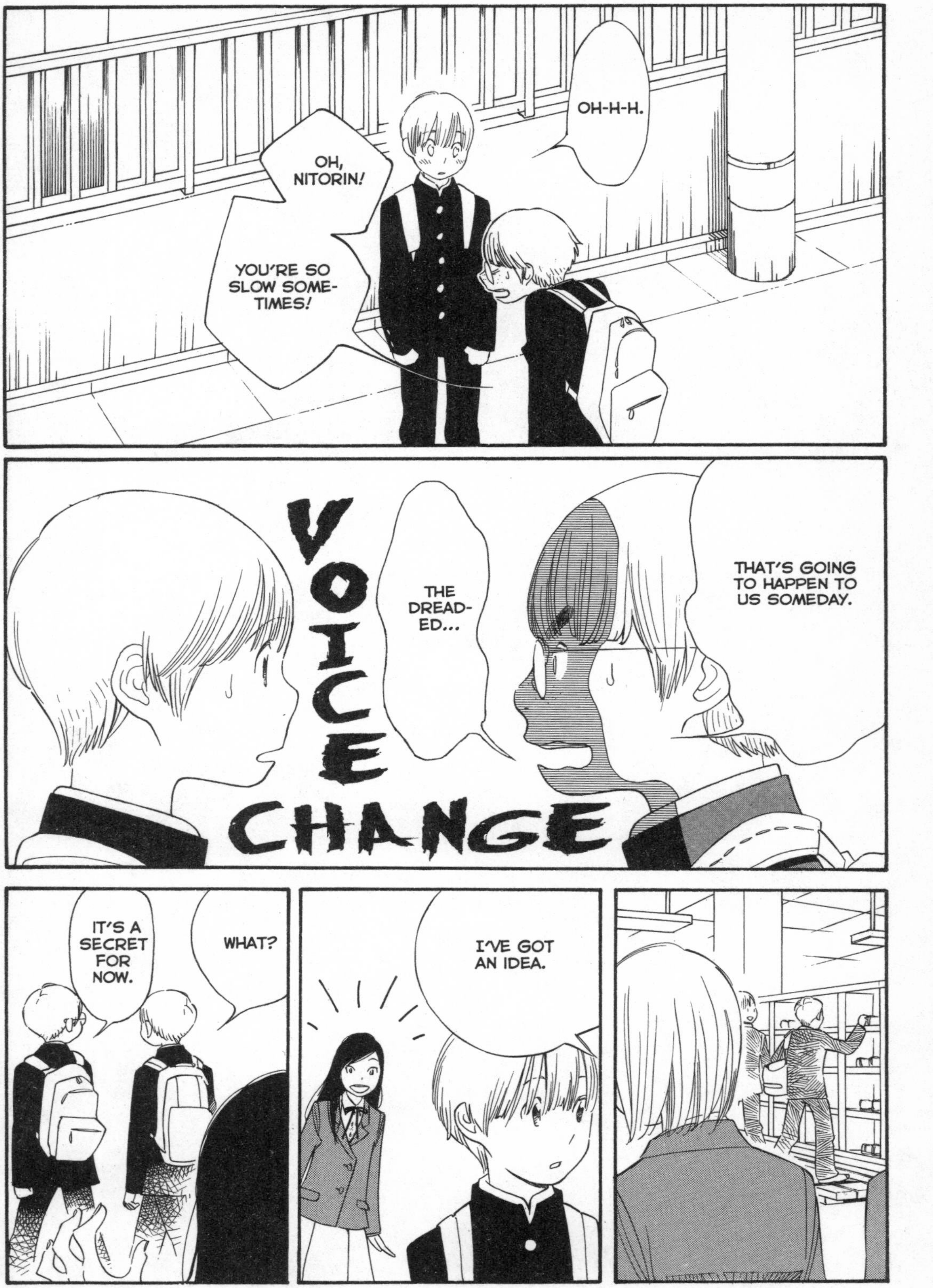
OH-H-H.
OH, NITORIN!
YOU'RE SO SLOW SOME-TIMES!
THAT'S GOING TO HAPPEN TO US SOMEDAY.
THE DREADED...
VOICE CHANGE
I'VE GOT AN IDEA.
WHAT?
IT'S A SECRET FOR NOW.

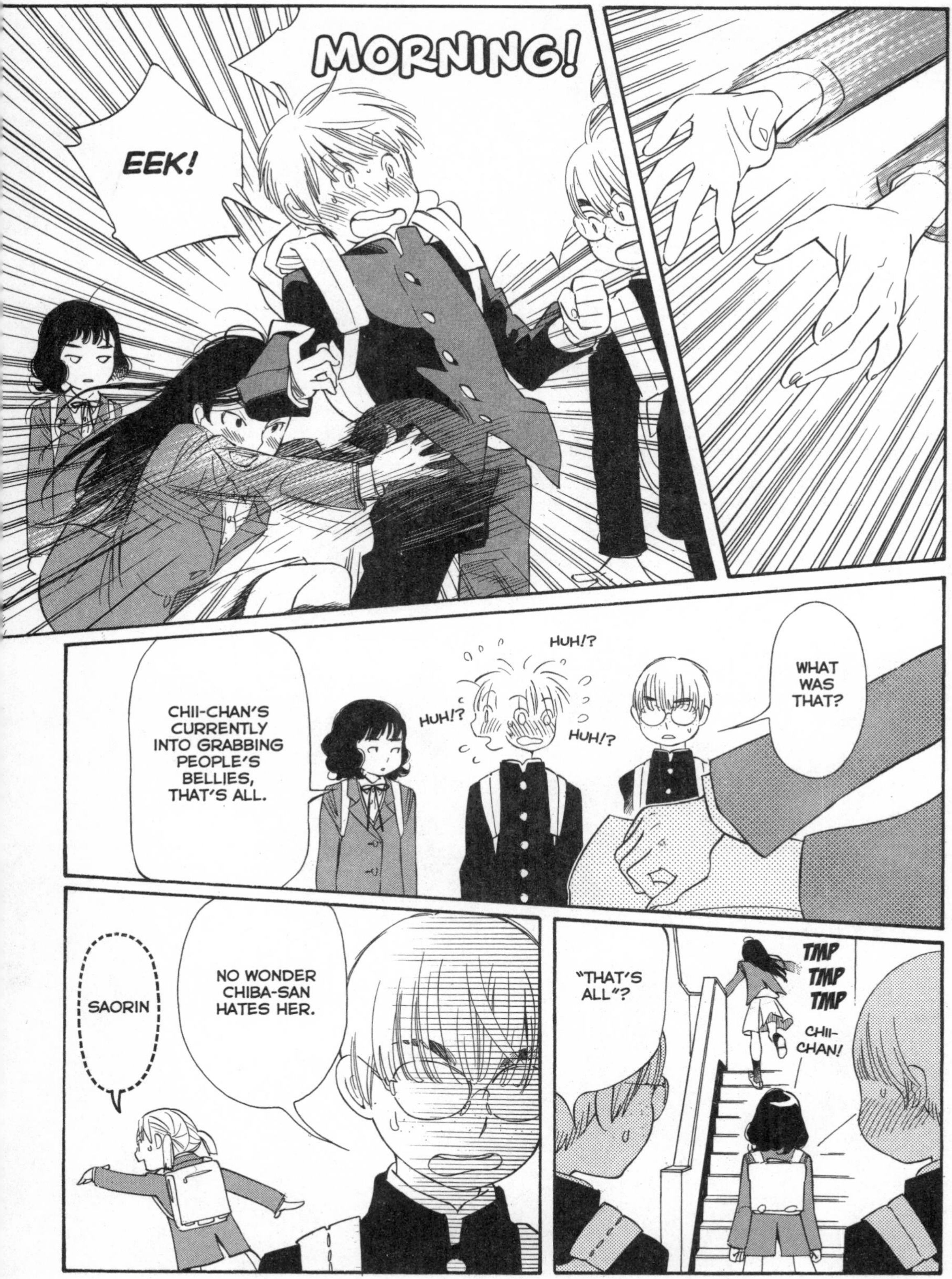
MORNING!
EEK!
WHAT WAS THAT?
HUH!?
HUH!?
HUH!?
CHII-CHAN'S CURRENTLY INTO GRABBING PEOPLE'S BELLIES, THAT'S ALL.
TMP TMP TMP
"THAT'S ALL"?
CHII-CHAN!
NO WONDER CHIBA-SAN HATES HER.
SAORIN

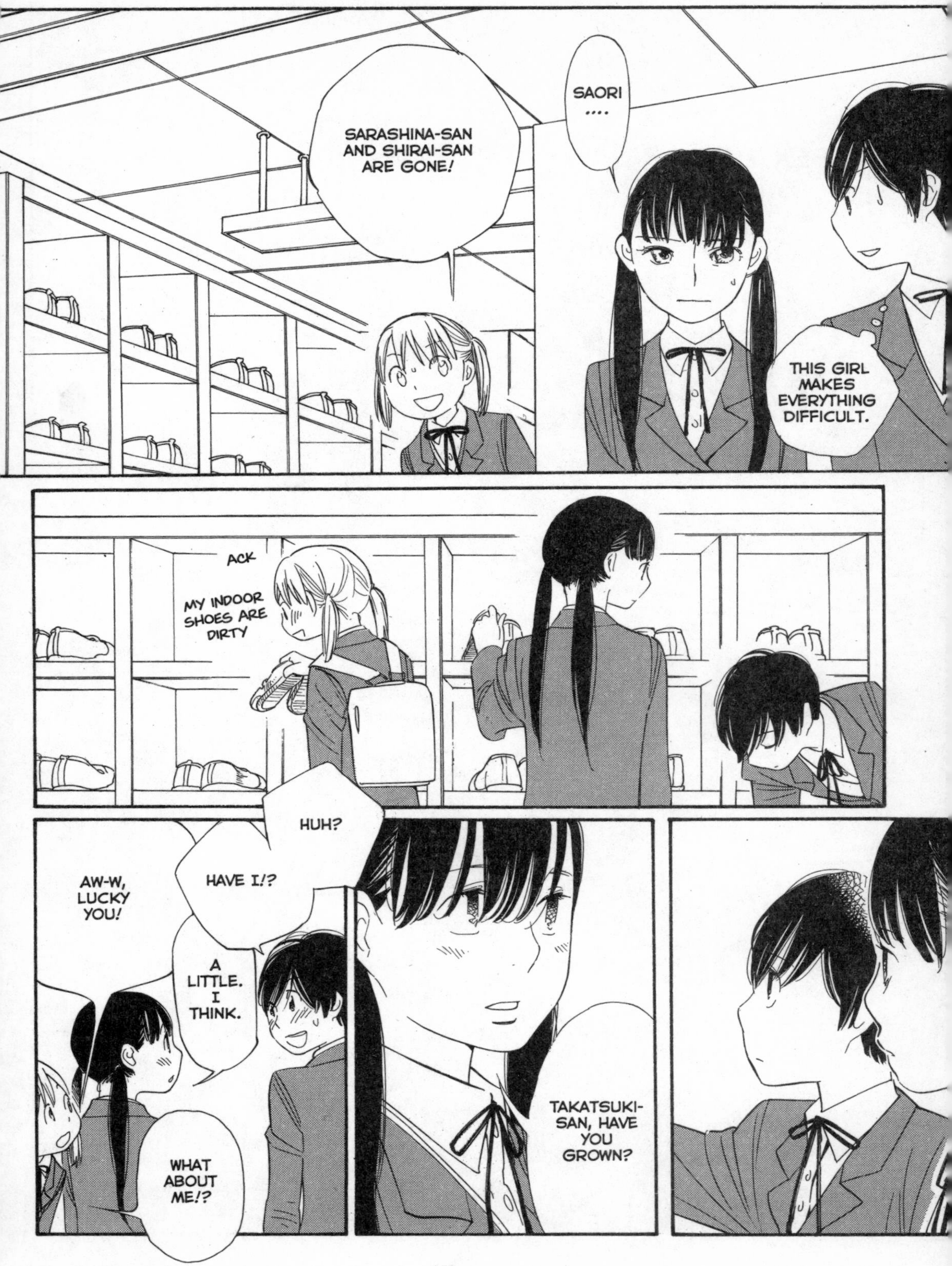
SAORI ....
THIS GIRL MAKES EVERYTHING DIFFICULT.
SARASHINA-SAN AND SHIRAI-SAN ARE GONE!
ACK
MY INDOOR SHOES ARE DIRTY
TAKATSUKI-SAN, HAVE YOU GROWN?
HUH?
HAVE I!?
A LITTLE. I THINK.
AW-W, LUCKY YOU!
WHAT ABOUT ME!?

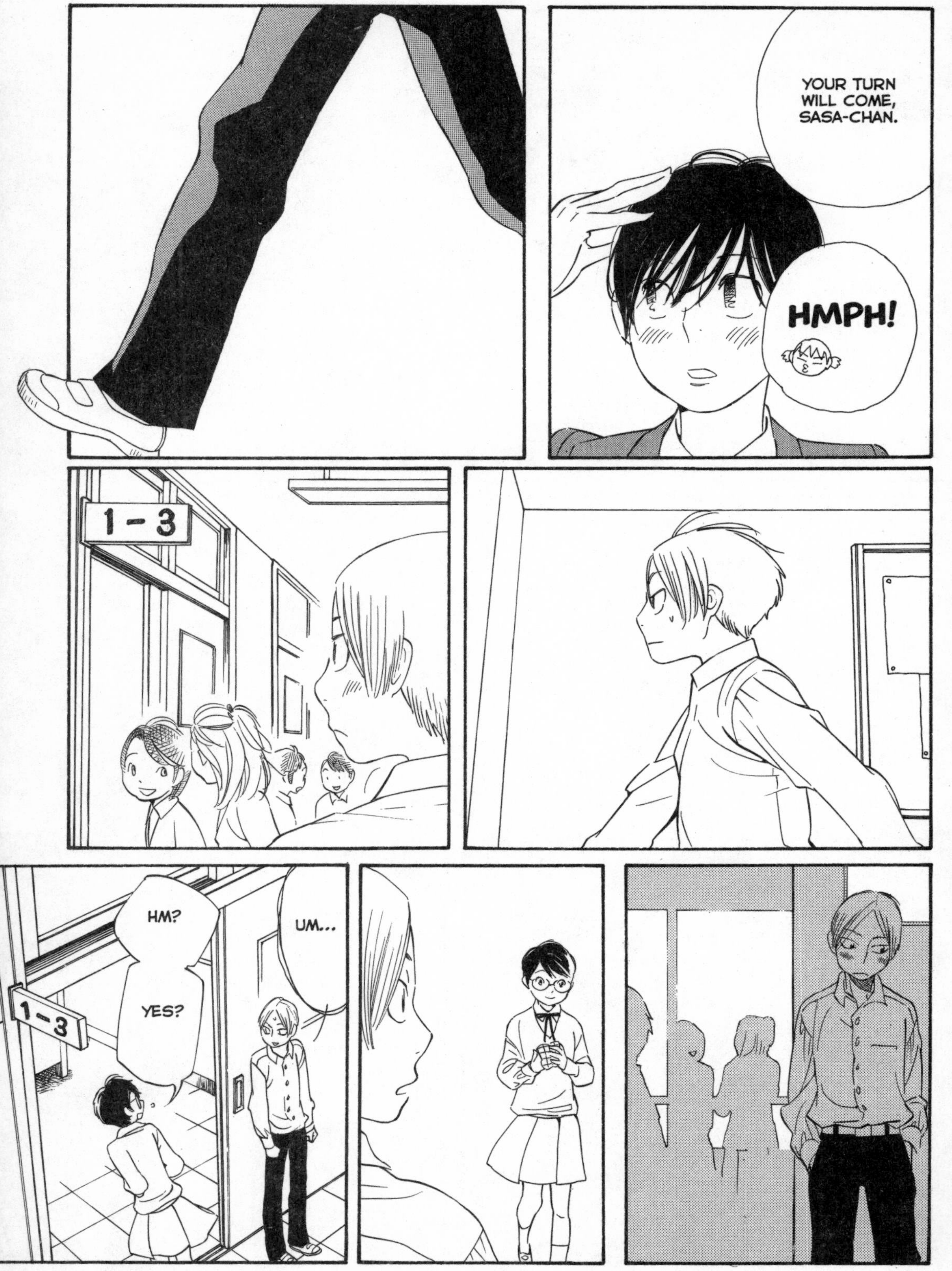
YOUR TURN WILL COME, SASA-CHAN.
HMPH!
1 - 3
UM...
HM?
YES?
1 - 3

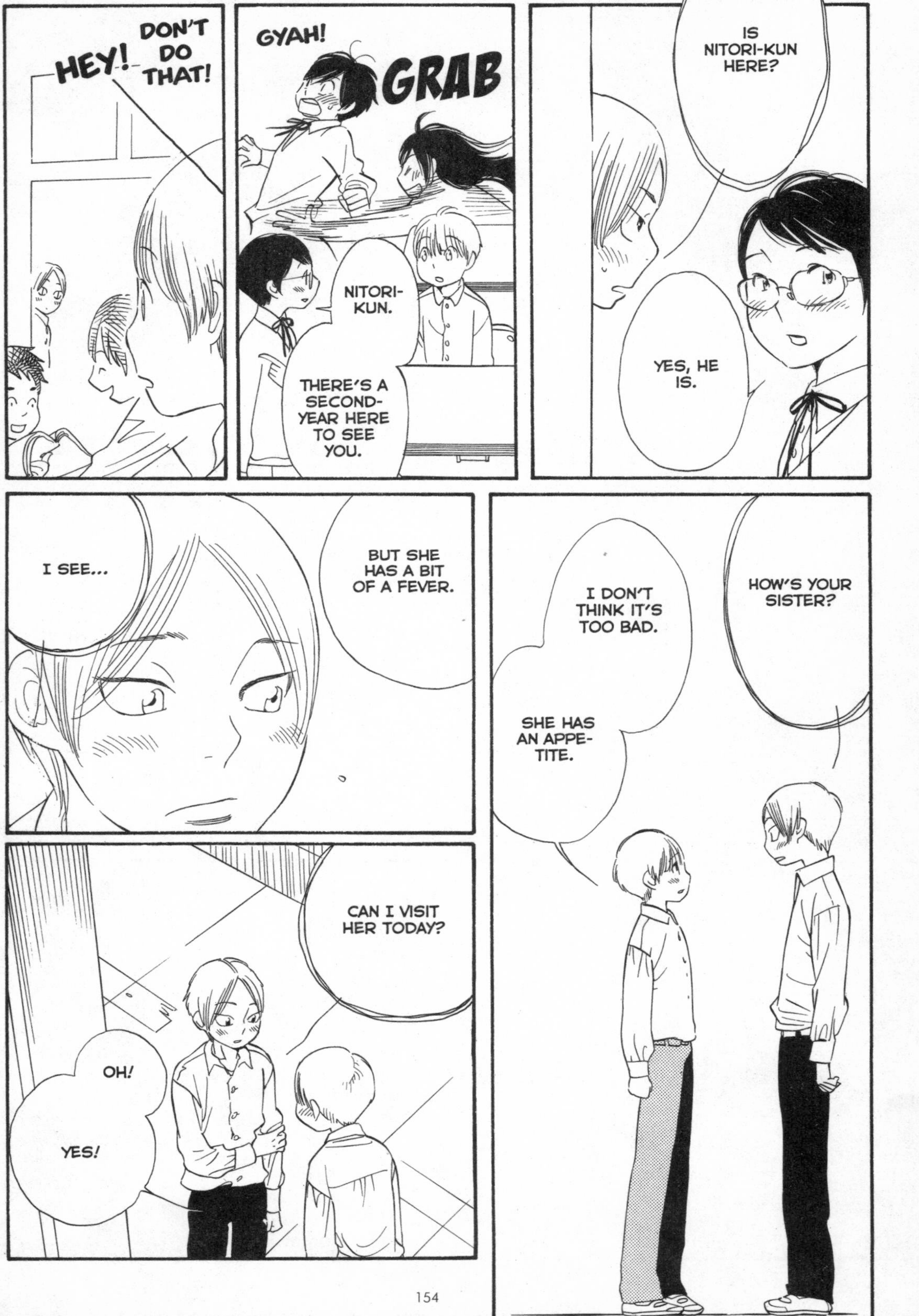
IS NITORI-KUN HERE?
YES, HE IS.
GRAB
GYAH!
NITORI-KUN.
THERE'S A SECOND-YEAR HERE TO SEE YOU.
DON'T DO THAT!
HEY!
HOW'S YOUR SISTER?
I DON'T THINK IT'S TOO BAD.
SHE HAS AN APPETITE.
BUT SHE HAS A BIT OF A FEVER.
I SEE...
CAN I VISIT HER TODAY?
OH!
YES!

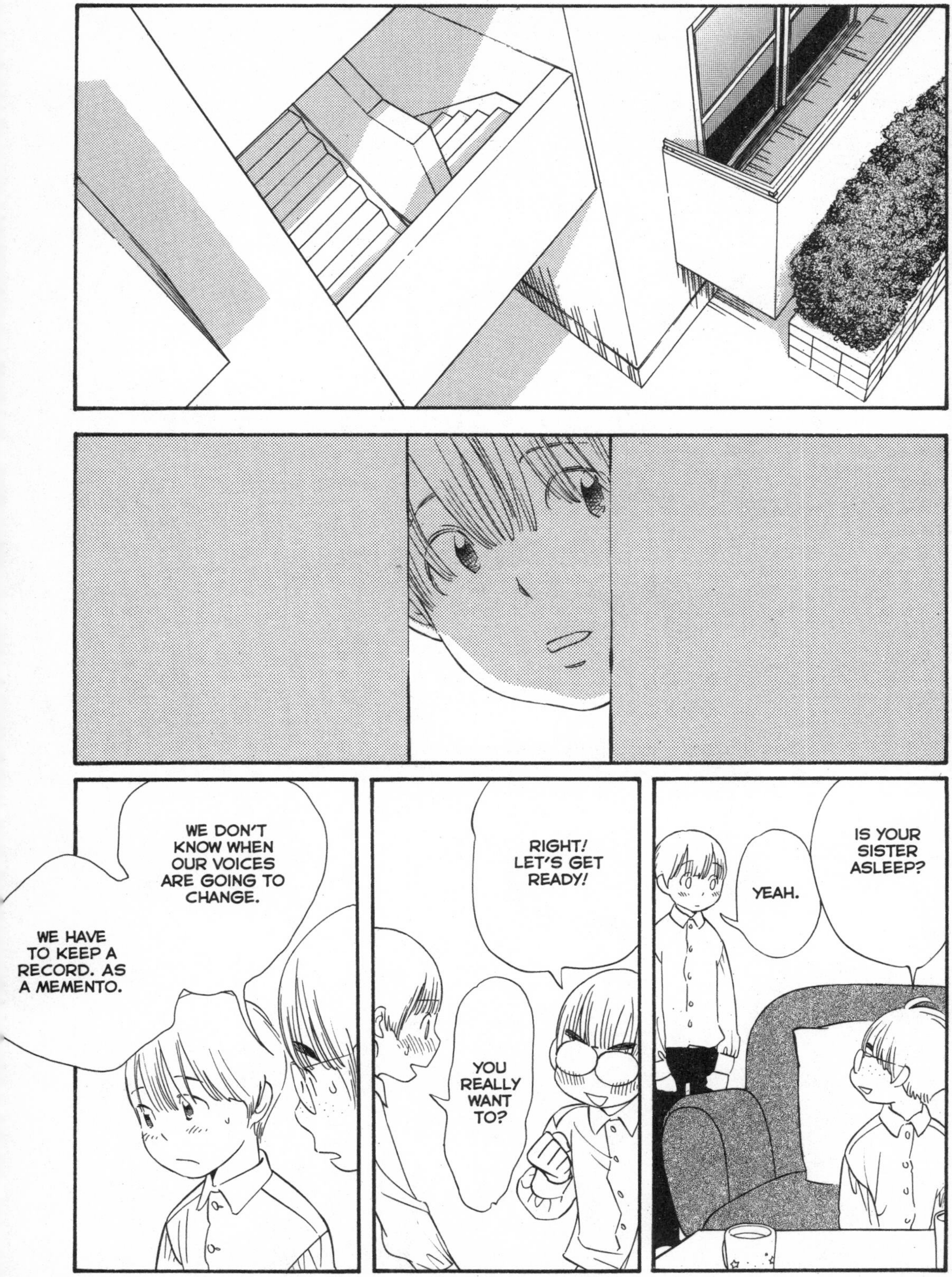
IS YOUR SISTER ASLEEP?
YEAH.
RIGHT! LET'S GET READY!
YOU REALLY WANT TO?
WE DON'T KNOW WHEN OUR VOICES ARE GOING TO CHANGE.
WE HAVE TO KEEP A RECORD. AS A MEMENTO.

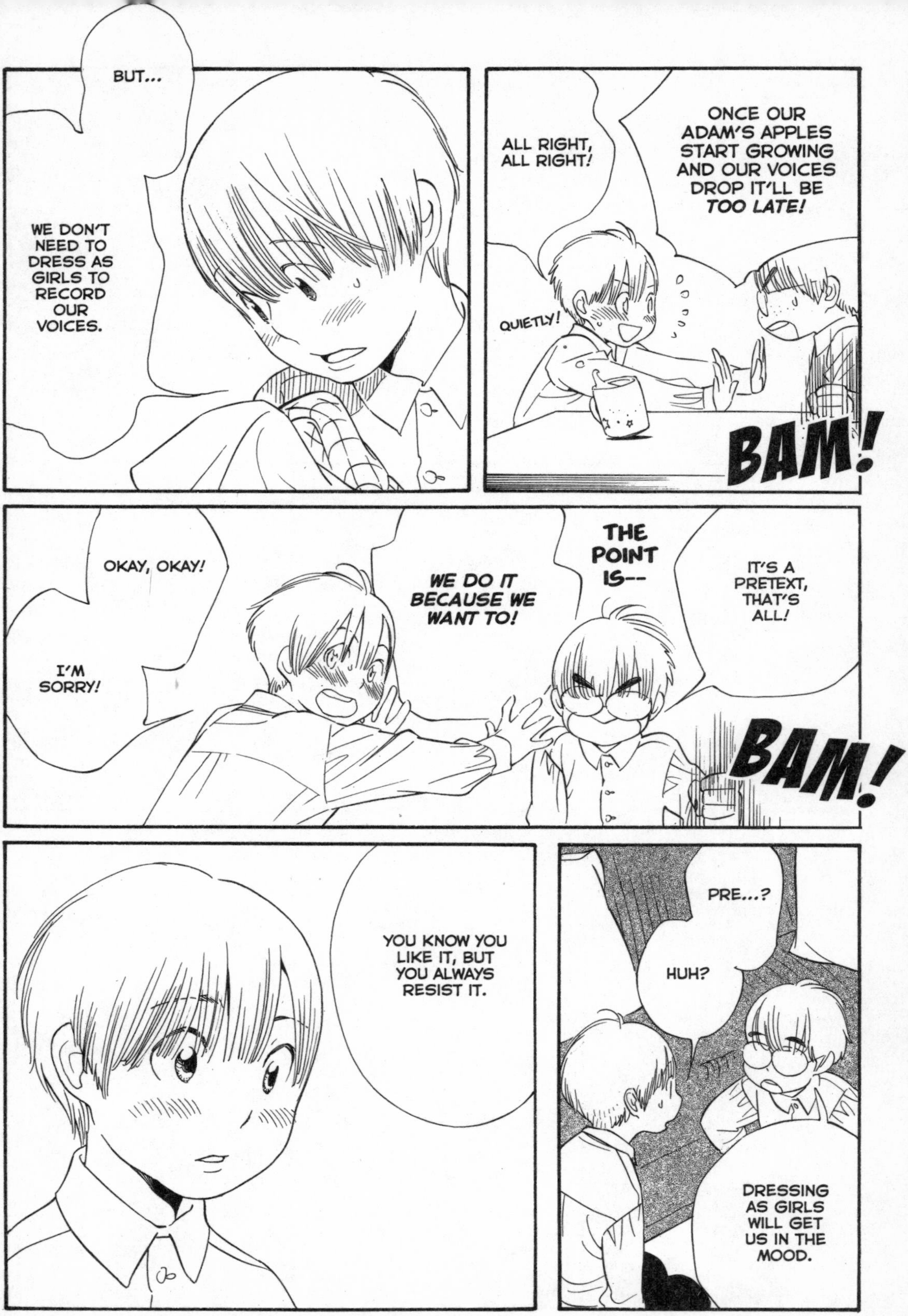
BUT...
WE DON'T NEED TO DRESS AS GIRLS TO RECORD OUR VOICES.
ALL RIGHT, ALL RIGHT!
QUIETLY!
ONCE OUR ADAM'S APPLES START GROWING AND OUR VOICES DROP IT'LL BE *TOO LATE!*
BAM!
OKAY, OKAY!
I'M SORRY!
WE DO IT BECAUSE WE WANT TO!
THE POINT IS--
IT'S A PRETEXT, THAT'S ALL!
BAM!
YOU KNOW YOU LIKE IT, BUT YOU ALWAYS RESIST IT.
PRE...?
HUH?
DRESSING AS GIRLS WILL GET US IN THE MOOD.

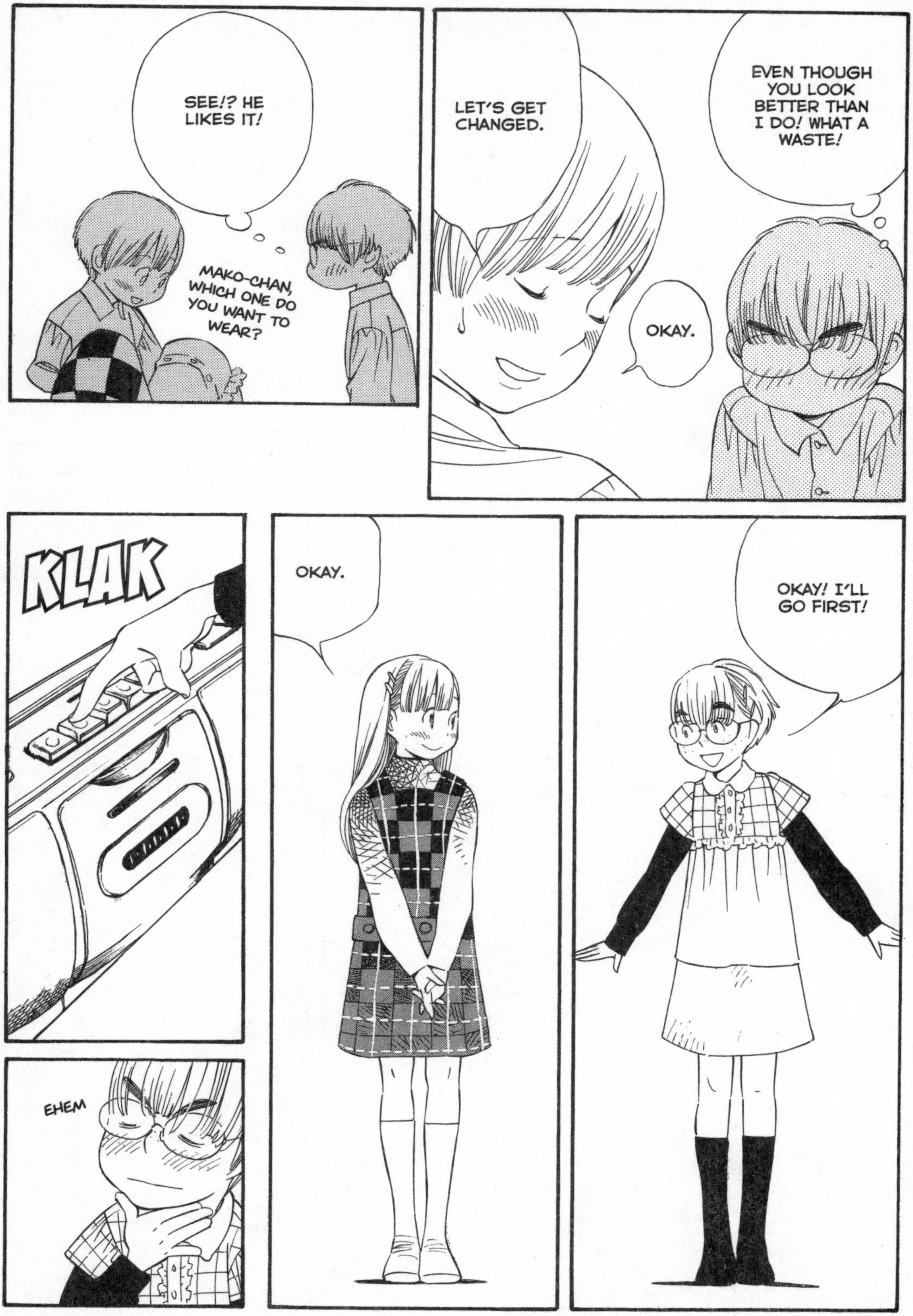
EVEN THOUGH YOU LOOK BETTER THAN I DO! WHAT A WASTE!
LET'S GET CHANGED.
OKAY.
SEE!? HE LIKES IT!
MAKO-CHAN, WHICH ONE DO YOU WANT TO WEAR?
OKAY! I'LL GO FIRST!
OKAY.
KLAK
EHEM

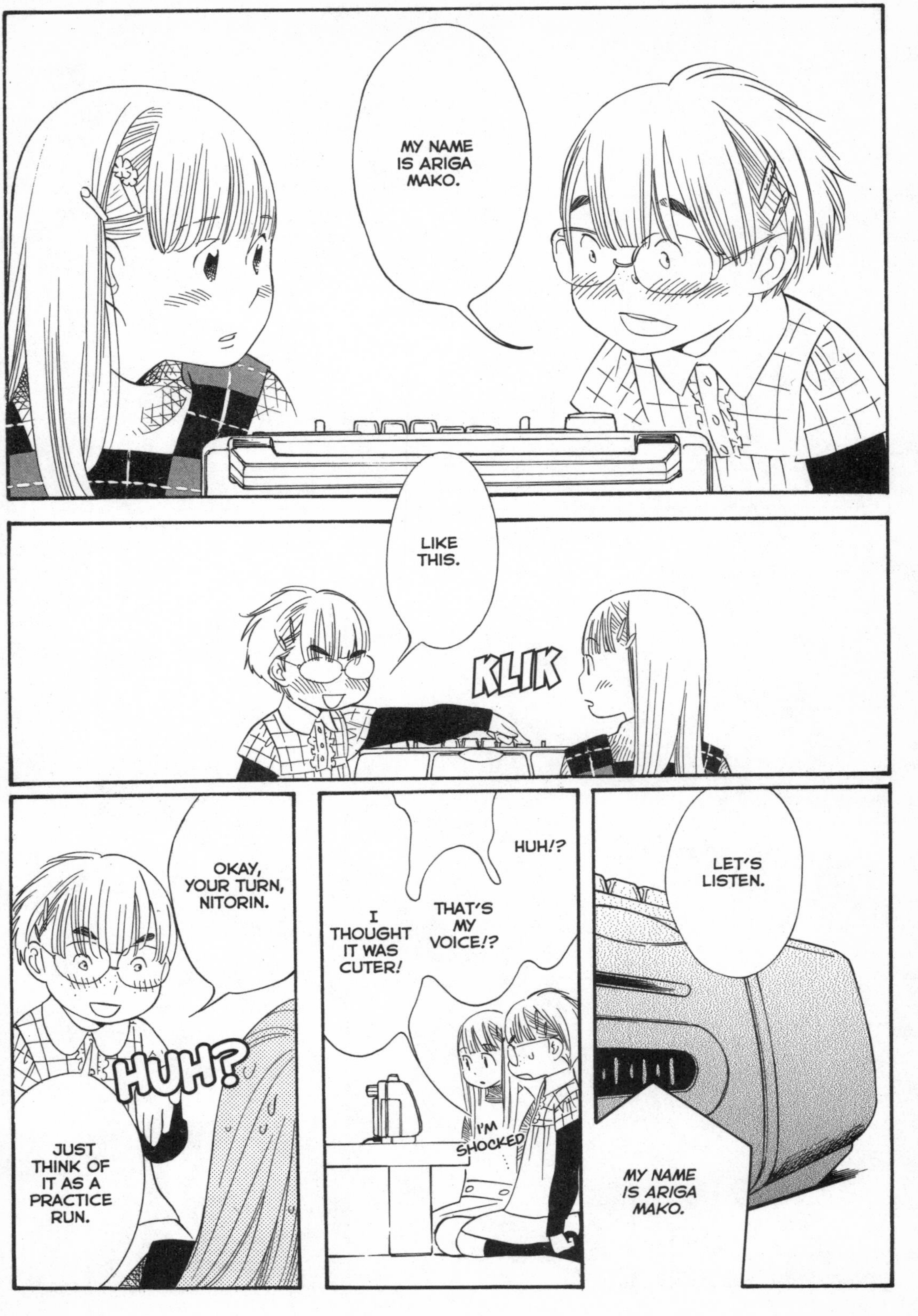
MY NAME IS ARIGA MAKO.
LIKE THIS.
KLIK
LET'S LISTEN.
MY NAME IS ARIGA MAKO.
HUH!?
THAT'S MY VOICE!?
I THOUGHT IT WAS CUTER!
I'M SHOCKED
OKAY, YOUR TURN, NITORIN.
HUH?
JUST THINK OF IT AS A PRACTICE RUN.

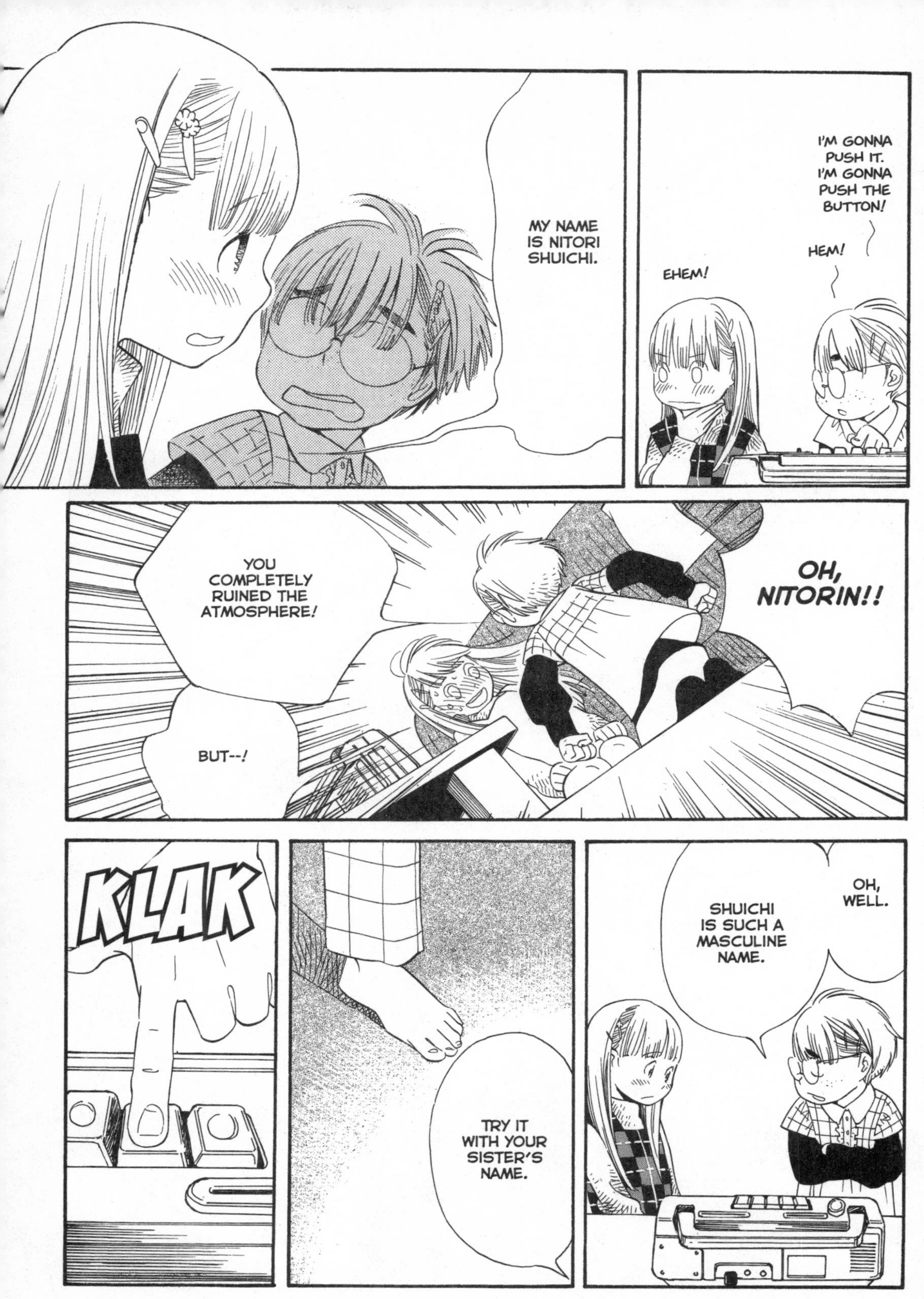
I'M GONNA PUSH IT. I'M GONNA PUSH THE BUTTON!
HEM!
EHEM!
MY NAME IS NITORI SHUICHI.
OH, NITORIN!!
YOU COMPLETELY RUINED THE ATMOSPHERE!
BUT--!
OH, WELL.
SHUICHI IS SUCH A MASCULINE NAME.
TRY IT WITH YOUR SISTER'S NAME.
KLAK

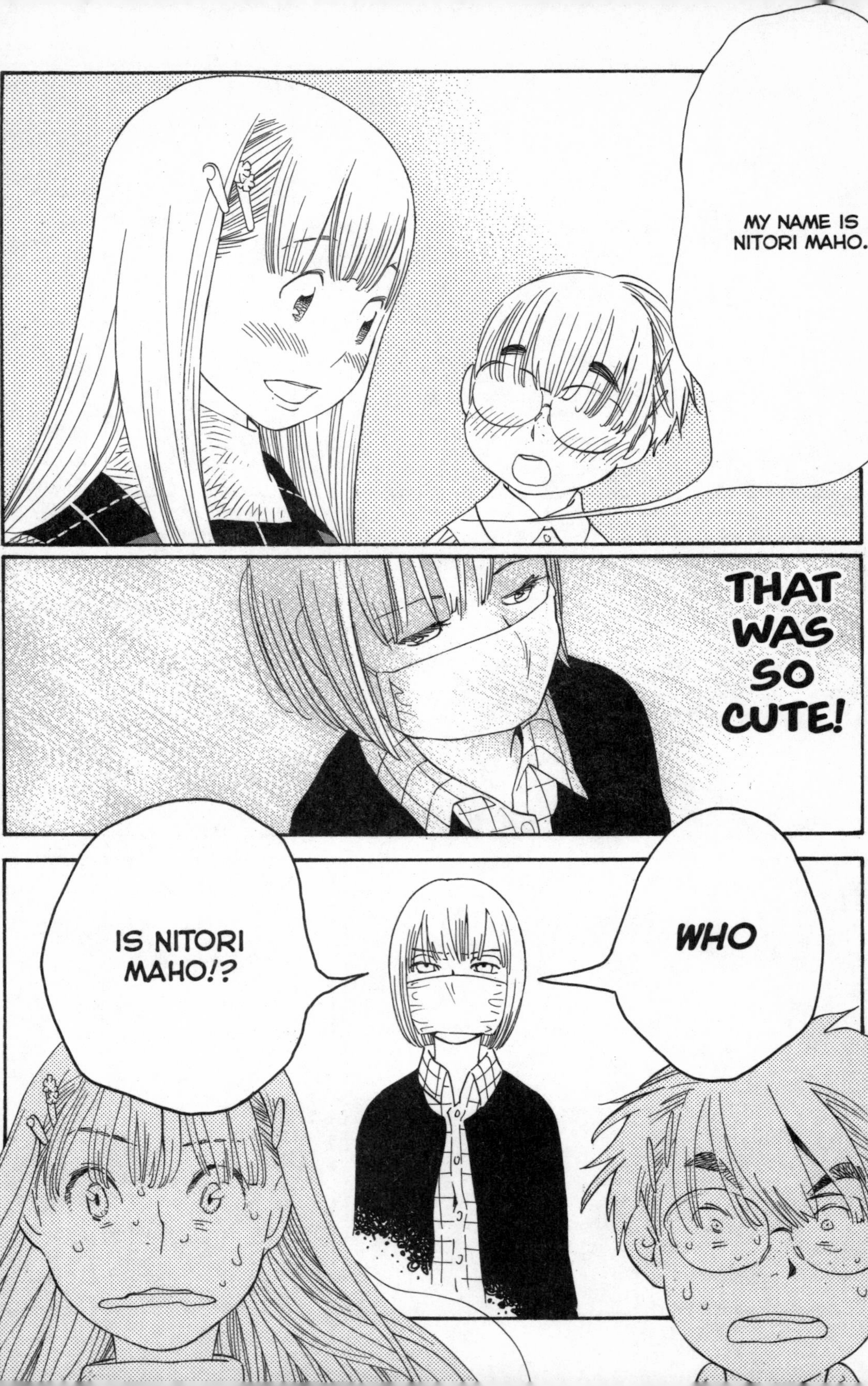
MY NAME IS NITORI MAHO.
THAT WAS SO CUTE!
WHO
IS NITORI MAHO!?

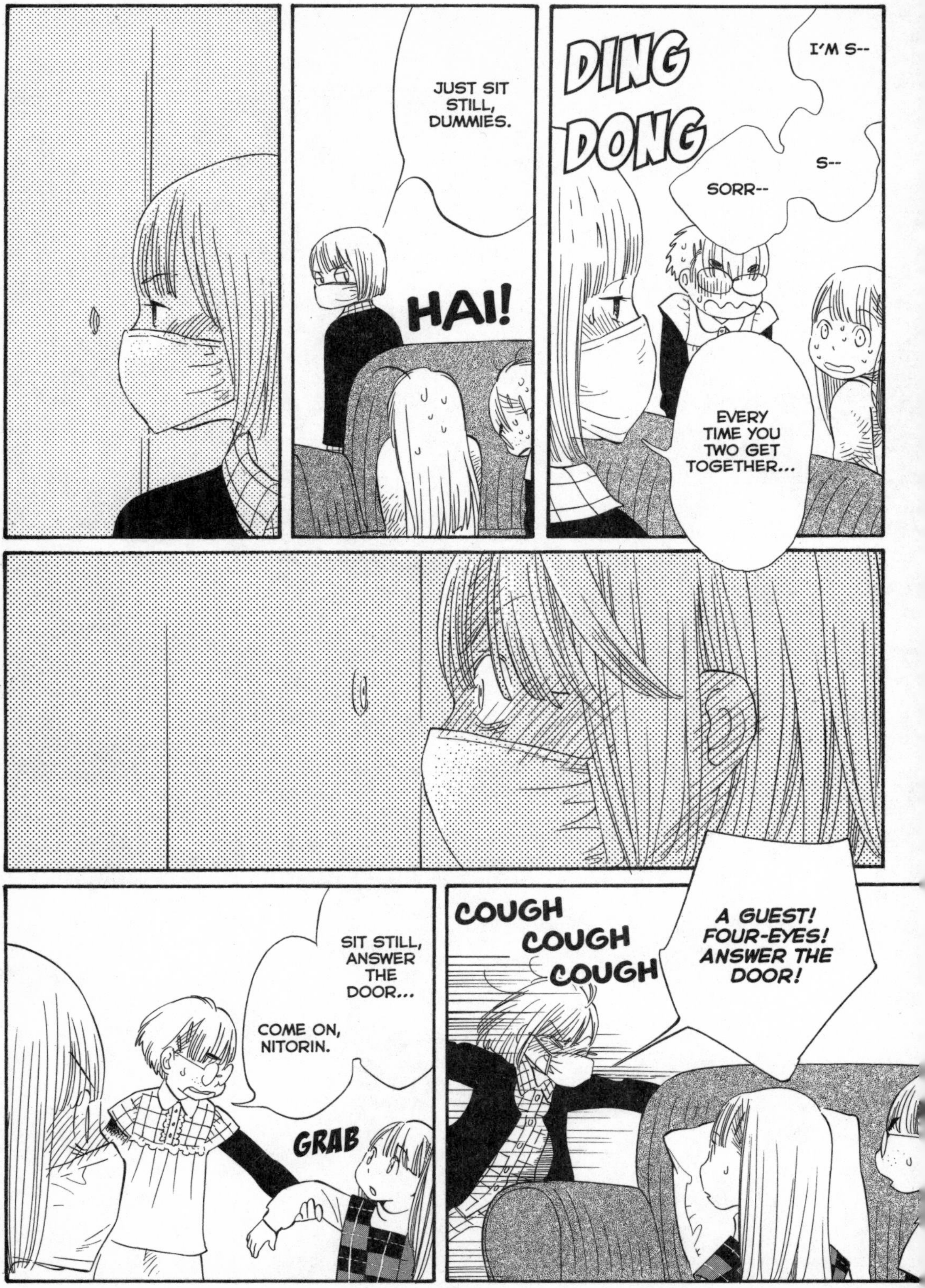
I'M S--
DING DONG
S--
SORR--
EVERY TIME YOU TWO GET TOGETHER...
JUST SIT STILL, DUMMIES.
HAI!
A GUEST! FOUR-EYES! ANSWER THE DOOR!
COUGH COUGH COUGH
SIT STILL, ANSWER THE DOOR...
COME ON, NITORIN.
GRAB

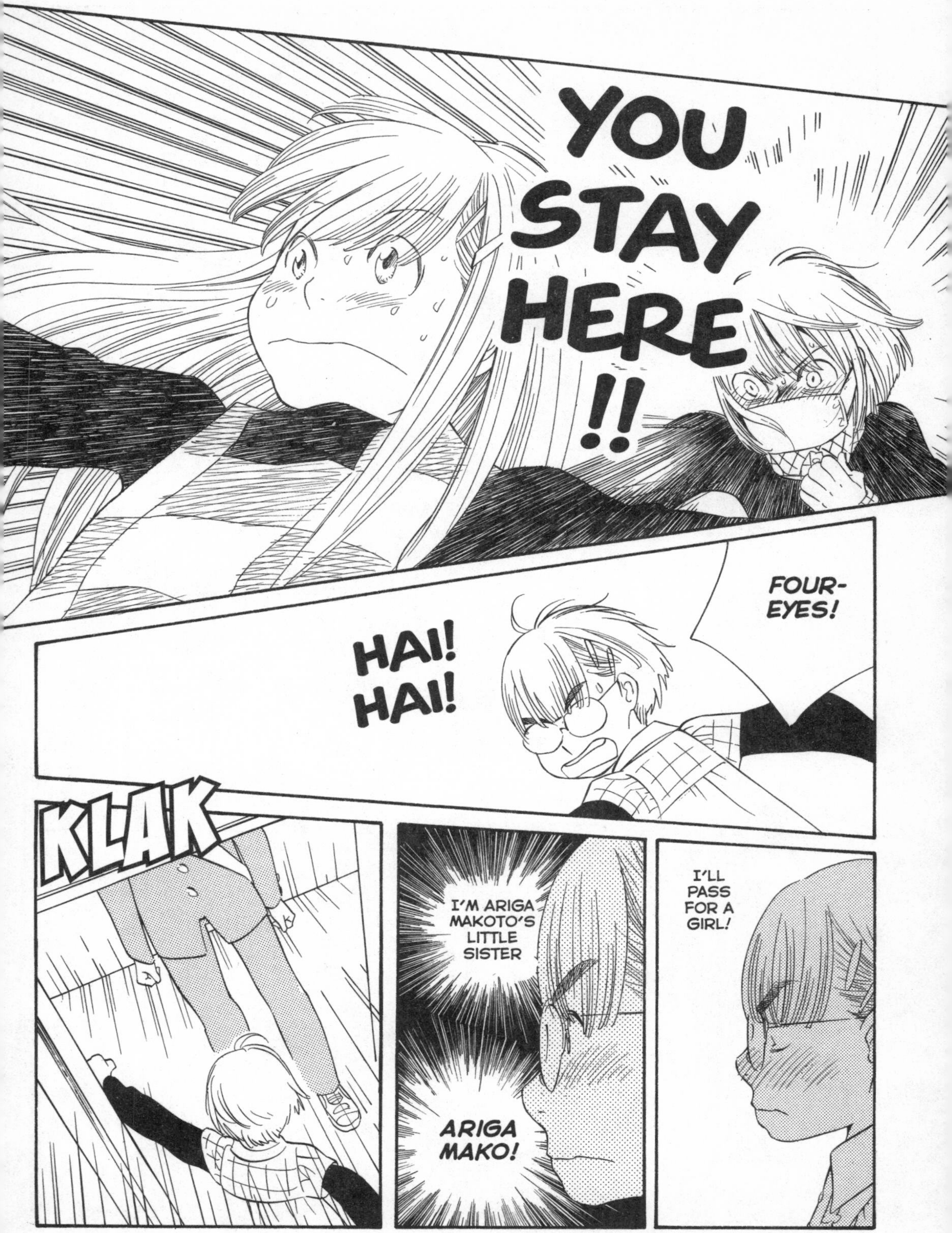
YOU STAY HERE!!
FOUR-EYES!
HAI! HAI!
I'LL PASS FOR A GIRL!
I'M ARIGA MAKOTO'S LITTLE SISTER
ARIGA MAKO!
KLAK

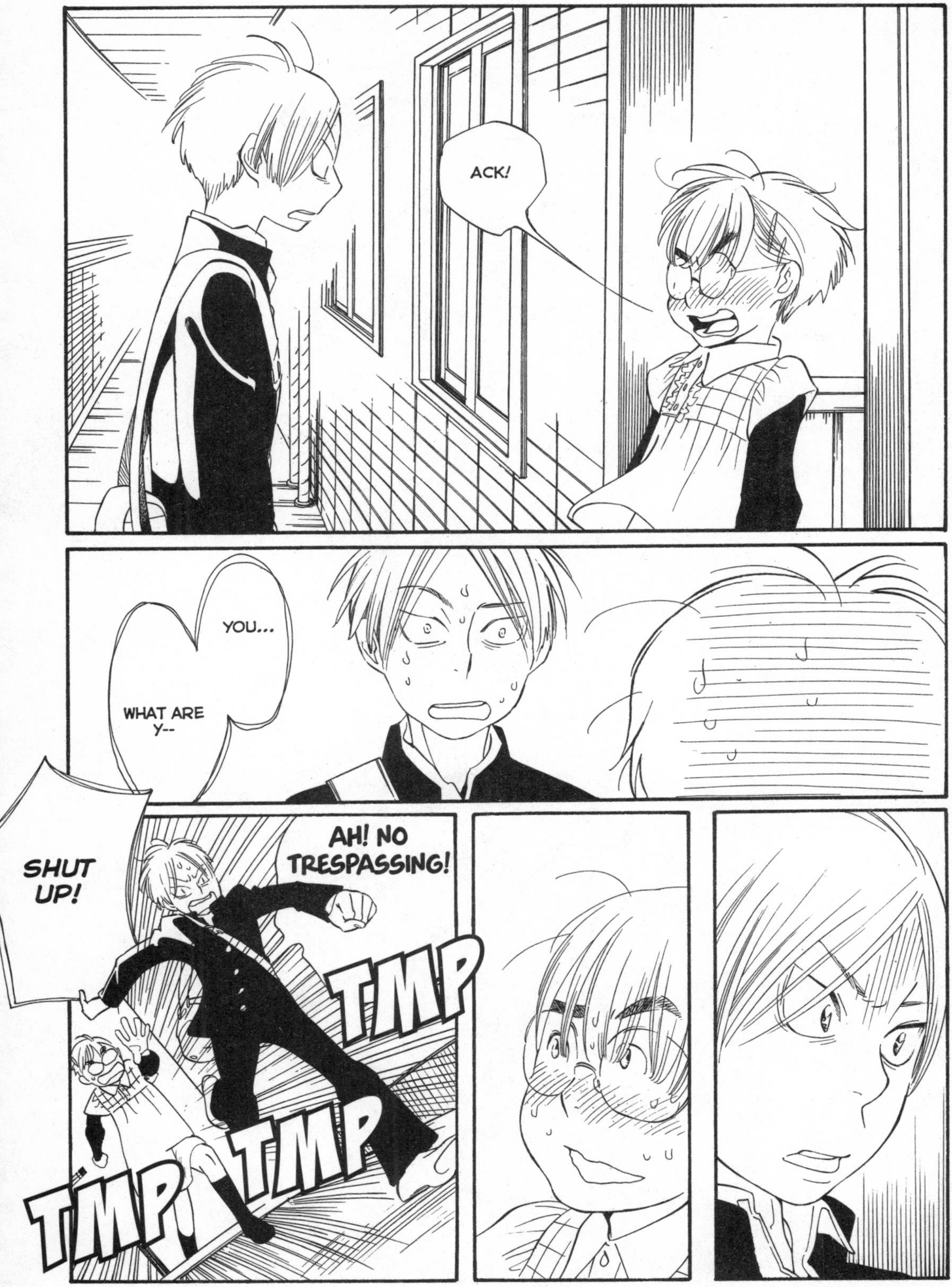
ACK!
YOU...
WHAT ARE Y--
AH! NO TRESPASSING!
SHUT UP!
TMP
TMP
TMP!

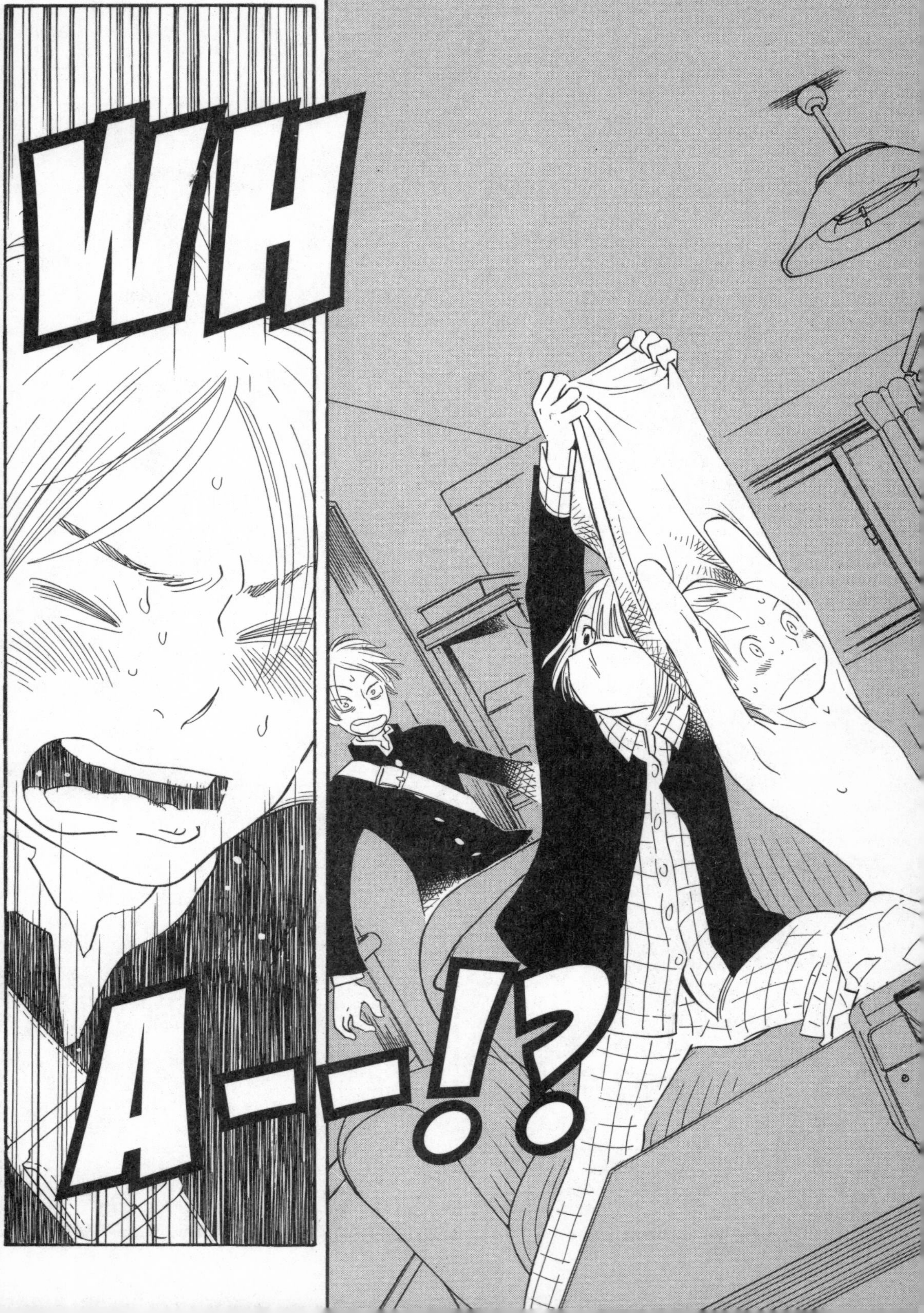
WH
A--!?

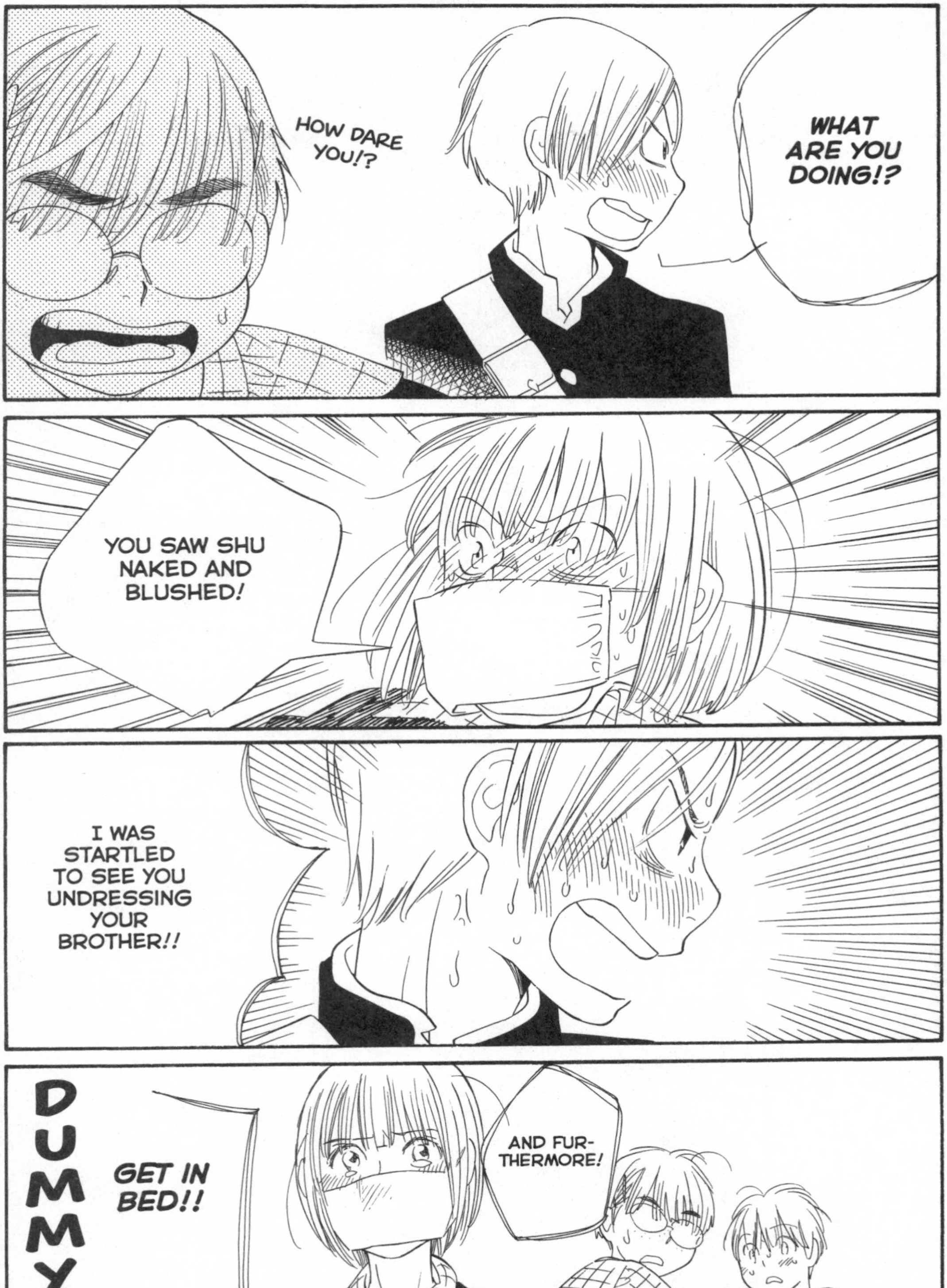
WHAT ARE YOU DOING!?
HOW DARE YOU!?
YOU SAW SHU NAKED AND BLUSHED!
I WAS STARTLED TO SEE YOU UNDRESSING YOUR BROTHER!!
AND FUR-THERMORE!
GET IN BED!!
DUMMY!

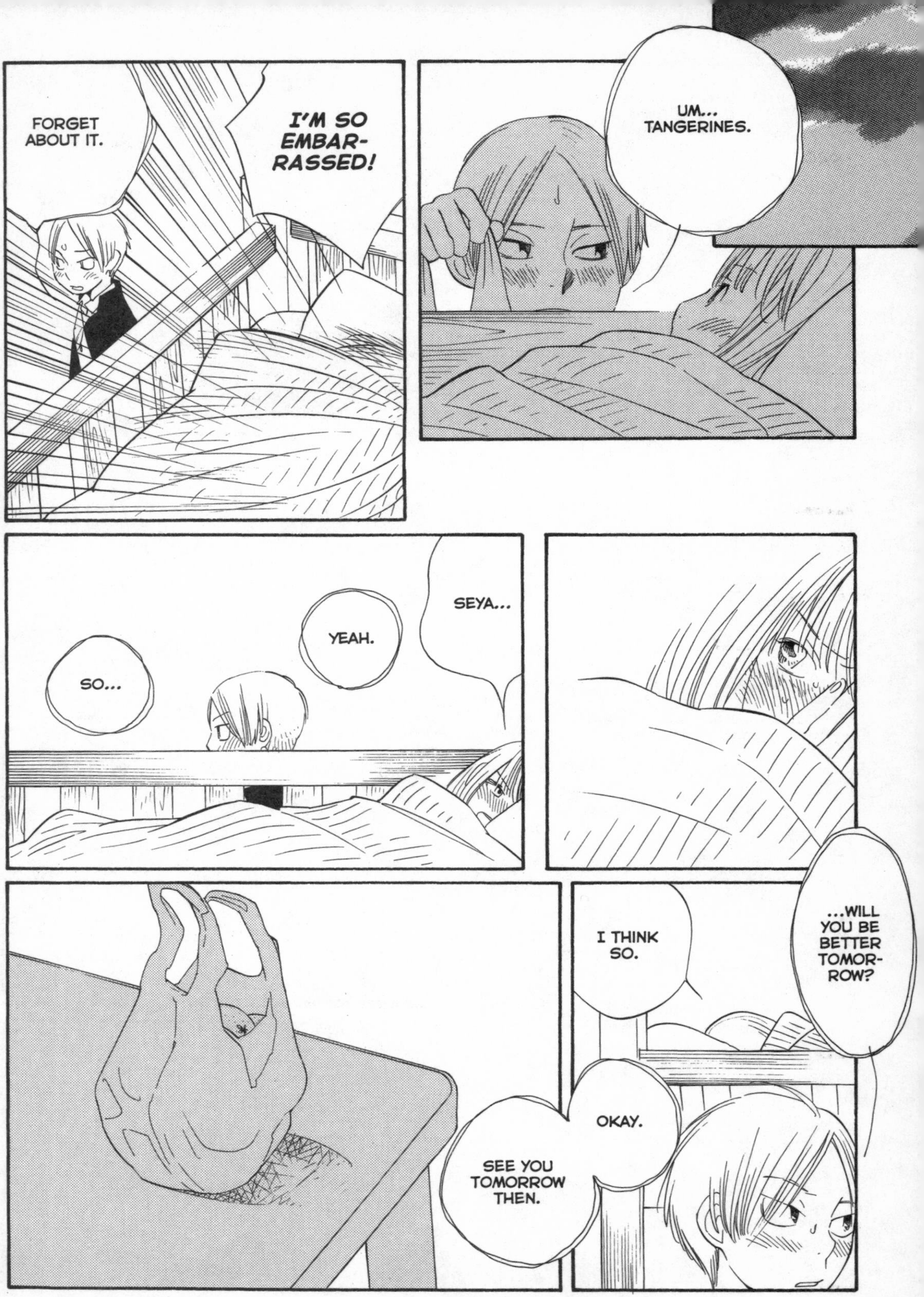
UM... TANGERINES.
I'M SO EMBARRASSED!
FORGET ABOUT IT.
SEYA...
YEAH.
SO...
...WILL YOU BE BETTER TOMORROW?
I THINK SO.
OKAY.
SEE YOU TOMORROW THEN.

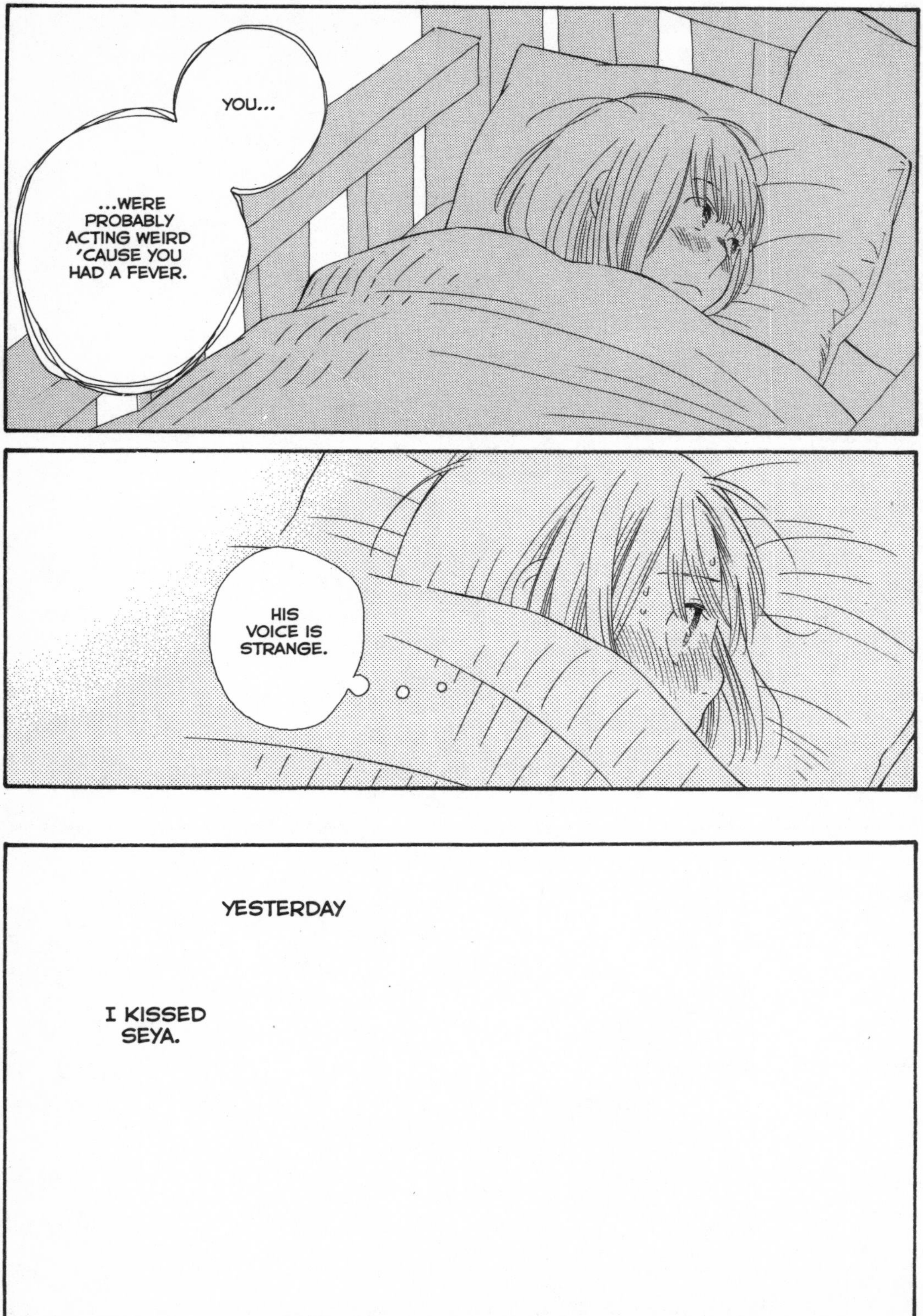
YOU...
...WERE PROBABLY ACTING WEIRD 'CAUSE YOU HAD A FEVER.
HIS VOICE IS STRANGE.
YESTERDAY
I KISSED SEYA.

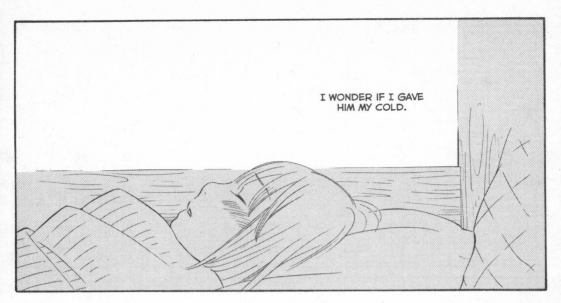

I WONDER IF I GAVE
HIM MY COLD.

40

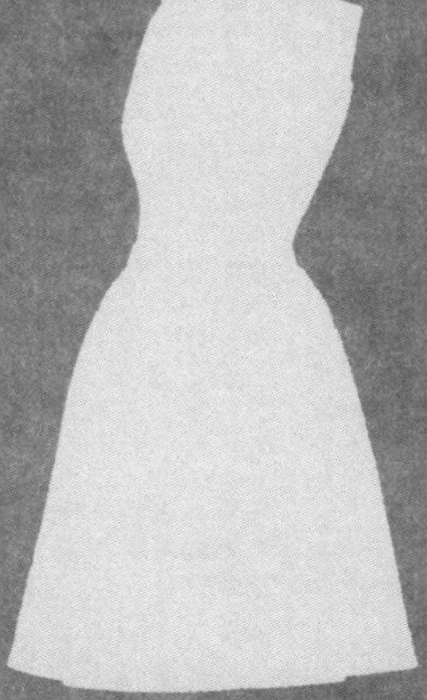

The Door to Summer

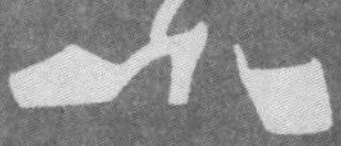

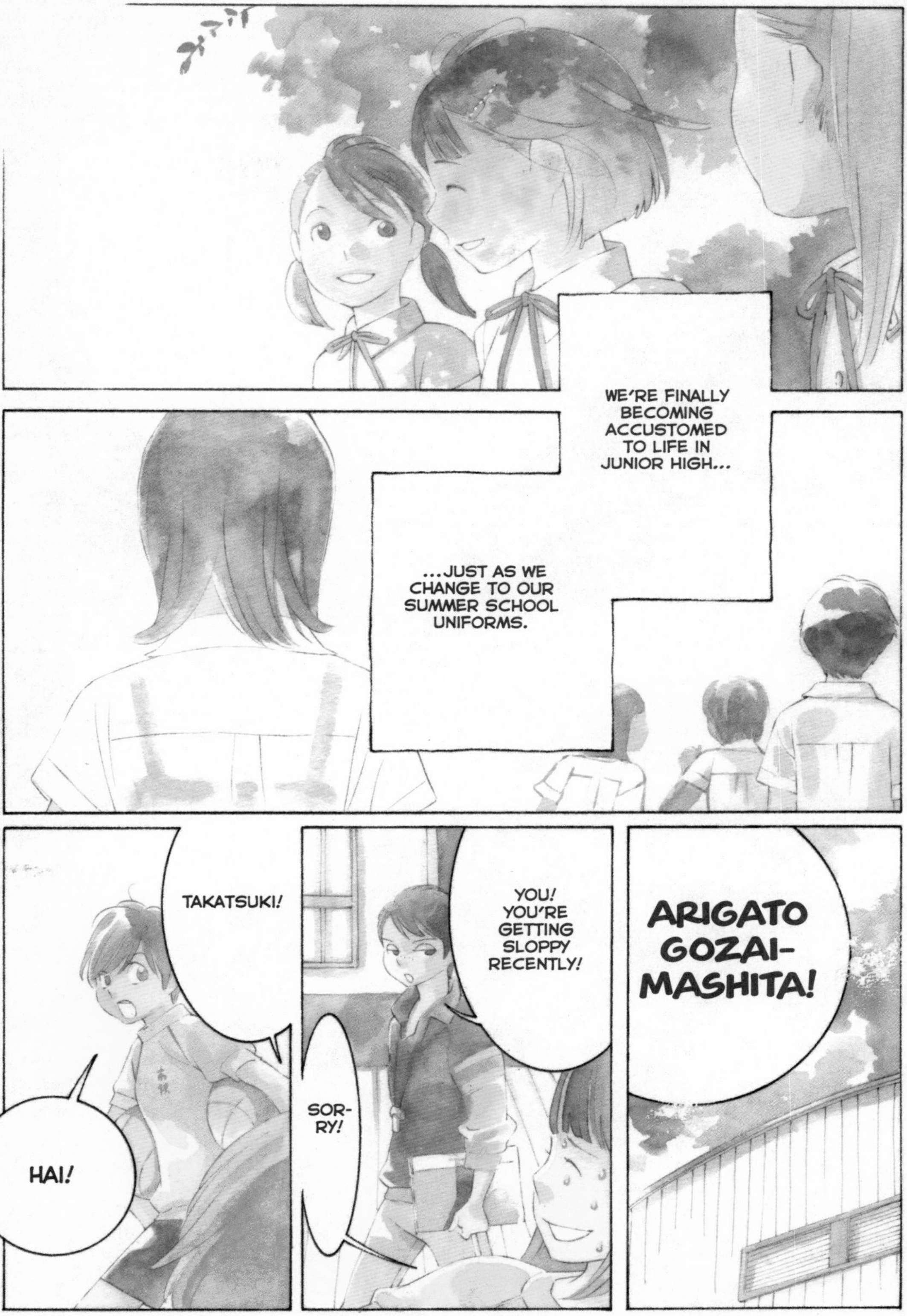
WE'RE FINALLY BECOMING ACCUSTOMED TO LIFE IN JUNIOR HIGH...
...JUST AS WE CHANGE TO OUR SUMMER SCHOOL UNIFORMS.
ARIGATO GOZAI-MASHITA!
YOU! YOU'RE GETTING SLOPPY RECENTLY!
SOR-RY!
TAKATSUKI!
HAI!

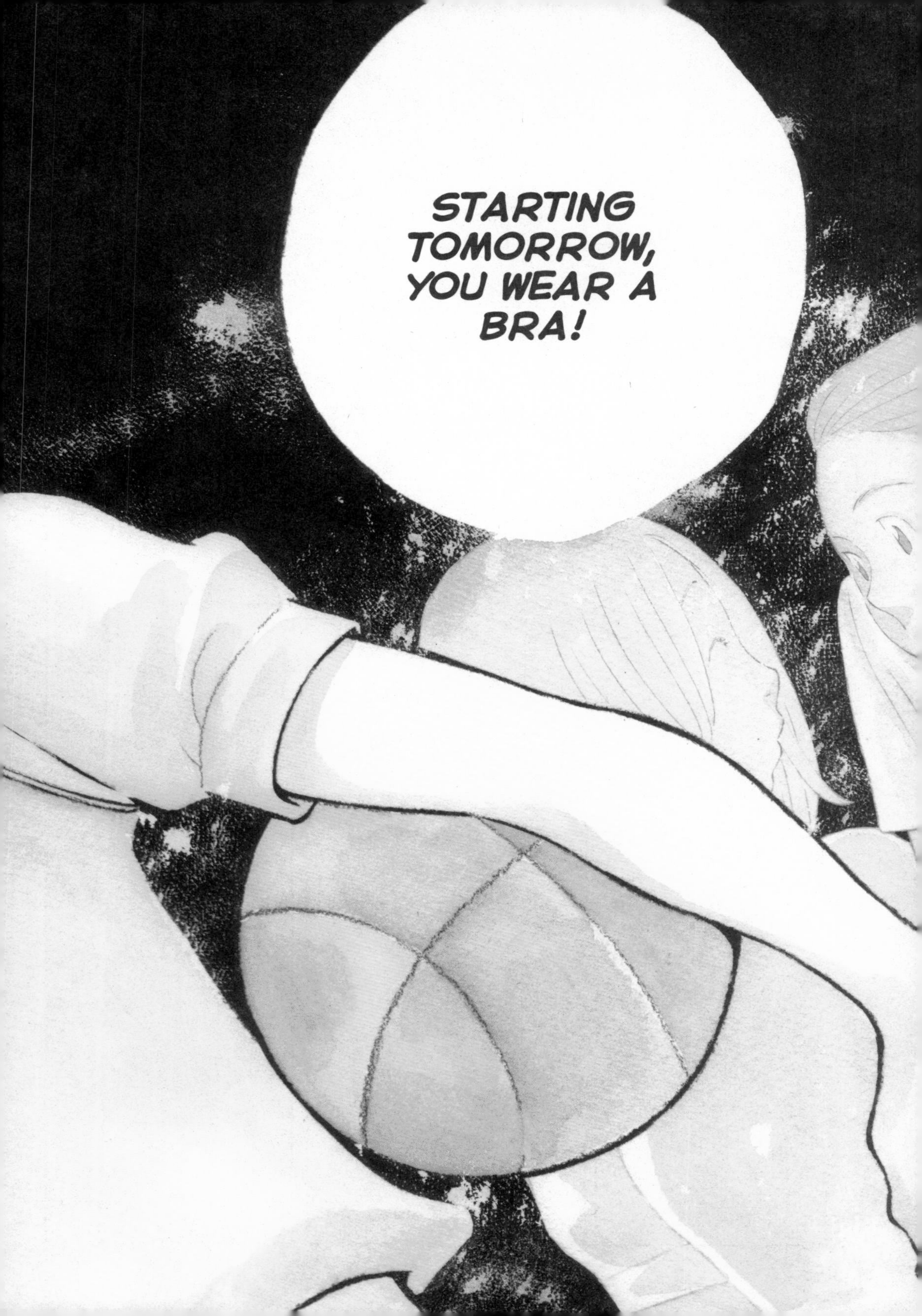
STARTING TOMORROW, YOU WEAR A BRA!

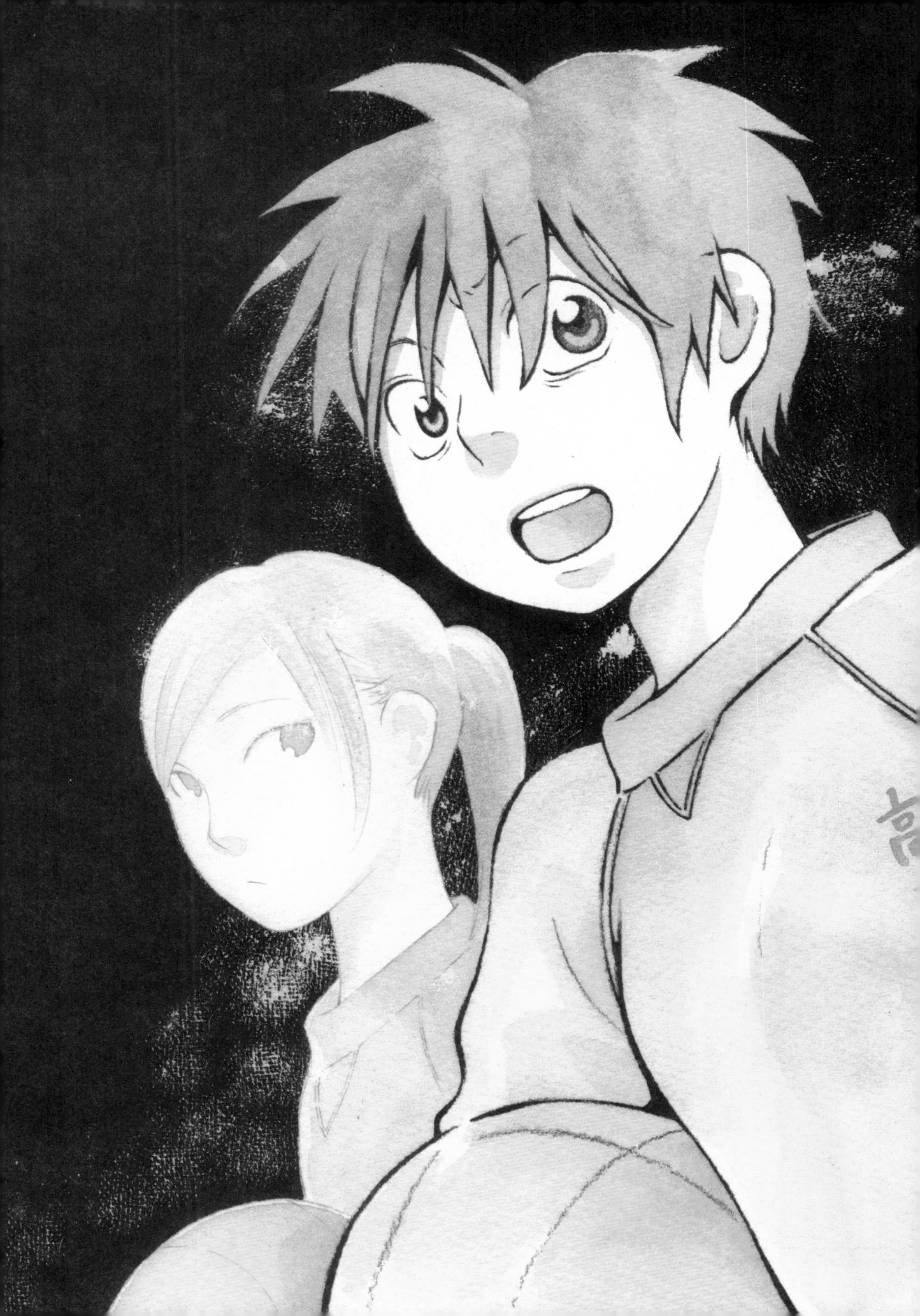

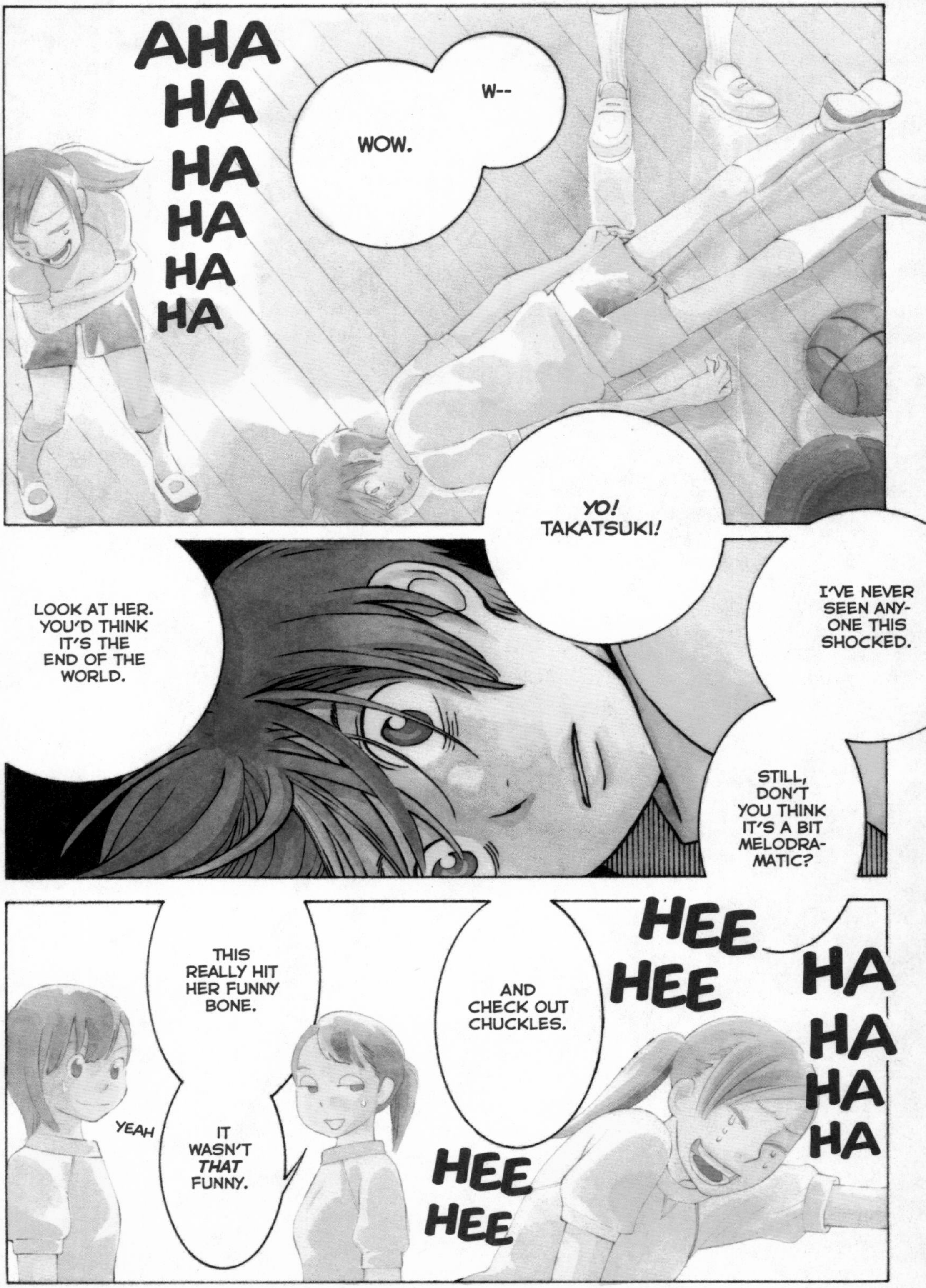
W--
WOW.
AHA HA HA HA HA HA
YO! TAKATSUKI!
I'VE NEVER SEEN ANY-ONE THIS SHOCKED.
LOOK AT HER. YOU'D THINK IT'S THE END OF THE WORLD.
STILL, DON'T YOU THINK IT'S A BIT MELODRA-MATIC?
HEE HEE
HA HA HA HA
AND CHECK OUT CHUCKLES.
HEE HEE
THIS REALLY HIT HER FUNNY BONE.
IT WASN'T *THAT* FUNNY.
YEAH

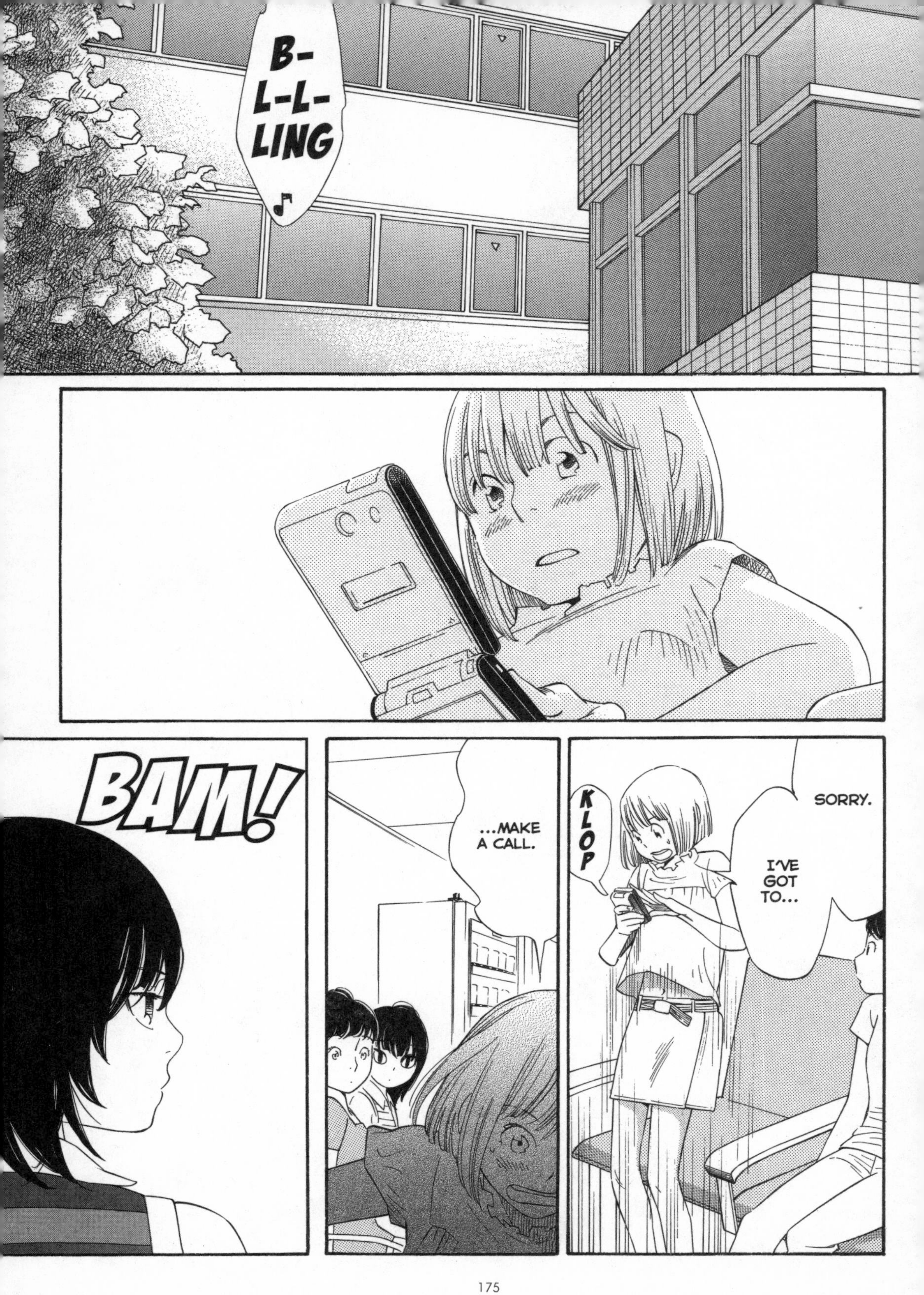
B-L-L-LING ♪
SORRY.
I'VE GOT TO...
KLOP
...MAKE A CALL.
BAM!

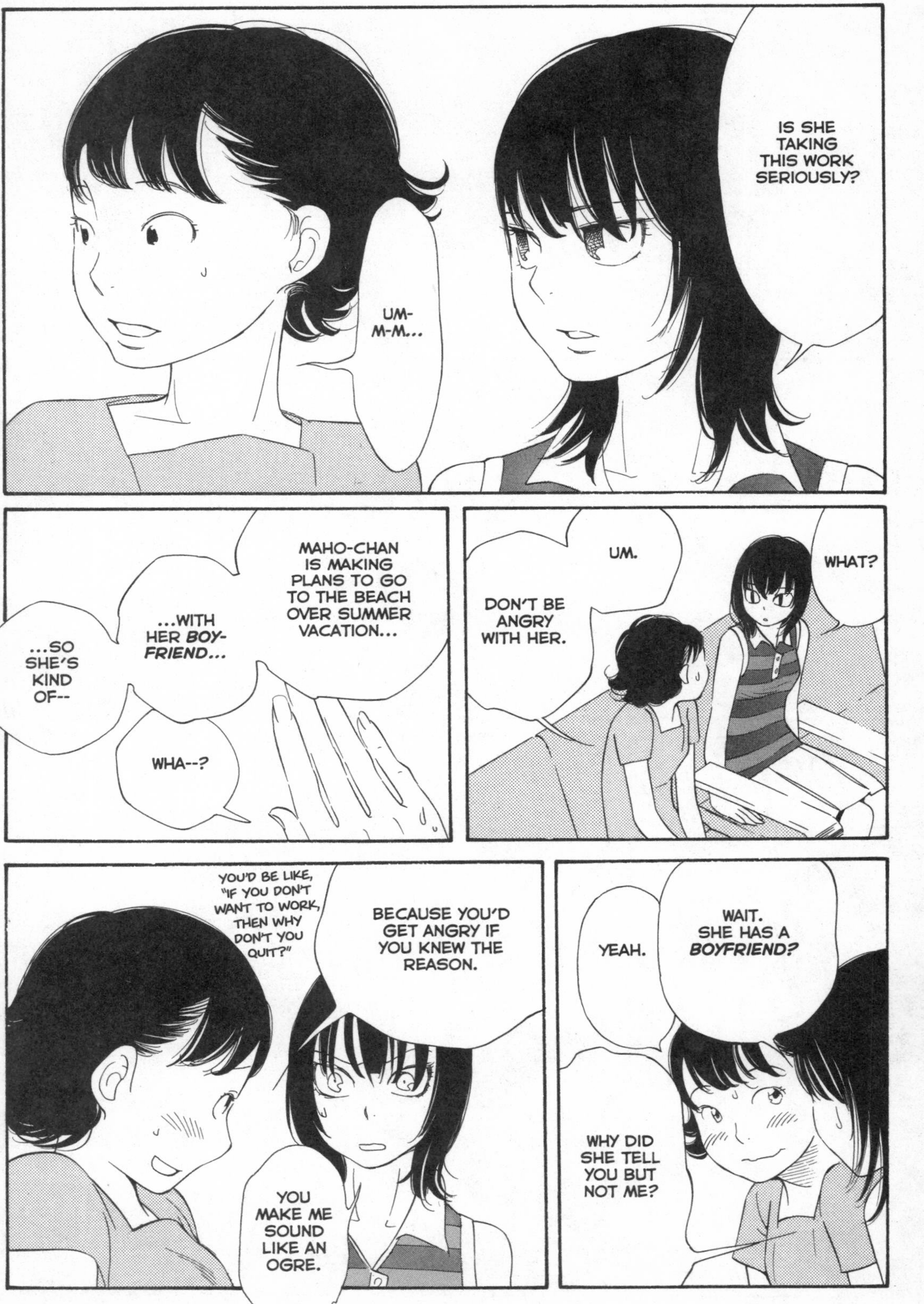
IS SHE TAKING THIS WORK SERIOUSLY?
UM-M-M...
WHAT?
UM.
DON'T BE ANGRY WITH HER.
MAHO-CHAN IS MAKING PLANS TO GO TO THE BEACH OVER SUMMER VACATION...
...WITH HER *BOY-FRIEND*...
...SO SHE'S KIND OF--
WHA--?
WAIT. SHE HAS A *BOYFRIEND?*
YEAH.
WHY DID SHE TELL YOU BUT NOT ME?
BECAUSE YOU'D GET ANGRY IF YOU KNEW THE REASON.
YOU'D BE LIKE, "IF YOU DON'T WANT TO WORK, THEN WHY DON'T YOU QUIT?"
YOU MAKE ME SOUND LIKE AN OGRE.

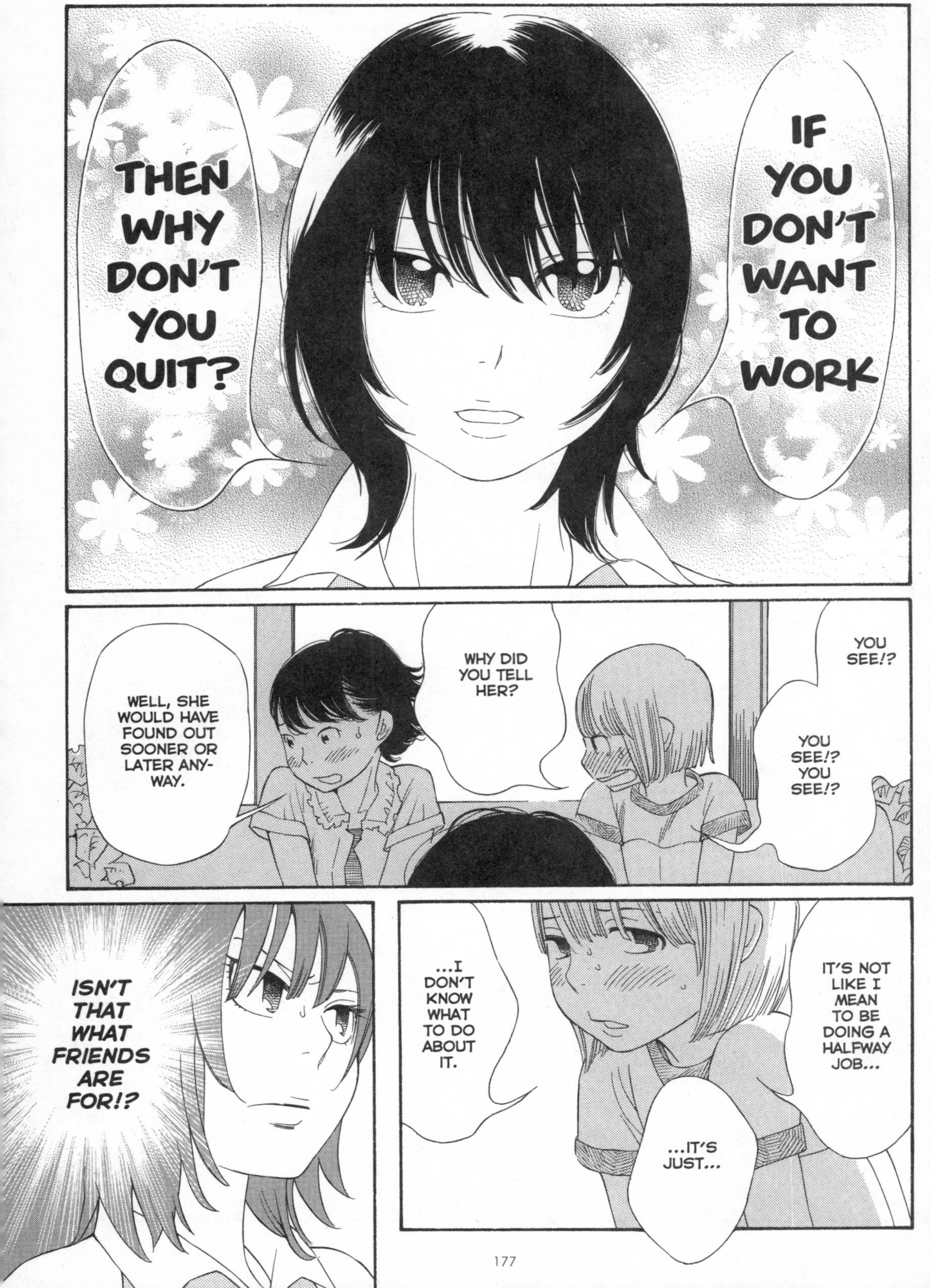
IF YOU DON'T WANT TO WORK
THEN WHY DON'T YOU QUIT?
YOU SEE!?
YOU SEE!? YOU SEE!?
WHY DID YOU TELL HER?
WELL, SHE WOULD HAVE FOUND OUT SOONER OR LATER ANY-WAY.
IT'S NOT LIKE I MEAN TO BE DOING A HALFWAY JOB...
...I DON'T KNOW WHAT TO DO ABOUT IT.
...IT'S JUST...
ISN'T THAT WHAT FRIENDS ARE FOR!?

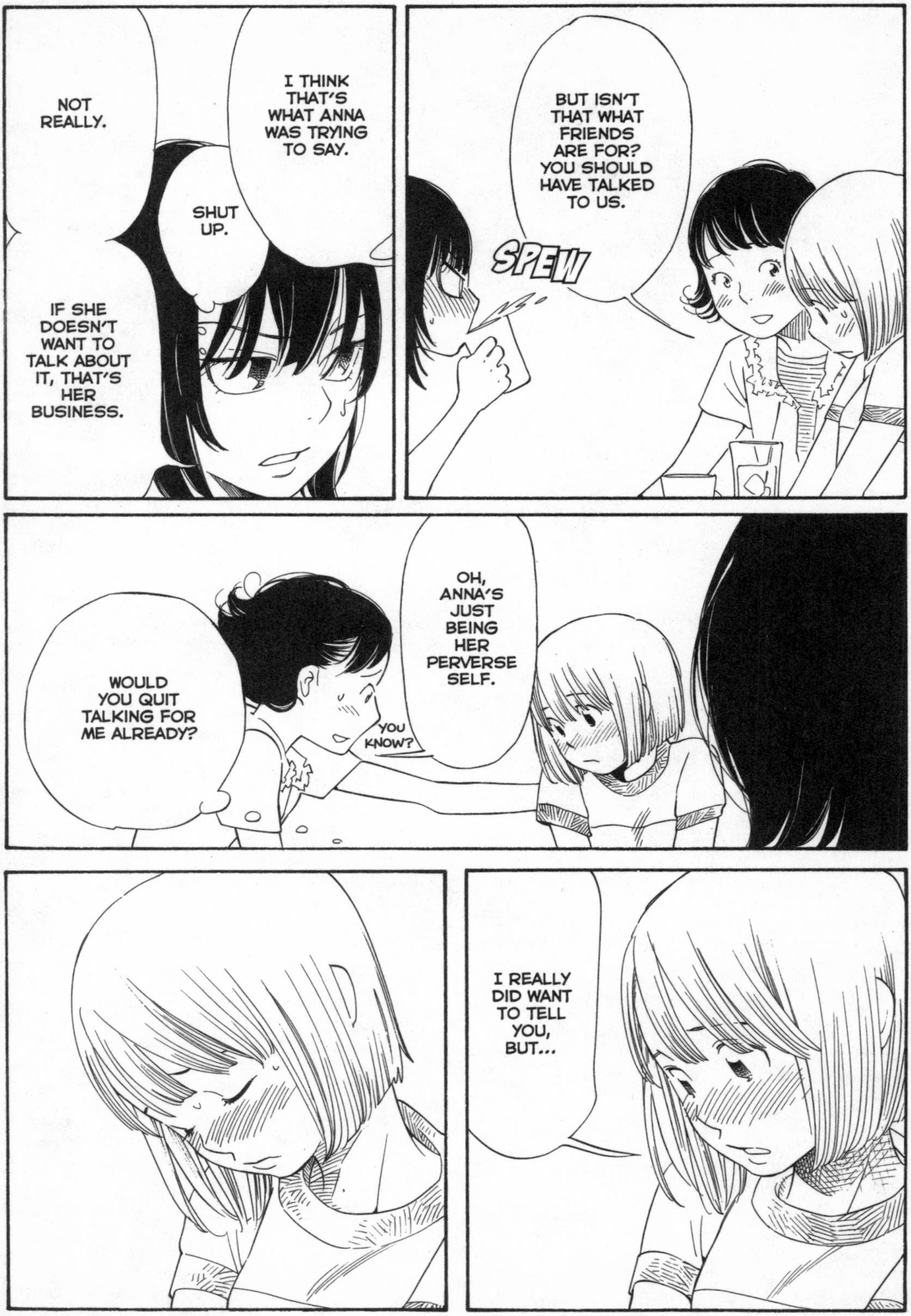
BUT ISN'T THAT WHAT FRIENDS ARE FOR? YOU SHOULD HAVE TALKED TO US.
SPEW
I THINK THAT'S WHAT ANNA WAS TRYING TO SAY.
SHUT UP.
NOT REALLY.
IF SHE DOESN'T WANT TO TALK ABOUT IT, THAT'S HER BUSINESS.
OH, ANNA'S JUST BEING HER PERVERSE SELF.
YOU KNOW?
WOULD YOU QUIT TALKING FOR ME ALREADY?
I REALLY DID WANT TO TELL YOU, BUT...

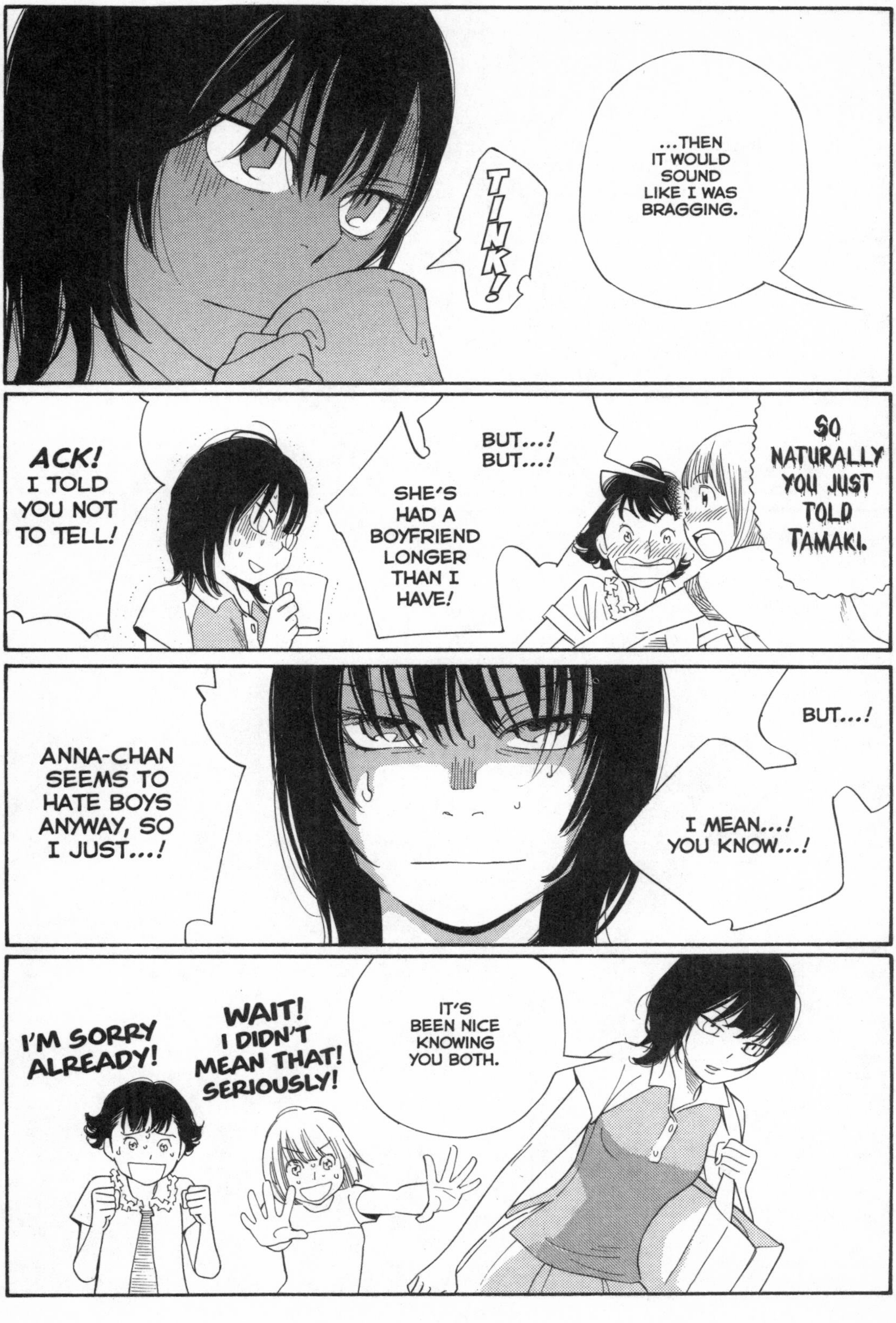
...THEN IT WOULD SOUND LIKE I WAS BRAGGING.
TINK!
SO NATURALLY YOU JUST TOLD TAMAKI.
BUT...! BUT...!
SHE'S HAD A BOYFRIEND LONGER THAN I HAVE!
ACK! I TOLD YOU NOT TO TELL!
BUT...!
I MEAN...! YOU KNOW...!
ANNA-CHAN SEEMS TO HATE BOYS ANYWAY, SO I JUST...!
IT'S BEEN NICE KNOWING YOU BOTH.
WAIT! I DIDN'T MEAN THAT! SERIOUSLY!
I'M SORRY ALREADY!

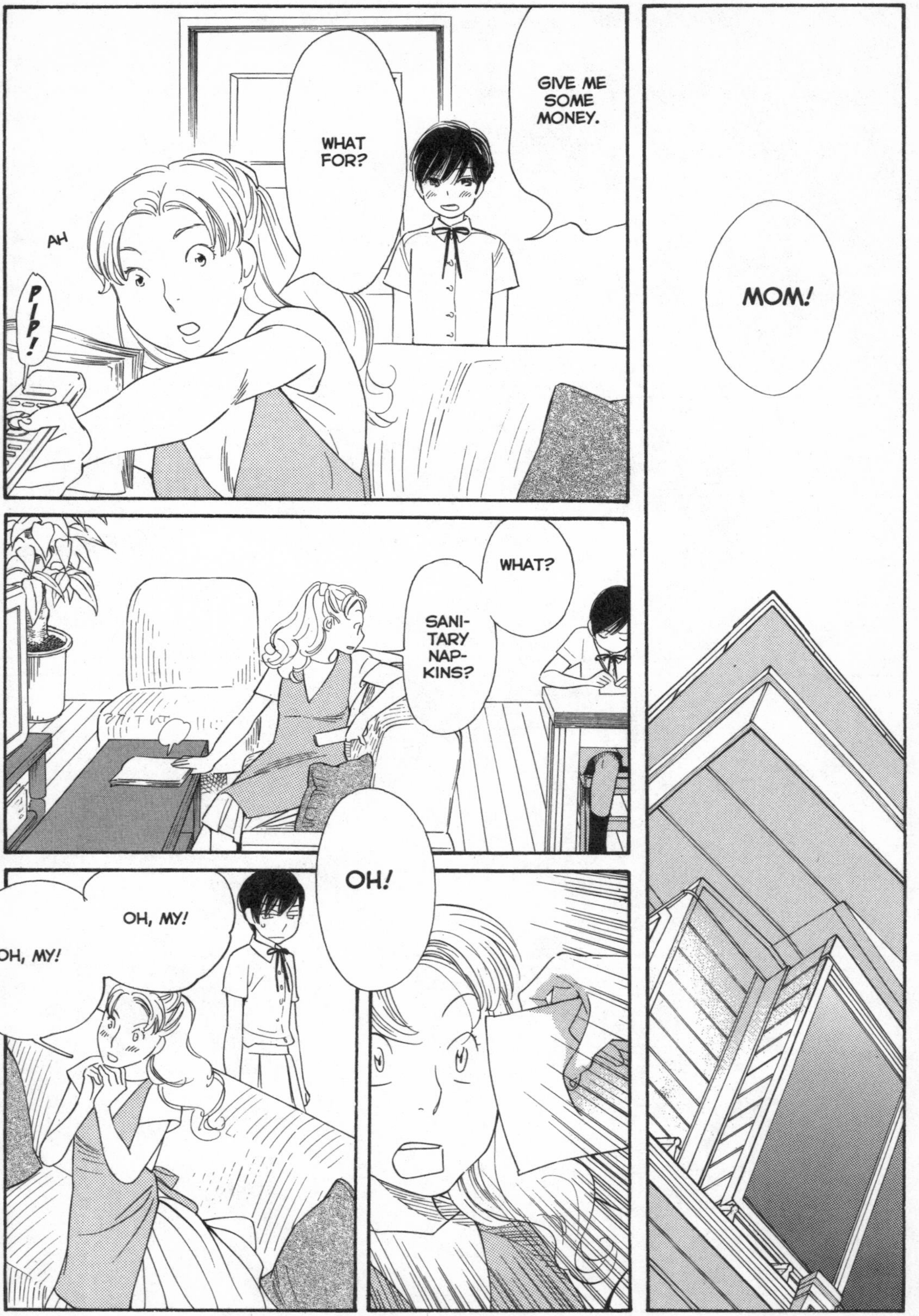
MOM!
GIVE ME SOME MONEY.
WHAT FOR?
AH
PIP!
WHAT?
SANITARY NAPKINS?
OH!
OH, MY!
OH, MY!

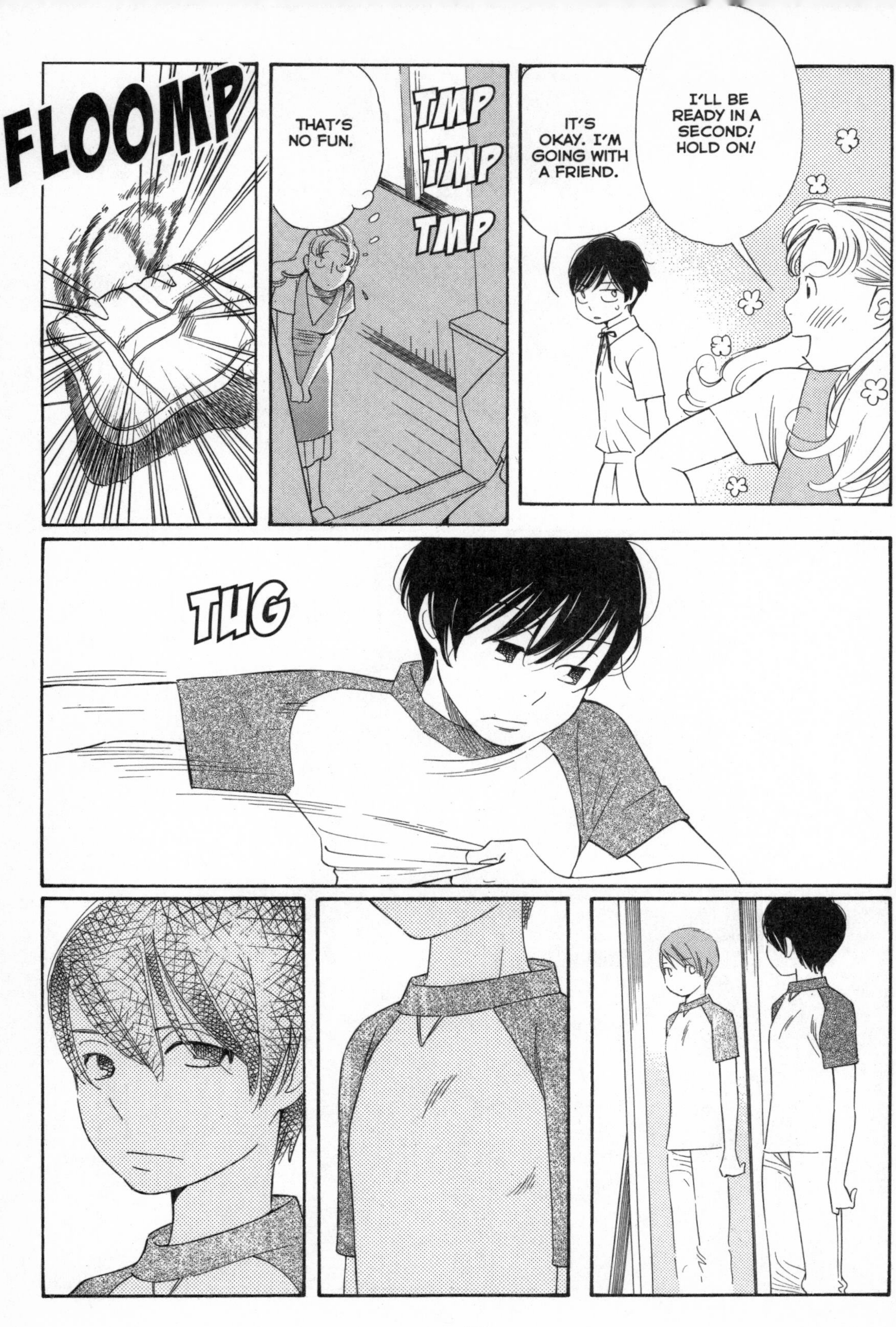
I'LL BE READY IN A SECOND! HOLD ON!
IT'S OKAY. I'M GOING WITH A FRIEND.
TMP TMP TMP
THAT'S NO FUN.
FLOOMP
TUG

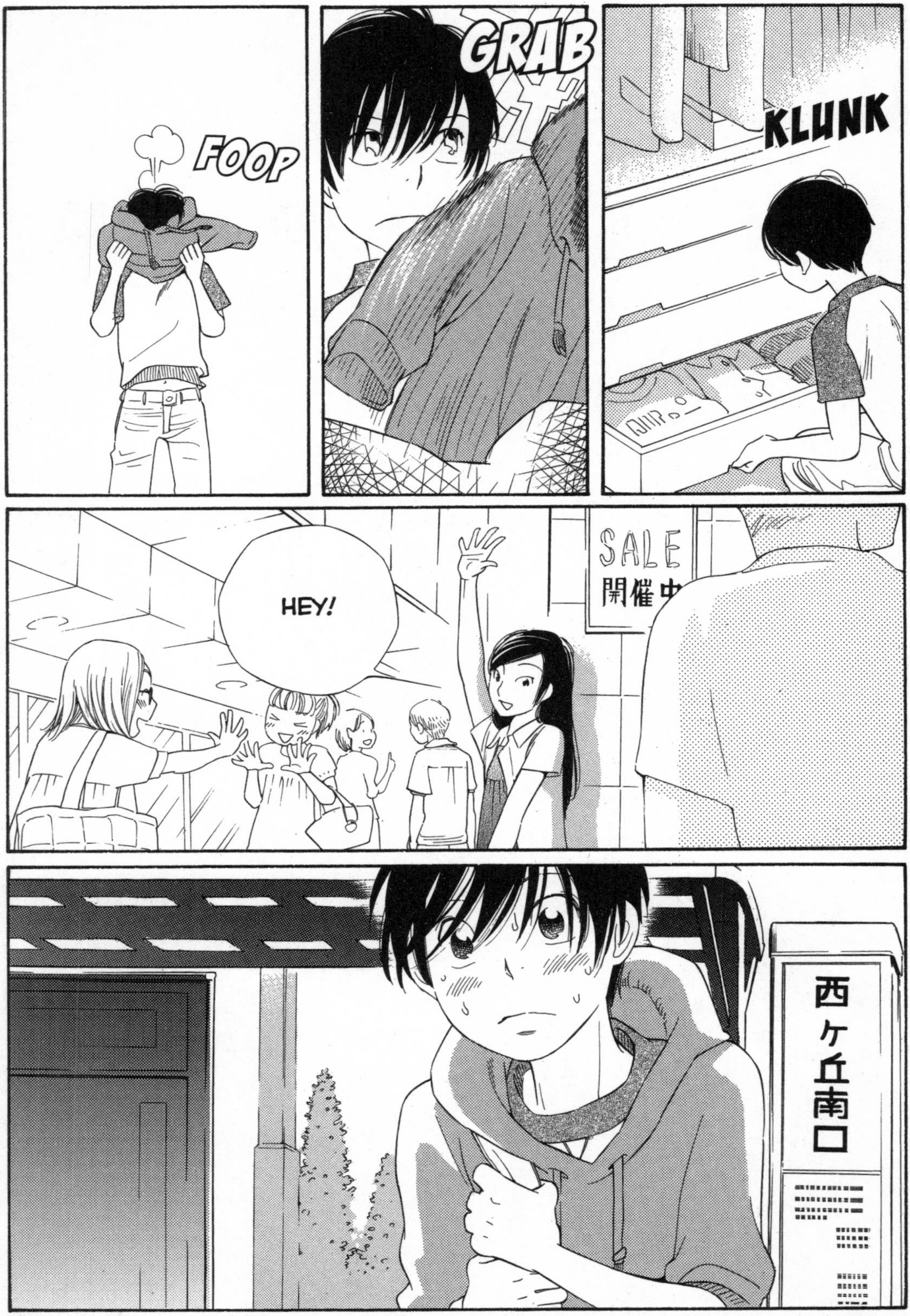
KLUNK
GRAB
FOOP
SALE
開催中
HEY!
西ヶ丘南口

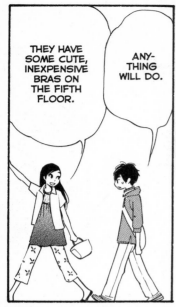

WHERE'S SHIRAI-SAN?
I DIDN'T INVITE HER.
YOU LOOK HOT.
I WAS RUNNING!
OH, COME ON. WHAT KIND DO YOU WANT?
ANY-THING WILL DO.
THEY HAVE SOME CUTE, INEXPENSIVE BRAS ON THE FIFTH FLOOR.
SALE
THIS'LL DO.

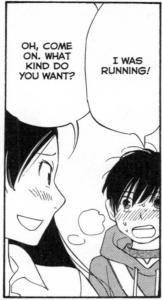

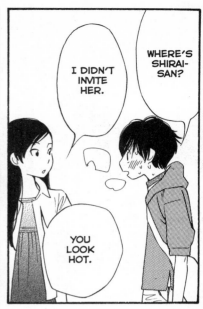

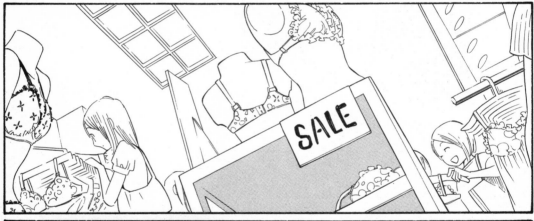

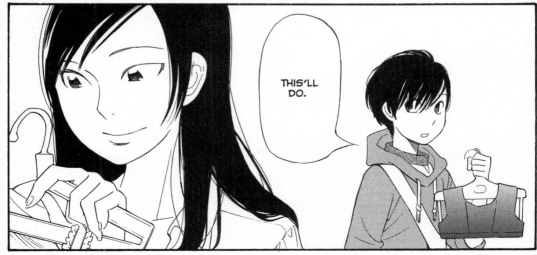

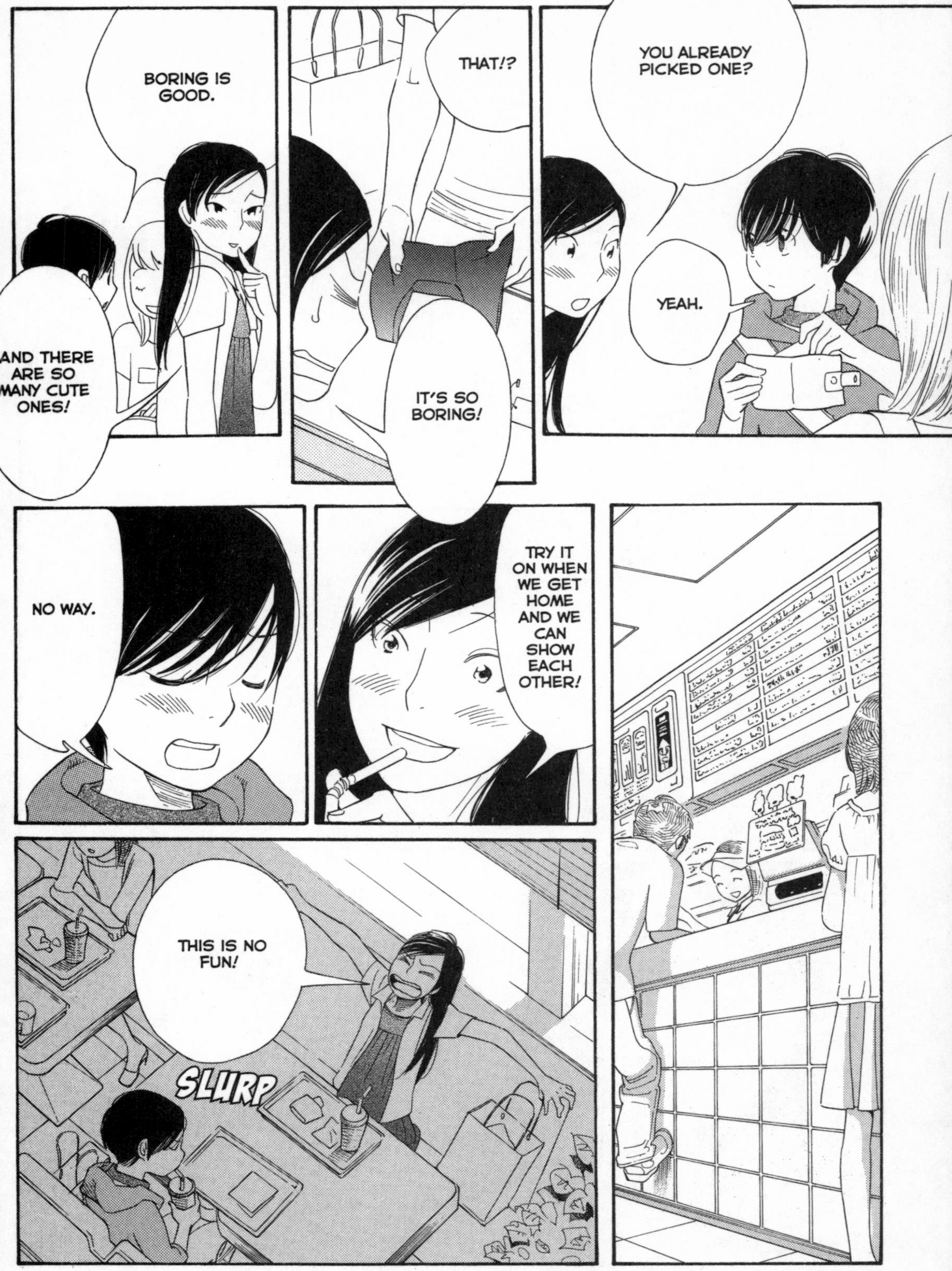
YOU ALREADY PICKED ONE?
YEAH.
THAT!?
IT'S SO BORING!
BORING IS GOOD.
AND THERE ARE SO MANY CUTE ONES!
TRY IT ON WHEN WE GET HOME AND WE CAN SHOW EACH OTHER!
NO WAY.
THIS IS NO FUN!
SLURP

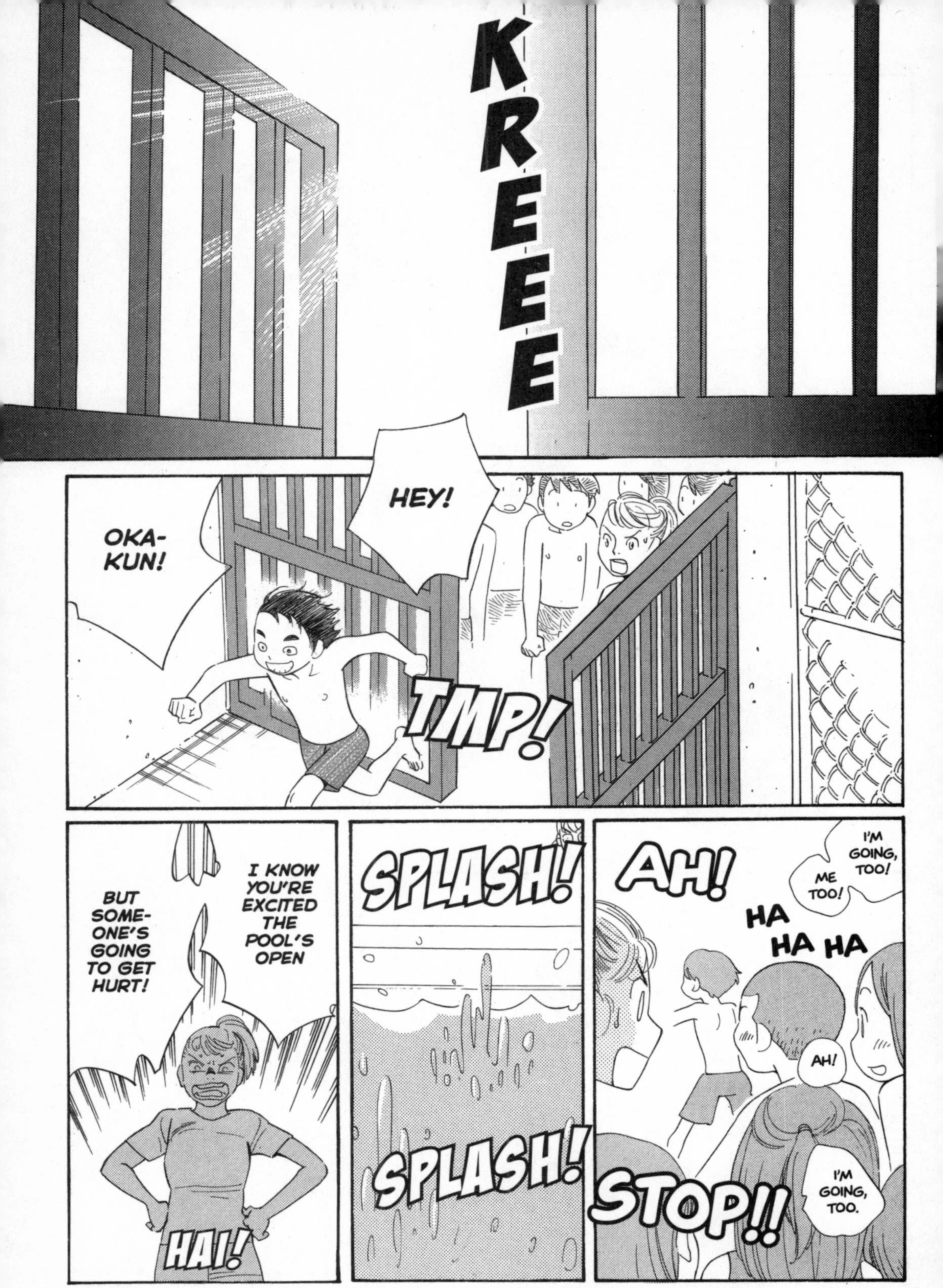
KREEE
HEY!
OKA-KUN!
TMP!
I'M GOING, TOO!
ME TOO!
AH!
HA HA HA
AH!
I'M GOING, TOO.
STOP!!
SPLASH!
SPLASH!
I KNOW YOU'RE EXCITED THE POOL'S OPEN
BUT SOMEONE'S GOING TO GET HURT!
HAI!

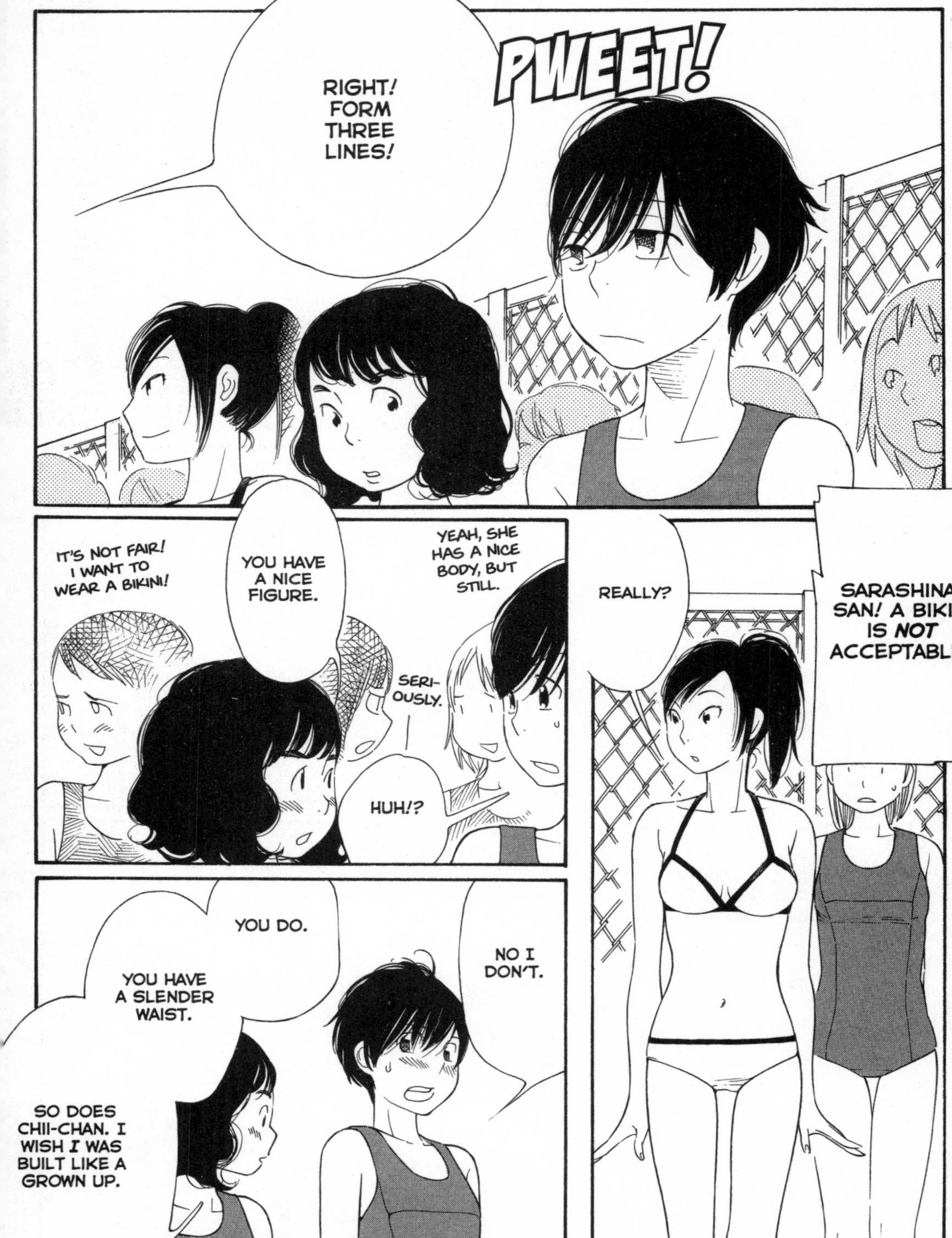
PWEET!
RIGHT! FORM THREE LINES!
SARASHINA-SAN! A BIKINI IS NOT ACCEPTABLE!
REALLY?
YEAH, SHE HAS A NICE BODY, BUT STILL.
YOU HAVE A NICE FIGURE.
IT'S NOT FAIR! I WANT TO WEAR A BIKINI!
SERI-OUSLY.
HUH!?
NO I DON'T.
YOU DO.
YOU HAVE A SLENDER WAIST.
SO DOES CHII-CHAN. I WISH I WAS BUILT LIKE A GROWN UP.

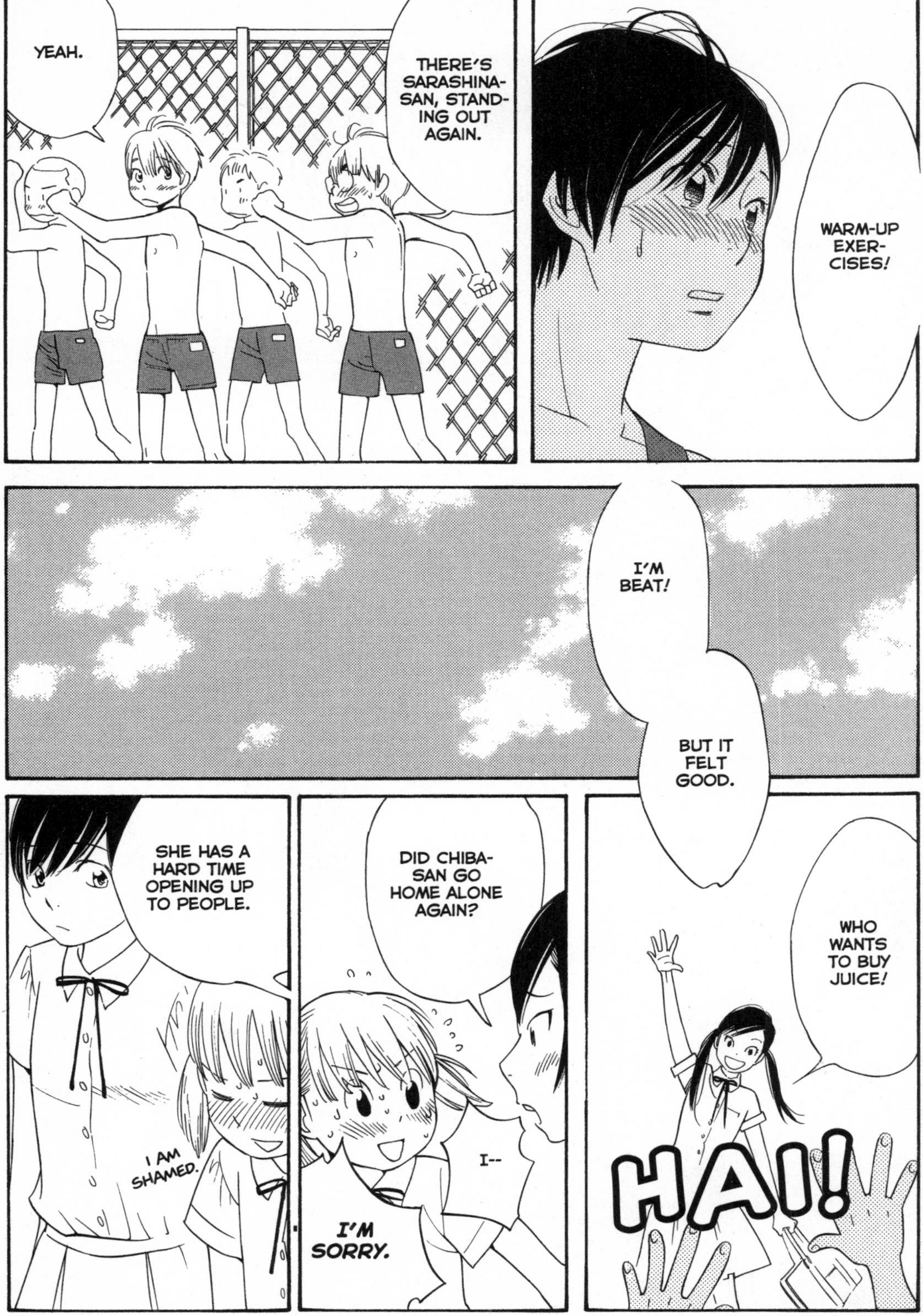
WARM-UP EXERCISES!
THERE'S SARASHINA-SAN, STANDING OUT AGAIN.
YEAH.
I'M BEAT!
BUT IT FELT GOOD.
WHO WANTS TO BUY JUICE!
HAI!
DID CHIBA-SAN GO HOME ALONE AGAIN?
I--
I'M SORRY.
SHE HAS A HARD TIME OPENING UP TO PEOPLE.
I AM SHAMED.

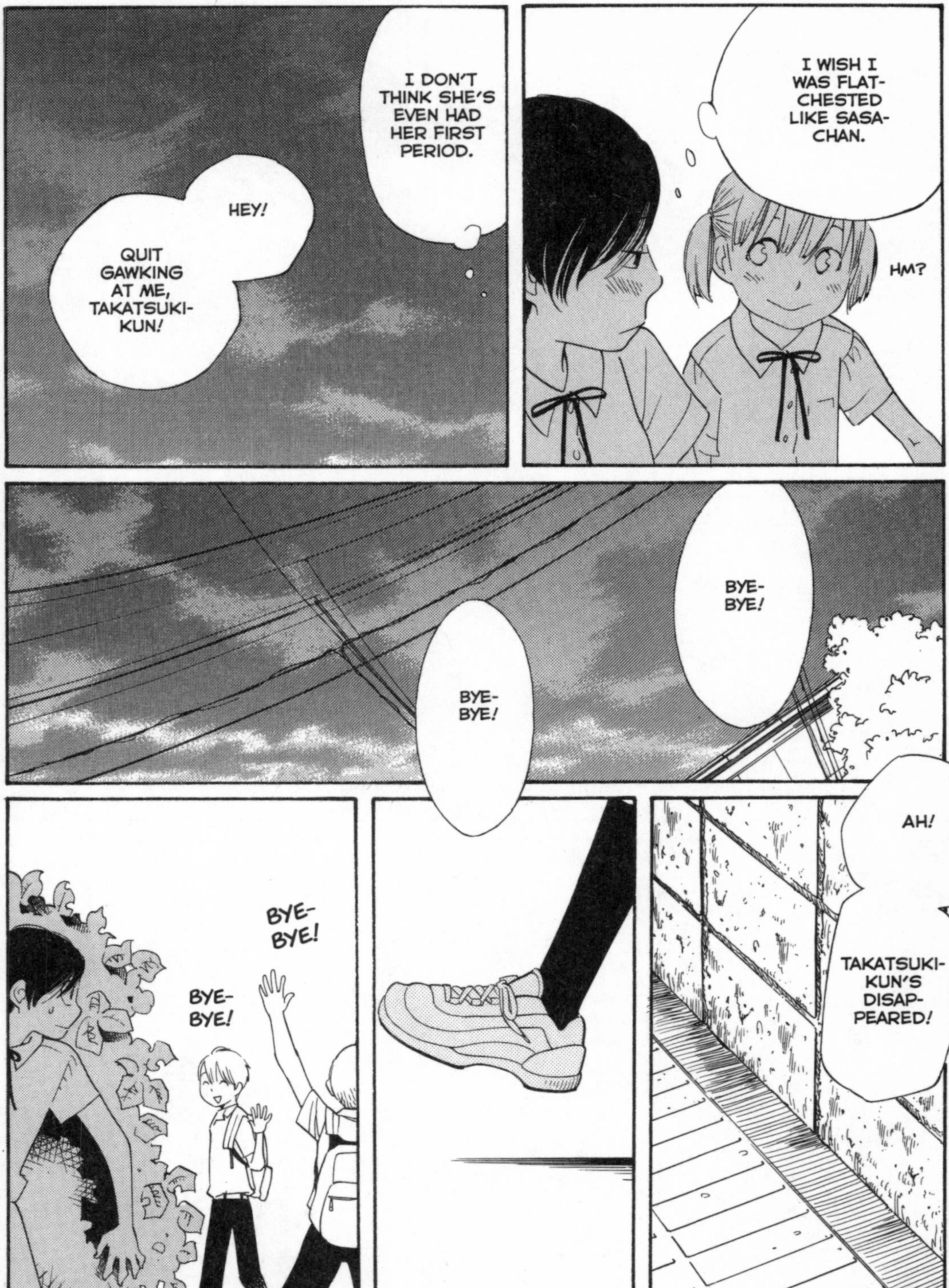
I WISH I WAS FLAT-CHESTED LIKE SASA-CHAN.
HM?
I DON'T THINK SHE'S EVEN HAD HER FIRST PERIOD.
HEY!
QUIT GAWKING AT ME, TAKATSUKI-KUN!
BYE-BYE!
BYE-BYE!
AH!
TAKATSUKI-KUN'S DISAP-PEARED!
BYE-BYE!
BYE-BYE!

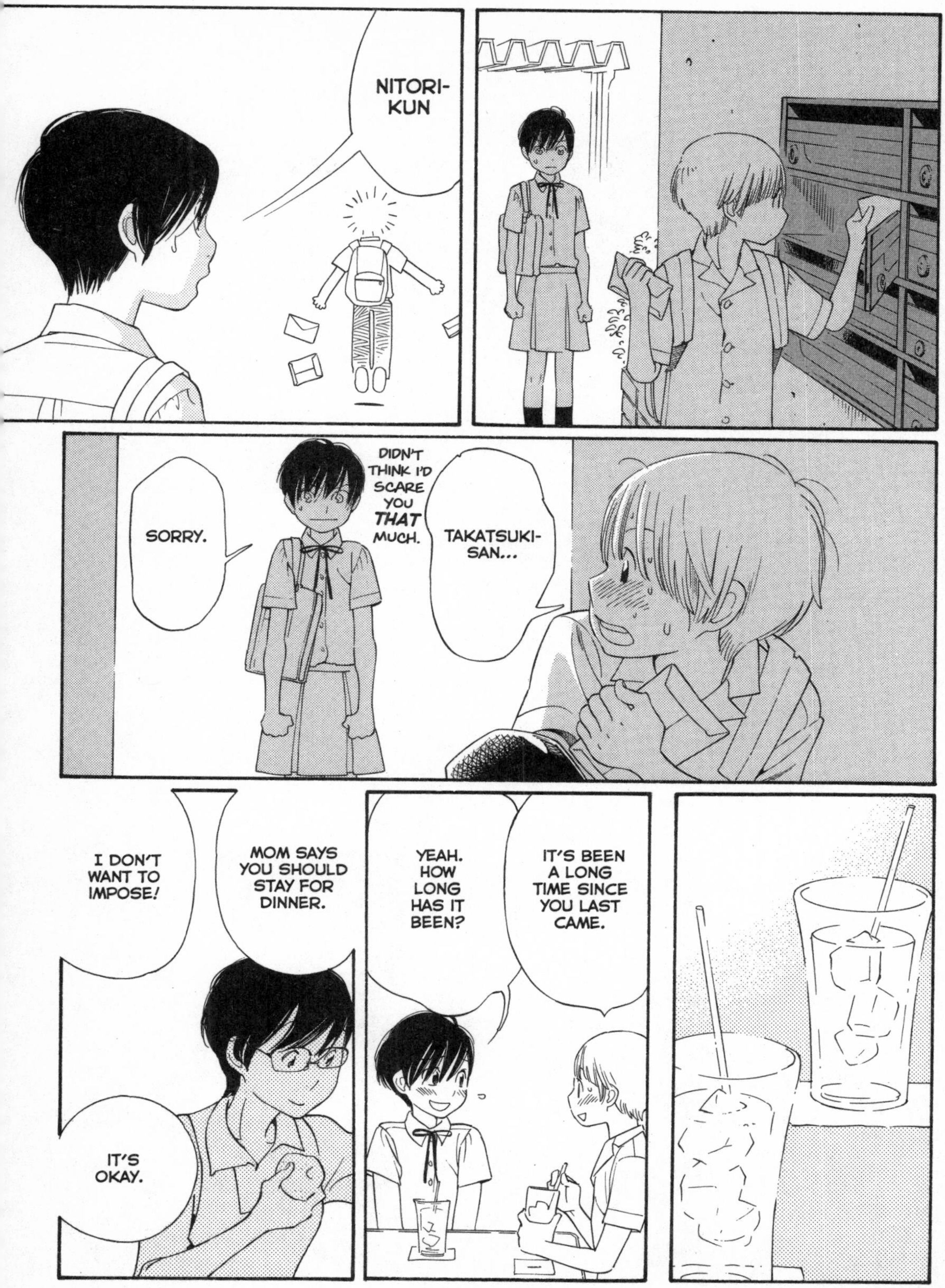
NITORI-KUN
TAKATSUKI-SAN...
DIDN'T THINK I'D SCARE YOU *THAT* MUCH.
SORRY.
IT'S BEEN A LONG TIME SINCE YOU LAST CAME.
YEAH. HOW LONG HAS IT BEEN?
MOM SAYS YOU SHOULD STAY FOR DINNER.
I DON'T WANT TO IMPOSE!
IT'S OKAY.

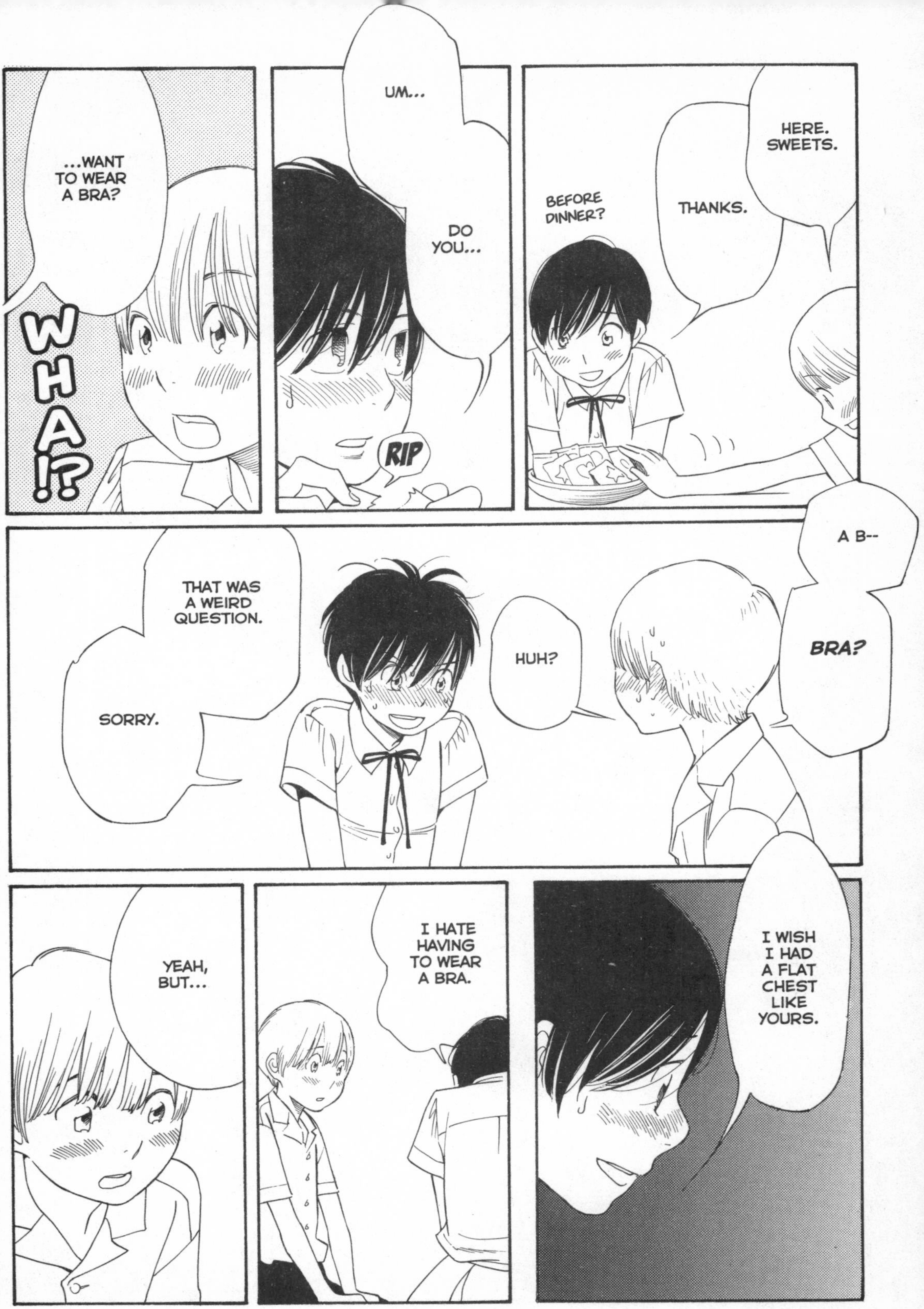
HERE. SWEETS.
THANKS.
BEFORE DINNER?
UM...
DO YOU...
RIP
...WANT TO WEAR A BRA?
WHA!?
A B--
BRA?
HUH?
THAT WAS A WEIRD QUESTION.
SORRY.
I WISH I HAD A FLAT CHEST LIKE YOURS.
I HATE HAVING TO WEAR A BRA.
YEAH, BUT...

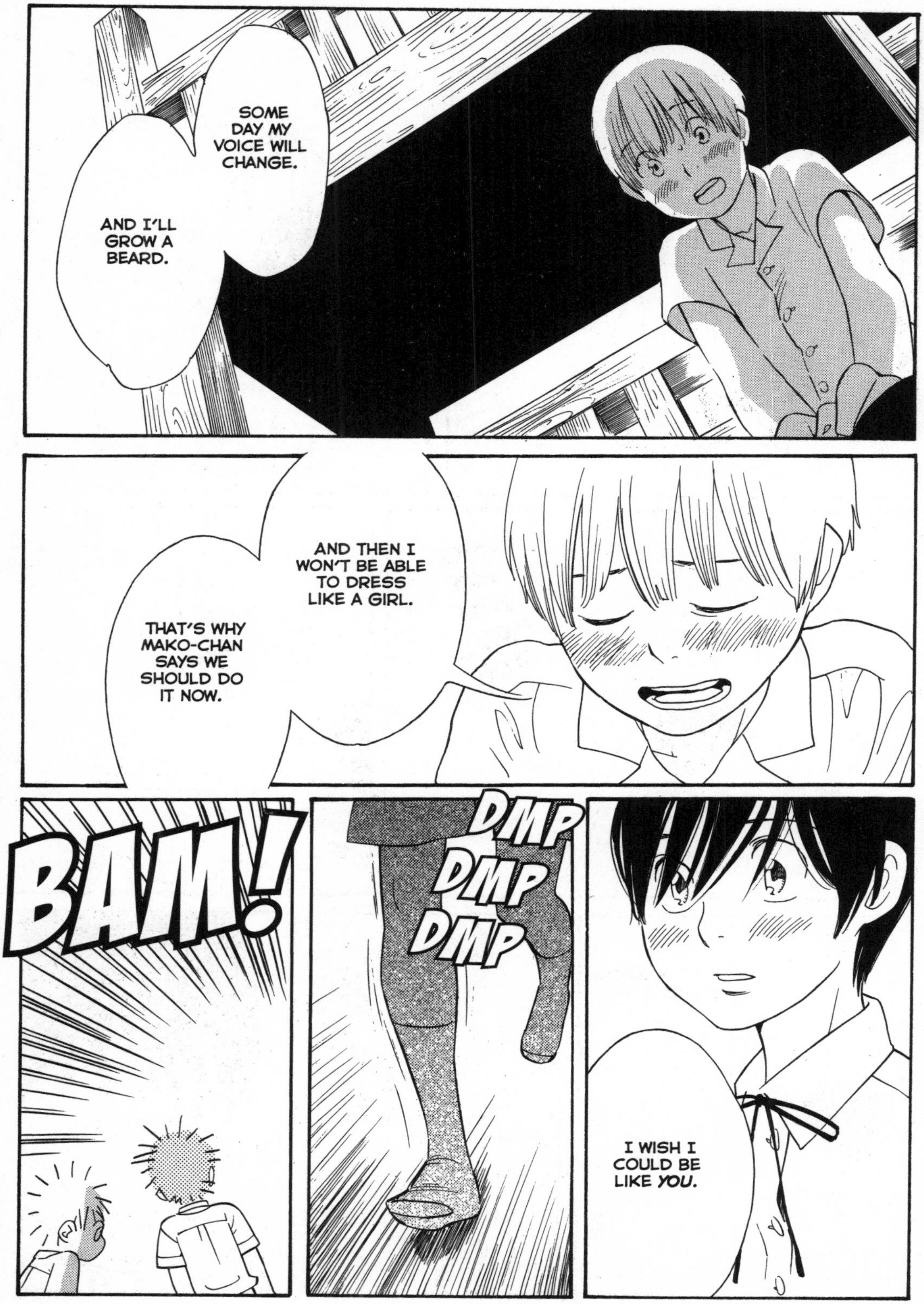
SOME DAY MY VOICE WILL CHANGE.
AND I'LL GROW A BEARD.
AND THEN I WON'T BE ABLE TO DRESS LIKE A GIRL.
THAT'S WHY MAKO-CHAN SAYS WE SHOULD DO IT NOW.
I WISH I COULD BE LIKE *YOU*.
DMP DMP DMP
BAM!

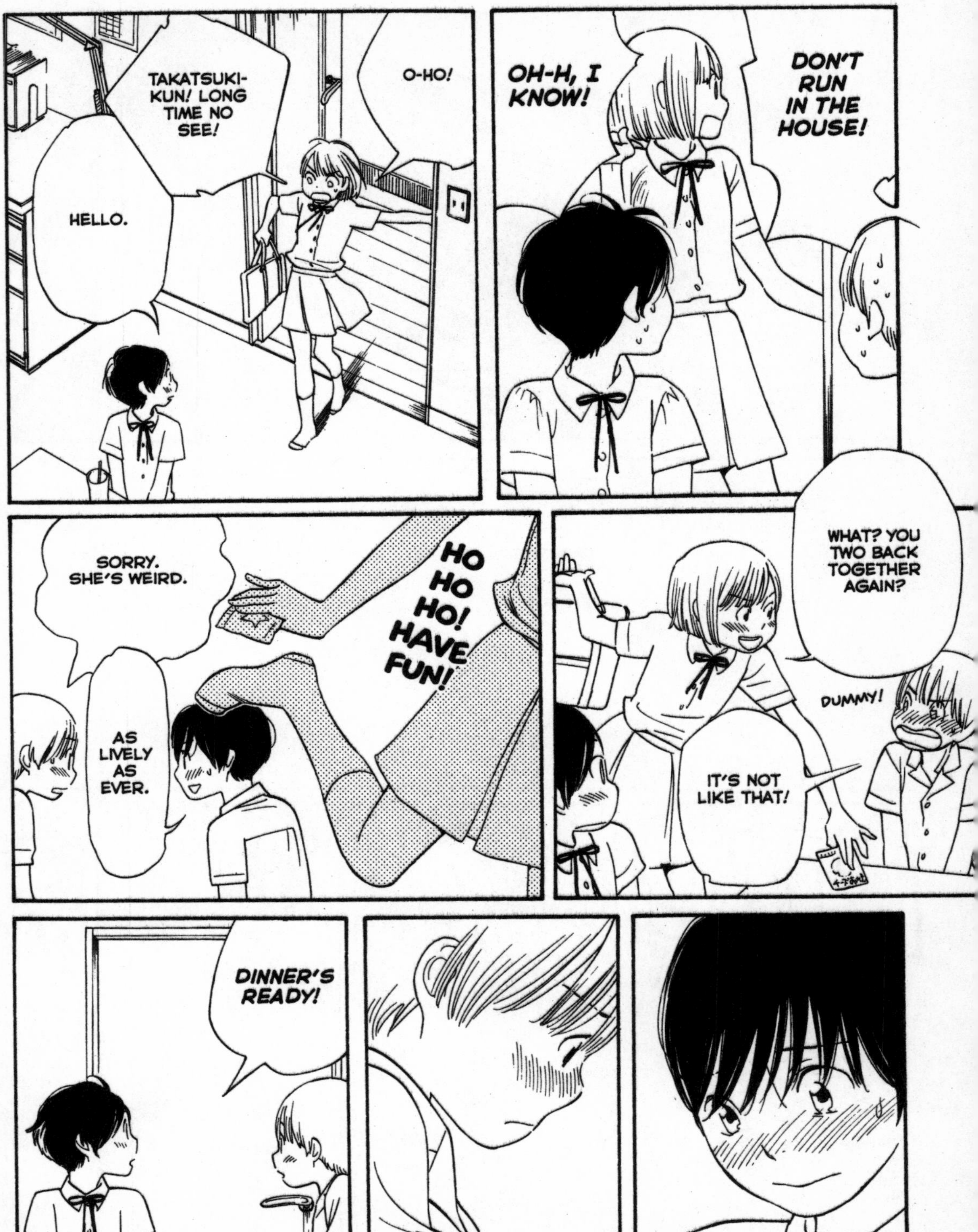
DON'T RUN IN THE HOUSE!
OH-H, I KNOW!
O-HO!
TAKATSUKI-KUN! LONG TIME NO SEE!
HELLO.
WHAT? YOU TWO BACK TOGETHER AGAIN?
DUMMY!
IT'S NOT LIKE THAT!
HO HO HO! HAVE FUN!
SORRY. SHE'S WEIRD.
AS LIVELY AS EVER.
DINNER'S READY!

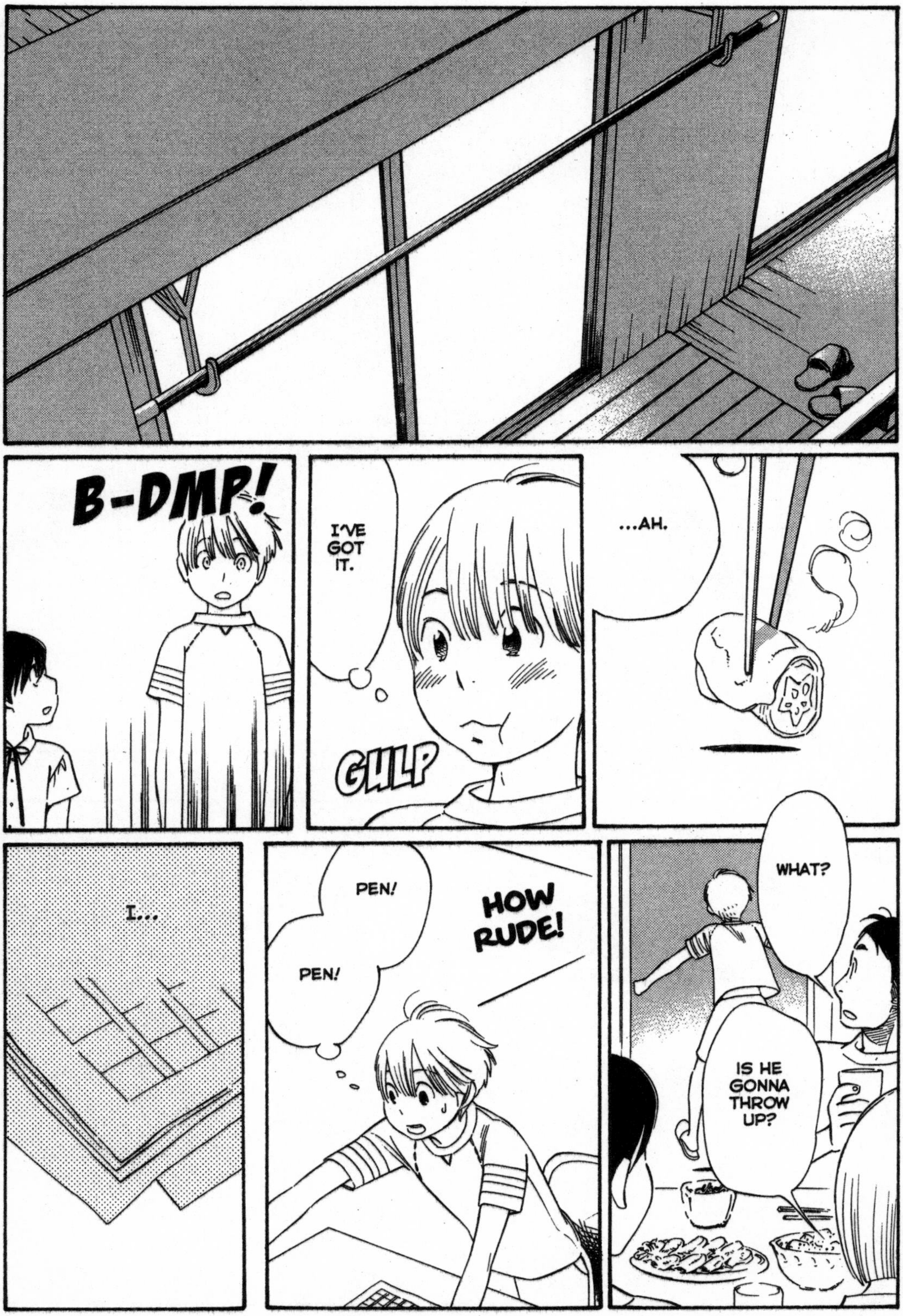
...AH.
I'VE GOT IT.
GULP
B-DMP!
WHAT?
IS HE GONNA THROW UP?
HOW RUDE!
PEN!
PEN!
I...

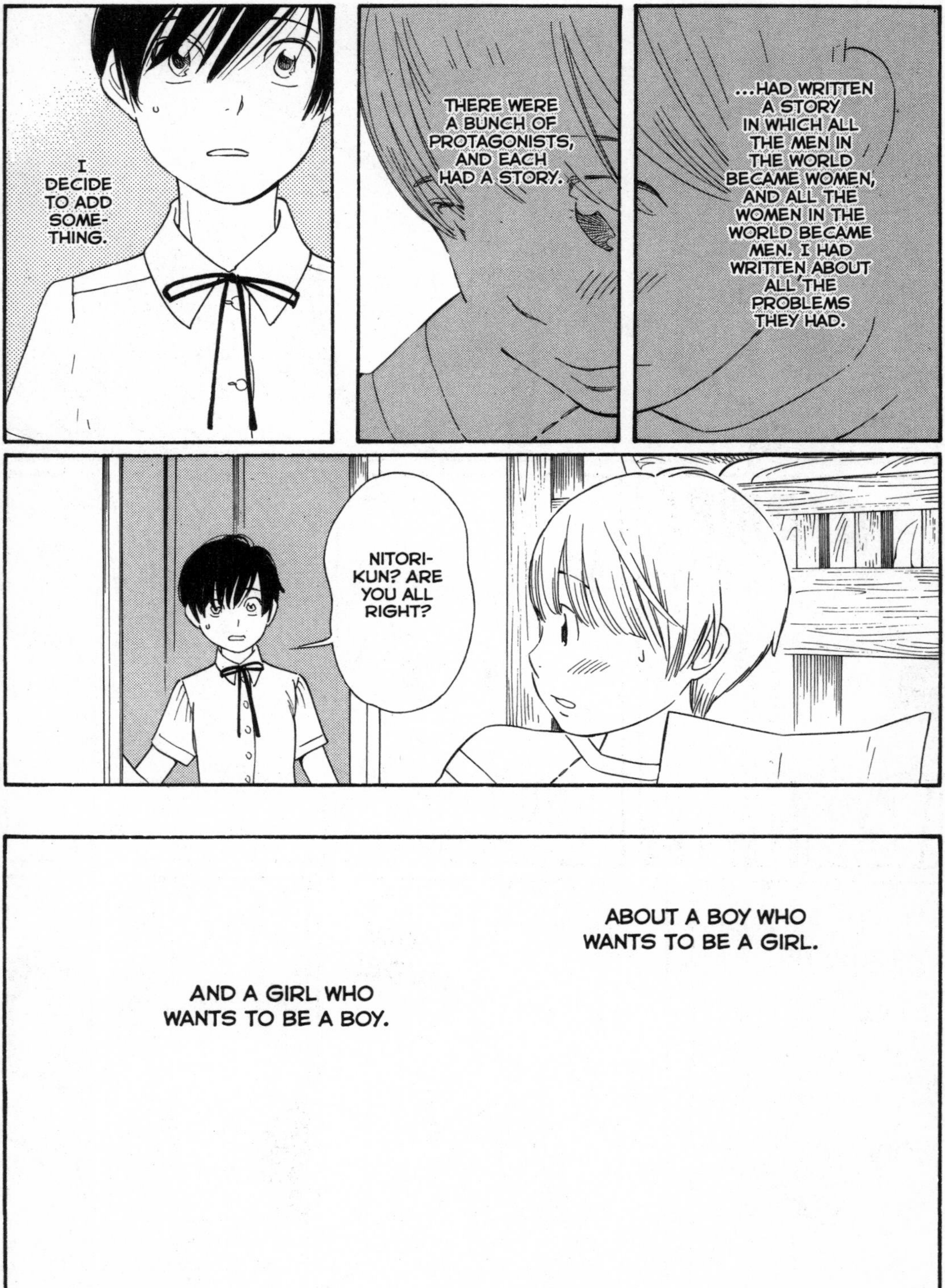
...HAD WRITTEN A STORY IN WHICH ALL THE MEN IN THE WORLD BECAME WOMEN, AND ALL THE WOMEN IN THE WORLD BECAME MEN. I HAD WRITTEN ABOUT ALL THE PROBLEMS THEY HAD.
THERE WERE A BUNCH OF PROTAGONISTS, AND EACH HAD A STORY.
I DECIDE TO ADD SOME-THING.
NITORI-KUN? ARE YOU ALL RIGHT?
ABOUT A BOY WHO WANTS TO BE A GIRL.
AND A GIRL WHO WANTS TO BE A BOY.

41

Tensions Build (Again)

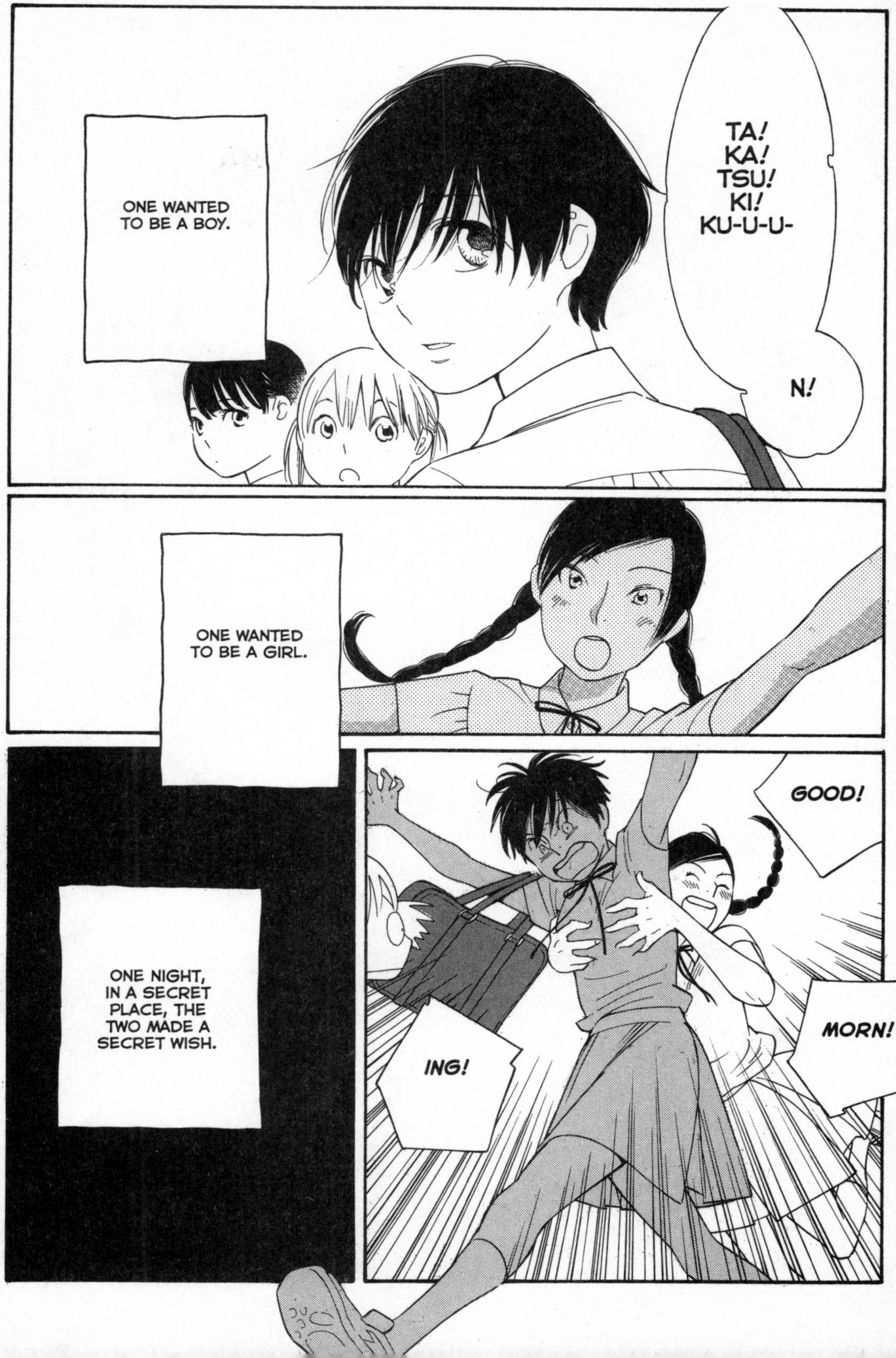
TA! KA! TSU! KI! KU-U-U- N!
ONE WANTED TO BE A BOY.
ONE WANTED TO BE A GIRL.
GOOD!
MORN!
ING!
ONE NIGHT, IN A SECRET PLACE, THE TWO MADE A SECRET WISH.

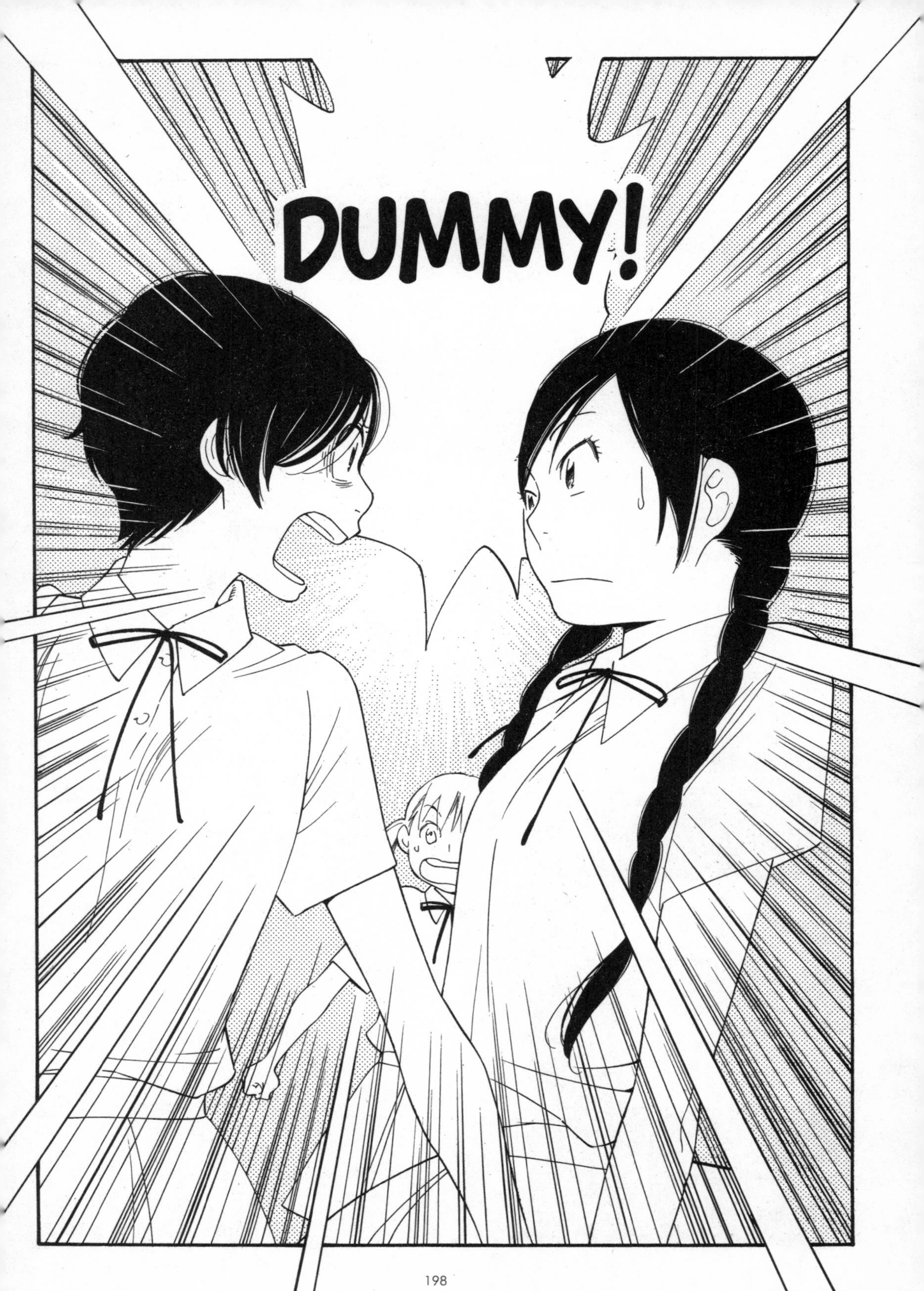
DUMMY!

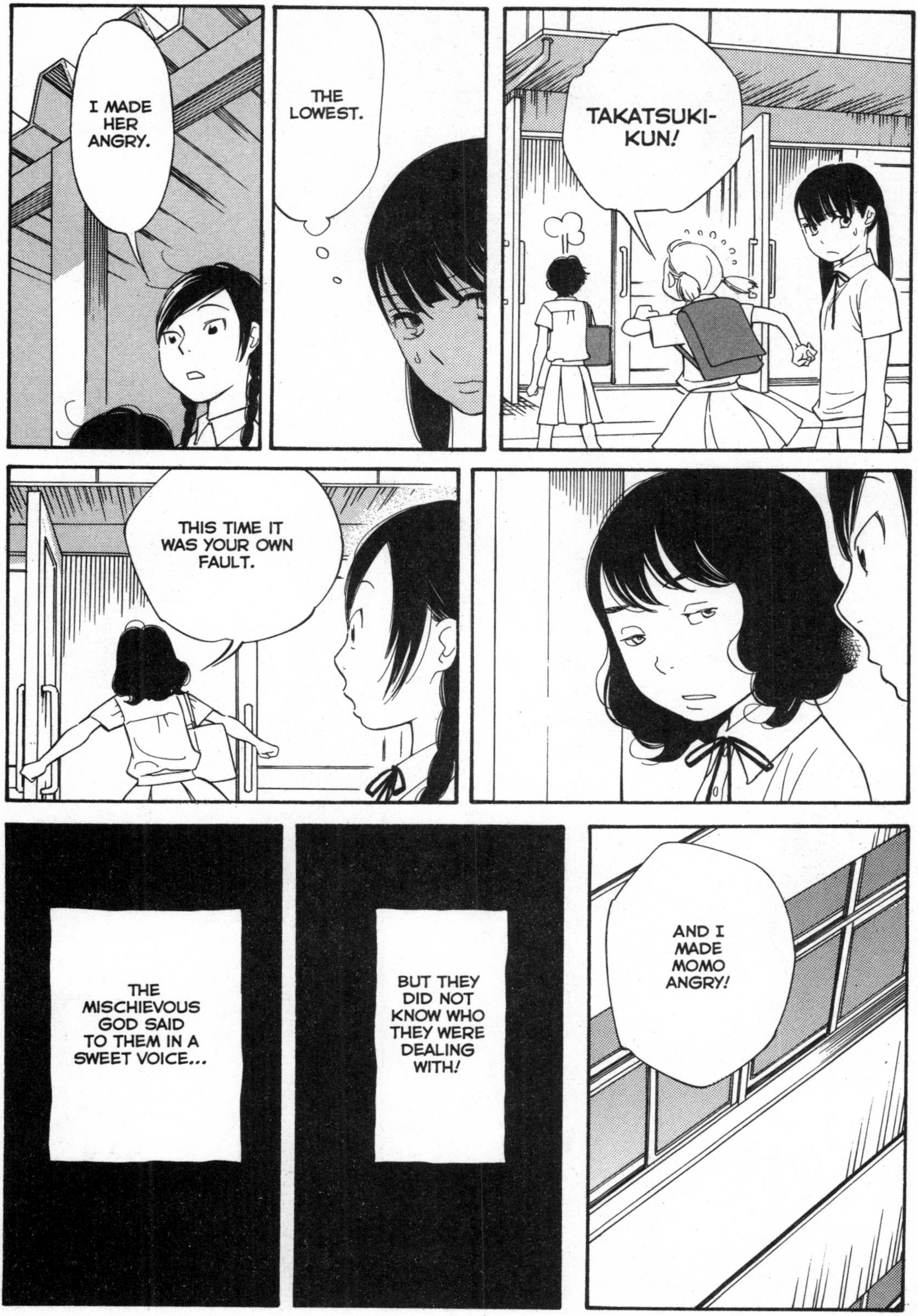
TAKATSUKI-KUN!
THE LOWEST.
I MADE HER ANGRY.
THIS TIME IT WAS YOUR OWN FAULT.
AND I MADE MOMO ANGRY!
BUT THEY DID NOT KNOW WHO THEY WERE DEALING WITH!
THE MISCHIEVOUS GOD SAID TO THEM IN A SWEET VOICE...

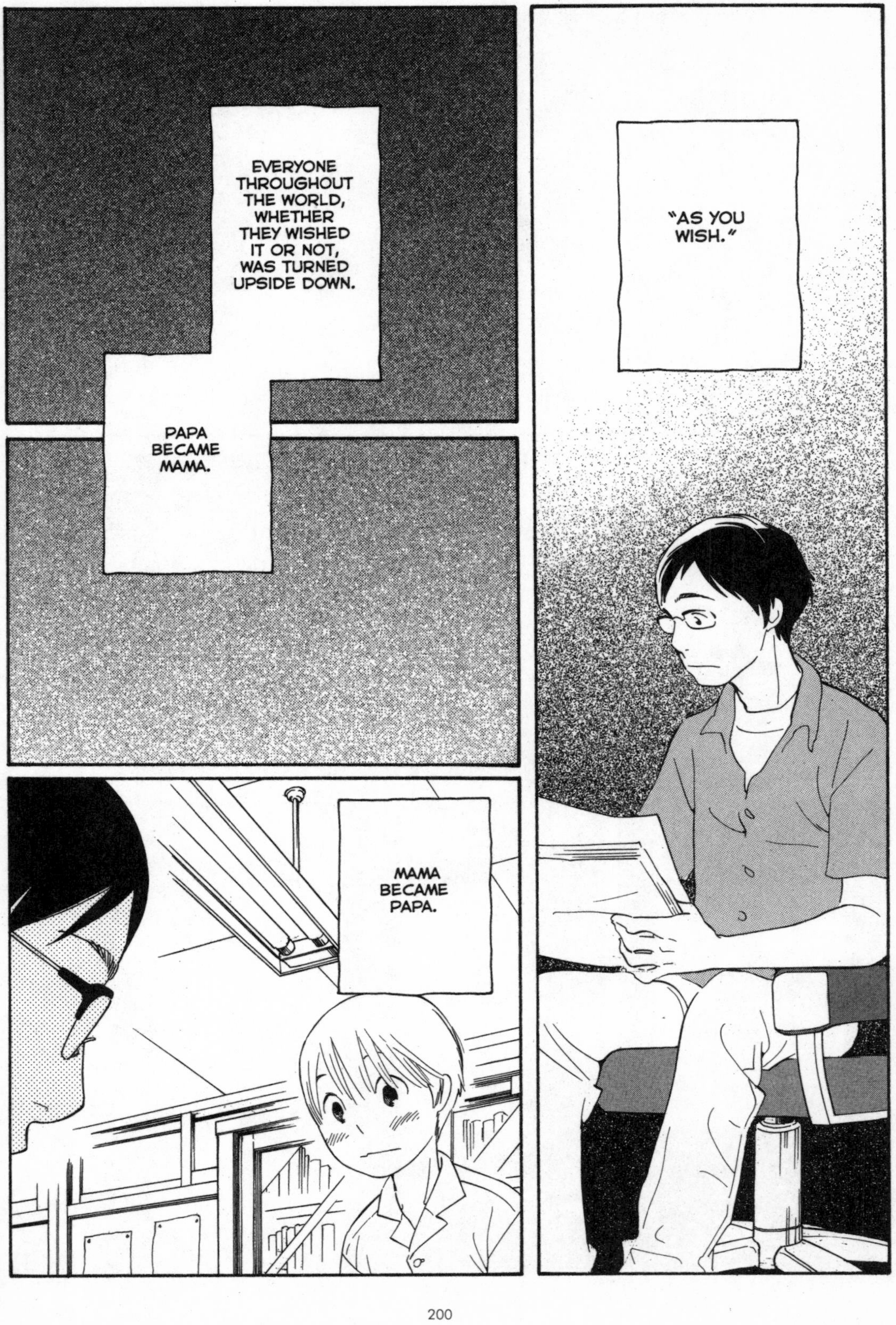
"AS YOU WISH."
EVERYONE THROUGHOUT THE WORLD, WHETHER THEY WISHED IT OR NOT, WAS TURNED UPSIDE DOWN.
PAPA BECAME MAMA.
MAMA BECAME PAPA.

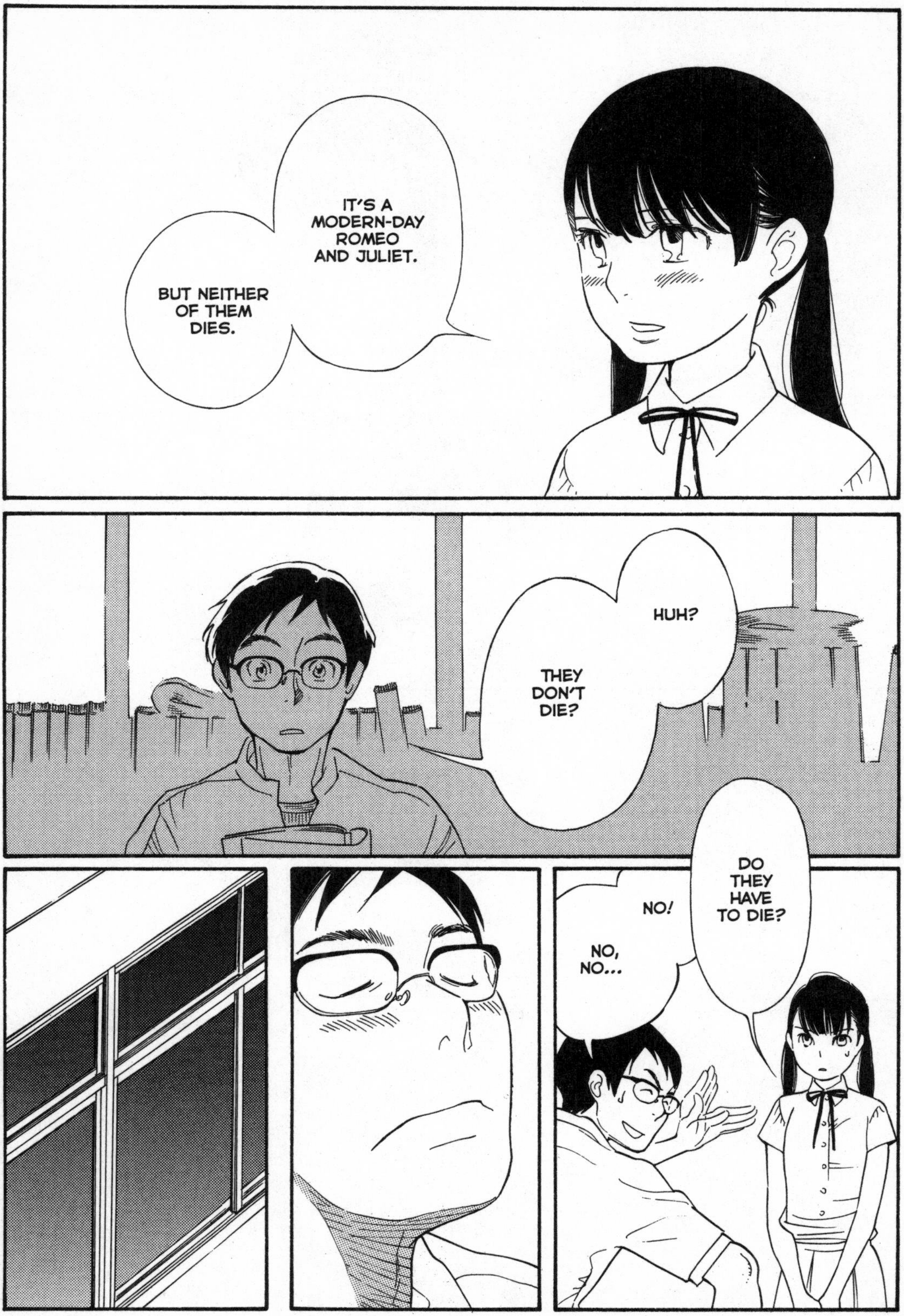
IT'S A MODERN-DAY ROMEO AND JULIET.
BUT NEITHER OF THEM DIES.
HUH?
THEY DON'T DIE?
DO THEY HAVE TO DIE?
NO!
NO, NO...

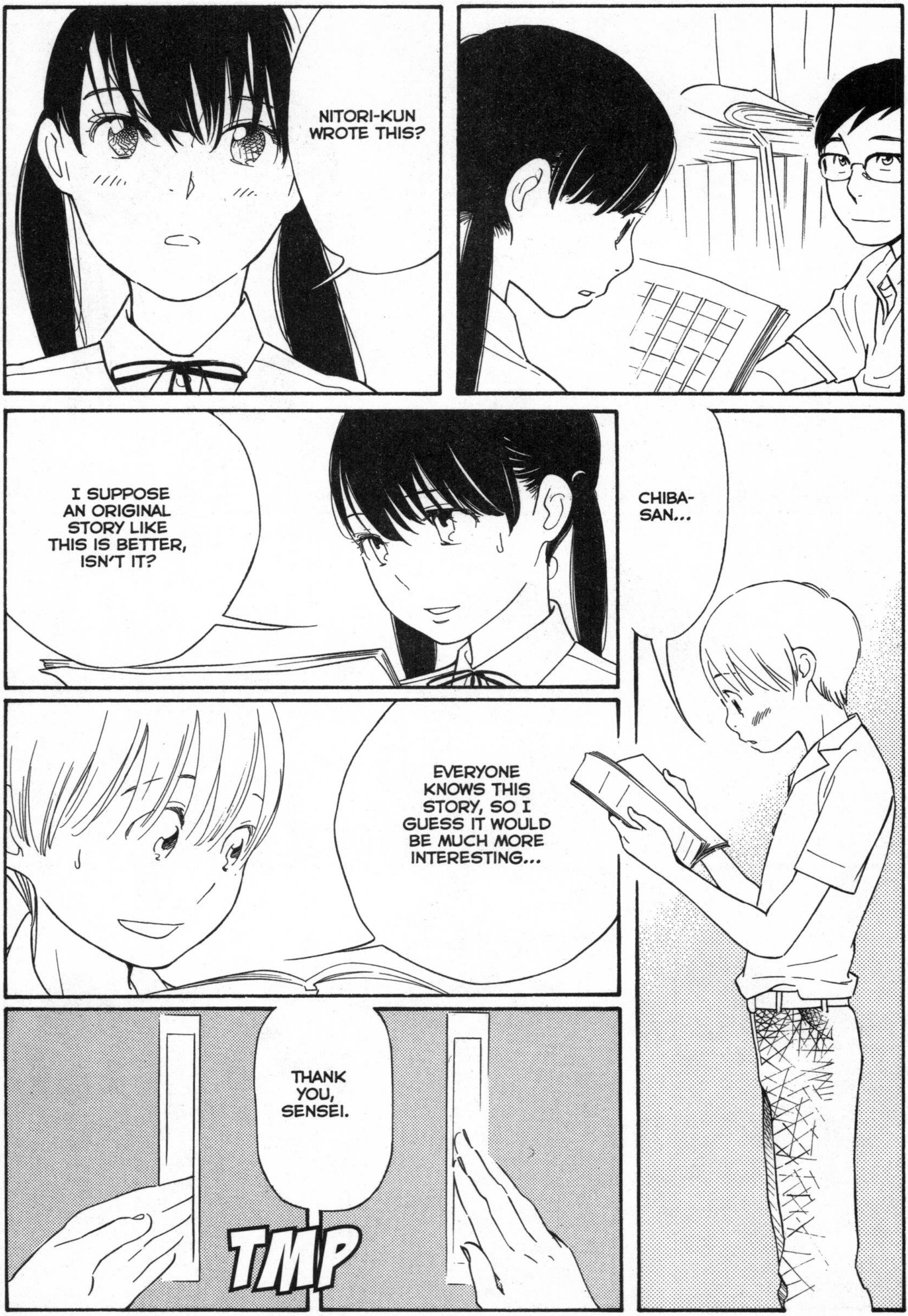
NITORI-KUN WROTE THIS?
CHIBA-SAN...
I SUPPOSE AN ORIGINAL STORY LIKE THIS IS BETTER, ISN'T IT?
EVERYONE KNOWS THIS STORY, SO I GUESS IT WOULD BE MUCH MORE INTERESTING...
THANK YOU, SENSEI.
TMP

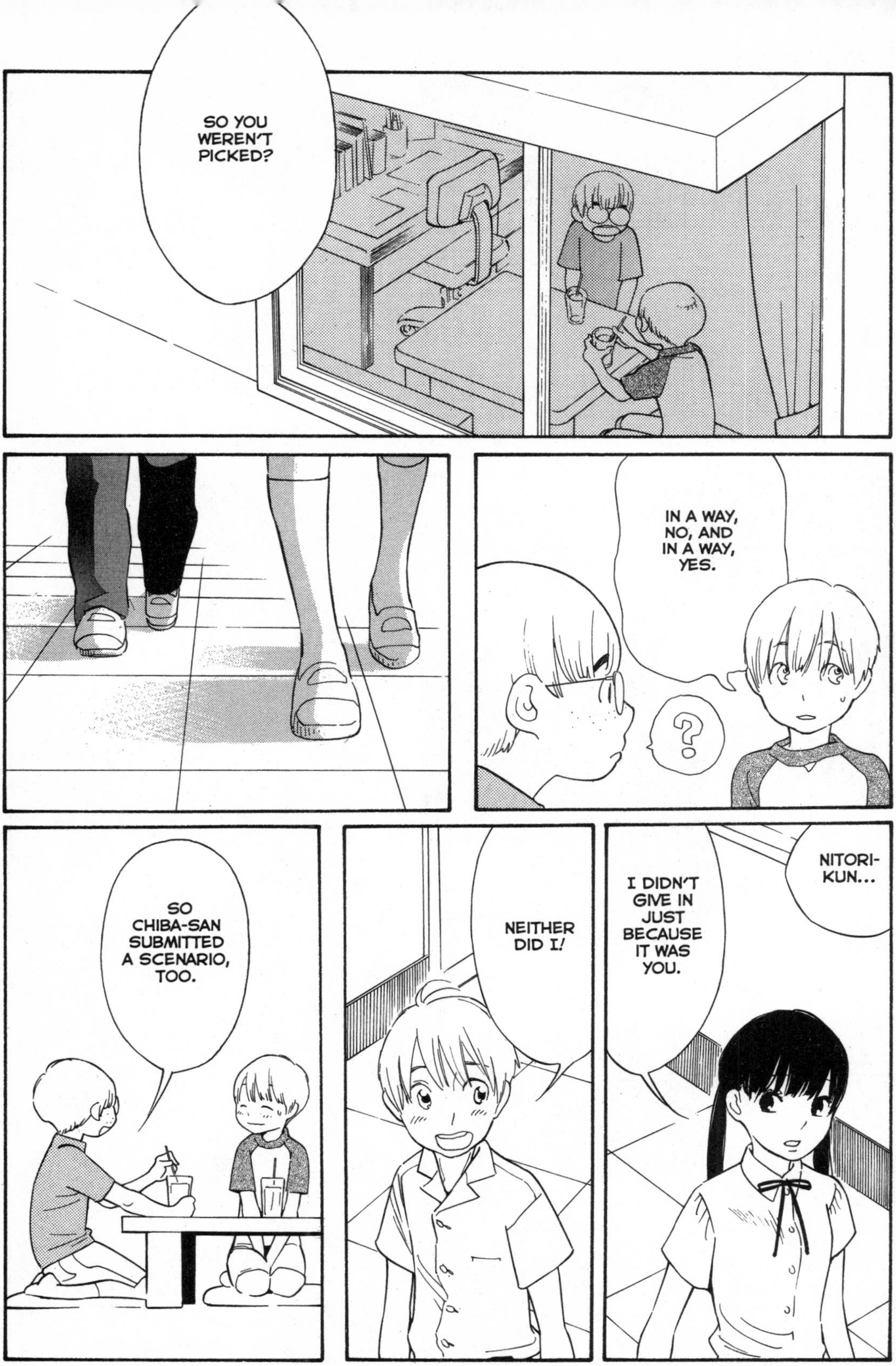
SO YOU WEREN'T PICKED?
IN A WAY, NO, AND IN A WAY, YES.
?
NITORI-KUN...
I DIDN'T GIVE IN JUST BECAUSE IT WAS YOU.
NEITHER DID I!
SO CHIBA-SAN SUBMITTED A SCENARIO, TOO.

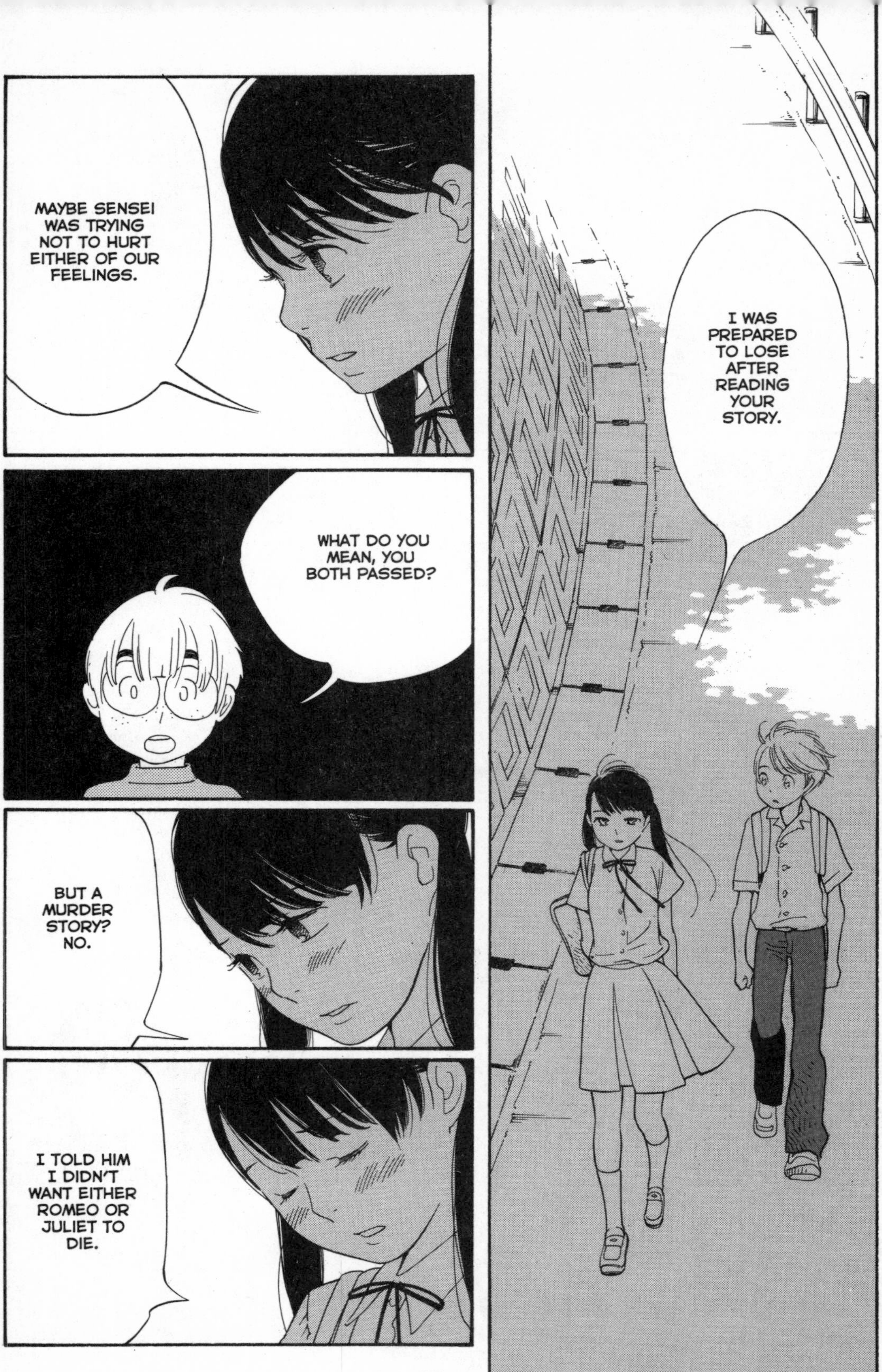
I WAS PREPARED TO LOSE AFTER READING YOUR STORY.
MAYBE SENSEI WAS TRYING NOT TO HURT EITHER OF OUR FEELINGS.
WHAT DO YOU MEAN, YOU BOTH PASSED?
BUT A MURDER STORY? NO.
I TOLD HIM I DIDN'T WANT EITHER ROMEO OR JULIET TO DIE.

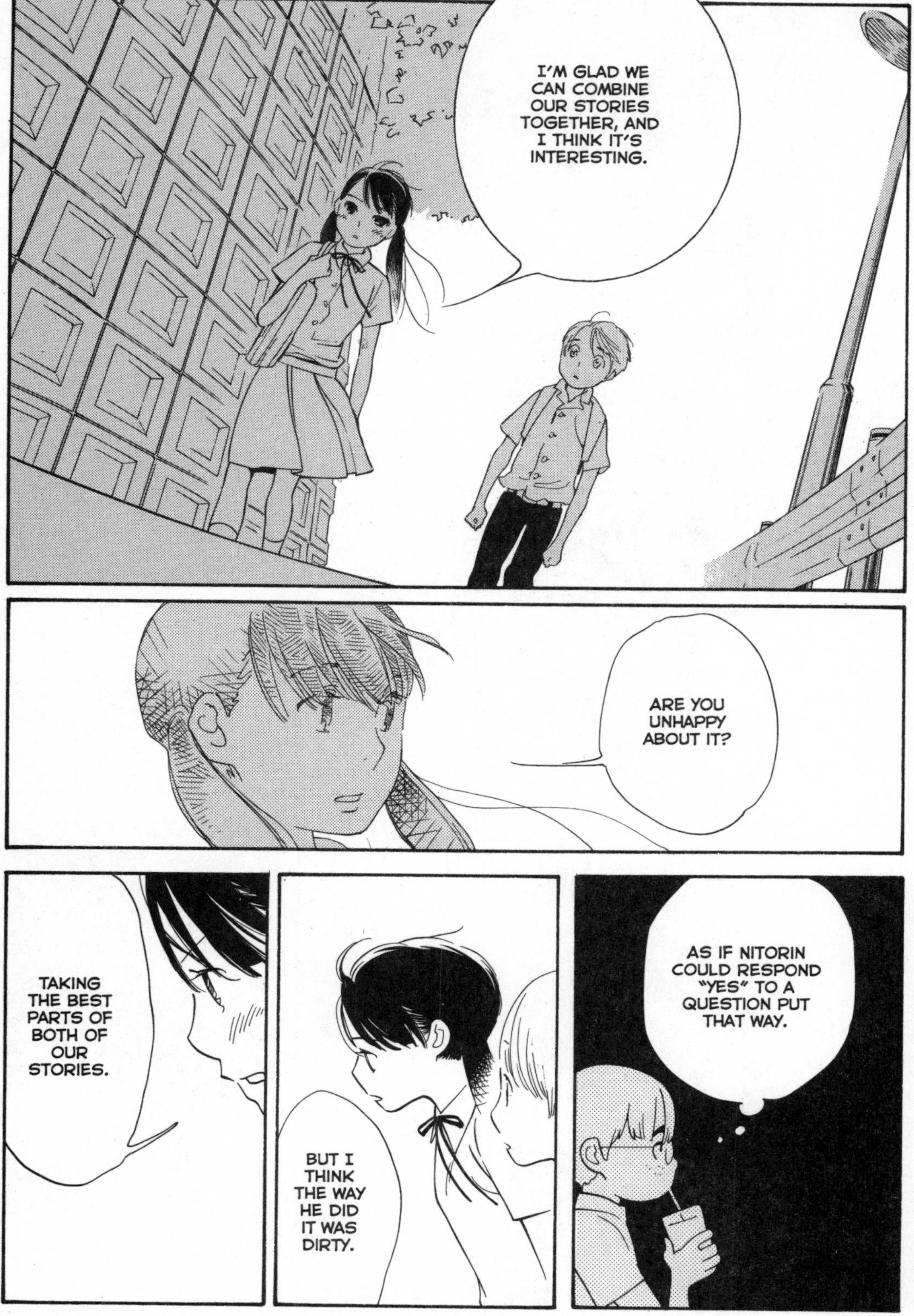
I'M GLAD WE CAN COMBINE OUR STORIES TOGETHER, AND I THINK IT'S INTERESTING.
ARE YOU UNHAPPY ABOUT IT?
AS IF NITORIN COULD RESPOND "YES" TO A QUESTION PUT THAT WAY.
BUT I THINK THE WAY HE DID IT WAS DIRTY.
TAKING THE BEST PARTS OF BOTH OF OUR STORIES.

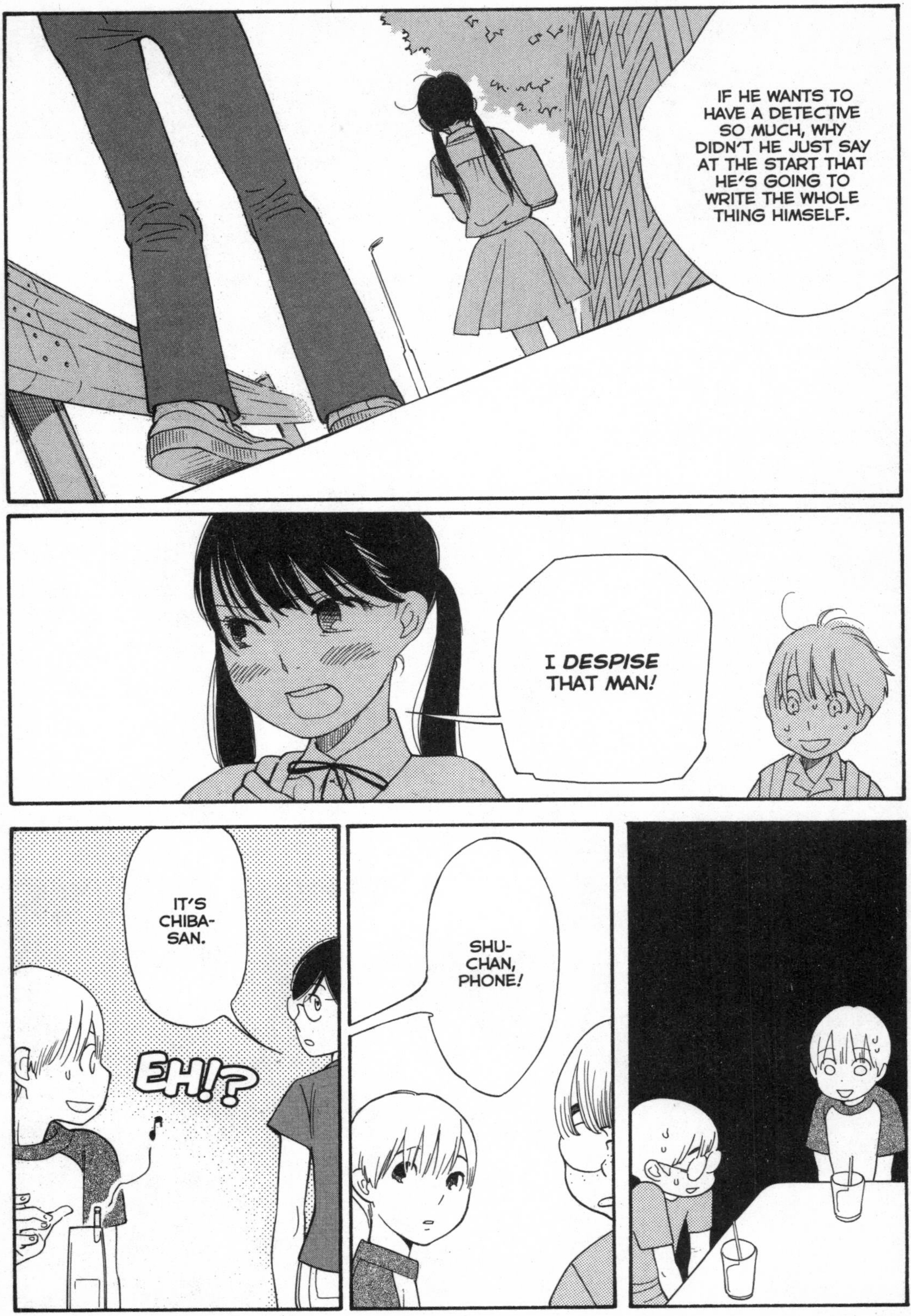
IF HE WANTS TO HAVE A DETECTIVE SO MUCH, WHY DIDN'T HE JUST SAY AT THE START THAT HE'S GOING TO WRITE THE WHOLE THING HIMSELF.
I *DESPISE* THAT MAN!
SHU-CHAN, PHONE!
IT'S CHIBA-SAN.
EH!?

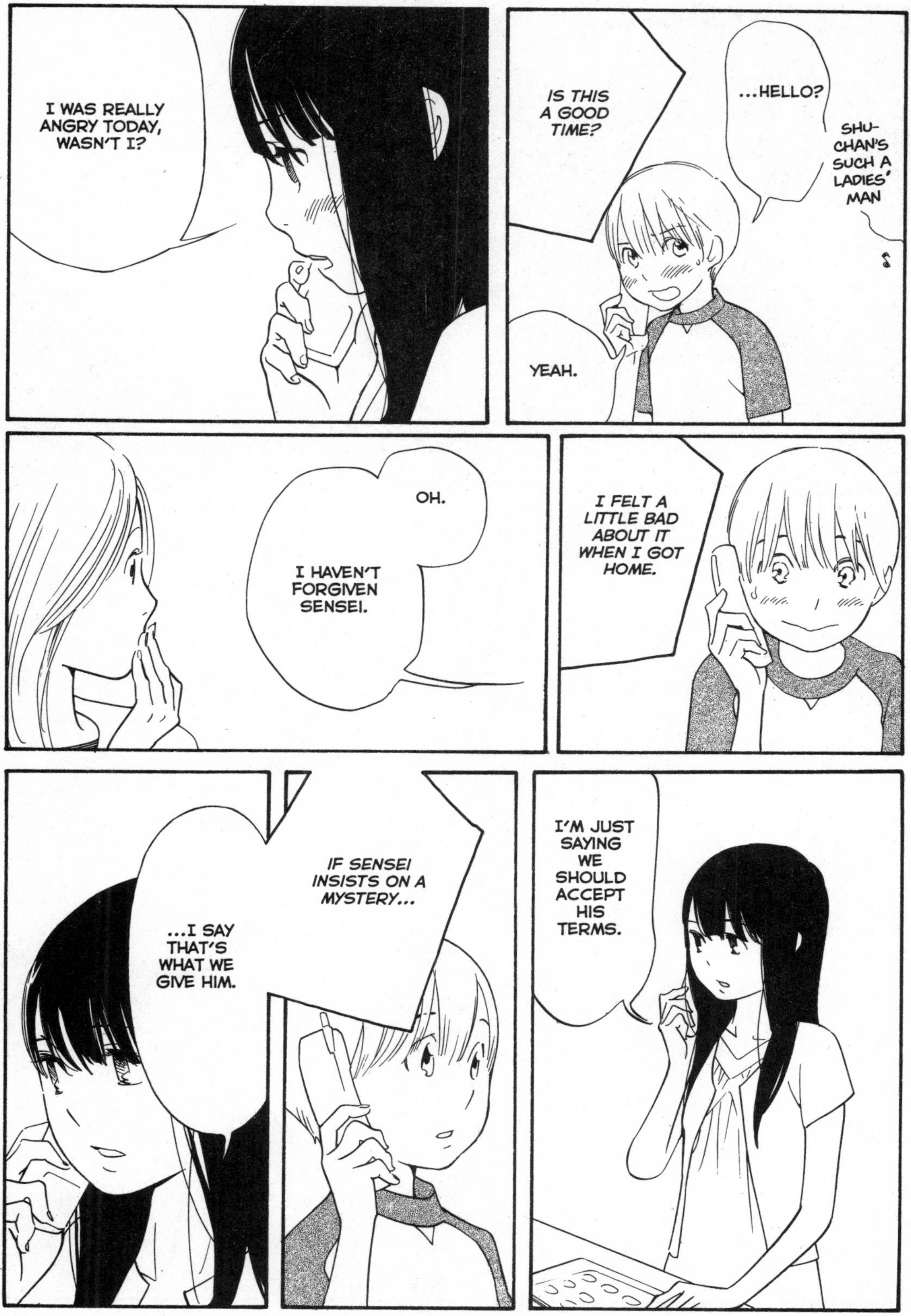
...HELLO?
SHU-CHAN'S SUCH A LADIES' MAN
IS THIS A GOOD TIME?
YEAH.
I WAS REALLY ANGRY TODAY, WASN'T I?
I FELT A LITTLE BAD ABOUT IT WHEN I GOT HOME.
OH.
I HAVEN'T FORGIVEN SENSEI.
I'M JUST SAYING WE SHOULD ACCEPT HIS TERMS.
IF SENSEI INSISTS ON A MYSTERY...
...I SAY THAT'S WHAT WE GIVE HIM.

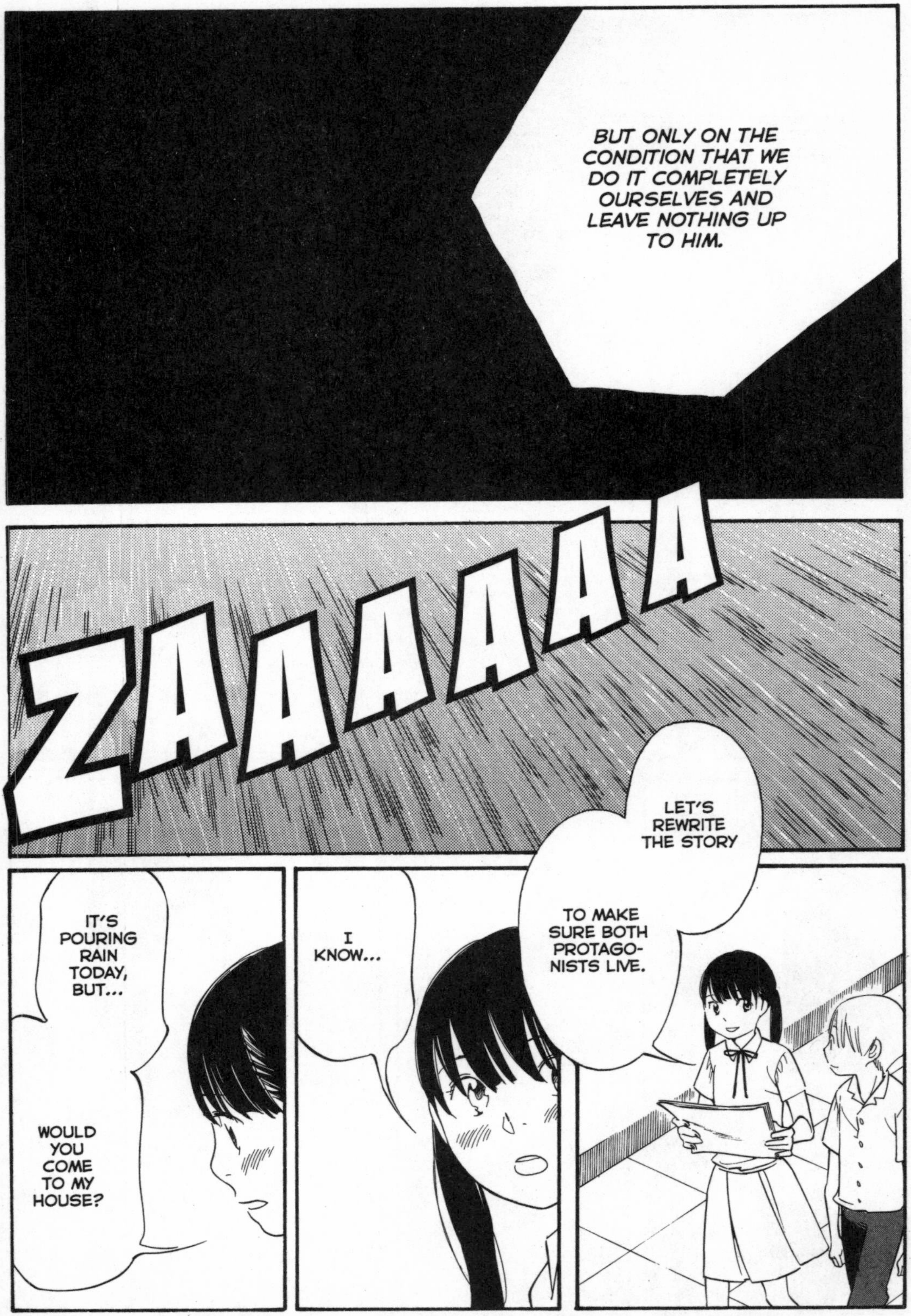
BUT ONLY ON THE CONDITION THAT WE DO IT COMPLETELY OURSELVES AND LEAVE NOTHING UP TO HIM.
ZAAAAAA
LET'S REWRITE THE STORY
TO MAKE SURE BOTH PROTAGO-NISTS LIVE.
I KNOW...
IT'S POURING RAIN TODAY, BUT...
WOULD YOU COME TO MY HOUSE?

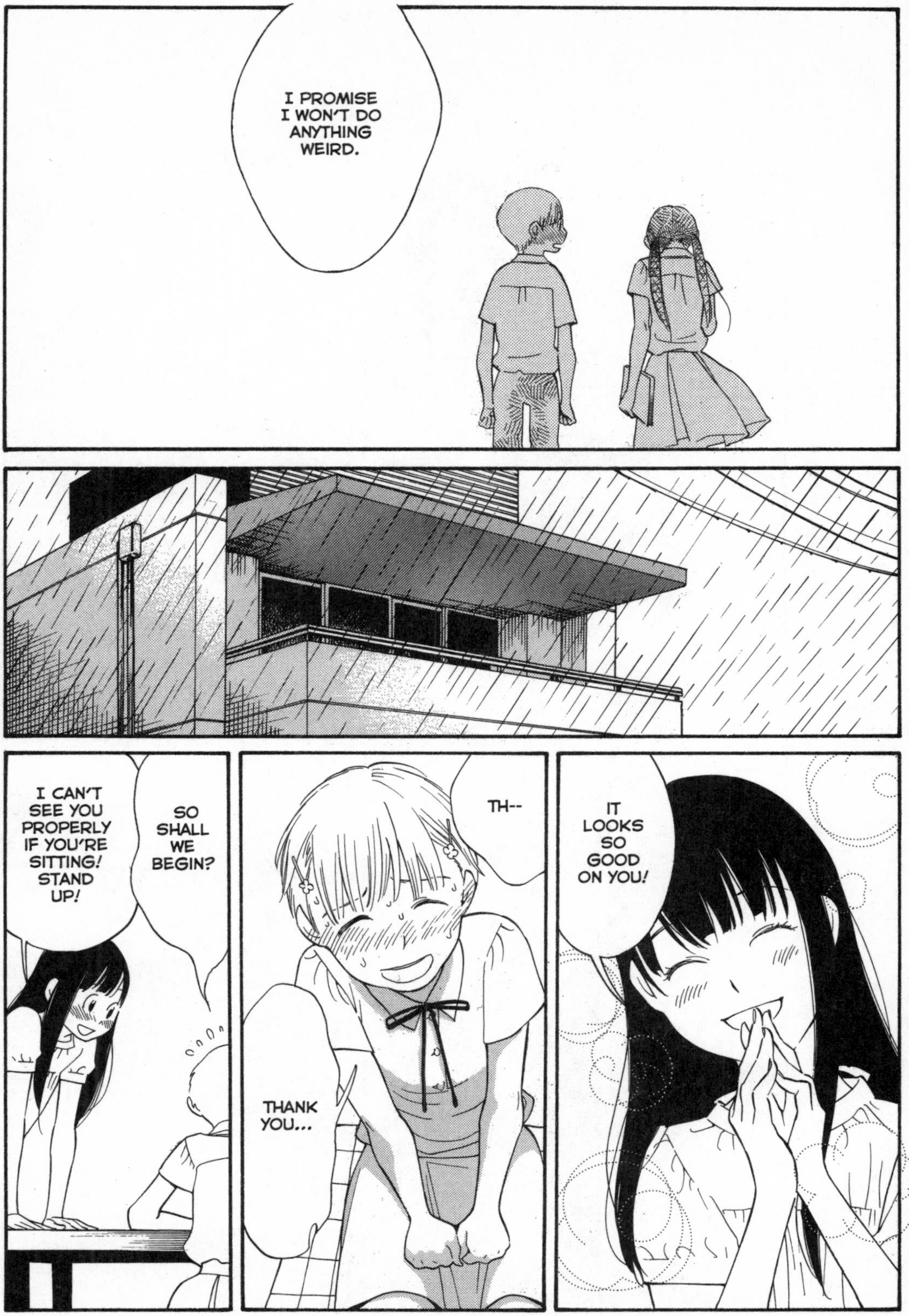
I PROMISE I WON'T DO ANYTHING WEIRD.
IT LOOKS SO GOOD ON YOU!
TH--
THANK YOU...
SO SHALL WE BEGIN?
I CAN'T SEE YOU PROPERLY IF YOU'RE SITTING! STAND UP!

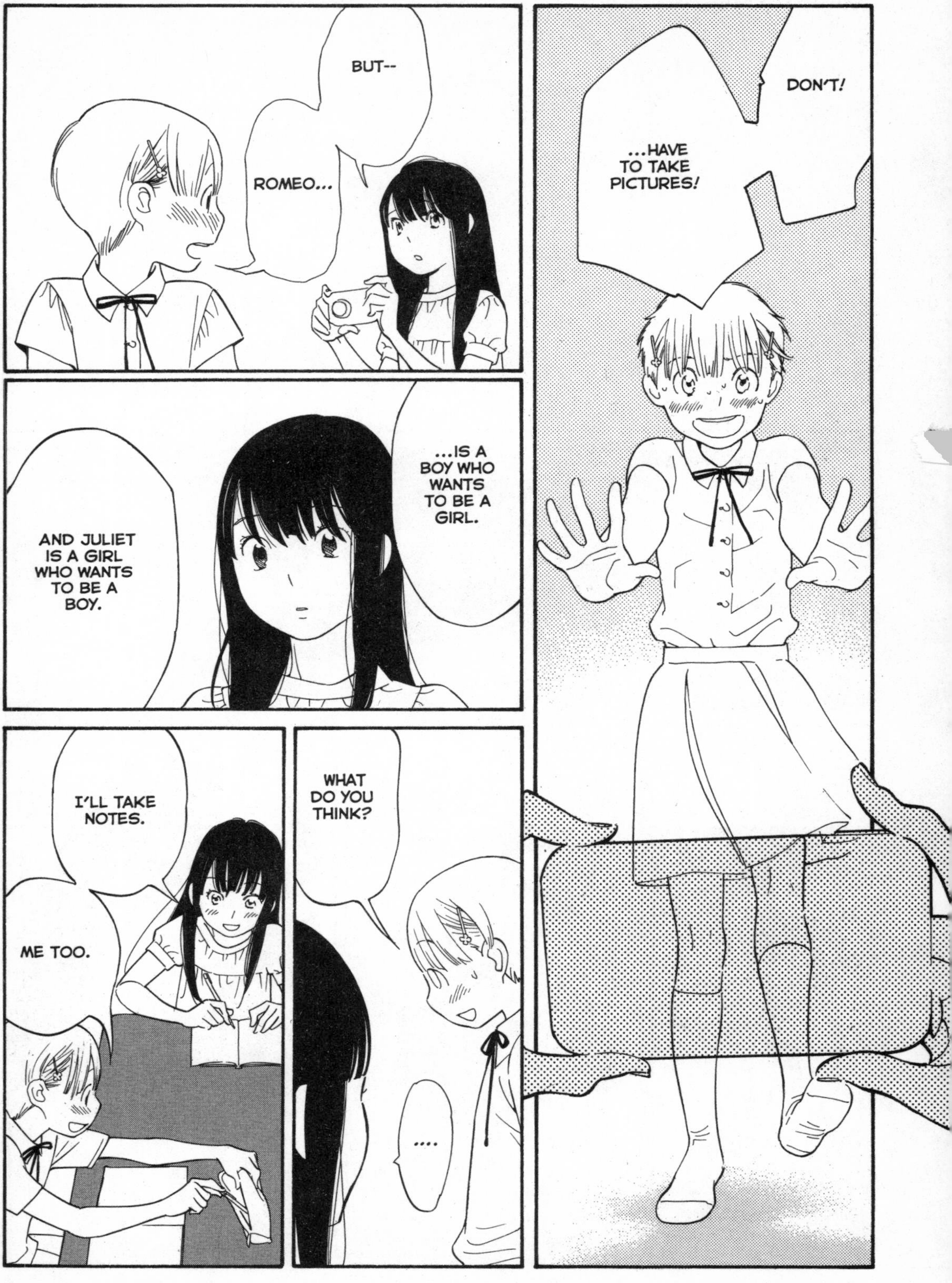
DON'T!
...HAVE TO TAKE PICTURES!
BUT--
ROMEO...
...IS A BOY WHO WANTS TO BE A GIRL.
AND JULIET IS A GIRL WHO WANTS TO BE A BOY.
WHAT DO YOU THINK?
....
I'LL TAKE NOTES.
ME TOO.

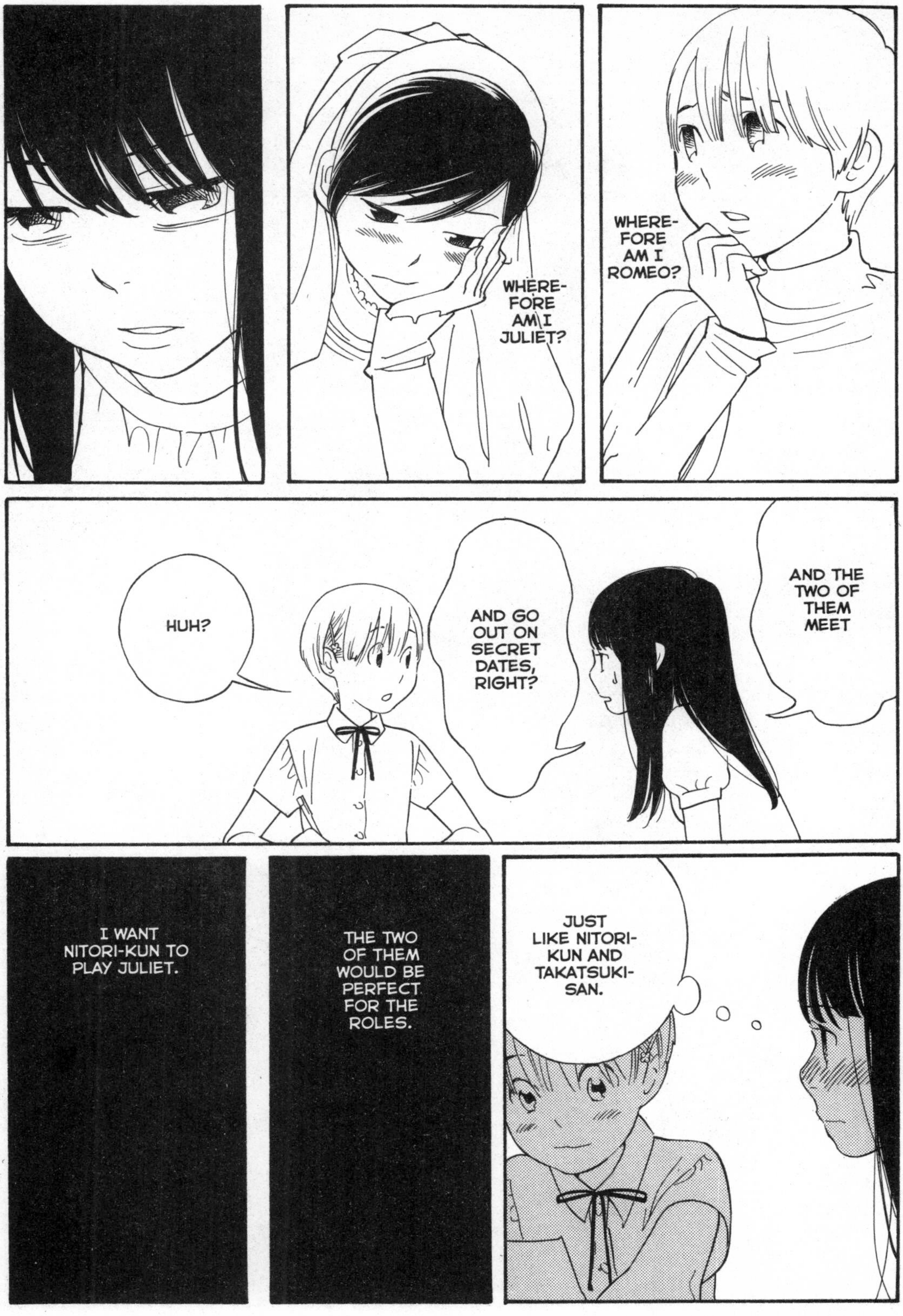
WHERE-FORE AM I ROMEO?
WHERE-FORE AM I JULIET?
AND THE TWO OF THEM MEET
AND GO OUT ON SECRET DATES, RIGHT?
HUH?
JUST LIKE NITORI-KUN AND TAKATSUKI-SAN.
THE TWO OF THEM WOULD BE PERFECT FOR THE ROLES.
I WANT NITORI-KUN TO PLAY JULIET.

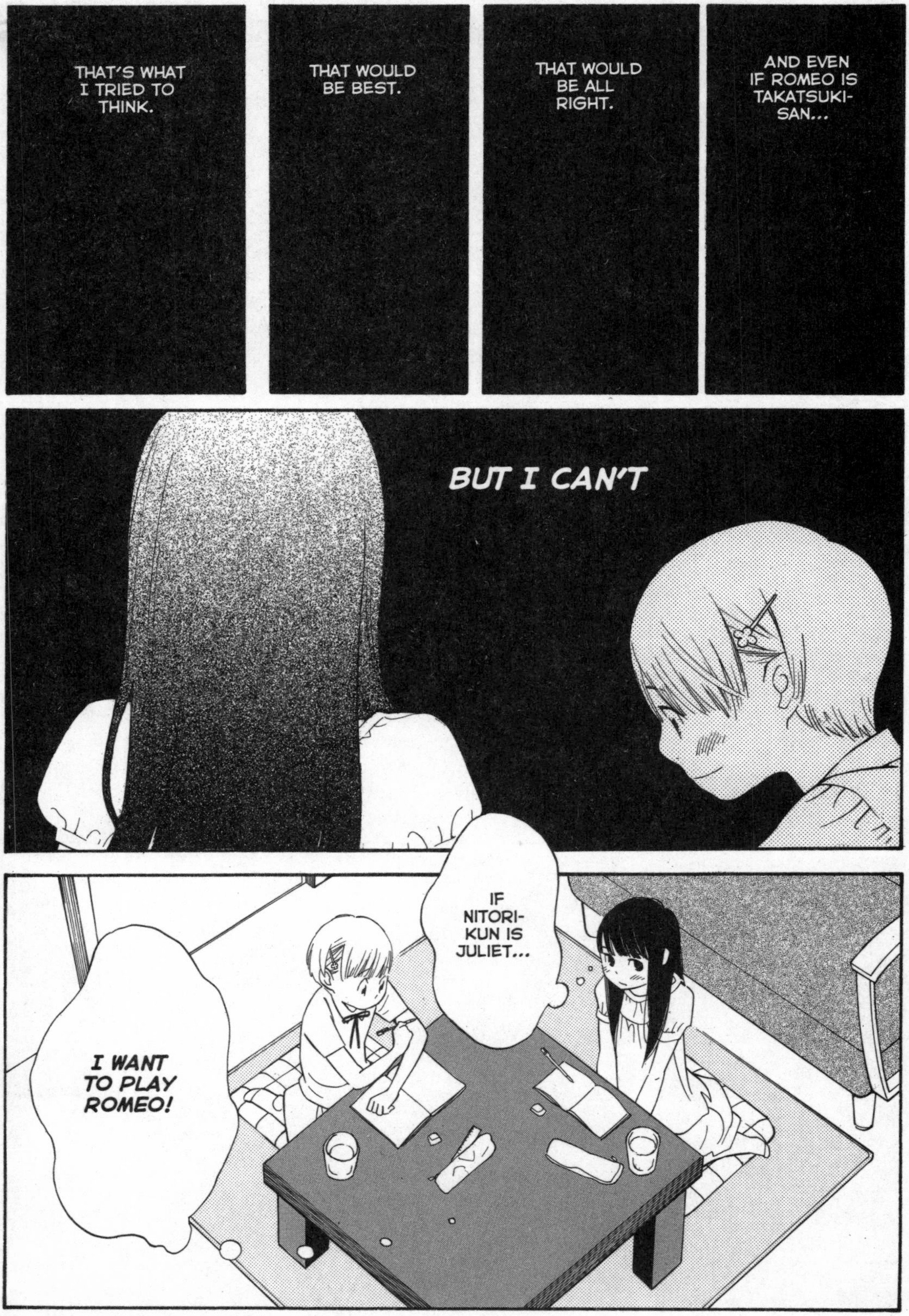
AND EVEN IF ROMEO IS TAKATSUKI-SAN...
THAT WOULD BE ALL RIGHT.
THAT WOULD BE BEST.
THAT'S WHAT I TRIED TO THINK.
BUT I CAN'T
IF NITORI-KUN IS JULIET...
I WANT TO PLAY ROMEO!

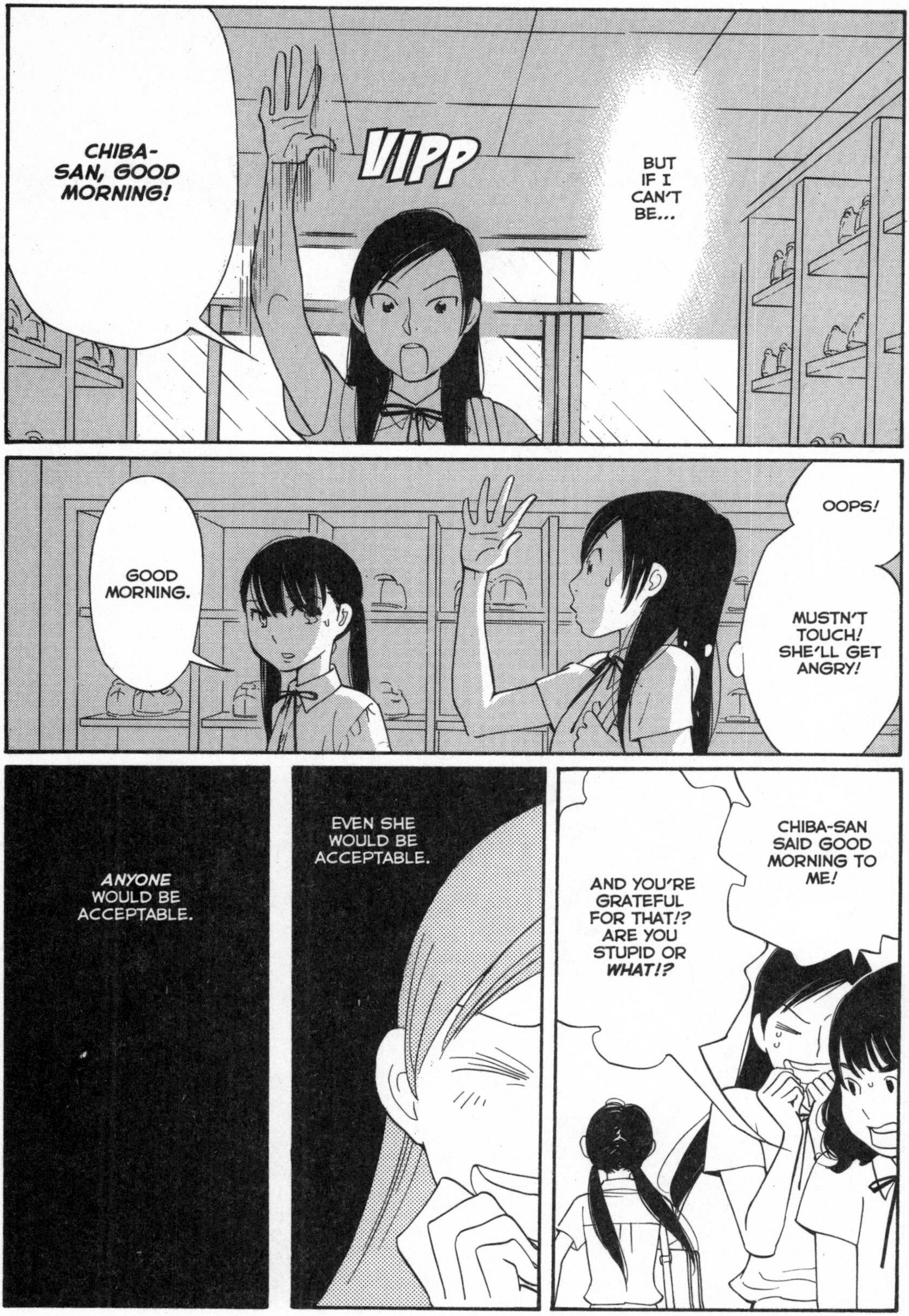
BUT IF I CAN'T BE...
VIPP
CHIBA-SAN, GOOD MORNING!
OOPS!
MUSTN'T TOUCH! SHE'LL GET ANGRY!
GOOD MORNING.
CHIBA-SAN SAID GOOD MORNING TO ME!
AND YOU'RE GRATEFUL FOR THAT!? ARE YOU STUPID OR *WHAT!?*
EVEN SHE WOULD BE ACCEPTABLE.
ANYONE WOULD BE ACCEPTABLE.

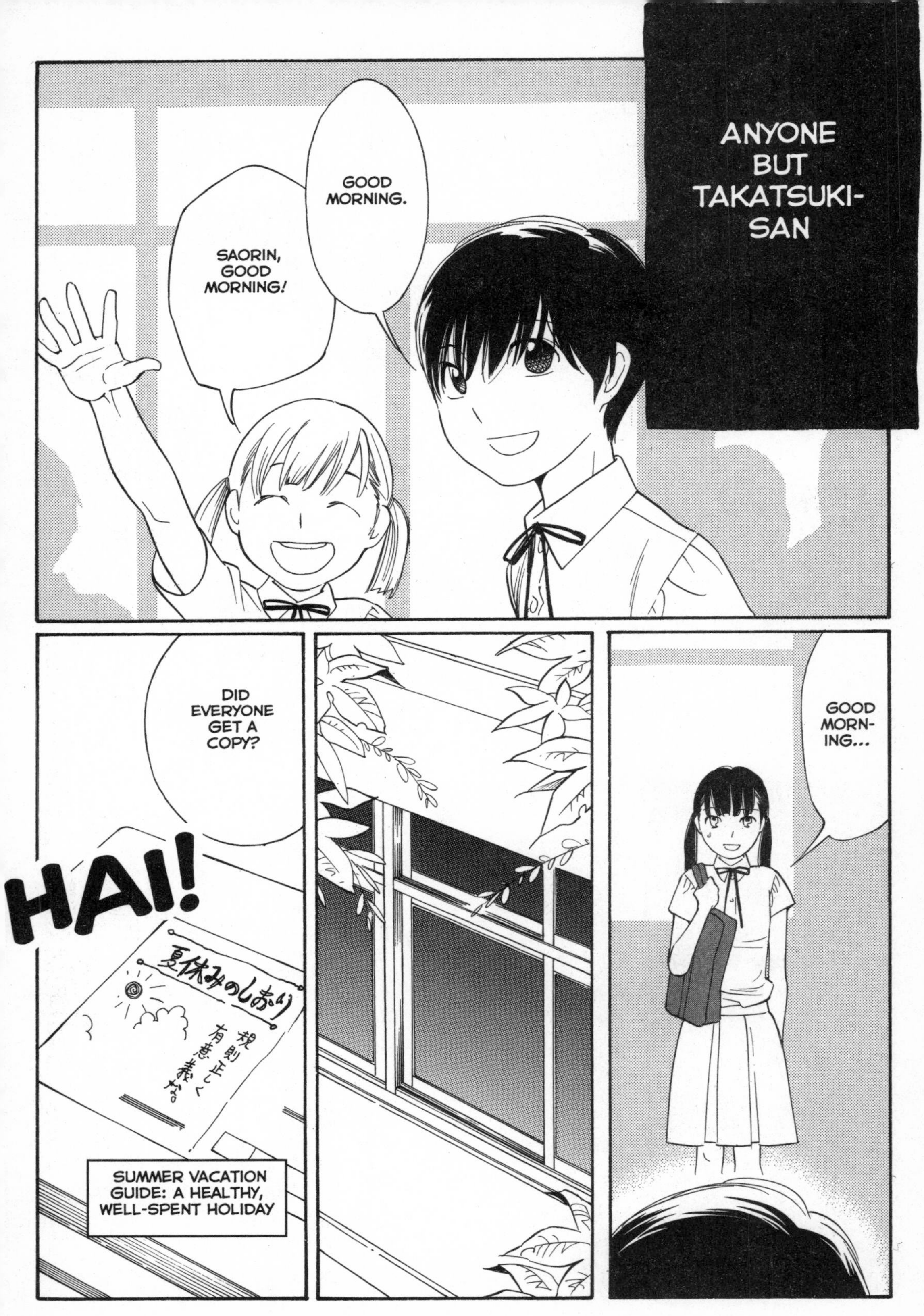
ANYONE BUT TAKATSUKI-SAN
GOOD MORNING.
SAORIN, GOOD MORNING!
GOOD MORN-ING...
DID EVERYONE GET A COPY?
HAI!
夏休みのしおり
規則正しく
有意義な
SUMMER VACATION GUIDE: A HEALTHY, WELL-SPENT HOLIDAY

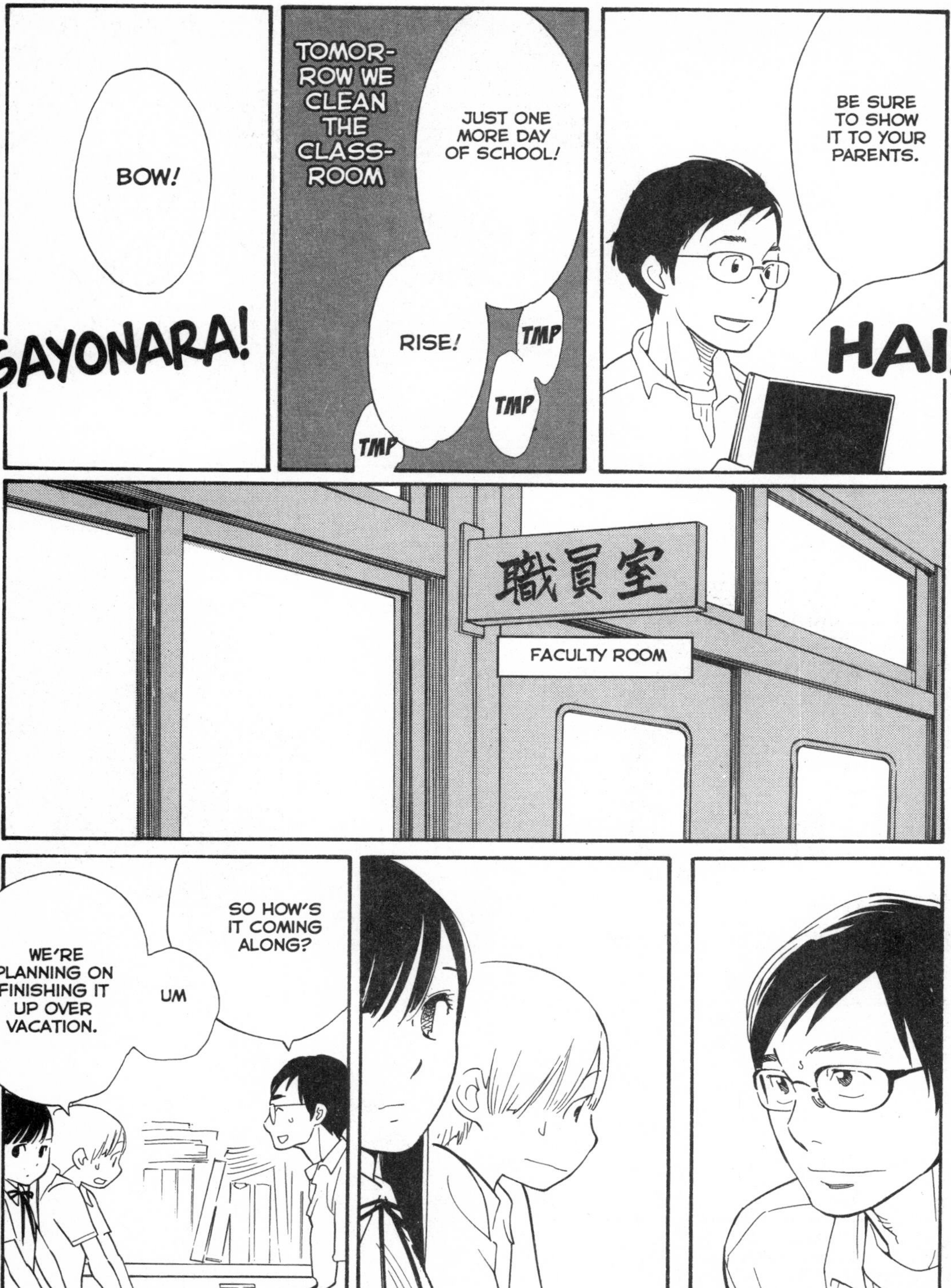
BE SURE TO SHOW IT TO YOUR PARENTS.
HAI!
JUST ONE MORE DAY OF SCHOOL!
TOMOR-ROW WE CLEAN THE CLASS-ROOM
RISE!
TMP
TMP
TMP
BOW!
SAYONARA!
職員室
FACULTY ROOM
SO HOW'S IT COMING ALONG?
UM
WE'RE PLANNING ON FINISHING IT UP OVER VACATION.

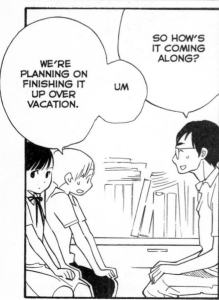

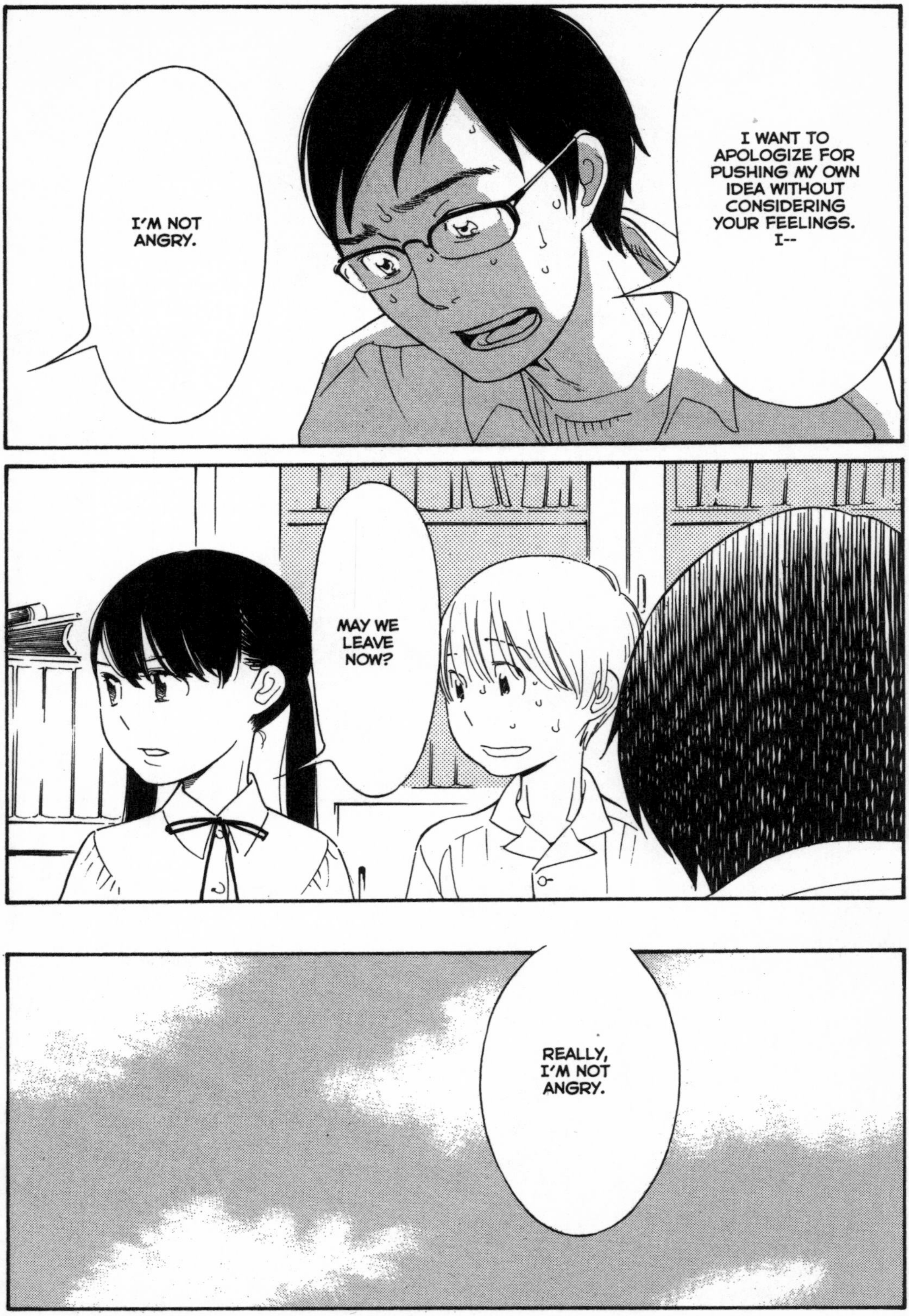
I WANT TO APOLOGIZE FOR PUSHING MY OWN IDEA WITHOUT CONSIDERING YOUR FEELINGS. I--
I'M NOT ANGRY.
MAY WE LEAVE NOW?
REALLY, I'M NOT ANGRY.

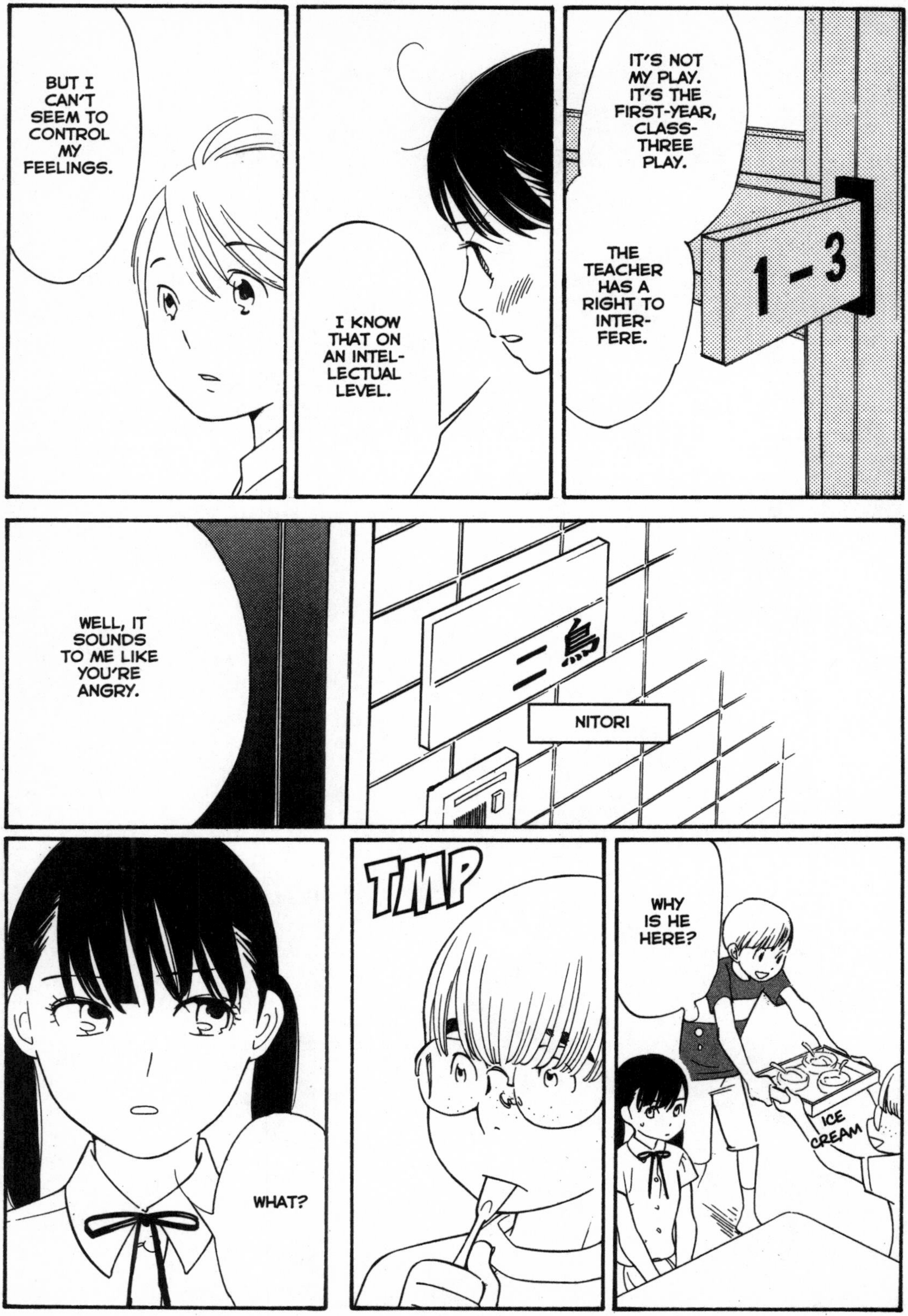
IT'S NOT MY PLAY. IT'S THE FIRST-YEAR, CLASS-THREE PLAY.
1-3
THE TEACHER HAS A RIGHT TO INTERFERE.
I KNOW THAT ON AN INTELLECTUAL LEVEL.
BUT I CAN'T SEEM TO CONTROL MY FEELINGS.
二鳥
NITORI
WELL, IT SOUNDS TO ME LIKE YOU'RE ANGRY.
WHY IS HE HERE?
ICE CREAM
TMP
WHAT?

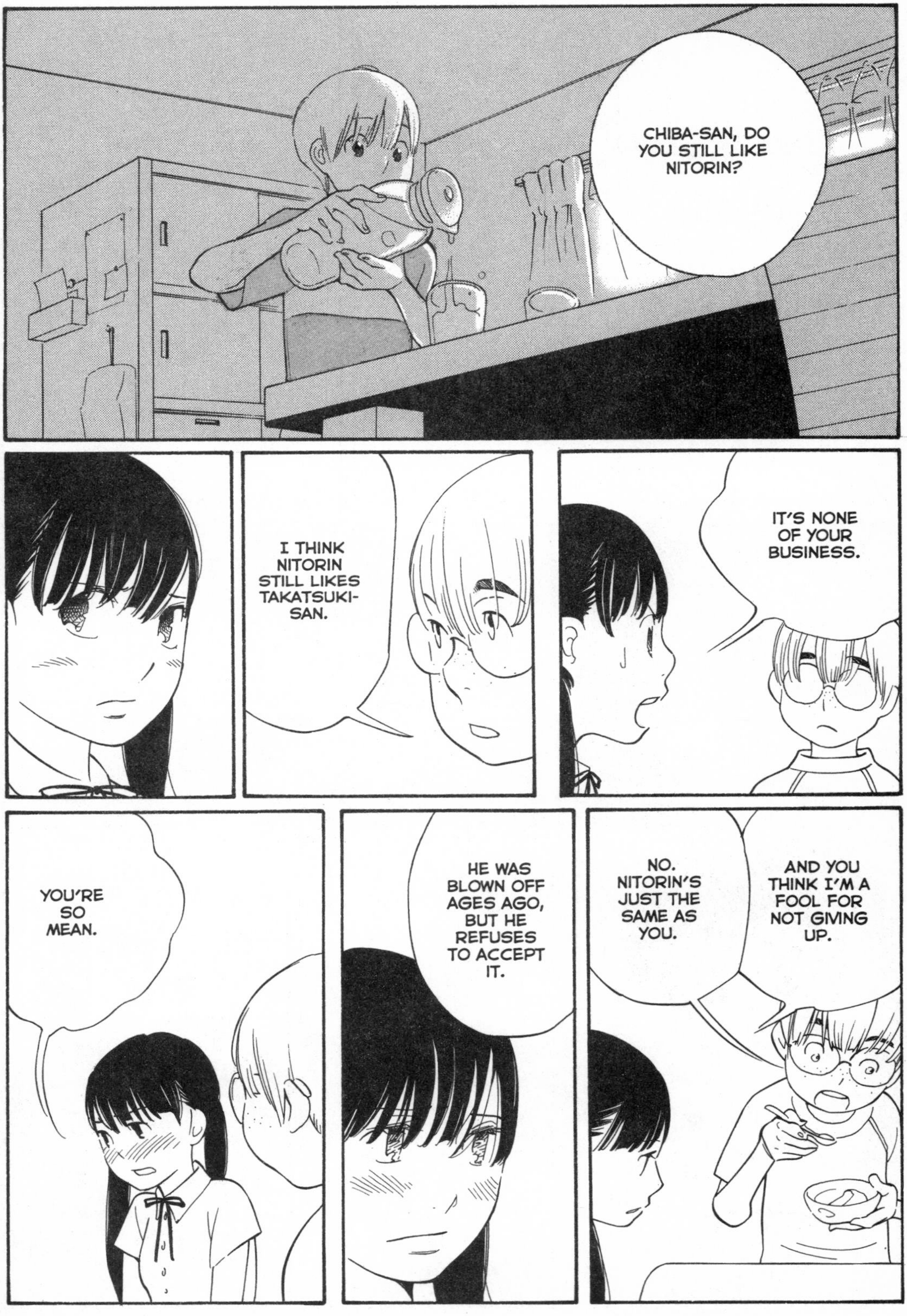
CHIBA-SAN, DO YOU STILL LIKE NITORIN?
IT'S NONE OF YOUR BUSINESS.
I THINK NITORIN STILL LIKES TAKATSUKI-SAN.
AND YOU THINK I'M A FOOL FOR NOT GIVING UP.
NO. NITORIN'S JUST THE SAME AS YOU.
HE WAS BLOWN OFF AGES AGO, BUT HE REFUSES TO ACCEPT IT.
YOU'RE SO MEAN.

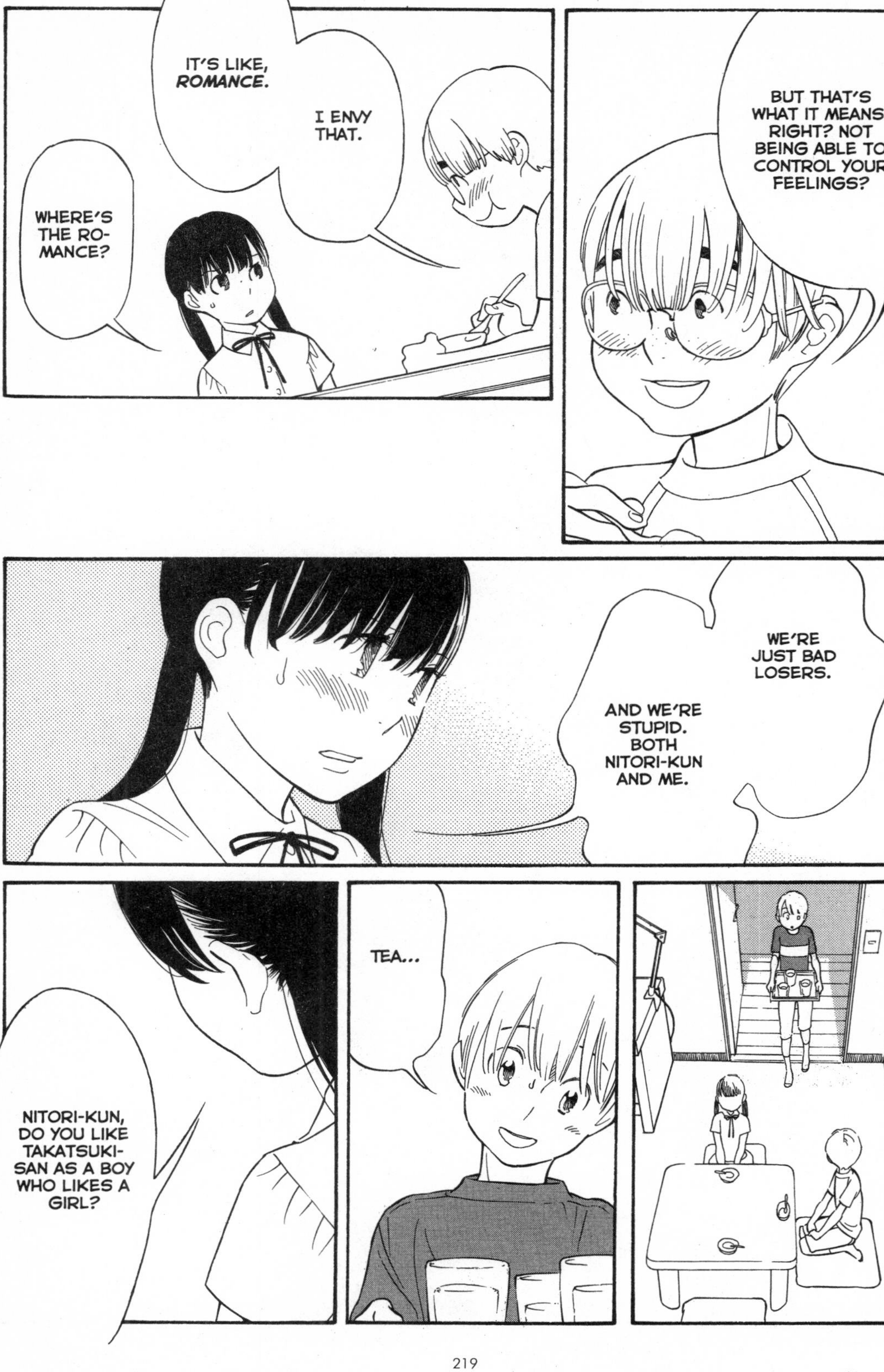
BUT THAT'S WHAT IT MEANS, RIGHT? NOT BEING ABLE TO CONTROL YOUR FEELINGS?
IT'S LIKE, *ROMANCE*.
I ENVY THAT.
WHERE'S THE RO-MANCE?
WE'RE JUST BAD LOSERS.
AND WE'RE STUPID. BOTH NITORI-KUN AND ME.
TEA...
NITORI-KUN, DO YOU LIKE TAKATSUKI-SAN AS A BOY WHO LIKES A GIRL?

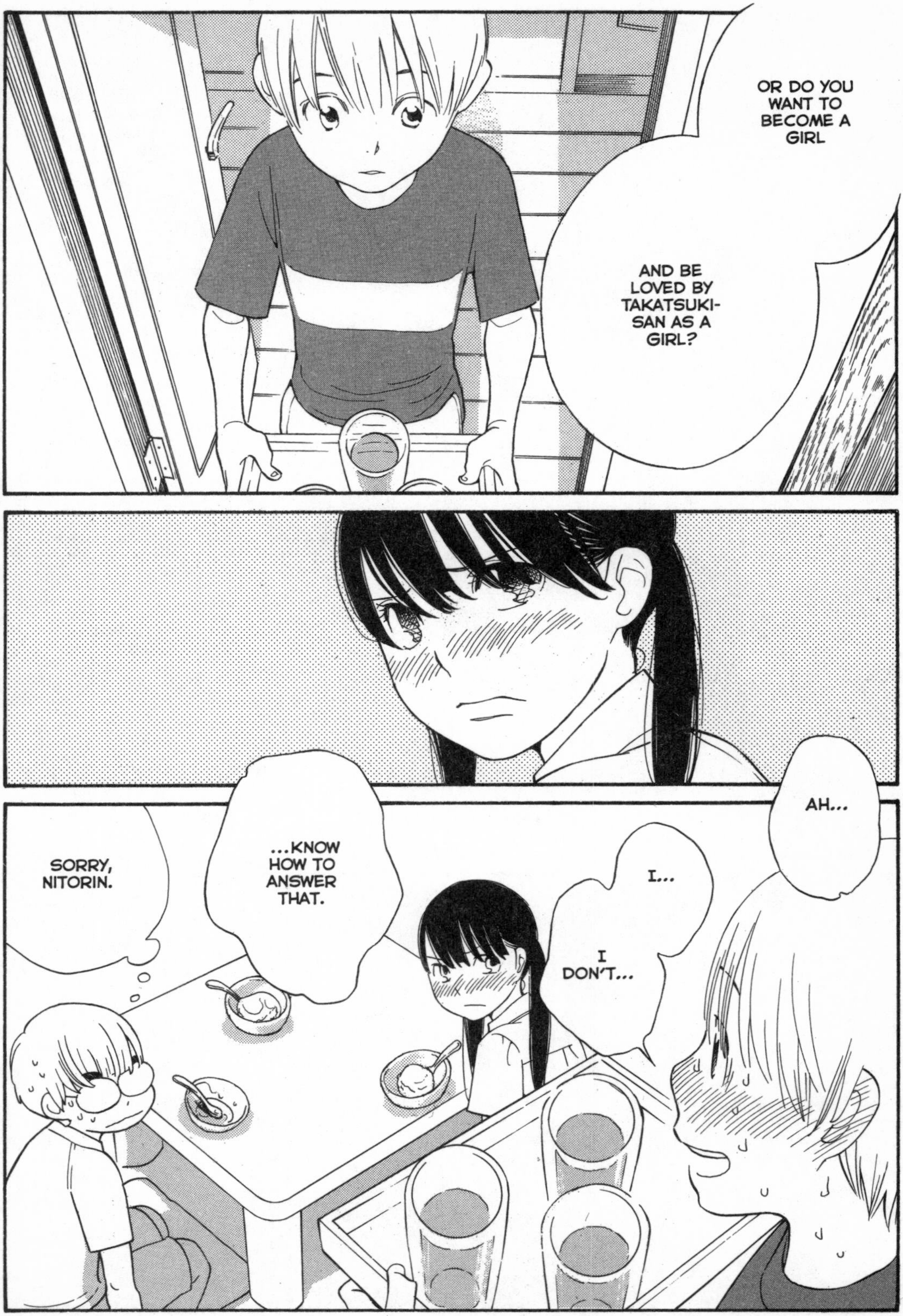
OR DO YOU WANT TO BECOME A GIRL
AND BE LOVED BY TAKATSUKI-SAN AS A GIRL?
AH...
I...
I DON'T...
...KNOW HOW TO ANSWER THAT.
SORRY, NITORIN.

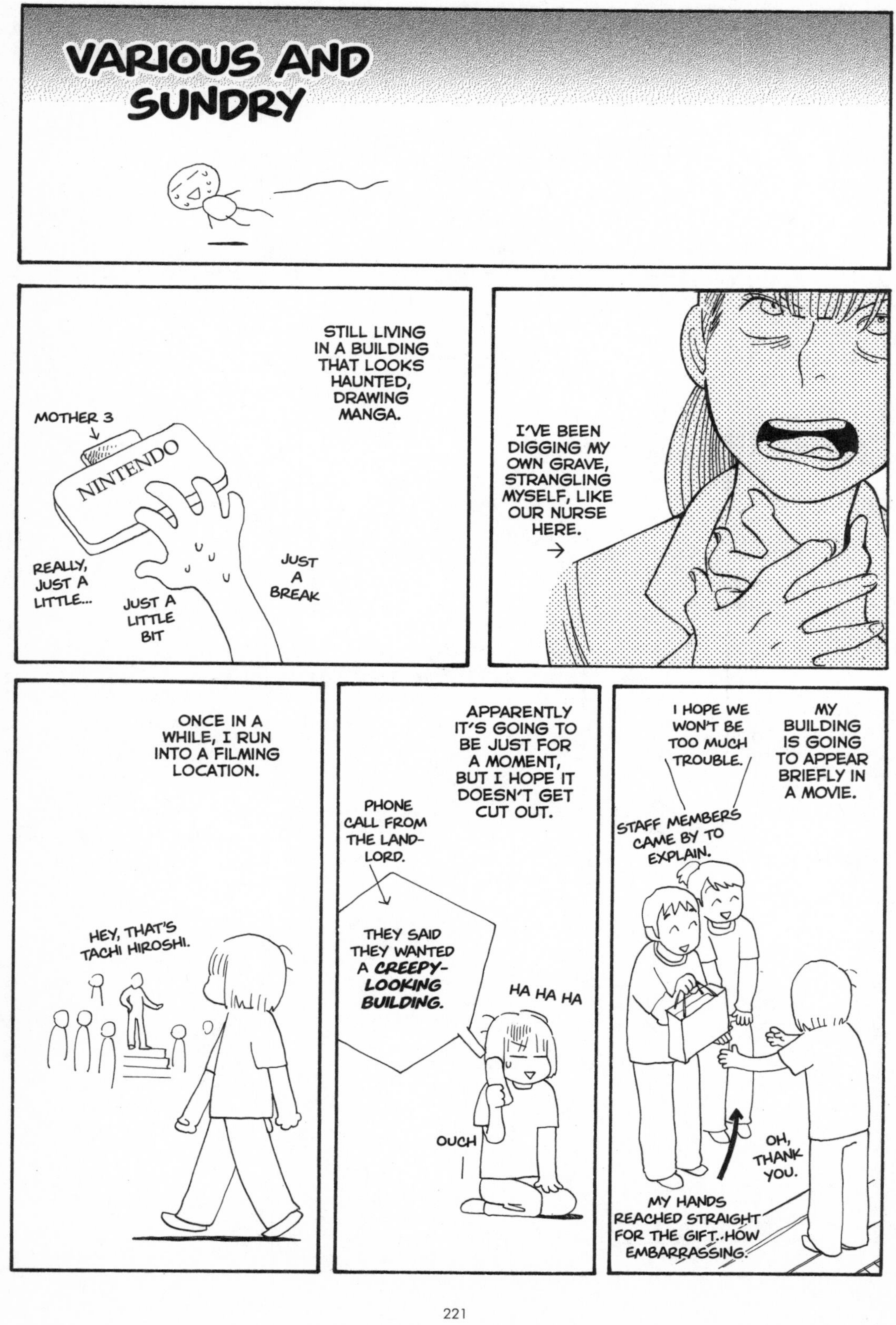
VARIOUS AND SUNDRY
I'VE BEEN DIGGING MY OWN GRAVE, STRANGLING MYSELF, LIKE OUR NURSE HERE.
STILL LIVING IN A BUILDING THAT LOOKS HAUNTED, DRAWING MANGA.
MOTHER 3
NINTENDO
JUST A BREAK
REALLY, JUST A LITTLE...
JUST A LITTLE BIT
MY BUILDING IS GOING TO APPEAR BRIEFLY IN A MOVIE.
I HOPE WE WON'T BE TOO MUCH TROUBLE.
STAFF MEMBERS CAME BY TO EXPLAIN.
OH, THANK YOU.
MY HANDS REACHED STRAIGHT FOR THE GIFT. HOW EMBARRASSING.
APPARENTLY IT'S GOING TO BE JUST FOR A MOMENT, BUT I HOPE IT DOESN'T GET CUT OUT.
PHONE CALL FROM THE LANDLORD.
HA HA HA
THEY SAID THEY WANTED A **CREEPY-LOOKING BUILDING.**
OUCH
ONCE IN A WHILE, I RUN INTO A FILMING LOCATION.
HEY, THAT'S TACHI HIROSHI.

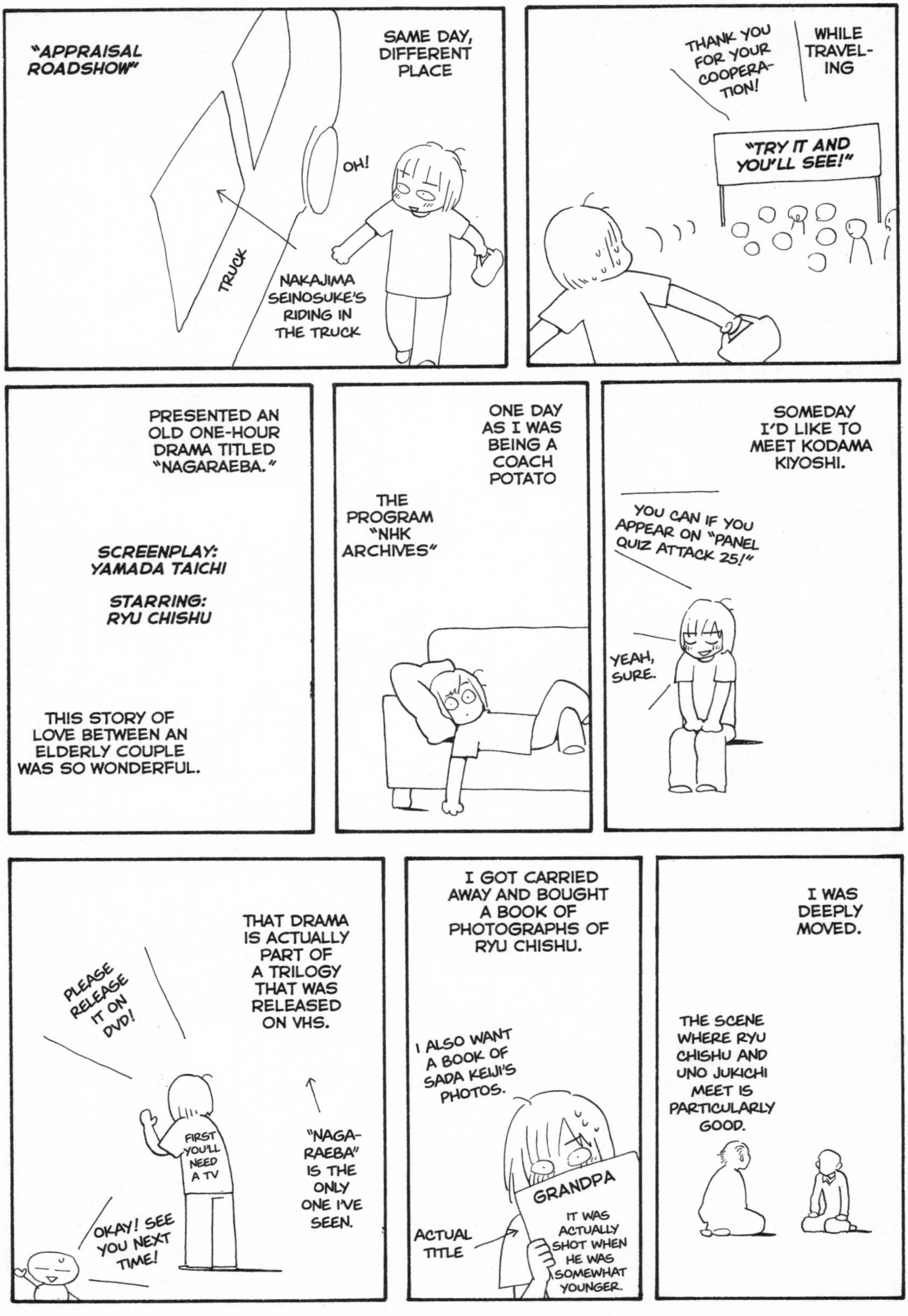
WHILE TRAVELING
THANK YOU FOR YOUR COOPERATION!
"TRY IT AND YOU'LL SEE!"
SAME DAY, DIFFERENT PLACE
"APPRAISAL ROADSHOW"
OH!
TRUCK
NAKAJIMA SEINOSUKE'S RIDING IN THE TRUCK
SOMEDAY I'D LIKE TO MEET KODAMA KIYOSHI.
YOU CAN IF YOU APPEAR ON "PANEL QUIZ ATTACK 25!"
YEAH, SURE.
ONE DAY AS I WAS BEING A COACH POTATO
THE PROGRAM "NHK ARCHIVES"
PRESENTED AN OLD ONE-HOUR DRAMA TITLED "NAGARAEBA."
SCREENPLAY: YAMADA TAICHI
STARRING: RYU CHISHU
THIS STORY OF LOVE BETWEEN AN ELDERLY COUPLE WAS SO WONDERFUL.
I WAS DEEPLY MOVED.
THE SCENE WHERE RYU CHISHU AND UNO JUKICHI MEET IS PARTICULARLY GOOD.
I GOT CARRIED AWAY AND BOUGHT A BOOK OF PHOTOGRAPHS OF RYU CHISHU.
I ALSO WANT A BOOK OF SADA KEIJI'S PHOTOS.
GRANDPA
IT WAS ACTUALLY SHOT WHEN HE WAS SOMEWHAT YOUNGER.
ACTUAL TITLE
THAT DRAMA IS ACTUALLY PART OF A TRILOGY THAT WAS RELEASED ON VHS.
"NAGARAEBA" IS THE ONLY ONE I'VE SEEN.
PLEASE RELEASE IT ON DVD!
FIRST YOU'LL NEED A TV
OKAY! SEE YOU NEXT TIME!

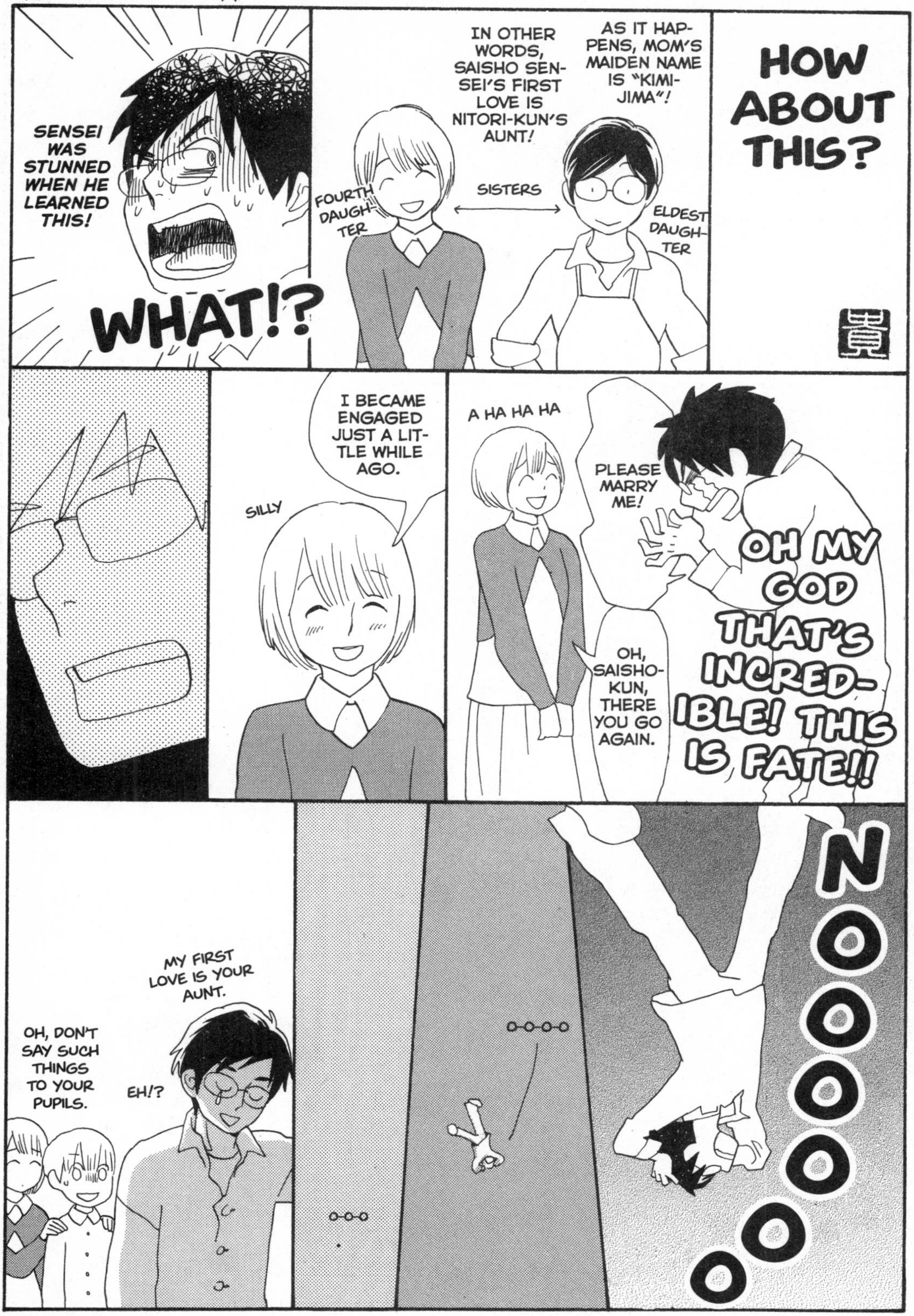
HOW ABOUT THIS?
AS IT HAPPENS, MOM'S MAIDEN NAME IS "KIMI-JIMA"!
IN OTHER WORDS, SAISHO SENSEI'S FIRST LOVE IS NITORI-KUN'S AUNT!
ELDEST DAUGHTER
SISTERS
FOURTH DAUGHTER
SENSEI WAS STUNNED WHEN HE LEARNED THIS!
WHAT!?
A HA HA HA
PLEASE MARRY ME!
OH MY GOD THAT'S INCREDIBLE! THIS IS FATE!!
OH, SAISHO-KUN, THERE YOU GO AGAIN.
I BECAME ENGAGED JUST A LITTLE WHILE AGO.
SILLY
NOOOOOOOO
O-O-O-O
O-O-O
MY FIRST LOVE IS YOUR AUNT.
EH!?
OH, DON'T SAY SUCH THINGS TO YOUR PUPILS.

THE END

STOP!

THE MANGA IN THIS BOOK IS "UNFLIPPED," MEANING PAGES RUN BACK-TO-FRONT AND PANELS START AT THE TOP RIGHT AND END AT THE BOTTOM LEFT. TURN THIS PAGE AND YOU'LL BE AT THE END OF THE STORY. FLIP THE BOOK AROUND FOR A MUCH MORE SATISFYING READING EXPERIENCE.

PRONUNCIATION
GUIDE

VOWELS

a	as in "father"
i	as in "spaghetti"
u	as in "put"
e	as in "them"
o	as in "pole"

"Long" vowels are usually indicated by a macron ("ō"), circumflex ("ô") or diaeresis ("ö"), although sometimes the vowel is simply repeated. In personal names, a long "o" is sometimes represented as "oh." In cases where one vowel is followed immediately by a different vowel, but is not in the same syllable, they are often separated by a dash or apostrophe to indicate the end of one syllable and beginning of another. Here are common pairs of vowels that sound to the English-speaker's ear like one syllable (and thus are not separated):

ai	as in "my"
ei	as in "ray"
oi	as in "toy"
ao	as in "cow"

CONSONANTS *that require clarification*

g	as in "get" (never as in "age")
s	as in "soft" (never like "rise")
t	as in "tale" (never like "d")
ch	as in "church"

ACCENTS

Most English words have "accented" and "un-accented" syllables. This is generally not the case in Japanese, which is more "flat." When English speakers encounter a new word, they tend to accent the first syllable if it has two syllables, the second if it has three, and after that they wing it. If you can't resist accenting a syllable in a Japanese word, accent the first and you'll be fine.

HONORIFICS
GUIDE

This translation retains certain Japanese honorifics that (hopefully) will help the reader to better grasp the atmosphere and, more importantly, the relative relationships of the characters to each other. Here's a simple glossary of the honorifics you'll find.

-san: The best-known and most common honorific, it is, in most cases, neutrally polite and applicable to both sexes and between people of differing ages. Some women or girls can be very intimate, yet never stop addressing each other as -san. In school or in the workplace, -san is more commonly used in addressing girls and women. When in doubt, surname + san will get you through most situations.

-kun: A form of address used most commonly in speaking to younger boys or men, but which can also be used in speaking to younger girls or women. Some bosses will address all their subordinates as -kun, regardless of the subordinate's gender. As a rule, it is never used to address someone older, even if that person is "junior" to the speaker within the school or workplace. School teachers are generally expected to address girls as -san and boys as -kun, though some male teachers will gruffly call a pupil by his or her surname, with no honorific.

-chan: An affectionate, diminutive form of -san. It is commonly used among family members for both sexes, and for girls among close friends. When it is used in speaking to or of a boy or man among friends, it is usually because it has become part of a nickname. Despite all the rules of who should address whom in what manner, when it comes to nicknames (which are very common in Japan), anything goes.

sensei: This is both a title and an honorific, used to address a teacher or any accomplished scholar, writer, or artist. It can be applied with equal validity to your aerobics teacher and a Nobel Prize Laureate.

Note that given names are generally used only by family members or fairly close acquaintances or friends. For the most part, Japanese call each other by their surnames. In particular, boys in the same grade are likely to call each other by surnames, without any honorific, or by nicknames. Girls are more likely to err on the side of politeness. Calling someone with whom you are not intimate by his or her given name is considered presumptuous and can be seen as rude.

The honorifics I've introduced should not be taken at face value in every case. Japanese will sometimes use them in inappropriate situations, either consciously (with irony or malice) or unconsciously (because they have misread the nature of a relationship). Honorifics can also be omitted as a show of contempt. (Addressing someone older than yourself without using an honorific is akin to a slap in the face.)

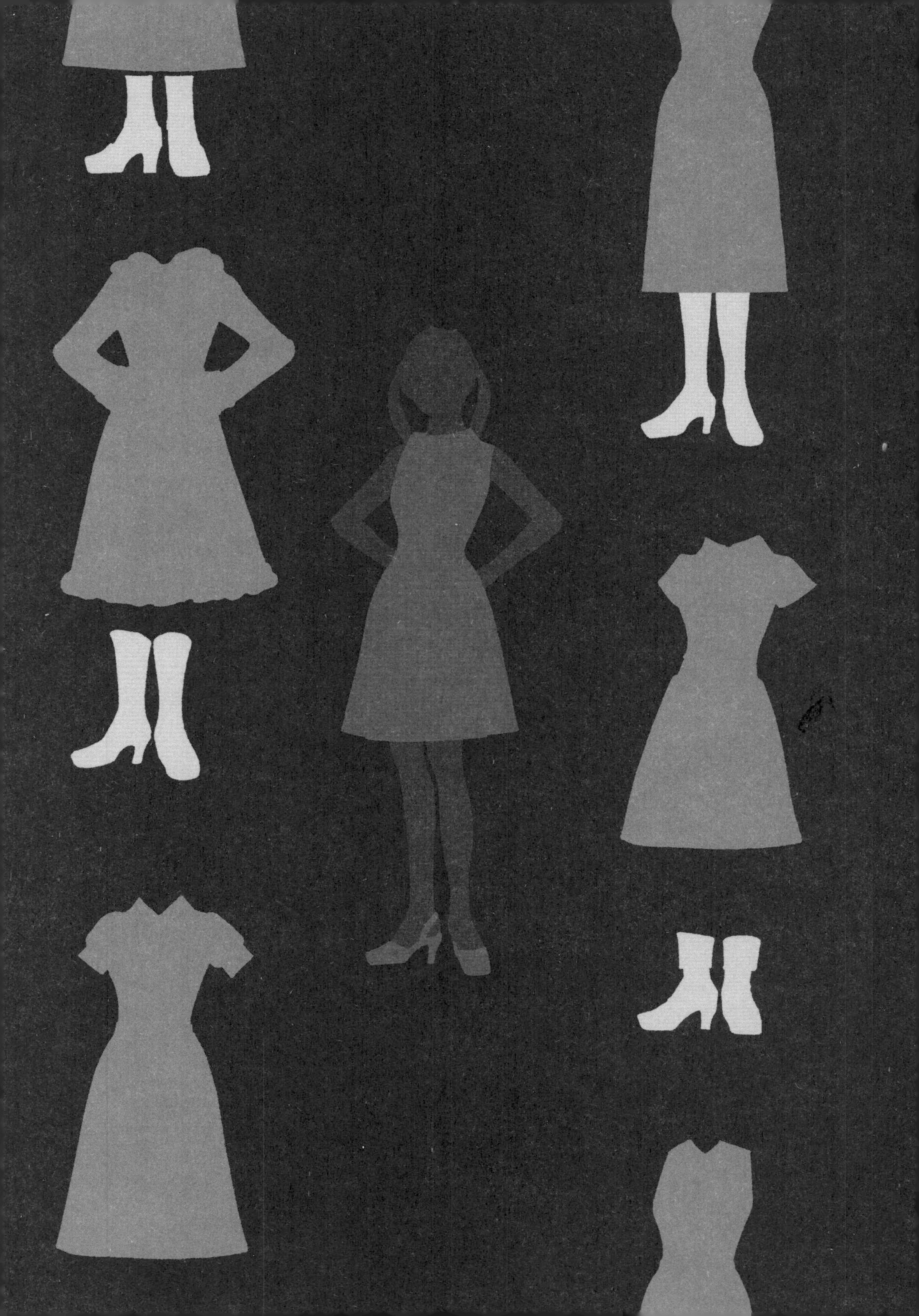